DATE DUE

OCT 24 '98			
MAY 15 '96			

the
study
of... american | contemporary
CULTURE |CONFLICTS

the study of... american
CULTURE | contemporary
CONFLICTS

edited by Luther S. Luedtke

everett / edwards, inc.
post office box 1060 / deland, florida 32720

Library of Congress Cataloging in Publication Data

Main entry under title:

The Study of American culture.
    1. United States--Civilization--20th century--Addresses, essays,
lectures.   I. Luedtke, Luther S.
E169.1.S94   973.9   75-3004
ISBN 0-912112-28-X

TABLE OF CONTENTS

ACKNOWLEDGEMENTS

Except for Chapters 3 and 10, the essays that appear in this volume were first presented as lectures to the American Studies Institute at the University of Southern California in the summer of 1973 or have been written in response to discussions that took place on that occasion. The three-week conference was sponsored by the American Studies Program of the University of Southern California and by the National American Studies Faculty of the American Studies Association. As Director of the Institute and editor of its proceedings, I have stored up more obligations than I can discharge here. Nonetheless, I must acknowledge some of my weightier debts.

The American Studies Institute was assisted by a generous grant from the National American Studies Faculty. I am grateful to the National Faculty for its support and particularly to Director John A. Hague, who lent his personal energy and good judgment in all stages of planning the Institute and in seeing this collection to print. At the University of Southern California I wish to thank especially John E. Cantelon, Paul E. Hadley, Robert B. Kaplan, Mary K. Ludwig, David H. Malone, and John A. Schutz for their advice and encouragement, and the College of Continuing Education for furnishing administrative services for the Institute. Over the past year the contributing authors have lightened the task of editing by their sympathetic response to various suggestions. The sixty members of the Institute, who gathered from fourteen states to examine the condition of contemporary American Studies, also are colleagues here. Throughout, Carol Lindstrom Luedtke has been my constant companion and critic.

Acknowledgement is made to the following publishers for permission to quote from copyrighted materials: to Harcourt Brace Jovanovich, Inc. for verses from "Little Gidding" by T. S. Eliot; to Farrar, Straus & Giroux, Inc. for Askia Muhammad Toure's chant from *Natural Process: An Anthology of New Black Poetry*, edited by Ted Wilentz and Tom Weatherly; to Alfred A. Knopf, Inc. for verses from "Lytton Strachey, Also, Enters into Heaven" in *Opus Posthumous* by Wallace Stevens, edited with Introduction by Samuel French Morse, copyright © 1957 by Elsie Stevens and Holly Stevens; and to Doubleday & Co., Inc. for "Barbie Doll," which was originally published in *Poems of the People* and later appeared in *To Be of Use,* copyright © 1969, 1971, 1973 by Marge Piercy. Museums, motion picture studios, and other holders of copyright have permitted use of the graphic materials in this book. They are acknowledged adjacent to the illustrations.

Finally, I am deeply grateful to the Deans of the Division of Humanities and the Division of Social Sciences and Communication at the University of Southern California, whose last-minute support enabled this book to be printed.

L.S.L.

INTRODUCTION

When the young man in Longfellow's poem "A Psalm of Life" exhorted his fellows — "Let us, then, be up and doing" — he phrased an apt motto for the American Studies movement. Since the 1930s, teachers and scholars in American Studies have contributed actively to both the practical and the imaginative understanding of our nation's history and consciousness. While as a type pragmatic and creative, they also have become increasingly critical in the last years of the social and methodological implications of their work, and of scholarship in the related disciplines. American Studies is continually changing form as scholars try out new subject matter and theories of knowledge in their search for a penetrating vision of the American cultural experience. There is, therefore, a double reason for spokesmen to come together to evaluate the contemporary state of this still emerging discipline: first to inform newcomers to the field, and second to provide models by which experienced teachers and scholars may wish to assess their own theories and practices. The following essays, most of which originated in the American Studies Institute at the University of Southern California in 1973, are presented with both audiences in mind.

This anthology begins with familiar themes and interdisciplinary combinations that long have been the mainstays of American Studies, then proceeds to popular and experimental subjects, and concludes with more theoretical inquiry. To an extent the sequence of essays thus recapitulates both the history and the developing style of the field. All the areas or types of work that legitimately claim to be American Studies are not, of course, represented here. Each reader will question the absence of other perspectives he considers important. But taken together, the statements show the breadth of cultural knowledge that has been achieved in American Studies, its critical self-awareness, and the vitality of the personalities and topics that it contains.

The first three chapters demonstrate various forms of a period study of American culture. In "An Approach to the Thirties" Daniel Aaron recreates the tone, the rhythms, the social and political ethos of that decade of "armies" and "new masses" through its literary and political manifestos. William Jordy's "Four Approaches to Regionalism in the Visual Arts of the 1930s" examines the artistic, literary, and social events of the same period, using painting, photography, architecture, and public planning to document the themes of regionalism, nationalism, and internationalism characteristic of the decade. Arthur Wertheim's essay on "Constance Rourke and the Discovery of American Culture in the 1930s" explores the awakening of this gifted scholar to regionalism and the vernacular arts at a time when cultural anthropologists began to give new importance to popular and folk elements in the explanation of national culture.

In "Thought and Social Change" Sydney Ahlstrom investigates the interaction of ideas and intellectual (or "spiritual") history with social, political, and institutional developments. History and culture come into being through the agency of human *intentionality,* he suggests; and the past is best regarded as an ideal construction shaped by the explanatory theories of the day. Professor Ahlstrom's essay and John Cotter's invitation to "Archaeology and Material History: A Personal Approach to Discovery of the Past" span an arc from the theoretical to the concrete, from the scholar-oriented to the student-centered. Professor Cotter encourages students to explore history by way of everyday artifacts and to join in the conservation of our material heritage. The methodic study of material data, he advises, also is a primary way of evaluating our historical judgments against the evidence left us by the past.

The next three essays — on man and technology, woman in American, and popular literature — look to frontier areas where much of the liveliest teaching and writing in American Studies is occurring. Engaged with popular attitudes and new forms of documentation, their authors share a concern for the habits of thought that broadly unify our culture and the values that move it. Roderick Nash, a pioneer in environmental studies, briskly reviews myth-making statements on "Machines and Americans" from literature, film, and popular lore. Technology as an instrument of national mission, he demonstrates, has been regarded with both hope and anxiety. In "Some Paradox! Some Irony!" Betty Chmaj draws from a variety of the popular and high arts to reconstruct images and stereotypes of woman in America since 1930. How do we explain, she asks, the paradoxes between the social conditions of women and the images that have been portrayed? What implications do the disparities between image and reality have for the process of historical generalization? Following Professor Chmaj's examination of female stereotypes across the arts, John Cawelti takes a theoretical approach to "Literary Formulas and Their Cultural Significance." After he has defined the major terms of this relationship, he begins to work out the problems of situating popular literature in formulaic and generic patterns that will show the extent to which it reveals and is shaped by culture.

Jay Martin and Jay Mechling speak for two fields that have become more prominent in modern American Studies: Comparative Cultures, and the New Ethnography (or cognitive anthropology). By plotting the course of American literary nationalism against the "Ethnic Poetics" of Black America and a revolutionary Latin American culture, Professor Martin constructs a theoretical model for perceiving what was characteristic in our own movement. He proposes that a national aesthetic develops in the gap between political and cultural independence; furthermore, he claims, the structure of literary and social revolutions is such that we may be able to predict social behavior from the tone and form of literary manifestos. Jay Mechling then inquires whether a paradigm revolution in the "third generation" of American Studies is about to replace the Myth/Symbol/Image school of criticism — long the favorite mode of explanation in American Studies, but now under siege — with a more satisfactory methodology derived from cognitive anthropology. As an example of the New Ethnographical approach, he introduces linguistic models and related forms of analysis to challenge the popular assumption that Relativity Theory was incorporated and expressed by a significant number of thinkers in the United States. This study in methods of proof and disproof voices the concern that many of our cultural judgments will not stand up to forms of scientific testing that have become available.

The last two essays have been written in response to the preceding statements and to discussions of practice and theory that were held by seminars of high school, college, and university teachers at the American Studies Institute. Robert Merideth approaches American Studies as an advocate of *disciplinarity* and *cultural revolution* and insists that the presuppositions — both philosophical and political — that scholars bring to their work must be defined and justified. Rendering the assumptions of the earlier essays "problematic," he applies a radical educational philosophy influenced by Paul Goodman and Ivan Illich to ten cases of teaching American Studies in the high school. My own essay represents a more traditional concept of American Studies than Professor Merideth's strategy of social transformation. This final commentary, a *vade mecum* through several current controversies in American Studies, asserts the continued importance of humanistic attitudes and demonstrates American Studies to be a forum for unresolved struggles over theories of knowledge in contemporary literary, historical, and sociological studies.

Luther S. Luedtke

CHAPTER 1

An Approach to the Thirties

By Daniel Aaron

DANIEL AARON, Professor of English and Chairman of the Committee on the History of American Civilization at Harvard University, has written widely in the areas of American history, politics, and the arts. From 1972 to 1974 he was President of the American Studies Association. While a member of the English Department at Smith College (1939-1971), Professor Aaron became a Guggenheim Fellow, a Fellow at the Center for Advanced Studies in the Behavioral Sciences, and a visiting professor at the University of Helsinki, Warsaw University, Sussex University, and the Salzburg Seminar in American Studies. Among his major writings are: *Men of Good Hope: A Story of American Progressives* (1950); with Richard Hofstadter and William Miller, *The United States: The History of the Republic* (1st ed. 1957); *Writers on the Left: Episodes in American Literary Communism* (1961); co-editor with Robert Bendiner, *The Strenuous Decade: A Social and Intellectual Record of the 1930's* (1970); and *The Inner Civil War: American Writers and the Civil War* (1973).

In the essay following, Daniel Aaron recreates the tone, the rhythms, the social and political ethos of the 1930s, a decade of "armies" and "new masses."

The decade of the 1930s is still a part of the "visitable past" — to use Henry James's expression — but from our vantage point in the 1970s (and even more so from the perspective of students) it is *dead* (even if expertly embalmed): it is *history*. When Murray Kempton wrote a book on the 30s some years ago, it wasn't out of contempt that he referred to the figures he discussed in his controversial volume as "Ruins" and "Monuments."

All the same, the decade is still contemporary and, in a measure, recoverable, and much remains to assist the historical imagination. The faces of the 30s — both the famous and the anonymous — stare back at us from the pages of history texts, anthologies, old films, albums of photography. Forms and shapes arise from novels and short stories and plays, from the volumes of reportage on strikes and parades and hearings that feature the more violent and flamboyant events of the period. The curious can also get a sense of the times from the advertisements in representative periodicals.

It is worth pointing out in this connection, by the way, that recent fashion styles have attempted — or are attempting — to recover the 30s look. As early as 1967, what *Business Week* called "spiffy new styles" and fabrics with "George Rafty" stripes were being featured along with ads depicting "Clifton Webb and Adolphe Menjou-type characters in creased-down hats with wide floppy brims, form-following double-breasted suits, and black-and-white bluchers." Films like *Bonnie and Clyde* encouraged the backward glance. A woman's shop in Chicago a few years ago advertised a "$195 two-piece Garbo outfit — antelope suede pants and a cobra vest." I leave it to the reader to decide the symbolic meaning of retrospective *chic*. Was the dress of the 30s more masculine than current styles? Does the present mode of argyle socks, bell-bottom trousers, square two-toned shoes, and butterfly bow ties indicate a retreat from the epicene style to the dress of sexually differentiated periods? At any rate we might direct our students' attention to the clothing ads or comic strips of the 20s and the 30s if only to suggest to them the vagaries of fashion and to arouse their suspicions that there may be a few links between their America and the America of forty years ago.

An obvious but often unreliable way to re-see the 30s is to read the memoirs and reminiscences that are now appearing in such profusion. Highly personal and idiosyncratic, they can be quite absorbing – even the bad ones – but they must be read with caution. Most of the memorialists are one-eyed, or at least they wear blinkers, and their conscious or unconscious omissions are sometimes more revealing than what they recall.

Take Eugene Lyons, for instance – author of a forgotten book called *The Red Decade.* For him the 30s were one long, drawn-out Communist conspiracy with all the writers and artists playing the roles of dupes and scoundrels. Or take Mike Gold, novelist, playwright, poet, columnist, Communist Party literary pundit – labelled by one unfriendly wit as the Al Jolson of American Communism, by another as the Cerberus of the Plebes. For him the 30s were heroic times when writers and intellectuals sloughed off their mean egotisms and for a brief interval consecrated themselves to humanity. Mike Gold remembered acts of courage and beauty as well as acts of betrayal.

Or take Lionel Trilling. He looks back on the 30s as a period marked by "moral urgency," by a sense of crisis and a concern for personal salvation. He believes (and I think rightly) that the politics of the radical literary intelligentsia in the Age of the Great Depression was "social and moral rather than political." They were concerned, he argues, (and the same would be true of other writers and artists in other times and countries) with "the ironic discrepancy, eventually the antagonism between life as it was . . . and the desire to make life as good as it might be." Their eventual disenchantment with their radical hopes, he concludes, came with the realization that if radical politics "affirmed freedom," political conduct often denied it.

Well, what can we learn from such books? And why should they be mistrusted as guides to the past? Because more often than not the autobiographies of men and women who flourished in the 30s are apologias exasperating in their self-absorption. If the author happens to be a Hemingway or a Dos Passos or any other figure of artistic substance, it doesn't particularly matter whether he or she has been selective, protective, and disingenuous. These writers have established their credentials in other ways. But for figures — literary or otherwise — whose importance lies principally in their having lived through the 20s and 30s and been privy to the events which concern us, we are chiefly interested in what they saw and (more important) remembered. A book like John Houseman's *Run-Through,* an urbane and well-written autobiography of a man who figured significantly in theatrical life in America during the 1930s, is in addition an informal history of the Federal and Mercury Theatres that wonderfully evokes people and places. Malcolm Cowley's reminiscences may be guardedly selective but they are also amusing and colorful. He succeeds very well in re-creating the 30s atmosphere. So does Edmund Wilson with his reportorial flair and reflective consciousness. But an autobiography like Albert Halper's *Good-Bye, Union Square,* despite its occasional flashes of 30s personalities and landscapes, is vainglorious, self-centered, self-defensive, and novelistic. So is *The Confessions of Edward Dahlberg,* a peevish book of far less interest than that author's autobiographical *Because I Was Flesh.*

Hence in approaching the memoirs, autobiographies, and recollections of the 30s, one might keep in mind the caveat of Erik Erikson that the man past his forties is likely to distort the past wilfully. He re-shapes the past or remembers it selectively or blots it out so that he can make the necessary adjustments to himself-in-maturity. Whether Erikson is right or not, any one who uses the memoir as a mirror of the past might consider the following questions: What is true and what is fictive in this memoir? Is the memoir an apologia or an attempt to re-see objectively what took place in the author's past? How does the author's conception of himself compare with his contemporaries' opinion of him? What is the significance of the form, structure, and style of the memoir? How are events that occurred decades before recorded? Are conversations repeated verbatim? What motivates a man to tell about his past? Does the picture of the author as conveyed in the memoir correspond to the inadvertent picture of himself projected in his other works? Is he hard on himself? Easy on himself? Does he seem typical or atypical of the 30s decade?

The last question — whether the author is typical of his time or atypical — suggests a more important one: is the 30s decade as readily definable as historians have made it out to be? Do the designations given to the 30s by cultural historians — "The Age of Convictions," "The Angry Decade," "The Red Decade," "The Strenuous Decade," "The Age of the Great Depression," "The Roosevelt Era" — really apply?

Each of these designations is tinged with a social or political implication, and I suppose it's natural that the 30s should *seem* to be all of a piece. If there is something artificial and arbitrary in dividing history into decades, more than most decades in American history the 30s *do* lend themselves to this kind of compartmentalization.

The decade opened dramatically with the Stock Market Crash of 1929. It ended, in effect, with the outbreak of the Second World War — a war signalized by the signing of the non-aggression pact between the Soviet Union and Nazi Germany in 1939. During the intervening years, political and social and economic events exploded (or seemed to) more violently than in the 20s or the 40s.

The student of the 30s is struck by the sustained note of crisis. He turns over the pages of the newspapers and magazines of the period and finds them filled with catastrophes of all kinds, economic and natural. The banks fail and the soil blows away. It is a decade of spectacular crimes — the Lindbergh kidnapping and the exploits of John Dillinger. The disorders are massive and collective; the panics are both financial and psychological.

It is worth noting, too, that this is the decade of *armies.* There were the military armies, of course, like the kind that burned out the Bonus Marchers camped on Washington's

Anacostia flats. On the orders of President Hoover, this army, commanded by General Douglas MacArthur and his two aides, Major Dwight Eisenhower and George S. Patton, conquered the Bonus "army" — a squalid episode Malcolm Cowley described at the time in a hot article. It appropriately inaugurated what Auden called in one of his poems — "a low dishonest decade." Then there were the armies of the National Guard employed to oust the sit-down strikers holding out in the plants of Michigan and Ohio — and the armies of labor in the throes of organization; and the armies of the unemployed moving from city to city; and the armies of protestors (sometimes Communist led, sometimes not) marching to demand jobs or resist evictions; and the armies of farmers organized to prevent foreclosures and to impede the operations of the courts.

If one went to the movies in the 30s — a national pastime of central importance — one could not only see these armies but hear them. And one could hear the leaders who addressed their mammoth congregations. Many of the sights and sounds of those days have been preserved. We can listen to the voices of the dead on tapes and recordings — FDR's "Fire-Side Chats," the harangues of Adolf Hitler, Paul Robeson's renditions of the songs of the Spanish Loyalists. It's useful to keep in mind, I think, that the Silent Films ended by 1929 and that 1930 began the era of sound and the microphone. News Reels recorded in film and sound the dictators' marching millions and artfully staged mass-meetings. No one who lived through the decade can forget the series of documentary films sponsored by the Luce publications, "The March of Time" — which caught the violence and dynamism of the decade. Each was narrated by a stern-voiced melodramatic broadcaster who ended every report with the Luce refrain: "Time . . . marches on."

What the newsreels showed in their American sequences was a people thinking and acting in groups — perhaps because of a widely shared feeling that one had to organize or die. Massive group action could be seen in the adoring adherents of the would-be American Fuehrers — the followers of Huey Long and Father Charles Coughlin, of Dr. Francis Townsend.

The "Enemy" — many things to many people — whether at home or abroad provoked the response of the aggregate. Hemingway's Harry Morgan, the hero of his novel *To Have and Have Not* (1937), put the message succinctly in his dying moment: "No matter how — a man alone ain't got no bloody fucking chance." It was the greatest leader of them all, Franklin Roosevelt, who summoned Americans to mobilize against the Depression as if they were repelling a foreign invasion.

Warren Susman in an illuminating essay on the 1930s makes the point that the impulse to cohere during the Depression, to act in concert when the body-politic seemed to be disintegrating, was assisted by new techniques and machinery having to do with mass communication. The 30s was pre-eminently the decade of the radio, and no one mastered its art more adroitly than the father figure and social physician, FDR. The ingratiating voice of President Roosevelt — reassuring, humorous, sarcastic, indignant, portentous — has been recorded for posterity, but how can one convey to students for whom television has supplanted the radio (except for music listening) its immense significance? The bodiless voice of the 30s can still arouse strong emotions in anyone who remembers those days, whether one is listening to Amos 'n Andy, Fred Allen, Edgar Bergen or Adolf Hitler, John L. Lewis, or Huey Long. On radio, the political speech or a human drama takes on special dimensions. The listener, deprived of the picture, must provide his own background for the voice; and the skillful broadcaster must suggest through intonation, emphasis, and accent what the listener can't see.

I can remember as a boy listening to Father Charles Coughlin's divisive harangues — called sermons — that emanated from the Shrine of the Little Flower, Royal Oak, Michigan, on Sunday afternoons. It was almost impossible *not* to hear these demagogic recitals about the crimes of the banking fraternity and the currency manipulators. Once I walked eight long Chicago blocks in early summer — all the way from University Avenue to the lake — and I didn't miss a single word of his talk. His unctuous voice sounded from the open windows of hundreds of apartment buildings.

I missed the famous — or notorious — radio performance of Orson Welles, the production of H. G. Wells's *The War of the Worlds* which many people, I dare say, have heard in its recorded version. That was a 30s phenomenon if ever there was, both the company of actors and the performance. The performers belonged to Orson Welles's Mercury Theatre company (another one of those famous "groups" in a decade of "groups"), the same company that staged Shakespeare's *Julius Caesar* in the Fascist setting of Mussolini's Rome and Hitler's Third Reich. Considering the close links between art and life in the 30s, was it so extraordinary that the Welles broadcast should have touched off mass hysteria?

It came, as a matter of fact, just after the Munich crisis — the apogee of all the 30s crises — in the fall of 1938, when it looked as if a world-wide war (if not a war of the worlds) was about to start. For several weeks before Neville Chamberlain capitulated to Hitler over Czechoslovakia, people all over the world had their ears glued to their sets as Hitler ranted at Nazi rallies and Mussolini threatened and radio announcers kept breaking into other programs to announce new developments in the crisis: "We interrupt our program in order to bring to our listeners the world-awaited talk on Germany's foreign policy." For the first time Americans were able to listen to the sound of history being enacted. The reports of such correspondents as William Shirer and Edward Murrow and announcers like H. V. Kaltenborn may seem less vivid than our more sophisticated coverage today, which provides us with our daily doses of armed violence in Southeast Asia or the Middle East or Northern Ireland, but it was exciting enough to listen to Hitler chanting *Blut, Boden, Deutschland* as he worked himself into a frenzy (we thought it was very funny at first — rather like Charlie Chaplin's clever parody in *The Great Dictator*) and then hear the antiphonal response of his followers — the sounds billowing out of the radio: *Sieg Heil! Sieg Heil!*

The radio performance of *The War of the Worlds* sent thousands of terrified Americans into the streets, convinced that hordes of Martian invaders (not German or Japanese invaders, mind you) were about to incinerate God's chosen people.

Given the pervasive hysteria of the times, given the verisimilitude of the performance and the fact that Americans in the 30s had become attuned to skillfully presented radio dramas, and given the frequency of "on-the-spot" radio broadcasts interrupting scheduled programs to notify the radio audience of horrendous news events, it's understandable why uneasy and gullible people should listen with particular attention when someone — announced as the Secretary of the Interior and sounding rather like FDR himself — should declare solemnly:

> "Citizens of the nation: I shall not try to conceal the gravity of the situation that confronts the country, nor the concern of your government in protecting the lives and property of its people. However, I wish to impress upon you — private citizens and public officials, all of you — the urgent need of calm and resourceful action. Fortunately, this formidable enemy is still confined to a comparatively small area [the Martians had only destroyed New Jersey], and we may place our faith in the military forces to keep them there. In the meantime placing our trust in God, we must continue the performance of our duties, each and every one of us, so that we may confront this destructive adversary with a nation united, courageous, and consecrated to the preservation of human supremacy on this earth. I thank you."

I know of no important literary figures who fled to the streets upon hearing this announcement, but writers — like other Americans — experienced their share of turmoil and fear. Sometimes they seemed to react to real or imagined crises facing them and society no less hysterically than the dupes of Orson Welles. Perhaps, more than most of their countrymen, they were called upon (or they *felt* called upon, in many cases) to "take sides."

In a general sense, all times and periods are "political," and most writers with strong ethical or moral concerns usually take a position vis-a-vis the standing order. No matter whether the writer defends or attacks it — or tries to avoid any sort of commitment — he is in effect taking a position, as radicals were quick to point out in the 30s. Throughout the decade, a sustained controversy took place between those who cautioned the engaged writer that Art and Propaganda

were mutually exclusive and those who argued just as
vehemently that all great artists wrote purposefully — that
tendentious literature was not necessarily mechanical and
shallow literature. During the 30s, politics — both domestic
and foreign — invited or compelled the writer to take a stand,
to declare his allegiance. The months after the Stock Market
Crash were full of deprivation and suffering. Unemployment
and other symptoms of economic and social collapse were no
longer quarantined in the cities or in the barren reaches of
the hinterland. The New Deal experimented with schemes to
alleviate the national crisis and to restore hope. It met with
some success. But the misery of the forgotten third of a
nation became everybody's business. It was revealed in the
stories and photographs and films and speeches about
breadlines,   evictions,   strike-breaking,   farm-foreclosures,
vigilantism — in what Diana Trilling called "the grim idiot
face of capitalism."

Not surprisingly, the writers who were discovering the
ugly facts of the Depression themselves, and writing about
them passionately, felt involved in the social scene more than
they ever had before. And not simply the Communists; Lewis
Mumford once observed in a letter to me:

> The moving idea during the thirties was not the vision of socialist
> transformation of our country. What made people [he was referring
> chiefly to writers and intellectuals] join all sorts of movements from
> technocracy to communism, from the Douglass plan to socialism was
> the desire to repair the broken down machinery of our society and
> overcome the poverty and misery and fear that visited even the middle
> classes and the once affluent professional classes. So badly had the
> dominant economic and political organizations failed that they were
> willing to try anything in order to correct injustices and restore life to
> our paralyzed economic limbs, as a person stricken with a fatal disease
> is willing to try anything, from homeopathy to surgery, provided it
> promises relief. The spectacle of human suffering was so widespread
> and inescapable that only the stupid or the hard-hearted could accept
> the existing order as the last word.

The violence and confusion in the political developments
of Europe — which matched the violence and confusion at
home — also affected writers and intellectuals of all political
persuasions. The response of writers and artists to Vietnam or
to the politics of current China or the USSR or the Middle

East or India seems far less intense and serious than the response of their counterparts in the 30s to Japanese expansionism, to the African adventures of Mussolini, to the frightening diplomatic triumphs of Hitler, to the proud claims of the USSR and the fearful rumors of trials and executions in that country, to the revolution in Spain.

In order to define and to isolate what is really typical of the 30s, then, one must pay particular attention to the *political ingredient*, no matter how indirect, in all of the social events of the period, including the lively arts and even sports. Politics occupied writers in different ways and in different degrees, of course. Some even conveyed personal revulsions, unhappy love affairs, injured pride in the metaphors of politics; but very few remained untouched by the events swirling about them or succeeded in isolating themselves behind their private bastions.

Americans have always been a future-minded people, but in times of crisis (or moral or cultural dislocation) they have looked to the past for direction or as a way to determine at what point the nation went wrong. In the 1930s, when the country seemed to have lost its bearings and special interests waged a kind of domestic civil war, writers and intellectuals as well as politicians sought ways to remind a fragmented society of its common traditions and culture.

For the Right-Wingers, the past to be resurrected came out in the form of star-spangled patriotism lampooned broadly in Sinclair Lewis's *It Can't Happen Here* and in Nathanael West's *A Cool Million.* The brand of "America Firstism" marketed by Col. McCormick's *Chicago Tribune* and the newspapers of William Randolph Hearst differed only in degree from the chauvinist propaganda of the totalitarian states.

Communist leaders, stigmatized as un-American by their critics and linked in the popular mind with foreign ideologies, sought to counteract these impressions (at least during the United Front period) with the claim that Communism was 20th century Americanism. They named their schools and clubs and organizations after famous Americans whom they

converted into ancestors: Tom Paine, Walt Whitman, Thomas
Jefferson, Abraham Lincoln, John Brown. Communist or
fellow-traveling historians and historical novelists re-wrote
American history as a set of variations on the class struggle.

In the South, a group of writers and teachers (largely
centered at Vanderbilt University in Nashville) drew
anti-Marxist or anti-Communist conclusions from American
history. The Nashville Agrarians were no defenders of the
national brand of financial or industrial capitalism, whose
triumph had been assured, they believed, by the victory of
the North in 1865. They were not about to substitute for the
bankrupt American system the servile state of the
Communists and projected a scheme for a society of small
property-holders happily abiding in a decentralized America.
The Agrarians proposed to restore the social values of the
historic South amidst "the very clash and thunder of partisan
views." (I'm quoting Donald Davidson.) In the biographical
narratives of Allen Tate, Andrew Lytle, and Robert Penn
Warren, studies of Stonewall Jackson, Bedford Forrest, and
John Brown, the Agrarians detected the causes for the
collapsing economy in 1930 and the economic, political, and
moral debacle which followed.

I have been suggesting that in the 1930s history was a
grab bag. Contesting groups representing the entire political
spectrum reached into it and fumbled for evidence to sustain
their preconceptions. Whitman, Tom Paine, Emerson, Mark
Twain were "for today," as the *New Masses* put it. The very
zeal with which partisans searched for links with what they
regarded as authentic American traditions — the passion with
which such poets as Carl Sandburg in *The People, Yes* or
Archibald MacLeish in *Land of the Free* used history as a
kind of national restorative — would seem to indicate that
the searchers were motivated by something stronger than
historical curiosity. The past dredged up in poetry and fiction
and drama, in films and song, in biography and mural
painting proclaimed American virility and toughness, the
resiliency of a people familiar with man-made or natural
disasters and able to cope with crises.

Reviewed in this light, the Federal Art Project (the history of which is now coming out in pieces) takes on a special significance. It was assumed by many at the time (and the view persists) that the huge New Deal experiment in publicly supported art projects was one of "the lesser plagues of the Great Depression" (the description is Harold Rosenberg's) and that the millions expended to provide jobs for "loafers, trouble-makers, and self-declared geniuses" could be most charitably justified as benevolent "boon-doggling."

This is not the place for even a perfunctory survey of the WPA arts projects in sculpture and painting, music, drama, and design, but one undertaking carried out under the auspices of the Federal Writers' Project (1935-1943) deserves at least a brief look: the American Guide Series.

The series — a vast, untidy operation inaugurated by the publication of the Idaho Guide in 1937 and closing with the appearance of the Oklahoma Guide five years later — received exhaustive comment from its admirers and critics. Bernard De Voto called it "the largest-scale experiment in literary cooperation ever made in the United States." An army of researchers, writers, and administrators (about 12,000 in all), only a small proportion of which were bona fide writers, were involved in its production. With the publication of each volume, friends and foes of the Writers' Project had no trouble in enumerating its errors and deficiencies. Yet the very size and scope of the series stilled what one reviewer called "picayunish" criticism. Soon it became evident that the Guides were not only a compendium of towns and cities and collections of road-tours. They were also a new kind of human and historical geography, a Whitmanesque kaleidoscope of a country as mysterious as China.

No one to my knowledge has attempted to assess the response of the readership to the State Guides and lesser Guides. On the whole, they seemed to have been well received, even by those who hated all of the other WPA art projects. State officials handed out copies to schools and libraries in their respective states; some of the Guides made the "best-seller" lists. But I'm more concerned with their symbolic import. For many readers, the Guides were simply containers of fascinating minutiae and oddities — the inside story of Calamity Jane, for example, or a North Carolina tax once levied on owners of beaver hats and gold-headed canes, or the inscription on the tomb of a Civil War veteran, N. Grigsby, of Harper, Kansas:

> Through this inscription I wish to enter my dying protest against what is called the Democratic Party. I have watched it closely since the days of Jackson, and know that all the misfortunes of our nation have come to it through the so-called party — therefore beware of this party of treason.

More discerning readers, however, valued the Guides as repositories of "invaluable antiquarian material that might have perished" and "heighten our national self-consciousness."

No hard evidence exists to prove the Guides served this purpose, but such responses (and there were a good many in the 1930s) support the hypothesis that in this decade history served a therapeutic function.

It is not surprising that, at a time when the country was threatened from within and without by real or fancied enemies and apprehensive about its future, American artists and intellectuals should take "a backward glance o'er travelled roads." Paradoxically, however, in this allegedly radical and potentially revolutionary decade, the composite view of the American past emerging from their work was markedly less iconoclastic and irreverent than the retrospective view in the Menckenian twenties.

As the Depression deepened, the debunking tone (briefly heard in magazines like *Americana* and *Ballyhoo*) faded away. The shift in attitude can be illustrated in the fate of two novels I have already mentioned, Nathanael West's *A Cool Million* (1934) and Sinclair Lewis's *It Can't Happen Here* (1935). Both deal with the coming of Fascism to America, but beyond this common theme, the two books are totally unlike.

West, the sardonic satirist, spoofs the Horatio Alger myth, commercialized patriotism, and the celebratory

"Pageant-of-America" view of history. Symbolic of his fascist-America is a brothel operated by one Wu Fong, educated at Yale-in-China and fluent in Italian. The brothel features a decor of various regional styles: Pennsylvania Dutch, Old South, Log Cabin Pioneer, Victorian New York, Western Cattle Days, California Monterey, Indian, and Modern Girl.

Nothing so indecorous or irreverent can be found in Lewis's splenetic novel. His story of the rise and fall of a dictator is a testament of faith, a celebration of the old national virtues. The authentic American hero, an idealized representative of the middle class, is not dismembered and destroyed like West's Lemuel Pitkin. He endures and saves his country, which is at bottom sound and uncorrupted.

West's novel failed dismally despite a few understanding reviews. The left-wing critics who might have been expected to relish the author's savage anti-fascist message found his black humor malapropos. In contrast they found much to praise in *It Can't Happen Here,* despite Lewis's slurring references to the Communists. The lesson was plain. The writer who wanted to be heard in the 30s dared not sell America short.

The most sensational political novel of the decade, *The Grapes of Wrath,* reached a vast audience in spite of conservative hostility, because it aroused humanitarian indignation without undermining confidence in the redeemable collective. Steinbeck's novel incorporates most of the strains of the 30s I've been alluding to. Its subject is a migrant army. It abounds with disasters. It celebrates the toughness and essential goodness of ordinary people. It is marked by "moral urgency." It relates the Depression crisis (the overwhelming fact of the decade) to America's democratic heritage and is more evangelical than radical, more New Dealish than socialist. Above all it is thirty-ish in its message: that the people must put aside private greed and cooperate to save their country and their souls.

The appeal of the 1930s shows no signs of abatement even while the American stage is being swathed in the bunting of its Revolutionary Bicentennial. The popularity of *The Waltons* on television and Studs Terkel's *Hard Times* in oral history manifests the general nostalgia for a decade which we all can revisit in memory, either at first or second hand. Deep structural changes occurred in those epoch-making years that have given the inarticulate a voice and steered the nation in a new direction. Yet, perhaps more than any other feature, it is the sense of human wholeness about the 1930s that fascinates us still: the synthesis of creative imagination and rational planning – of moral, social, and political wisdom. It is this wholeness that continues to make the 1930s an ideal enterprise for the student of American culture.

BIBLIOGRAPHICAL NOTE

This essay draws upon a small library of books on the 1930s. A convenient although already dated bibliography is included in *The Strenuous Decade: A Social and Intellectual Record of the Nineteen-Thirties,* ed. Daniel Aaron and Robert Bendiner (Garden City, New York: Anchor Books, 1970). Allusions are made directly to Murray Kempton, *Part of Our Time: Some Ruins and Monuments of the Thirties* (New York: Simon & Schuster, 1955); Eugene Lyons, *The Red Decade* (Indianapolis: Bobbs-Merrill Company, 1941); Michael Gold, *The Hollow Men* (New York: International Publishers, 1941); Lionel Trilling's afterword to Tess Slesinger, *The Unpossessed* (New York: Avon, 1966); John Houseman, *Run-Through* (New York: Simon & Schuster, 1972); Malcolm Cowley, *A Second Flowering* (New York: Viking Press, 1973), in addition to Cowley's pieces in *The Strenuous Decade;* Warren I. Susman, "The Thirties" in *The Development of an American Culture,* ed. Stanley Coben and Lorman Ratner (Englewood Cliffs, N.J.: Prentice-Hall, 1970), a key article for understanding the decade. Houseman's book contains the best account of the Martian 'invasion' as well as the most vivid description of theatrical life in the 30s. References to Lewis Mumford can be found in the author's

"The Treachery of Recollection" in *Essays in History and Literature,* ed. Robert H. Bremner (Columbus: Ohio State University Press, 1966). Jerre Mangione, *The Dream and the Deal: The Federal Writers' Project, 1935-43* (Boston: Little, Brown & Company, 1972) is the most readable and complete account of that episode. Some recent books apposite to this essay are: William Stott, *Documentary Expression and Thirties America* (New York: Oxford University Press, 1973), and Richard H. Pells, *Radical Visions and American Dreams* (New York: Harper and Row, 1973), a conscientious survey of the decade.

CHAPTER 2

Four Approaches to Regionalism in the Visual Arts of the 1930s

By William H. Jordy

WILLIAM H. JORDY is Professor of Art and a member of the American Civilization Committee at Brown University, where he currently presents courses on modern architecture and the history of art. A graduate of the doctoral program in American Studies at Yale University and a former Guggenheim Fellow, he is also a member of the Society of Architectural Historians and the College Art Association. Among his published works are: *Henry Adams: Scientific Historian* (1952); Montgomery Schuyler, *American Architecture and Other Writings,* edited with Ralph Coe; *American Buildings and Their Architects: Progressive and Academic Ideals at the Turn of the Twentieth Century* (1971); and *American Buildings and Their Architects: The Impact of European Modernism in the Mid-Twentieth Century* (1972).

This essay examines the artistic, literary, and social events of the 1930s, using painting, photography, architecture, and public planning to document the themes of regionalism, nationalism, and internationalism characteristic of the decade.

In the visual arts during the 1930s surely regionalism was
a cardinal issue. Publications bracketing the period testify to
the pervasiveness of the theme. At the threshold of the
decade, there were Benton MacKaye's *The New Exploration*
(1928), Twelve Southerners' *I'll Take My Stand* (1930) and
W.P. Webb's *The Great Plains* (1931); toward its end Lewis
Mumford's *The Culture of Cities* (1938), Donald Davidson's
The Attack on Leviathan (1938) and Harold Odum's
magisterial compendium on the subject, *American Regionalism* (1939). In the visual arts specifically, to mention
examples only from painting, photography, architecture and
planning, on which this discussion will center, the theme of
regionalism immediately conjures up the midwestern trio of
painters Thomas Benton, Grant Wood, and John Curry. It
brings to mind murals in government buildings on local lore,
local history or local industry, customarily executed in a
mixture of archaic cubism and primitivized Quattrocento
styles that rather intensified the provincial flavor, while
trying to monumentalize the image. It recalls the painstaking
exactitude of the delineators of artifacts from the national
garret which added up to the Index of American Design. It
also calls up the work of the documentary photographers of
the period, and especially three books that epitomized the
regional flavor of much of the documentation of the time:
Margaret Bourke-White's *You Have Seen Their Faces* (1937)
with Erskine Caldwell, Dorothea Lange's *An American
Exodus* (1939) with Paul Taylor, and Walker Evans's *Let Us
Now Praise Famous Men* (1941) with James Agee. Turning
to architecture, there is the work of Frank Lloyd Wright, of
course. His so-called Usonian houses and scheme for
Broadacre City accounted for part of the immense revival of
interest in his work, both from professionals and laymen,
following the period of relative neglect and obscurity that
characterized his career during most of the twenties. In
architecture, too, Walter Gropius and Marcel Breuer, toward
the end of the decade, adapted the European modernism of
the "International Style" to the carpentered vernacular and
fieldstone walls of New England. Or a bit later, a group
around San Francisco adapted the same modernism to a

redwood vernacular that came to be labeled the "Bay Area Style." And — just to conclude this selection from the grab bag of thirties regionalism with the most heroic example of the lot — there was, of course, the Tennessee Valley Authority. All of these examples were in some significant manner permeated with regional concerns; all comment on the theme.

But regionalism is a changing conception, assuming different meanings in different contexts. The difference, in turn, depends on the focus of the polemic. In the visual arts, four possible foci can be distinguished in the use of the term during the decade. First, regionalism may be seen as a *reformist conceptual tool* for certain ills afflicting the entire country. Second, it may be seen as an *adaptive or acclimatizing attitude* by which the cosmopolite adjusts to or learns from the local situation. Third, it may be seen as one pole of a dichotomy, as the *different America*. Or, finally, it may be seen as the embodiment of the *deeper America*.

Thus — to elaborate briefly on each of these attitudes by specific example — TVA was obviously viewed by its partisans as a regional enterprise in the sense of a reformist tool applicable to and beneficial for much of America. From the outset both Arthur E. Morgan and David Lilienthal repeatedly spoke of the Authority as a "laboratory" for what was to come (or should come) elsewhere. When Harold Ickes organized the National Resources Committee within the Department of Interior with the idea that at last a central planning agency would determine national priorities in accord with a comprehensive rationale rather than with pork barrel expediency, the Board recommended no fewer than 17 major river authorities. [1]

Beside such use of regional thinking as a means of effecting mammoth change, *ad hoc* regionalism as a component in the creative adjustment of the outsider to an unfamiliar area is relatively mundane, and a phenomenon that occurs at all times. There are periods, however, when the regional aspects of the creative act are especially conspicuous, transcending the mere means of accommodation to become its core. This is the case, for example, with the

transformation that the German emigres Walter Gropius and
(more especially) Marcel Breuer effected in their modern
houses, just before and after World War II, once they had
reached New England.[2] Comparison of Breuer's Harnisch-
macher House in Wiesbaden (1932) with, say, the Robinson
House in Williamstown, Massachusetts (1946-47) makes the
point. (Figs. 1, 2.) The taut, apparently thin surfaces of the
earlier house with its sharp edges, its pencil-thin window
mullions, its pipe railings, its abstract compactness of shape
crisply set against its landscape setting typify the "machine
image" that marked the so-called International Style of
European modern architecture of the twenties. Just as surely,
Breuer's Robinson House in New England (a bit late for our
period, to be sure, but an outstanding example of ideas
initiated during the thirties) shows the progressive absorption
of elements from his new environment. Indigenous carpentry,
fieldstone walls, shed roofs, and the generous spread of the
building on its site, but with the sort of laconic starkness
with which the New England house typically confronts the
field that surrounds it: these are insignia of the locality.
Quite consciously, as he himself has admitted, Breuer altered
his European manner under the impact of his new situation.

To be sure, this example of regional transformation, like
others, is less pure than the starkest comparison indicates.
Even among the most devout adherents of the machine image
of the twenties, there were European architects who tended
from the early thirties onward to turn for inspiration toward
regional vernacular styles with their more traditional shapes,
closer relation to the earth, and rough-textured materials. So
Breuer was preconditioned in Europe to appreciate the New
England vernacular tradition. The Robinson House therefore
reflects a double development. It is part of a widespread
tendency in Europe itself to move away from the polemical
imagery of modernity in earlier buildings toward a more
comfortable, more popular and less elitist, vocabulary of
form. But this European preconditioning was given impetus
toward and particularity of regional expression in New
England. Moreover, and especially in the general fervor for

regional ideas at the time, Breuer's design could be assimilated into the larger cause. Much the same could be said of the redwood and shakes vernacular tradition that modified International Style modernism in the San Francisco area around 1940.[3] These assaults of the indigenous on the most strident modernity of the International Style substantially modified it. It should be added, however, that the architects who adjusted the International Style to local traditions were circumspect regionalists. Regional influences were important, yes; but they adamantly maintained the cosmopolitan bases for their designs.

Commitment is of the essence with respect to the third of the four approaches to regionalism that characterized the omnibus movement in the thirties. Of the gamut of varieties of regionalist sentiment, this was the most extreme. Whereas the other two represented enthusiastic projections from the local to the national, this brand of regionalism would husband the provinciality and use the difference to establish a dialogue between nation and region. The conspicuous proponents of this most separatist point of view — at its radical extreme more akin to the exclusive position of nineteenth-century "sectionalists" than to the cooperative position of twentieth-century regionalists — were the self-styled Southern Agrarians.[4] Published in 1930, *I'll Take My Stand* became the catechism of the movement. The attribution of this collection of essays to "Twelve Southerners" underscored its shared conviction. So did a prefatory manifesto subscribed to by all the contributors.

At the core of the Southern Agrarian movement was a group who had originally come together as teachers and students at Vanderbilt University in informal gatherings to read and criticize their own poetry. As the group became more self-aware and more ambitious, it sponsored the publication of a journal, *The Fugitive,* which became a focus for *avant garde* poetry, its importance extending far beyond the brief period of its existence from 1922 to 1925. All from the South, the group members were conscious of their Southern background while at Vanderbilt, in the sense that they lived it, and their poetry almost inevitably sprang from this inheritance. With time, the attrition of individual careers inevitably eroded the group, as most of them moved away from Vanderbilt (many to northern states). In their new situations they became, if anything, more aware of that part of themselves that they had left behind, and more deeply concerned about the New South industrialism that threatened Old South agrarianism. They continued to correspond, occasionally to meet, the composition of the group undergoing some change in the course of time — if, indeed, "group" is not too strong a term to characterize what had become a diffuse point of view, but fiercely held and brought to focus in *I'll Take My Stand.* Of the contributors to this volume the best known are John Crowe Ransom, Donald Davidson, Allen Tate and Robert Penn Warren. The introductory essay by Ransom strikes the tone for the book in its very title, "Reconstructed but Unregenerate." Although there is no comparable statement in the visual arts of regionalism as the different America, *I'll Take My Stand* is so useful as a baseline against which to appraise the nature of "regionalist" contributions by artists and architects that Ransom's essay merits quotation to epitomize the sentiment of the whole. "The Southern idea today is down, and the progressive or American idea is up." [5] He went on to compare the South to England, a country that had done its pioneering long ago, and settled into an easy, civilized rapport with tradition.

> The pioneering life is not the normal life, whatever some Americans may suppose. . . . Boys are very well pleased to employ their muscles almost exclusively, but men prefer to exercise their minds. . . . For it is the character of a seasoned provincial life that it is realistic, or successfully adapted to its natural environment, and that as a consequence it is stable, or hereditable. But it is the character of our urbanized, anti-provincial, progressive, and mobile American life that it is in a condition of eternal flux. Affections, and long memories, attach to the ancient bowers of life in the provinces; but they will not attach to what is always changing. . . . Progress never defines its ultimate objective, but thrusts its victims at once into an infinite series. Our vast industrial machine, with its laboratory centers of experimentation, and its far-flung organs of mass production is like a Prussianized state which is organized strictly for war and can never consent to peace. Or,

returning to the original figure, our progressives are the latest version of those pioneers who conquered the wilderness, except that they are pioneering on principle, or from force of habit, and without any recollection of what pioneering is for. 6

Ransom and his cohorts realized that the South existed at a watershed, the Old South rapidly giving way to the New. They dug in their heels, taking their (hopeless) stand against the trend. Eventually, in 1937, Davidson rounded out the earlier volume with his *The Attack on Leviathan,* but, to repeat, no comparable attack came from the painters. There was no Southern Agrarian school of painters. A few photographers discovered the rotting plantation house, and incidentally hastened the day of restoration for some of them; but there was no exceptional regional commitment in the photographs. The movie version of *Gone With the Wind,* released in 1939, might also be cited; but this was dominant America cashing in on the difference.

Whereas the arch-enemy to the Southern Agrarians was dominant America, to other regionalists maintaining a more widely held position the arch-enemy was of course Europe. (How ironic, and how revealing, that the Southern Agrarians should identify themselves *with* Europe: the most out-spokenly provincial point of view among the regionalists come full-circle, as it were, to hold hands with the interna-tionalists!) Those who adhered to this brand of regionalism did not oppose the nation. On the contrary, they found in regionalism the deeper, more authentic America. The focus for this position is not the South, but the mid-West. In the visual arts, it is the position most visibly occupied by the triumvirate of midwestern painters, Benton, Wood and Curry, together with the architect, Frank Lloyd Wright.

Here is Benton, the most articulate of the three painters, writing reminiscently in 1951, when he added a section to his *An Artist in America,* to bring it up-to-date:

John Steuart Curry and Grant Wood rose along with me to public attention in the thirties. They were very much a part of what I stood for and made it possible for me in my lectures and interviews to promote the idea that an indigenous art with its own aesthetics was a growing reality in America . . .

We were different in our temperaments and many of our ideas but we
were alike in that we were all in revolt against the unhappy effects
which the Armory Show of 1913 had had on American painting.[7] We
objected to the new Parisian aesthetics which was more and more
turning art away from the living world of active men and women into
an academic world of empty pattern. We wanted an American art which
was not empty, and we believed that only by turning the formative
processes of art back again to meaningful subject matter, in our cases
specifically American subject matter, could we expect to get one . . . .

The term [Regionalism] was, so to speak, wished upon us. Borrowed
from a group of southern writers who were interested in their regional
cultures, it was applied to us somewhat loosely, but with a fair degree
of appropriateness. However, our interests were wider than the term
suggests. They had their roots in that general and country-wide revival
of Americanism which followed the defeat of Woodrow Wilson's
universal idealism at the end of World War One and which developed
through the subsequent periods of boom and depression until the new
internationalisms of the Second World War pushed it aside. [8]

Although Benton went on to admit that this Americanism of the twenties had its dark side "suggestive of an
ugly neo-fascism"[9] (he cited the Ku Klux Klan, Red Baiting,
the repressive settling of strikes as instances), he believed it
also had its beneficent side. It was the creative aspect of
regionalism, the American identifying himself with a place,
finding (to reverse Gertrude Stein) a *there* there, which, in his
opinion, had come to characterize the healthiest tendencies
in American painting in the thirties. Not that he denied that
foreign ideas had always played a role in American culture;
but the foreign ideas in contemporary painting, mostly
imported from Paris as either the geometrization of form in
Cubism, or as the flat, brilliantly colored planes of Fauvism,
had, in his opinion, become overly intellectual. Instead of an
open, understandable, "collective" art, modern art had
adopted a public-be-damned attitude. So much was
the reasonable, if hardly reasoned, opinion which became
congealed as Benton's fixed position, even as the founding of
the Museum of Modern Art in New York in 1929 brought
into being one of the most phenomenally successful
educational enterprises the United States has ever known. It
promptly popularized what Benton found hermetic. Moreover, there is no blinking the fact that Benton had his uglier
side, as when he castigated the homosexuals that infested

New York galleries and museums. He himself could be (and was) condemned for remarks that skirted Nazi attacks on "degenerate art," although in fairness it should be added that Benton (and to a lesser degree the other two midwesterners) were liberal with respect to most political and economic issues.

Of course Benton had been to Paris before the war, and he had tried to become a modernist himself. Wood and Curry, too, went to Paris in the twenties: Wood a bit lost as to what stance to adopt with respect to modern art (but eventually opting for tradition), Curry never at any time straying from a conservative position. The styles of all three indicate that it was *modern* European art they abhorred. *Traditional* European art was another matter, as indeed regional points of view must, in some respect, lean heavily on tradition.

Without investigating the matter of Benton's style in any detail,[10] suffice it to say that the grotesque linear patterning that gives such vehement animation to his forms, the intense elongation of figures, jumps in scale and space, and the extravagant spot-light effect of the illumination, all derive from European mannerism of the sixteenth century, most specifically perhaps from El Greco, who was undergoing rediscovery in the early twentieth century. (Fig. 3.) Surely the solids modeled in mechanical fashion from light to dark and set in opposition to the precipitous perspective of the space is ultimately Renaissance, although the ghastly, nightmarish quality of the light and the runaway aspect of the space could also have been absorbed from European surrealism of the Salvador Dali sort. There are rudimentary evidences, too, of Benton's earlier interest in cubism, learned when he was still imagining a career for himself as a modernist.

Or to be even more brisk with the Renaissance borrowings of Curry:[11] the oval organization of a composition like his familiar *Tornado Over Kansas* (1928), the heroic idealization of farmer and wife, as well as the kind of grandiose landscape depicted here is a provincializing of Rubens. (Fig. 4.) Curry was also enamored of the Venetians (especially evident in his later paintings) and among the moderns affected by Delacroix, Gericault, Turner, Daumier, and Courbet; in short, by no influences much beyond the mid-nineteenth century. Nor were these influences transmuted into as much of a personal style even as Benton's. Instead Curry aggrandized his representational content by the husks of great styles from the past. His painting is popular, in a double sense: his viewers' familiarity with the American scene is augmented by their familiarity with the styles of great painting from the past. The most rewarding aspects of the painting are illustrative. Curry feels farm life intensely for having grown up in it. He is capable of such acute, if sentimental, observations as the saving of the household pets in the underground ark, while the barnyard animals are forced to brave the holocaust. Each of the pets (dog, cat, and guinea pigs) reacts in a characteristic way to the epic of fright and rescue.

With Wood, a comparable relationship of content to style occurred. [12] (Fig. 5.) In his case it was Flemish and German late medieval/early Renaissance painters like the Van Eycks or Memling that furnished inspiration. Wood stylized their archaic stiffness into stereometric simplification, as he also stylized and patterned their microscopic realism of detail. Like the others, but especially like Benton, he was fascinated by the formalistic gaucheries of daguerreotypes, nineteenth-century prints, and other folk arts, an interest that intensified the sense of quaintness and pastness. It may be worth mentioning, too, that at one point in his life Wood made house models surrounded by sponge trees for a local real estate man, the better to entice customers. A sense of toys pervades Wood's imagery, as a sense of stage flats in Benton's works may recall his brief sojourn as a set designer for the movies.

Clearly these are men of different temperaments, working in very different styles. What unites them is their common interest in local subject matter, and the deliberate adaptation of traditional European styles to their themes, with varying admixtures of influences from folkish sources.

Frank Lloyd Wright also saw himself as a midwestern regionalist. Convinced that what was most creative in America stemmed from its heartland, he vociferously opposed the European modernism which the then recently established Museum of Modern Art had christened in an exhibition of 1932 as the "International Style." To Wright this was the "cardboard style," a chill, intellectual, mechanistic architecture extracted from the modernist art of purified cubism. Nor was he, anymore than the painters, guiltless of attacks on European modernism that would have gladdened the heart of an arch-conservative. This despite liberal convictions, like theirs, that in his case embraced (among many) Henry George, Edward Bellamy, Samuel Butler, William Morris, as well as Thoreau, Whitman and Jefferson. Moreover, Wright's approach to the house was as laden with traditional sentiment as their pictures. [13] The hearth core, the sheltering roof, the casement windows, the close spread to the ground, the expansion to nature, the natural materials: what real estate man's cliché for "home" does Wright not include? The superficial answer of course is that he does not overlay this traditional cluster of homey attributes with Cape Coddy, Neo-Colonial, Half-Timber, or Latest Modern veneers. He invents architectural forms, rigorously abstract in themselves ("conventionalized" as he sometimes liked to say), that convey sentiments and induce experiences as entities, and as interwoven, interacting parts of a whole. If he is the greatest domestic designer in the entire history of architecture, it is because he began with a conception of the house so banally sentimental as to win the widest popular support — what one has "always wanted in a home" — and then transcended the banality by his creative act. There is nothing specifically "midwest" about Wright's houses of the thirties, nothing quite as specifically midwestern as their famous "prairie" prototypes before World War I. Indeed, the thirties saw Wright's clientele increasingly spread across the country, as the U.S. in "Usonian" may indicate; but the source of these houses was the earlier "prairie" house. If Wright spoke of his work as "American," alternatively he spoke of it as "midwestern"; or rather, consonant with the deeper Americanism of his kind of regionalism, he saw himself as "American" *because* he was "midwestern."

His simultaneous development of his scheme for Broadacre City,[14] beginning in 1934 and extending until 1954 (with only minor modifications, however, after 1937), is rather more conspicuously "midwestern" than his houses of the period. (Figs. 6, 7, 8.) It was a scheme that took its cue from the spread of the prairie and seems to have derived its large-scale rectangular grid of highways from the typical straight-line thrust of prairie highways with their right-angled crossings, which the flatness of the terrain and the geometry of landholding encouraged. Broadacre City was a city that encompassed the countryside, "nowhere and everywhere," as Wright phrased it. Its quarter-acre, half-acre, full-acre house sites provided for spreading houses with their mix of floral and vegetable gardens, so that every resident was half-Jeffersonian agrarian, half-suburbanite. Community centers, each with its regional rather than cosmopolitan cultural institutions, were dropped at intervals in the grid. So were enclaves of industry located along the super-highways. Wright seems to have been influenced by Henry Ford's recommendations in the twenties for industry of modest size like the sort founded by self-made men in the smaller midwestern cities, as typified by the Larkin Company in Buffalo or the S. J. Johnson Wax Company in Racine, for which Wright executed two of his best known commissions. If work fell off in such factories (Ford was even more specific on this point than Wright), then the workers could fall back on the land to tide them over.

If one part of Wright's Broadacre scheme centered in a midwestern idyll of small industry embowered in a mix of suburb and farm, the other part was the buzzing transport that, in a particularly midwestern style, held the spread together. On the grid of the superhighways, terminating in *cul de sac* roads within superblocks, Wright's big-wheeled designs for the auto-of-the-future moved like gay toys hither and thither, supplemented overhead by space ships bouncing like tops from the earth-floor in hopping arcs. No trolleys, no trains, boasted Wright; all transport was to be highly individualistic, constantly shuttling in all directions with houses graded not only by land size (quarter-, half- and one-acre plots) but by automobile ownership (one-, two- and three-unit garages).

To Wright, like the midwestern painters, the heartland provided inspiration to the nation. "The country is the city," in his words. "The city is the country." As Broadacre City spread, it would physically, as well as experientially, blanket the nation. All America would become suffused with, identical with, the deeper America of the heartland.

Now just such indiscriminate spread (agrarian or not), just such mobility, just such dependence on the machine, were anathema to Southern Agrarians. In their battle with the national Leviathan the Southern Agrarians counted on support from the Western Agrarians, but they realized that Westerners were uncertain allies because the West had always been more committed to Leviathan than the South. It was not only that the West, except portions of the southwest bordering on the South, did not have the "peculiar institution" of slavery and had not been defeated in a Civil War. It was also that the West, for all its agrarian and populist sentiments, had always looked to national help when the South was willing (or forced) to go it alone.

As Donald Davidson pointed out,[15] in the South it was individuals who moved from settled areas and took western lands. It was local leaders like John Sevier and Andrew Jackson who took on the Indians, and local leaders along the frontier who even conducted militant foreign policy. Further north in the West federal troops pushed out the Indians. Federal regulations laid out homesites. Federal grants threaded the northern half of the West with railroads at the expense of the South which, with its convenient waterborn transport by way of rivers and ocean, had never plumped for internal improvements like the other sections. It was this largesse of federal support to internal improvements that bound the agricultural interests of the northern part of the West so firmly to midwestern and eastern metropoli. Across the northern portion of the West, too, the "damned Yankee" moved, infecting the frontier with his biases. Therefore, much as the Southern Agrarian might believe that he must cooperate with the midwestern agrarian, he realized that the midwesterner was an unreliable ally. Wright's Broadacre City made this unreliability clear. So did Benton's complaint that he found the regionalist label too exclusive for his taste.

So here, then, are four approaches to regionalism in the visual arts as they influenced the thirties:

    (1) regionalism as a technological tool;
    (2) regionalism as an adaptive technique;
    (3) regionalism as an alternative to nationalism;
    (4) regionalism as a deepened national consciousness. [16]

If these comprise the gamut of uses to which the regionalist concept may be put, what unites these diverse appeals to the regionalist theme? In a word, it is concern for the *indigenous.* This was the key-word for Benton MacKaye in *The New Exploration,* first published in 1928. MacKaye was a forester; aside from his remarkable book, he is best known for his work in establishing the Appalachian Trail. A thread through the mountain wilderness from Mt. Washington in New Hampshire to Mt. Mitchell in North Carolina, it was conceived as a trail with occasional shelters along the way, and more occasional campers' villages, these to be supplied by valley farms. The entire wilderness spine, in turn, backed the line of town, city and metropolitan settlement along the Atlantic Coast.

This balance that should occur between city and country is the theme of *The New Exploration.* Behind MacKaye's book lay his own devotion to the American wilderness, and to the ideas of those, like Thoreau and George Perkins Marsh, who shared this feeling; his awareness, too, of the work of Ebenezer Howard and those followers who developed the idea of the greenbelt town; most specifically, perhaps, the theory of Patrick Geddes, the Scottish regionalist who strongly advocated a balanced relationship between city and country. [17] Geddes spoke of the "valley section" as the regional ideal of civilization: the valley bottom (to telescope an intricate scheme) containing cities and transportation

ribbons interspersed with bottom land agriculture, the
uplands dotted with smaller villages and farming appropriate
to fertile hillsides, higher up the woodlands, still higher the
wilderness. (Fig. 9.) The kind of balance natural to the well
managed "valley section" became for Geddes the epitome of
that large equilibrium between farm and city, field and
forest, man and nature, toward which all planning should
tend.

If Geddes's example strongly influenced MacKaye's *The
New Exploration,* it also pervaded the thinking of a group to
which MacKaye belonged, in which indeed he may have
initially learned of Geddes's work. This was the Regional
Planning Association of America.[18] The RPAA was not a
governmental organization of any sort, but a small, informal
study group of architects, land planners, environmentalists,
economists, housing specialists and a real estate developer
interested in planning. They met irregularly from 1932 to
1933. Aside from MacKaye, the best known members of the
group were Clarence Stein, the architect and town planner
ultimately responsible for, among others, Radburn, New
Jersey; his land-planning colleague, Henry Wright; the
popular economist Stuart Chase; and, most prominent of all,
the social analyst Lewis Mumford. Centered in New York,
with some of its members also on Governor Alfred Smith's
State Commission for Housing and Regional Planning, the
RPAA used New York State as a case study. For them the
state combined the virtues of familiarity and accessibility. It
also contained an ideal mix of land use ranging from all
degrees of urbanization, through a comparable gamut of
farming operations, to mountains and wilderness, with the
entire area given its principal unity by the inverted-L-shaped
corridor of the Hudson and Mohawk River valleys. The
RPAA published its findings as informally as it conducted its
inquiries, principally in the *Survey Graphic* of May 1, 1925;
then in MacKaye's *The New Exploration* of 1928; eventually,
in the final chapters of Mumford's *The Culture of Cities* of
1938, which chart the ideal toward which he believed the
planning of the future should tend.

Geddes, whose ideas Mumford especially brought to the RPAA, hypothesized that modern civilization had passed from what he termed a *paleotechnic* phase to a *neotechnic* phase: from the need to centralize dirty, coal-burning industry in the squalid cities of the nineteenth century to the possibility of burning coal at the minehead with the transmission of this energy as clean electrical power to dispersed industry anywhere. The gasoline engine and electrical communication accelerated the trend toward dispersal. Regional planning was therefore as appropriate to the new age as city planning had been (or should have been) to the nineteenth century. To Geddes's phases, paleotechnic and neotechnic, Mumford added two others and publicized them in *The Culture of Cities*. In Mumford's terminology, an *eotechnic*, or dawn, phase of technology preceded the paleotechnic. One hoped a *biotechnic* phase would succeed the neotechnic, when at last technology would exist in a symbiotic relationship with the biosphere. In the *Survey Graphic* publication in the mid-twenties, the schematic map of New York State with neotechnic data and biotechnic implications assumed an emblematic quality for the thinking of the RPAA. (Fig. 10.)

At the time of this publication, population in New York State was still being drawn away from the hinterland towns toward the industrial cities tied to railroad lines along the river valley for need of coal and transport.

In *The New Exploration* MacKaye noted a similar migration in New England from hinterland farms and towns to the cities on the railroads. So the central thesis of the RPAA that the advent of electricity, the automobile, and the radio would reverse this trend and usher in a new era of mobility and decentralization was timely in the mid-twenties, and not the tired commonplace it seems today; timely in the double sense of pin-pointing the trend as it began to appear, and realizing the momentous opportunity that then − just then − existed. These inventions would reverse the flow away from the hinterlands. They would enhance the reciprocity of city and country which is appropriate to regional planning; and through the new technology, they would enable the

1.
Marcel Breuer. Harnishmacher House. Weisbaden, Germany. 1932. (Courtesy of the architect.)

2.
Marcel Breuer. Robinson House. Williamstown, Massachusetts. 1946-47. (Copyright Ezra Stoller.)

3.
Thomas Hart Benton. *Arts of the West.* 1932. (New Britain Museum of American Art, New Britain, Connecticut. Harriet Russell Stanley Fund.)

4.
John Steuart Curry. *Tornado Over Kansas*. 1928. (Hackley Art Gallery, Muskegon, Michigan.)

5.
Grant Wood. *American Gothic*. 1930. (Friends of American Art. Art Institute of Chicago.)

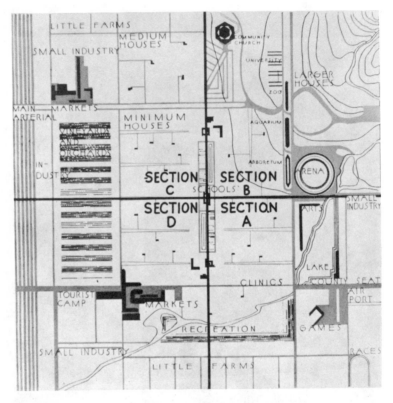

6.
Frank Lloyd Wright. *Broadacre City*. 1934-54. Schematic diagram of a
typical segment of the city.

7.
Frank Lloyd Wright. *Broadacre City*. Highway view showing car design. (The Frank Lloyd Wright Foundation, Museum of Modern Art, New York.)

8.
Frank Lloyd Wright. *Broadacre City.* Panoramic overview with sky craft. (The Frank Lloyd Wright Foundation, Museum of Modern Art, New York.)

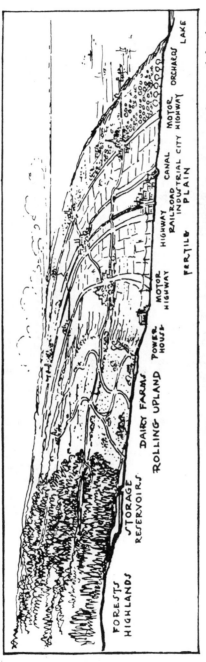

An "ideal section" based on a line drawn through Orleans and Genesee counties, but indicating sound regional development along most of New York state's northern frontier

9.
Diagram of the "valley section" patterned after the regional thinking of Patrick Geddes. (*Survey Graphic*, May 1, 1925.)

FORESTS
HIGHLANDS

STORAGE
RESERVOIRS

DAIRY FARMS

ROLLING UPLAND

POWER
HOUSE

MOTOR
HIGHWAY

HIGHWAY

CANAL

RAILROAD

MOTOR
HIGHWAY

INDUSTRIAL CITY

ORCHARDS

FERTILE
PLAIN

LAKE

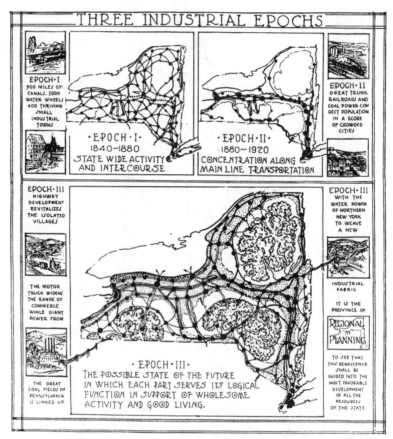

10.
Schematic map of New York State summarizing the ideas of the Regional Planning Association of America, and later used as a key illustration by Lewis Mumford in *The Culture of Cities*. (*Survey Graphic*, May 1, 1925.)

11.
Walker Evans. *Post Office, Sprott, Ala.* 1936. (Courtesy of the Library of Congress.)

12.
Walker Evans. *Gas Station, Reedsville, W. Va.* 1936. (Courtesy of the Library of Congress.)

13.
Thomas Hart Benton. *Boomtown.* 1928. (Memorial Art Gallery of the University of Rochester. Marion Stratton Gould Fund.)

14.
Dorothea Lange. Photograph of migrating "oakies" from *An American Exodus*.
Published in 1939. Dorothea Lange Collection. The Oakland Museum.)

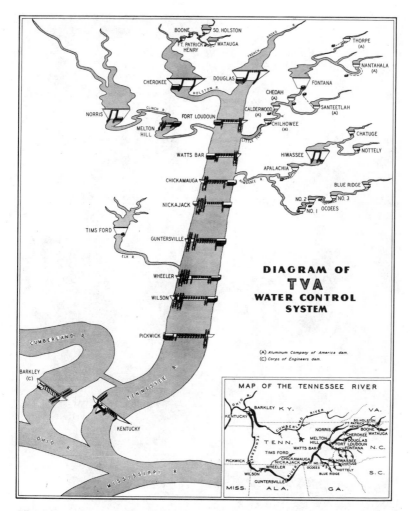

15.
Diagrammatic overview of the Tennessee Valley Authority System.
High storage dams appear upstream on the tributaries. Low naviga-
tional control dams with locks appear crossing the main river channel.
All dams provide power, and are presently supplemented by steam
plants to supply the vast amount of electricity required in the valley.
(Tennessee Valley Authority.)

16.
Thomas Hart Benton. *The Lord is My Shepherd*. 1920-21. (Whitney Museum of American Art. Photo by Geoffrey Clements.)

17.
John Sloan. *Three A.M.* 1909. (Philadelphia Museum of Art. Photo by
A. J. Wyatt.)

18.
Alfred Stieglitz. *The Terminal*, 1893. (Courtesy of Georgia O'Keeffe for the Alfred Stieglitz Estate.)

unconsciously poignant, improvisations by which the hinterland meets its initial onslaught — the dawn of the gas station,
of roadside billboards, of the "tourist cabin."

Evans especially is a master in depicting the starkness of
the confrontation.[22] Here is *Post Office, Sprott, Ala.* (Fig.
11.) The sense of gravel roads leading from nowhere to
nowhere, and then, suddenly, Sprott! It asserts its effort to
be a "place" in the pathetic dignity of this civic center *cum*
general store — literally a hollow dignity in the sense of the
thin board shell covering a meager interior, but with a certain
presence in the formality and "bearing" (so to speak) of the
gable with its two blind windows, so frailly supported, so
meagerly backed. And the whole ghostly scene of road,
building, and scraggly landscape is intensely peopled by the
gas pump, a mailbox, above all by the Coca Cola bottle.
Thanks to Coca Cola, in fact, the place has got its label.

Or here is *Gas Station, Reedsville, W. Va.* (Fig. 12.) The
row of gas pumps dominates the ramshackle rectangular
backdrop that is the building. The pumps, the building and
the signs make a counterpointed frieze of rectangular and circular elements. Peering within this layer-like organization of
intricate forms, one finally perceives the human figures
slouched in the shadowed box of space within the debris,
compressed between two of the pumps.

It is not merely that the presence of the automobile,
where invisible, is known by the artifacts it strews in its
wake. One also feels, in the electrifying intensity of these
images, the excitement of the photographer as *his* jallopy —
unseen but sensed — prowls the backroads and bursts in on a
world just then unique in the way in which the tenuous
"old" and the incongruent new collided on such a broad
front.

The jallopy is prominent in Benton's paintings, too.
Indeed, there is a sense of frenetic "coverage" in his work
that reminds us that he did in fact travel widely and rapidly
about the country making headlong sketches of passe
Americana. Often, as in Benton's *Boomtown* of 1928 — in
those days before traffic signals and the channeling of
roadways with painted lines — the jallopies seemed to lead

opening up of hinterlands which were too remote to have been usable in the past, or too poorly endowed with power or transportation resources.

What should be the nature of regional planning in this threshold situation? According to RPAA, the implications were two-fold, one negative, one positive. Negatively, RPAA argued that the old idea of regional planning as metropolitan planning for a major central city and the area around it was dead. This had been the focus of so-called regional planning from Daniel Burnham and Edward Bennett's *Plan of Chicago* for the Commercial Club of 1909 to the *Regional Plan of New York (City) and Its Environs* directed by Thomas Adams for the Russell Sage Foundation, which had spent the better part of the decade of the twenties preparing its eight-volume report. [19] Conceiving of the metropolis as the "hub" of a tributary area, such regional planning to RPAA was passe. Positively, RPAA argued that the central theme of future regional planning would be the reciprocal relationship that should occur among many cities large and small spread out in a comparable reciprocity with the country ranging in character from farm to wilderness. As Mumford put it in the *Survey Graphic,* "The hope of the city lies outside itself." [20] In short, if the reciprocity of Geddes's "valley section" could be maintained as a result of fresh regional thinking, then, in Mumford's terms, the neotechnic phase would transcend into the biotechnic. The hope of the nation lay in this new regionalism.

If RPAA and *The New Exploration* both focused their attention on the by-passed hinterlands, as the vacuum that would be filled in one way or another, for good or bad, another group, too, looked at the hinterlands from a different perspective. In a series of momentous photographs of the thirties, many of them done for the Farm Security Administration by such photographers as Evans, Lange, and Bourke-White, the hinterlands were captured at the moment of impending change. [21] These are images of life and artifacts "in the sticks"; but a sense of the invading jallopy pervades them. Not that the camera always catches the jallopy: one senses it, however, in the graceless, but haunting and the helter-skelter life of colonies of black bugs, much as they later appeared in *Bonnie and Clyde*. (Fig. 13.) The mobility of the jallopies, the clouds of dust they trailed along the backroads, was also at the heart of the most prominent example of negative regionalism of the period. In *An American Exodus*, Lange memorably photographed them as they chugged out of the Dust Bowl, a bedraggled procession of machines, human beings, and possessions mimicking the saga of earlier pioneers. [23] (Fig. 14.) What a contrast, this disheartened migration — where the only heartening aspect was the *possibility* of migration — to the exhilarating gaiety of movement in all directions undergirding Broadacre City! Yet, of course, what affinities too.

To meet the regional challenge of the automobile, the decade of the thirties saw nothing more substantial really than the development of the limited access highway. [24] As early as 1906, when the car population of the United States already totaled 105,000 vehicles, there was talk of such highways. Between 1916 and 1924 the Bronx River Parkway was opened in stages in Westchester County, linking plush suburbia to New York City. Characteristically, the "parkway" first appeared as a means of easing the flow of passenger vehicles in and out of the central city, thereby establishing a pattern for such highways that worked against their effective use as the major regional planning tools they might have become. In 1930, in an article entitled "The Townless Highway," [25] MacKaye had argued against the use of such highways either as mere commutation routes to the metropolis or as the spines of "linear cities" such as Edgar Chambless had earlier advocated in calling for a utopian "Roadtown." MacKaye hoped that the limited access highway of the future would by-pass the densely clustered small towns or cities strung along it, each separated from the other by the ample countryside in between. [26] The new highway would thus become a neotechnical tool toward the realization of his ideal of the regional basis for civilization.

As for electricity, the other major element in the technology that conditioned the regional point of view of the

period toward planning, the contribution of the thirties is of
course most impressive. Indeed the Tennessee Valley Authority remains the pinnacle of American regional planning. (Fig.
15.) The familiar ingredients of the scheme and their
interrelationship need no more than listing. [27]

    1) *an intensive core*
         rivers and the dams

    2) *multiple interdependent functions reciprocally ben-
       eficial*
         dams to control floods
         dams to preserve a navigational channel
         dams to make power
         power to be used in part to create cheap nitrate
            fertilizer
         fertilizer to improve agriculture in the area
         agriculture not only to provide income for a poor
            area, but to prevent silting of the dam basins
         agriculture also to encourage forests on upper
            slopes as another economic resource and
            another means of preventing the erosion that
            silts dams
         power also to encourage industry
         industry to complement the agriculture of the
            region
         the dams to provide lakes for recreation – and so
            on: in David Lilienthal's phrase "a seamless
            web"

    3) *a balance of uses*
         farm and factory
         work and recreation
         residence and movement
         immediate use and conservation

    4) *finally, flexibility of operation and boundaries*
         ability to alter functional priorities and to move
            into new territory consonant with the pres-
            ervation of the region as an entity

In a way TVA represented an analog to the estate in Hyde Park. Roosevelt came to the Presidency committed to the idea of land as a basis for a civilized way of life. His father's business dealings in New York merely made Hyde Park possible: it was Hyde Park that counted. In a sense TVA could be seen as the country estate writ large, and transformed by an advanced technology. The dams take the place of the big house; the grounds expand to a river valley; the inhabitants of the "estate" are part of a balanced economy of work, residence and recreation, all stemming from the land, with the sense of the land omnipresent.

If, as Lilienthal maintained, the TVA was a "seamless web" of land, technology, and man, then once the machinery was in place and the cycle had begun, the critical factor became that of balance. Has the success of TVA, especially its industrial success, disrupted this balance? Within the period we are covering, the question did not arise. The plant was still building. The balance of uses, if weighted in any one direction, was not then so heavily weighted but that shifts could occur. During World War II, however, TVA did undergo tremendous change. It provided no less than 10 percent of all power used by industry during the war. The "seamless web" with its biotechnic implications became the "arsenal for democracy." The propaganda brochures shifted from farmers standing knee-deep in alfalfa (power lines in the background against the sky) to pretty girls in Ike jackets tallying the bombs in Valley warehouses ("greetings to Hitler and Hirohito").

This of course was the threat of Leviathan against which the Southern Agrarians had warned. [28] To introduce the new technology from the outside was in itself to alter the life and culture of the region, to change it irrevocably. One could at very least hope that some *new* balance could be maintained; but balance, the essence of creative regionalism in any technological program, is difficult where process is another essential.

Finally, what then can we make of such a sampling of the regional trend in the thirties as this brief survey discloses? In

the first place, of course, it is not quite the phenomenon of
the thirties to which easy generalization tends to assign it. If
the regional idea was conspicuous in the thirties and found its
apogee in the TVA, it is nonetheless true that the basic
ideology for the regional ideal in planning was well established in the thinking of the RPAA during the twenties. The
twenties, too, saw the formulation of the laissez faire
opposition to technological regionalism in the extremist
cultural position of the Southern Agrarian. To be sure, not
every component in our sample can be so neatly traced to the
twenties. Possibly a genesis for the photography of the
thirties could be determined in the twenties; certainly not in
the modern architecture of the decade. Suffice it merely to
focus on the case for the regionalist position in painting
during the twenties, partly because it is especially indicative
of the regionalist undertow throughout the decade and partly
because, in the visual arts during the thirties, painting came
to assume such a central position in the polemics for
regionalism.

In his 1951 postscript for a new edition of his *An Artist
in America,* Benton admitted the importance of the twenties
to his convictions. After quibbling again about the narrowness of the term for what he, Wood, and Curry (the last two
dead by then) had intended in their art, he went on to say
that the regional school of painting really owed its origins to
the widespread feeling of profound disillusionment with
Europe after World War I, and to an affirmative withdrawal
of America into itself following the dissipation of Wilsonian
idealism. He was certainly correct in maintaining that the
midwestern regionalists had fully formed their points of view
prior to 1930. In his own work he stated his position visually
at least as early as 1920, in *The Lord Is My Shepherd:* a
shabby elderly couple sitting down to a meager meal beneath
a sampler motto. [29] (Fig. 16.) Curry completed his most
familiar paintings, *Baptism in Kansas* and *Tornado in Kansas,*
in 1928 and 1929 respectively; Wood his *American Gothic* in
1930. Just to indicate that tendencies observed in these three
were not exclusively theirs, Charles Burchfield and Edward

Hopper might also be mentioned because they, too, before 1925, fully realized in their paintings the kind of small town realism for which they are known. Less polemically committed to a regionalist point of view than the midwestern trio, they were often grouped with them in such criticism of the thirties as Thomas Craven's, where, in fact, the borderline between "regional" and "American scene" painter was justifiably blurred. If Craven's phenomenally successful *Modern Art* and *Men of Art,* published in 1934 and 1936, gave wide publicity to his special enthusiasm for the midwestern artists as the hope for American art, he was already expressing this opinion in articles and reviews before 1925. So the regionalist position, as Benton maintained, had firmly established itself well before 1930.[30]

In fact, it could be argued that the realism of the twenties was a projection of the pre-World War I urban realism of The Eight (later absorbed into the Ashcan School), who had protested against European aesthetics and the lifeless standards of the National Academy of Design and, in their exhibition in 1908 at the Macbeth Gallery in New York City, had demonstrated a determination that the artist must paint the life he knows in all its unidealized details. It was as if the concern for the local scene that these men discovered in the streets of New York had been violently interrupted by the brief international interlude of the Armory Show and the sudden desire of Americans to head for Paris and become modernists. The flurry of modernist excitement just before and after the Armory Show was abetted in the United States by avant garde galleries, notably by Alfred Stieglitz's *291,* as well as by the arrival of European artists with the outbreak of the war, especially Marcel Duchamp and certain Dadaists. Finally, there were the returning Americans also scurrying out of Paris to escape the war.

The modernist flurry that occurred in the years immediately around 1920 was, in retrospect, just that: an intense moment of excitement and absorption.[31] Then America took over. In Paris the American painters had been surrounded by art; on their return home they were surrounded by America. The Dadaist group melted away. Duchamp himself largely abandoned art for chess. Stieglitz closed down. Among major American artists interested in the more abstract aspects of modernism around 1920 only Arthur Dove and Stuart Davis persisted as near-abstractionists throughout the decade, Davis ultimately becoming something of an influence on post-World War II American modernism. The normative course for the progressive American artist of the twenties, on the other hand, involved the use of cubism in various ways to create painterly equivalents to observed nature. Put another way, typically the American scene received some sort of cubist treatment. Such was the course taken by Hartley, Marin, Sheeler, Demuth, Dickinson, Spencer, for that matter by Hopper, and so on. For Benton, Wood, and Curry it was a much more conservative continuation of the tradition of The Eight: Benton making a reversal from his earlier commitment to modernism; Curry never a modernist at all; Wood in between on the issue.

There were three differences between the realism of The Eight and that which the midwestern trio began to develop in the twenties. First, The Eight were actually more revolutionary in a technical sense since their style depended on the kind of loose brush work and palpably painted surfaces of Manet and his followers. It was thus at least *retardataire* modernism that they practiced in contradistinction to the extensive Renaissance borrowings of the later group. If the realism of The Eight centered in urban scenes (and was continued into the thirties, notably by Reginald Marsh, another whose name was often linked to the midwesterners), the realism of the midwesterners of course focused on rural and small town subject matter. As a final difference, the emotional mood of the realism of The Eight contrasts markedly with that of the midwesterners.

For all its seaminess and vulgarity the city seen by The Eight is an ebullient, joyous place, full of the verve of community spirit, and totally at odds with the tiredness of Benton's *The Lord Is My Shepherd,* the anxiety of Curry's *Tornado in Kansas,* or the grimness of Wood's *American*

Gothic. These are characteristic of the darker mood that not quite invariably, but typically appears in the paintings of the midwestern regionalists, as comparable qualities also pervade the works of Burchfield and Hopper.[32] How different from John Sloan's *Three A.M.* of 1909. (Fig. 17.) In this, one of his less buoyant images, Sloan shows us two working girls in a dingy flat. Fatigue is the essence of the subject; but fatigue staved off by the excitement with which the girl who has come in from a date reports to her roommate, who rouses herself to prepare a late snack (with daring cigarette in hand). Here is seaminess, poverty, toil, but human fervor and rapport that transcend the situation. The same conclusion can be drawn from a comparison of Alfred Stieglitz's photographic "realism" of New York before the war — as, for example, in his familiar image of the horsecar in *The Terminal* of 1893 — with that of Evans. (Fig. 18.) What an expressive gulf exists between the steaming atmosphere that affectionately binds elements together in Stieglitz's print, with the soft blur of the tonality and the picturesque silhouetting, as opposed to the unflinching clarity and harshness of Evans's work, in which sentiment is not edged with residual prettiness and sentimentality, but derives from a tougher, more ironic vision. The literary parallels to such bitter-sweet images of provincial America are of course Sinclair Lewis's *Main Street* or Sherwood Anderson's *Winesburg, Ohio.*

The fascination of this hydra-headed regionalist interest, peaking from the mid-twenties to the mid-thirties, would therefore seem to center precisely in the confrontation between the dying rurality of the individual family farm and the small isolated village and emergent technological and institutional change at the moment when this rurality was decisively challenged in a watershed way. The outcome can be predicted, although there was possibility that somehow a balance might be struck. Highways had yet to reach the hinterlands; the automotive invasion had just begun. Alcoa and the other big corporations had only started to take over the Tennessee River valley, the factory farm was in the initial stages of its agricultural take-over, the prefabricated gas station of the major oil companies was a slick blight of the future; so were industrial parks, the proliferation of vacation lodges, ski tows, snowmobiles, trailers, country rock, and all the other phenomena by which the hinterlands fell to the twentieth century. The battle between invader and invaded was prolonged by the Depression, because of its stagnating effect on the economy; and, concomitantly, because it fostered the idea of subsistence on the land either as a measure of desperation or as a philosophy of life.

Those identified with the regionalist idea reacted to it in various ways: with nostalgia by some, with hope by others, with scorn, with despair, with clinical objectivity, and with some mixture of these and other oscillating emotions. How could it be otherwise? For most (not quite all) of those we have mentioned had themselves grown up on farms or had some intimate boyhood contact with what MacKaye termed the indigenous world. "Brought up on the family farm . . ." or "spent summers on grandfather's farm . . ." or "grew up in the small town of . . .": how regularly such phrases occur in the biographies of those who had spent boyhoods and girlhoods in the last decades of the nineteenth century. But this near-universal experience in youth was passing too. Even those happiest to say goodbye to all that could not, of course, quite escape the poignancy of a moment that was, after all, part of their lives.

When, in the visual arts, the pendulum again swung toward the "American scene" with the Pop-Art of the sixties and the Super-Realism of the seventies, it was not to the indigenous that artists turned, but to the urban, and in images with a sophisticated awareness of modern art. They in fact were, the vanguard. But wasn't it in the cards all along? In the end, Leviathan would triumph.

NOTES

1. Started as the Natural Resources Board to the Public Works Administration under Frederic A. Delano, President Roosevelt's uncle and a long-time city planner, the Board was transformed in 1934 into the National Resources Committee. This Committee acted as an overall planning agency until its demise during World War II. Its distinguished staff included such economists and planners as Charles Eliot, Wesley Mitchell and Gardner C. Means. In addition to its informational role the Committee was important in encouraging planning activity at all levels.

2. See William H. Jordy, "The Bauhaus in America," in Donald Fleming and Bernard Bailyn, eds., *The Intellectual Migration: Europe and America 1930-1960* (Cambridge, Mass., 1969); also Jordy, *American Buildings and Their Architects: The Impact of European Modernism in the Mid-Twentieth Century* (New York, 1972), chap. 4. On Breuer and the thirties, Vincent Scully, "Doldrums in the Suburbs," *Journal of the Society of Architectural Historians,* 24 (March 1965), 36-47, is also relevant, while the entire issue is pertinent insofar as it deals with aspects of modern architecture during the 1930s.

3. The label derives from an exhibition at the San Francisco Museum of Art in 1949. The catalog, *Architecture of the San Francisco Bay Region,* contains an introduction by Gardner Dailey and Clarence Mayhew, plus an appreciative essay by Lewis Mumford. See also "Domestic Architecture of the San Francisco Bay Area," *Architectural Record,* 106 (Sept. 1949), 119-126.

4. On the background of the group, see Louise Cowan, *The Fugitive Group* (Baton Rouge, La., 1959) and John M. Bradbury, *The Fugitives: A Critical Account* (Chapel Hill, N. C., 1958).

5. John Crowe Ransom, "Reconstructed but Unregenerate," in Twelve Southerners, *I'll Take My Stand* (New York, 1930), p. 3.

6. *Ibid.*, pp. 4-8 *passim.*

7. The famous Armory Show of 1913 (New York, Chicago, and Boston), officially called the International Exhibition of Modern Art, introduced the American public for the first time to the works of the avant garde movements, such as Impressionism, Symbolism, Cubism, and Fauvism, which had caused so much excitement in Europe.

8. Thomas Hart Benton, *An Artist in America*, 3rd ed. (Columbia, Mo., 1968), pp. 314f.

9. *Ibid.*, p. 315. For a negative appraisal of Benton's political and social position, see Meyer Schapiro's review of the original edition in *Partisan Review,* 4 (Jan. 1947), 53-57.

10. On Benton's art see the convenient compendium, *An American in Art: A Professional and Technical Autobiography* (Lawrence, Kan., 1969).

11. On Curry, the most comprehensive treatment is Lawrence E. Schmeckebier, *John Steuart Curry's Pageant of America* (New York, 1941).

12. On Wood, see Darrell Garwood, *Artist in Iowa: A Life of Grant Wood* (New York, 1944); also Hazel E. Brown, *Grant Wood and Martin Cone: Artists of an Era* (Ames, Iowa, 1972).

13. The best introduction to Wright's philosophy of house design for what he termed the "Usonian" house of the thirties appears in his own *The Natural House* (New York, 1954). The standard account is Henry-Russell Hitchcock, *In the Nature of Materials: The Buildings of Frank Lloyd Wright, 1887-1941* (New York, 1942), pp. 85-103 and plates.

14. The best critical account of Broadacre City is George Collins, "Broadacre City: Wright's Utopia Reconsidered," in James Marston Fitch, ed., *Four Great Masters of Modern Architecture* (New York, 1963). The most comprehensive initial publications readily available appeared in *Architectural Record*, 77 (April 1935), 243-54, and *American Architecture*, 146 (May 1935), 55-62. Wright published the scheme in book form in variant repetitions: *The Disappearing City* (New York, 1932), *When Democracy Builds* (Chicago, 1945), and *Living City* (New York, 1958). On the philosophy of subsistence agrarianism underlying Broadacre City, see Wright's publication with Baker Brownell, *Architecture and Modern Life* (New York and London, 1937). For additional critiques, see Meyer Schapiro's review of *Architecture and Modern Life* in *Partisan Review*, 4 (March 1938), 42-47; Percival and Paul Goodman, *Communitas* (New York, 1947); Robert C. Twombley, "Undoing the City: Frank Lloyd Wright's Planned Communities," *American Quarterly*, 24 (Oct. 1972), 538-49.

15. Donald Davidson, "Lands That Were Golden: II. The Two Wests," *American Review*, 4 (Nov. 1934), 29-55.

16. It is possible to mention a fifth: that is, the idea of subsistence living such as one finds in the writings of Ralph Barsodi and Baker Brownell, or in some of the ideology of the Farm Security Administration, especially the notion of "subsistence homesteads." Although such ideas are intimately related to regional thinking, they do not *necessarily* involve regional concepts and I have therefore omitted discussion of them here.

17. On Geddes, apart from *The New Exploration* see Marshall Staley, ed., *Patrick Geddes* (New Brunswick, N.J., 1972), which not only includes an anthology of Geddes's principal writings on regionalism, but a short biography by Abbie Ziffren.

18. On the RPAA, see Roy Lubove, *Community Planning in the 1920s: The Contribution of the Regional Planning Association of America* (Pittsburgh, 1963). On Lewis Mumford's ideas, see the convenient analysis in R. Allan Lawson's *The Failure of Independent Liberalism, 1930-1941* (New York, 1971), pp. 183-216.

19. The Regional Plan of New York (RPNY and not to be confused with RPAA) started operation in 1922.' In addition to the eight survey volumes published toward the end of the decade comprising the *Regional Plan,* the series included two additional volumes: *The Graphic Regional Plan: Atlas and Description* (1929)' and a summary volume by Thomas Adams, *The Building of the City* (1931). R. L. Duffus, *Mastering a Metropolis: Planning for the Future of the New York Region* (New York and London, 1930) is a popularization of RPNY material. For a convenient summary of RPNY in its relations with RPAA, see Lubove, chap. 7.

20. Lewis Mumford, "Regions to Live In," *Survey Graphic,* 54 (May 1, 1925), p. 151.

21. See William Stott, *Documentary Expression and Thirties America* (New York, 1973).

22. The Museum of Modern Art held a comprehensive retrospective of Evans's work: *Walker Evans* (New York, 1971), introduction by John Szarkowski.

23. On the Lange retrospective at the Museum of Modern Art, see *Dorothea Lange* (New York, 1966), introduction by George P. Elliott.

24. A convenient survey of the history of parkway and throughway design, together with a discussion of the visual integration of the highway into the countryside which is very germane to regional concerns, appears in Christopher Tunnard and Boris Pushkarev, *Man-Made America: Chaos or Control* (New Haven, Conn. and London, 1963), pp. 159-276.

25. First published in the *New Republic,* 62 (March 12, 1930), pp. 93-95, conveniently reprinted as an appendix to a new edition of *The New Exploration* (Urbana, Ill., 1962). The Chambless essay mentioned immediately below appeared in a privately printed book, *Roadtown* (New York, c. 1910).

26. Another ingredient in MacKaye's thinking on the "townless highway" was the city planning of autoless neighborhoods of Clarence Stein and Henry Wright, as especially embodied in their new town of Radburn, N.J., begun in 1928 and stopped by the Depression. It might have been mentioned as a major planning contribution of the period to the problem of the automobile, but it is not specifically directed at regional problems. For discussion, see Clarence Stein, *Toward New Towns for America* (New York, 1957), which contains a fine historical introduction by Lewis Mumford.

27. The classic statement of the TVA philosophy is David Lilienthal, *TVA: Democracy on the March* (New York, Evanston, and London, 1944). A new edition in 1953 contains an introductory essay by Lilienthal, "TVA Revisited." See also the statement by a later official of TVA: Gordon Clapp, *The TVA: An Approach to the Development of a Region* (Chicago, 1955). A sympathetic but critical account of one aspect of TVA is C. Herman Pritchett, *The Tennessee Valley Authority: A Study in Public Administration* (Chapel Hill, N. C., 1943).

28. See, for example, Donald Davidson, "The Political Economy of Regionalism," *American Review*, 6. (Feb. 1936), especially pp. 423ff.; also "Political Regionalism and Administrative Regionalism" *Annals of the American Academy of Political and Social Science*, 207 (Jan. 1940), pp. 140ff.

29. To be sure, this is a somewhat isolated forecast of things to come. Benton does not really become steadily committed to his regionalist/Americanist subject matter until around 1927-28. See especially, Milton Brown, *American Painting from the Armory Show to the Depression* (Princeton, N.J., 1955), p. 192.

30. On regionalist/American Scene developments during the 1920s, see *ibid.*, pp. 173-95; also Matthew Baigill, "The Beginnings of 'The American Wave' and the Depression," *Art Journal*, 27 (Summer 1968), 387-96. There was an international aspect to this fervor for American subject matter; see H. W. Janson, "The International Aspects of Regionalism," *Art Journal*, 2 (May 1943), 110-15, which centers on Munich and Neue Sachlichkeit influence on Wood during a European trip. On Craven's criticism in the mid-twenties, see Baigill, p. 388.

31. See, for example, Brown, pp. 103-95; also Barbara Rose, *American Art Since 1900, A Critical History* (New York and Washington, 1967), chap. 4.

32. It could be maintained that the *best* of the regionalist work of Benton, Curry, and Wood show qualities that give a love-hate tension to their approaches to their subject matter. As these painters increasingly wrapped themselves in red-white-and-blue, their paintings tended to become more saccharine. Wood's sardonic *Daughters of the Revolution* readily turned to the coy patriotism of themes derived from Paul Revere's ride or Parson Weems's yarn about Washington and the cherry tree. Benton came to favor rural idylls in which he depicted the themes of American folk songs or translated such Biblical legends as that of Susannah and the Elders into rustic peek-a-boo. Like Wood, Benton turned increasingly to the celebration of episodes from American history in his later work. Benton and Curry emphasize landscape in their late work. Especially revealing is Wood's original conception of *American Gothic* as satire on the straight-laced narrowness of American rural life. As his viewers reacted favorably to the painting, and the specific became submerged in the "representative," it was transformed for both Wood and its public into a virtuous image of stalwart Americanism. See Garwood, pp. 118-28. Baigill is also interesting on this point.

CHAPTER 3

Constance Rourke And The Discovery Of American Culture In The 1930s

By Arthur F. Wertheim

ARTHUR F. WERTHEIM majored in American Studies at Yale University before completing the M.A. and Ph.D. degrees in American Civilization at New York University. His book *The New York Little Renaissance: Iconoclasm, Modernism, and Nationalism in American Culture, 1908-1917* will be published by the NYU Press in the spring of 1976. An Assistant Professor of Cultural and Intellectual History at the University of Southern California, he won the Dart Award for innovative teaching in 1974 with an interdisciplinary course in women studies. At present he is preparing a series of essays on twentieth-century American social and literary critics.

The essay to follow explores the awakening of Constance Rourke to regionalism and the vernacular arts at a time when cultural anthropologists began to give new importance to popular and folk elements in the explanation of national culture.

Constance Rourke's historical essays during the Depression were devoted to discovering the roots of American culture. The seven volumes she published between 1927 and 1942 are closely linked to the intellectual climate of the 1930s, specifically to the themes of regionalism and nationalism in the arts and related fields, and her interest in the relationship of folk and popular culture to regional traditions led to the discovery of neglected aspects of Americana. The significance of her work is well described by Van Wyck Brooks: Constance Rourke "began to write at a moment when the American mind was intensely concerned with itself, present and future, a moment of self-recognition that was marked by a number of writers who were bent on exploring the culture and resources of the country."[1]

The concept of regionalism was shared by individuals throughout the arts and sciences during the thirties. The close association of geographical area and artistic expression was evident in the midwestern painting of Benton, Curry, and Wood and in the sectionalism of the Southern Agrarians. Social engineers such as the Distributionists supported the decentralization of industry on a regional basis, and planners proposed organizing the country into cohesive areas where Americans could gain a sense of tradition and community during the Depression. Since social critics blamed the economic crisis on the complexities of our urban-industrial economy, regional planning and associated cultural movements could be interpreted as a reaction against Eastern control over the economy and the arts. As a concept, regionalism was also used to justify the importance of rural folk and popular culture on the frontier and to recapture faith in an older America that was vanishing due to technological changes. By venerating nostalgically the agrarian tradition, regionalists such as Rourke found a sustaining sense of values during a time when belief in the American system was being shattered.[2]

Rourke was influenced by the historian Frederick Jackson Turner, whose innovative thesis relating sectionalism to the formation of American political and social institutions she lauded. Following Turner, she argued in the title essay of

The Roots of American Culture (1942) that our culture has been determined by environmental influences and not merely by a transit of civilization from Europe.[3] She thus shared with other regionalists a tendency to play down the impact of European culture. Rural traditions in New England, the South, and the Middle and Far West have combined to produce a rich national culture, and the unique factor in distinguishing our civilization from that of Europe has been the environment of the frontier. She was impressed in particular by Turner's idea of a succession of moving frontiers from the Atlantic to the Pacific which contributed to an indigenous culture.[4]

Her books, therefore, focus almost exclusively on the culture of the moving frontier and its impact on regional traditions. New England and the Ohio Valley serve as geographical backgrounds for *Trumpets of Jubilee* (1927), her first published work and a study of such popular figures of the mid-nineteenth century as Henry Ward Beecher, Harriet Beecher Stowe, Lyman Beecher, Horace Greeley, and P. T. Barnum. These leaders of the spirit, politics, and enterprise have a kinship, she wrote, "beyond that created by their vast popularity. They sprang from the soil of New England."[5]

Her second book, *Troupers of the Gold Coast* (1928), dealt with culture on the California frontier by tracing the career of the famous dancer and singer Lotta Crabtree. In it she interprets Lotta as a native talent of the wild West whose boisterous singing and sprightly dancing signify the spirit of the frontier. She also recreates the exciting life of traveling theater companies in gold rush mining towns and San Francisco music halls, and understands the early California theater to be an indigenous form of popular entertainment that grew out of regional community life.[6]

Her study of the artist Audubon in 1938 illustrated how the frontier determined the character and culture of this amazing man. Audubon is portrayed as an artist who lost his French manners while living in the wooded back country of Kentucky and Louisiana. In Rourke's book he changes slowly into a frontier figure, an expert rifleman at home in the woods and a teller of tall tales. Rourke saw these influences of freedom and romance reflected in his watercolors depicting wild birds and animals. She felt there a sense of drama and naturalism identifiable with frontier life, but her interpretation led to a somewhat distorted biography, as she failed to take into account European influences on Audubon's work and exaggerated his actual relationship to the frontier. "He was never wholly a scientist," she insisted; "he was what he claimed to be, an artist, a woodsman, even a backwoodsman, with more than a touch of the broad humor that had sprung up on the frontier." [7]

Her biography of Audubon reveals that she was as much an environmentalist as Turner although she criticized him for overemphasizing the degree of individualism on the frontier, an environment she thought much more conducive to collective experience and group solidarity. Unlike the social critics of the 1920s who had interpreted the frontier as a cultural wasteland, Rourke referred to the area as a place where "tranquility and balance was sustained . . . by close identities of race, religion, and memory, and by the immediate communal experience of settlement." Her ideas in this regard better reflected the crisis atmosphere of the Depression. During that decade the mood of the country's intellectual life changed from a concentration on the self to a concern for society, and the community and group became consummate symbols of unified effort at this time. Black Mountain College, the MacDowell art colony, and the Group Theater signified the new spirit of cooperative venture. Rourke expressed the importance of communitarianism to her generation when she wrote that "not merely the individual but the culture of a group, a town, a region may be significant of main tendencies." The arts flourish, she declared, when "small social unities have been established, and groups have come to feel common bonds because of long settlement together or because of a common fortune." [8]

Rourke believed that community life in a rural environment had nourished such artistic development. In her work she often discussed the number of model secular and religious groups that prospered in the early nineteenth century. In *Trumpets of Jubilee* she praised the Owenite and Fourier experiments for their communitarian spirit and traced Horace Greeley's involvement with the Phalanx movement. She was impressed with the concern for group ritual of such religious associations as the Millerites, Mormons, and Shakers. Of these, the Shakers best exemplified for her a community formed around a "richly integrated culture." Their unpretentious architecture, furniture, and crafts served both a utilitarian and an esthetic function, expressing religious belief and a basic sense of form identifiable with a pious life. In her pioneer essay on the Shakers in *The Roots of American Culture,* she was one of the first writers to recognize that this religious community "possessed the coherence and unity of a folk, the instinctive traditional habits and beliefs, and the arts that have belonged to folk-groups." [9]

As a devotee of folk art, Rourke had few followers in the 1920s, when interest in folk art was primarily limited to specialists, collectors, and occasional museum exhibitions. Except for the work of Gilbert Seldes, most cultural historians did not concern themselves with the subject of popular entertainment. Even her orthodox book reviews of serious American and foreign literature for the *Freeman* magazine during 1920-21 revealed that she was a perceptive but not yet an innovative critic. [10] Two essays she published in the *New Republic,* however, suggested that her work was about to take a new direction. An article analyzing the legend of Paul Bunyan showed her interest in frontier folklore; another discussed vaudeville as a legitimate art form that could be improved by more imaginative set designs. [11]

Her growing belief that folklore and popular entertainment were equally as important as formal literature and the fine arts reflected the influence of cultural anthropologists. Their investigations of customs and artifacts of primitive societies had helped discredit the stereotype that culture was an exclusive achievement of a literate elite. Under their influence, she became a cultural relativist who believed that patterns of behavior and thought were conditioned by environment. She avidly read Ruth Benedict's *Patterns of*

Culture (1934) and used ideas from the book to argue that
the arts should be studied in relationship to their regional
background. Cultural anthropology underwrote Rourke's
opinion that the United States has its own native artistic
expressions which have sprung from the common people in
various sections of the country. [12]

Rourke was also influenced by the eighteenth-century
German writer Johann Gottfried von Herder, who strengthened her conviction that culture originates as much from the
layers of society as from the intelligentsia. Herder's view that
culture reflects national patterns and communal organization
had an impact upon her writing. She praised him for
"insisting that the folk-arts laid a base for the fine arts in
form, spirit and expression, that folk-forms were the essential
forms in any communal group." [13] Herder's theories on the
integral relationship between the folk and fine arts and the
importance of a rich community life to cultural development
reappear throughout Rourke's own work.

Her birth and childhood in the Middle West had an even
deeper bearing on the formation of her views. A true
"daughter of the middle border," Rourke was born in
Cleveland, Ohio, in 1885, but spent most of her school years
in Grand Rapids, Michigan, while it was still a quaint
midwestern town. She was an excellent student, and her
mother, a school teacher and principal, created an atmosphere at home of book learning and intellectual curiosity.
Her college years were spent at Vassar College, from which
she was graduated in 1907, followed by several years' study
at the Sorbonne and work as a research reader in Europe.
Returning in 1910, she obtained a position as an English
instructor at Vassar but resigned her post in 1915 in order to
devote herself to free-lance writing. Instead of making her
headquarters in a large city such as New York, Rourke
returned to Grand Rapids, where she participated in civic and
social affairs. She remained there until the end of her life,
reveling in a community that had a rich regional tradition. [14]

Like her contemporaries Thomas Hart Benton and Frank
Lloyd Wright, Rourke viewed the Middle West as the true
heartland of America. Grand Rapids, she declared, was

similar to "at least two dozen villages in Michigan and elsewhere in the early Middle West that did not conform to" the idea that "life in our smaller towns and cities has been too meager to give the artist nourishment." She proudly described the cultural assets of her home town, particularly its practicing amateur and professional painters and the art gallery. Steamboat Gothic houses painted in bright colors and perched on wooded knolls gave the town a picturesque quality, and "enclosing fruit trees and country gardens" created a pastoral touch. By living in such a pleasant atmosphere, an artist would soon discover "that our towns and villages are not always stereotypes." Her sympathetic picture of the small town differed radically from the social critics of the 1920s who had revolted against the village because of its middle-class provincialism. She believed, instead, that rural small-town America could be a stimulating environment for the artist precisely because of its regional traditions and closeness to nature. "Surely something may be gained by the artist ... knowing a society at close range, from perceiving cycles of its effort, touches of its history, its distinctive flavor, its darker and more checkered aspects," Rourke declared. [15]

Her belief in the creativeness of regional traditions is reaffirmed in her 1938 study of the painter Charles Sheeler. The book restates the themes of her earlier work: the influence of regionalism on cultural development and the relationship of folk art to high culture. A major factor in Sheeler's work, she believed, was his attachment to the area of eastern Pennsylvania, where he grew up and began his career. He was impressed by the designs of Pennsylvania folk art and rural architecture, and Shaker buildings and furniture contributed to his basic sense of form. This influence of local folk material, she felt, did not make Sheeler a provincial painter. He was an artist in the American tradition; his painting "achieves a composite of qualities which could belong only to ourselves." [16] But as in her study of Audubon, she overemphasizes the impact of rural regionalism and is unable, for example, to understand the importance of technology and the industrial arts to Sheeler's work. In

Rourke's mind, Sheeler represents the artist who has been
nourished by regional traditions and influenced by local
subject matter — a modern-day Audubon whose art is
typically American.

The study of Sheeler discloses Rourke's belief that a
national culture could be created out of regional folklore.
That relationship between regionalism and nationalism might
seem at first contradictory, but for regionalists like Rourke
the real America was centered in the hinterland where local
cultural traditions surfaced unhindered by the artificial
pressures of urban civilization. The rural sections of the
country embodied both a "different America" and a "deeper
America," to borrow definitions of regionalism suggested by
William Jordy.

In this sense, her writing can be linked to the cultural
nationalism of the Depression years, when the idea of
"America! America!" sounded through much of our literature and art. American life was depicted in documentary
film, descriptive journalism, and WPA travel guides. Daniel
Aaron has pointed out that the discovery of the past had the
therapeutic value of reassuring the public of its ability to
survive the Depression. The deification of frontier superheroes suggested a vicarious identification with great individual feats during a time when the American dream of
personal success had collapsed, while a reaction against
machine technology led to a nostalgic glorification of our
rural past. Old ballads were revived and legendary frontier
heroes such as Davy Crockett, Mike Fink, Johnny Appleseed,
and Daniel Boone were immortalized. Folk festivals were
staged, folk singing increased in popularity, exhibitions of
folk art multiplied, and in 1935 the Index of American
Design was established. This fascination with American
folkways, which became a popular craze, also elevated the
literature of the masses. [17]

Rourke's writing during the 1930s well suited this
renaissance of folk culture. *American Humor* (1931), her
most influential book, is a perceptive interpretation of
folklore and popular entertainment on the frontier. Except

for a tendency to overstate the influence of comic folklore on formal American literature, her classic study is full of brilliant insights. Rourke rightly believed that the major motif in Western literature, from tall tales to the stories of Mark Twain, has been humor. It is also a dominant trait in the American character, epitomized by the frontiersman, whose comic sense enabled him to survive his everyday struggle against nature, and by the half-truths of tall-talk and frontier oratory. Comic exaggeration prevailed in the legendary tales of Davy Crockett, Mike Fink, and Sam Patch, while strolling actors performed burlesque and staged satirical melodramas for the amusement of the settlers. Frontier culture, in short, derived naturally from the rustic folk experience of the pioneer. [18]

Her preoccupation with folk materials led her next to study the exploits of Davy Crockett, who personified the ideal frontier hero. She was distantly related to George Mayfield, a friend of the scout, and as a young girl had heard stories of the backwoodsman's adventures. Using Crockett's *Almanacs,* narratives, letters, and speeches, Rourke presents the frontiersman as a mythical figure of courageous individualism. "By his character, his repartee, his stories, his exploits, he had captivated the popular imagination, and his name kept this afire," she eulogizes. "These stories constitute one of the earliest and perhaps the largest of our cycles of myth." [19] Unlike the persuasive arguments in *American Humor, Davy Crockett* is pure myth-making, a book for the juvenile market that cashed in on the enthusiasm for folk heroes during the Depression and provided one of the heroes the American youth needed.

Rourke became involved in various movements to bring folk art to the attention of the American public. She helped plan the 1934 St. Louis National Folk Festival in which folk songs, dances, and plays were presented from different areas of the country. To her, the festival was a "freely arranged" sequence of programs in which "the national arts appeared in elliptical outline with an effect of deeply set traditions." As a form of group enterprise, regional expression, and national

rite, the St. Louis pageant embodied the major cultural values
Rourke stressed in her books. [20]

During 1937 she also served as national editor of the
Federal Art Project's Index of American Design, a pictorial
record of American folk and decorative art. Furniture,
textiles, glass, ceramics, silver, cigar-store Indians, kitchen-
ware, toys, and tavern signs were some of the major items
recorded by artists on relief. Rourke's wide knowledge of
folk art enormously contributed to the project's success. She
hoped that the Index would reveal the rich folk culture of
America's regions, bringing "fresh light ... upon ways of
living which developed within the highly diversified communities of our many frontiers," and that this would in turn
give us "new knowledge of the American mind and tempera-
ment." The Index, she asserted, would also "offer an
education of the eye, particularly for young people, which
may result in the development of taste and a genuine
consciousness of our rich national inheritance." [21]

Throughout her career she urged the public to study the
arts for cultural purposes, in the hope that a greater
awareness of native culture would improve the quality of
society. To achieve this, she called for published studies on
American culture, a program of circulating art exhibititions,
and the preservation of cultural history material by museums
and libraries. Believing that education is a vital tool in
informing students about their culture, she urged high
schools and universities to establish courses in folklore and
folk music. "If we could open our past to young people . . .,"
she stated, "we might have a great literature and music and
art upon us before we know it." [22] Rourke's work uncovering
common traditions and culture during the 1930s thus carried
a special sense of mission and urgency.

When Constance Rourke died unexpectedly in 1941, she
was lauded by the intellectual community for having brought
"to the American present a greater and more informed
awareness of the American past, especially in the arts; for it
was her conviction that specific, integrated knowledge and
understanding of the past was indispensable to the creative

worker in any field." The past she recreated, however, was a very special one, and this contributed both strengths and weaknesses to her writing. If the fiction of the 1930s sometimes suffered from a sentimental belief in the value of living close to the land, Rourke's own work was weakened by the exaggerated generalization that rural regionalism was the major influence on American culture. By overestimating the impact of the frontier, she neglected the role of Europe and the city. Her dedication to the folk arts also caused her to overrate the influence of folklore on formal literature and painting. Nevertheless, her belief in the relationship of folklore and popular entertainment to American regional traditions led her to uncover neglected aspects of our national culture and to open new areas of scholarship. [23]

NOTES

1. Van Wyck Brooks, preface to *The Roots of American Culture and Other Essays* by Constance Rourke (New York: Harcourt, Brace & World, 1942), p. vi.

2. On the concept of regionalism, consult R. Allan Lawson, *The Failure of Independent Liberalism, 1930-1941* (New York: G. P. Putnam's Sons, 1971), pp. 135-37, 206-08.

3. At the time of her death in 1941, Rourke was working on a multivolume history of American culture. Brooks collected the pieces she had written and published them in *The Roots of American Culture.* The title essay of the book is the best exposition of Rourke's critical opinions.

4. Rourke discusses Turner in "The Significance of Sections," *New Republic,* 20 Sept. 1933, pp. 148-51.

5. Constance Rourke, *Trumpets of Jubilee* (1927; rpt. New York: Harbinger Books, 1963), p. viii.

6 Constance Rourke, *Troupers of the Gold Coast; or, the Rise of Lotta Crabtree* (New York: Harcourt, Brace, 1928).

7. Constance Rourke, *Audubon* (New York: Harcourt, Brace, 1936), p. 242.

8. Constance Rourke, *Charles Sheeler: Artist in the American Tradition* (New York: Harcourt, Brace, 1938), p. 32. Rourke, *The Roots of American Culture,* p. 51. Rourke, "The Significance of Sections," pp. 148-51.

9. See Rourke, *Trumpets of Jubilee,* pp. 180-275. Quoted from Rourke, *The Roots of American Culture,* pp. 236-37.

10. While on the *Freeman,* Rourke became acquainted with Brooks, the magazine's literary editor, and was no doubt impressed by his socio-historical criticism and desire to uncover a usable literary past. Yet she never shared his hierarchical concept of the arts nor his early negative opinions concerning the paltriness of American literature. Evidence suggests that Rourke's zealous cultural nationalism was a later influence on Brooks's more affirmative works of the thirties. In his *Autobiography* (New York: E. P. Dutton, 1965, p. 356), Brooks states that her work broadened his horizons. Yet he refutes John Chamberlain's inference that Rourke was a major influence on his later writing, in an exchange of letters with Lewis Mumford, published in *The Van Wyck Brooks-Lewis Mumford Letters: The Record of a Literary Friendship, 1921-1963,* ed. Robert E. Spiller (New York: E. P. Dutton, 1970), pp. 218-20.

11. Constance Rourke, "Paul Bunyan," *New Republic,* 7 July 1920, pp. 176-79; "Vaudeville," *New Republic,* 27 Aug. 1919, pp. 115-16.

12. Rourke refers to Benedict in *The Roots of American Culture,* pp. 49-50, 284. On the influence of cultural anthropology during the 1930s, see Robert M. Crunden, *From Self to Society, 1919-1941* (Englewood Cliffs, N. J.: Prentice-Hall, 1972), pp. 10-13; Warren I. Susman, "The Thirties," in *The Development of an American Culture,* ed. Stanley Coben and Lorman Ratner (Englewood Cliffs, N. J.: Prentice-Hall, 1970), pp. 183-84.

13. Rourke, *The Roots of American Culture,* p. 24.

14. The following sources contain biographical information on Rourke: Kenneth S. Lynn, "Constance Mayfield Rourke," in *Notable American Women, 1607-1950: A Biographical Dictionary,* ed. Edward T. James (Cambridge, Mass.: Belknap Press, 1971), II, 199-200; *National Cyclopaedia of American Biography* (New York: James T. White, 1933), XXXII, 100; Stanley J. Kunitz and Howard Haycraft, *Twentieth Century Authors* (New York: H. W. Wilson, 1942), pp. 1206-07.

15. Constance Rourke, "Art in Our Town," *Nation,* 30 March 1940, pp. 424-25. See also Constance Rourke, "Portrait of a Home Town," *New Republic,* 23 Feb. 1921, pp. 369-71.

16. Rourke, *Charles Sheeler,* p. 187.

17. For a good description of the period's cultural nationalism see Alfred Kazin, "America! America!" *On Native Grounds* (1942; rpt. Garden City, N. Y.: Anchor Books, 1956), pp. 378-406.

18. Constance Rourke, *American Humor: A Study of the National Character* (1931; rpt. Garden City, N.Y.: Anchor Books, 1953).

19. Constance Rourke, *Davy Crockett* (New York: Harcourt, Brace, 1934), p. 250.

20. Constance Rourke, "The National Folk Festival," *New Republic,* 30 May 1934, p. 73. See also Constance Rourke, "The National Folk Festival," *New Republic,* 5 June 1935, pp. 102-03.

21. Quoted from Holger Cahill, introduction to *The Index of American Design* by Erwin O. Christensen (New York: Macmillan, 1950), p. xvii. See also Constance Rourke, "Index of American Design," *Magazine of Art,* April 1937, pp. 207-11.

22. Constance Rourke, "Traditons for Young People," *Nation,* 20 Nov. 1937, pp. 562-64.

23. Obituary, *Nation,* 29 March 1941, p. 368. For an excellent criticism of Rourke's work see Stanley Edgar Hyman. "Constance Rourke and Folk Criticism," *The Armed Vision: A Study in the Methods of Modern Literary Criticism* (1948; rpt. New York: Vintage Books, 1955). pp. 114-31.

CHAPTER 4

Thought and Social Change: Reflections On Cultural Studies

By Sydney E. Ahlstrom

SYDNEY E. AHLSTROM, Professor of American History and Modern Religious History at Yale University, was Chairman of the American Studies Program from 1967 to 1971 and again in 1973-1974. He teaches in the History Department, the Department of Religious Studies, the American Studies Program, and the Divinity School at Yale and has frequently lectured abroad, including the Salzburg Seminar in 1947 and 1952 and the Kyoto American Studies Seminar in 1972. Professor Ahlstrom's special interest in American intellectual and religious history and the cultural history of New England have been expressed in *The Harvard Divinity School* (1954); *Theology in America*, in the *Religion in American Life* series (1961); *The American Protestant Encounter with World Religions* (1962); editor, *Theology in America: The Major Protestant Voices from Puritanism to Neo-Orthodoxy* (1967); and *A Religious History of the American People* (1972), which was awarded the National Book Award. His chief research interests at present relate to the religious dimensions and implications of European and American romantic thought.

In his essay here, Sydney Ahlstrom investigates the interaction of ideas and intellectual (or "spiritual") history with social, political, and institutional developments.

The lecture on which this essay is based was conceived as a response to somebody's utterly traditional deprecation of the fabled Ivory Tower wherein professors live out their lives.* My dissent from this stereotypical view was not intended to be a defense of professional conduct, however, but a consideration of the social and political consequences of pure academic scholarship. I was going to argue that most of the social change of the modern world, from the unleashing of atomic energy to the green revolution, and certainly including the communist revolution as well, has stemmed from one room or another of that Ivory Tower. This would be to bring support to Kenneth Boulding's observation that most of what has happened to the earth's biosphere in the last four hundred years has stemmed from increments of knowledge.

Having recently written a very large religious history of the American people, I was going to base my exposition on facts drawn from that controversy-filled realm. I had decided to stress the ways in which the abstruse and erudite critical work of biblical scholars, using a dozen disciplines from linguistics to sociology, undermined the authority of the most authoritative Book the world has ever seen and thereby profoundly altered the foundations of the chief institutional structures of Western civilization and exposed religious thought to the corrosive action of modernity and relativism.

One could have begun such an account with some reference to Laurentius Valla or with Martin Luther's interpretation of the homolegomena within the New Testament canon. These developments would have led naturally through a long series of predominantly European developments to the Fundamentalist Controversy that began in

---

*The title of the paper out of which the present essay developed was "Humanistic Scholarship as a Social Force in America." It was the third of my three lectures and workshop-sessions sponsored by the American Studies Institute at the University of Southern California in the summer of 1973. Heavy revisions seemed necessary because so many questions raised during that week entered into my final lecture that it could not easily stand alone. The present essay is in part a response to these many discussions and conversations, and I have tried to maintain the informal mood and manner of the original situation.

America with Theodore Parker's edition of DeWette's *Introduction to the Old Testament* in 1843. It would then have followed the widening and deepening conflict in the churches down to the 1920s by which time it was taking on concrete political dimensions. I could then have considered the work now being done on the exciting gnostic texts recently discovered in Egypt and the Sinai peninsula. A contemporary note might have been struck with an account of the present-day exile of faculty and students from America's largest Lutheran seminary, where historical studies of the Scriptures had become a divisive issue.

The emergence of Fundamentalism as an organized component of American evangelical Protestantism would then have led naturally to a consideration of Leon Festinger's general theory of "cognitive dissonance," which seeks to explain the sometimes feverish activity of groups who sense a great disparity between their views and those of the more well-informed public. [1] It would also tend to show the relevance of Peter Berger's notion of "cognitive deviance," which accounts for the tendency of these same groups to develop supportive communities and institutional self-protection. [2] In the light of such interpretations we would see more clearly how the clash of contradictory theological outlooks leads many Americans to defensive and even semihysterical forms of individual and group behavior which politicians and charismatic revivalists can successfully turn to their own purposes. One result of such an inquiry might be a much improved understanding of the social implications of scholarship. In a larger sense, moreover, it would have served as a case study on the social and political importance of *Geistesgeschichte,* or spiritual history. [3] In the light thus afforded, what we often call intellectual history would appear not as an epiphenomenal irrelevancy, but, on the contrary, as a fundamental necessity for all who want truly to understand how social and political movements are sustained.

These formulations, of course, suggest a certain affinity for Wilhelm Dilthey's concept of *Verstehen*[4] and for R. G.

Collingwood's famous dicta: "Historical knowledge ... has for its proper object thought"; "Of everything other than thought, there can be no history."[5] They would also show my great respect for the ways in which Max Weber sought to qualify and improve the more simple-minded kinds of economic determinism that were flourishing at the turn of the last century. In the process we would perhaps discover the degree to which economic and institutional developments are soaked in spiritual and valuational concerns.

Having thus tipped my cards, I would like to make clear that this overall course of action did not seem fruitful in the present context. I have thus decided not to pursue this investigation of biblical criticism and its social consequences, and for two reasons: first, because it would take years to prepare an adequate survey of this vast subject; and second, because even my brief resume of things *not* done has already provided an indication of a general problem that requires a different mode of discourse.

What follows, therefore, is a more abstract indication of the ways in which students of civilizations and national cultures might extend their inquiries beyond the more external and "objective" aspects of life and seek to understand the beliefs, attitudes, fears, hopes and illusions that combine to constitute human intentionality. The accomplishment of my purposes in stressing this need, however, will require a number of subcontentions that have often figured in methodological discussions. The order in which they should be introduced is debatable, but the main lines of an argument will, I trust, emerge.

Perhaps primary in a general discussion of cultural studies is the need to recognize that the distinctions and definitions that are commonly used to identify separate scholarly disciplines tend to be ambiguous, artificial, and idealized. When these ill-defined disciplines are segregated or grouped in distinct academic departments, the confusion tends to be not only compounded but ossified. To further darken matters, these departments are often grouped in three separate divisions or moved into separate schools. It is not my purpose here, of course, to complain about academic organization, but simply to suggest that bureaucratic necessities should not blind us to the fact that the study of human beings, individually and in society, historically and nomothetically, goes on in virtually all of these disciplines, departments, divisions, and schools. What goes on in each of them, furthermore, has a history, as do most of the objects of their study from the nebulae and stars to the earth and all living things. Only numbers and other beings like that (God is like that perhaps) are eternal and thus beyond history.

In our discussions, therefore, it is imperative that we view nearly all of these distinctions as potentially deceiving even when they are organizationally useful. And most deceiving of all in the present context is that very familiar distinction between the humanities and the social (or behavioral) sciences. Nearly all of the disciplines usually put in these categories are in pursuit of larger and better interpretations of human existence. A philosopher or historical theologian is as deeply concerned with human behavior as a sociological analyst of census returns. Historians are constantly being found on both sides of the half-imaginary divide, and so are political philosophers. There are scholars of art and literature who both use and seek to formulate nomothetic formulations, just as there are many nominalistic political scientists who have little interest in seeking to formulate laws of political behavior. Historically speaking, almost all of the disciplines grouped in the humanities and behavioral sciences emerged from theology, philosophy, and ethics; and at bottom most of them frequently betray their lineage. In cultural studies especially, these academic factions stand in need of a Geneva Conference. By the same token the practitioners of American Studies need to come to the conference table with those who study other countries and cultures and those who concentrate their attention on the interdisciplinary study of specific periods.

A vital corollary to the above observations that applies in diverse ways across the entire spectrum of disciplines is the fact that historical events, including the emergence of distinctive national cultures, come into existence through human agents. Human beings make up their minds and act.

They have motives (good or bad) for their doings. This fact, moreover, is recognized even by dogmatic determinists—who tend to concur with Jonathan Edwards that "if a volition may come to pass without a cause, . . . many other sorts of effects may do so, too."[6] In this sense most interpreters of human events, including historians, appear to be at least implicitly deterministic in that they constantly try to explain events, including human acts and decisions, in terms of antecedent circumstances or motives. Aside from their formal beliefs on this score, moreover, very few historians would say that A did B for no reason whatsoever. If we ignore human reasons, intentions, and purposes, we are not only writing very opaque history but are indulging in a species of inhumanism, treating persons like mute stones. On the other hand, if we lack this knowledge and even lack grounds for guessing, we are reduced to writing no more than annals or chronicles.

The great value of biographies stems from the fact that they do allow a kind of study that is otherwise often denied to the historian. They allow a careful consideration of a person's family relationships, nurture, education, psychic problems, and developing thought patterns. At their best they can provide almost all we can know about the vexing problem of intellectual influences. When the evidence is abundant, one can even expose or dismiss those spurious forms of influence wherein the acceptance of certain views follows simply on the discovery of a fellow spirit—perhaps a fellow spirit who writes more clearly, or more forcefully, or more beautifully. I am convinced that Francis Ellingwood Abbot and most of his poetically minded Harvard College friends were of this type when during the 1850s they idolized William Cullen Bryant and imitated his poetry. Yet the biographer may also discern authentic influence, that is, the impact of ideas or precise knowledge that disrupts or destroys a person's spiritual composure and forces a thorough-going intellectual restructuring. Returning to Abbot again (upon whose life I wrote a very long doctoral dissertation), one could observe this kind of genuine influence arise from his reading of Charles Darwin. Evolutionary thinking destroyed the conservative Unitarian synthesis to which he had been converted during the revivals of 1858 and set him to the lifelong project of constructing a viable form of "scientific theism." Variations on these alternatives are, of course, and have always been, almost infinite in number; and since the rise of psychology as a more or less scientific discipline, the number has if anything increased. The emergence of a more standardized post-Freudian vocabulary of interpretation, however, should not lull us into an assurance that our interpretations are less personal and more profound than those of Plutarch, Dilthey, or Lytton Strachey. [7]

In my more pessimistic moods I sometimes wonder if any other kind of study can supply our need for better knowledge of why human beings do what they do. In more optimistic moments, however, I write papers like the present one and suggest that the requisite methods can be applied in more comprehensive contexts if students of social movements will truly listen to the voices they hear.

The primary ground for confidence in this regard is perhaps best expressed in the principle that what applies to our knowledge of individual persons applies also to human being in its corporate form. Following a line of thought that Josiah Royce often stressed, we may say that the distinction between individual and corporate human being is not ontologically fundamental. [8] For historical purposes it is clearly not decisive. A group of people is not less real or less human than a person. One may say, therefore, that epistemology should follow ontology.

For the student of history and culture, an explanation of a politician's act is not inherently different from his explanation of a political faction's act, though the latter may be far more difficult, in that not everyone joins a faction for the same reason or reacts to political provocations in the same way. Ralph Barton Perry, who may well be the most astute American philosopher to have written a major work of cultural exposition, put the matter succinctly in his own attack on "epiphenomenalism."

> What is true of individual behavior is true of social behavior.
> As individual behavior depends on decisions embracing purposes
> and judgments so social behavior depends on common purposes
> and common judgments. Men act when they decide; they act
> together when they agree. Having gone so far, there is no just
> ground for denying the potency, the unique social potency, of
> those interrelations, reciprocities, and identities of emotion and
> expectation which constitute collective ideals .
>   In short, those practical leaders whose business it is to
> engineer the making of history pay to the causal efficacy of ideals
> the highest possible tribute. . . . If a factor such as an ideal makes
> *any* difference, then there may be situations in which it makes all
> the difference.[9]

What followed this forceful philosophical statement was a
large and perceptive book on the American ideological
experience, with special emphasis on the ways in which the
chief elements of the country's heritage—Puritan and Enlightened—were developed, appropriated, and fused. It must be
said, too, that his convictions about the substructural
importance of ideas and ideals did not prevent him from
taking good account of the nation's "practical leaders" and
of the concrete institutions through which American ideals
were expressed. My chief criticism would relate to his
inadequate treatment of Puritan convictions about work,
property, and personal economic freedom, for it was these
ideas above all which became so firmly objectified in the
federal constitution and in American institutional life.

Another way of stating this criticism of Perry would be
to commend an Hegelian mode of analysis and at the same
time to recommend Professor William Goetzmann's recently
published anthology on Hegelianism in America, which
provides a timely documentation of a long and lively
tradition in this country. [10] It seems to me that Hegel more
than any other thinker inaugurated a new era of dialectical
interpretation in which the subjective and objective, the ideal
and the material, the positive and the negative dimensions of
the historical process are comprehended. He more than any
other made us look to the whole sweep of Western history
(or Christendom) and made us see how its dominant ideas,
Graeco-Roman and Judaeo-Christian, functioned as a shaping
force in the development of Western beliefs, values, behavior

and institutions. He also shows us the superificality of seeing ideas and institutions or intellectual history and social history as opposed or as separated, or, worse still, as autonomous or self-sufficient modes of analysis. It is precisely because he brought these frequently opposed elements together that even Hegel's place in the idealistic tradition needs to be qualified. As scholars of Marxian thought have been saying, Spinoza may be as important in his intellectual lineage as Kant, Schelling, and Fichte. Hegel's idealism, more than any, holds up under the demand that Josiah Royce once placed upon any idealistic system of thought. It must meet "the presupposition of life, that we work in a real world where house-walls do not melt away as in dreams, but stand firm against the winds of many winters, and can be felt as real." As if in response to Royce, J. N. Findlay speaks, in a recent work, of "the toughness, the empirical richness, the logical brilliance, and the astonishing self-subversive movement of Hegel's thought." He also finds him "infinitely far from both Berkeley and Kant" and "more nearly a dialectical materialist than most Hegelians have realized."[11] I am, of course, no Hegel scholar, but I am testifying to a large recent literature on Hegel and the young Marx that has had a deservedly large influence on contemporary studies of culture and social change. One of the great values of this movement of thought is that it has broken down some of the senseless polarities that have featured much American theory and practice in the broad fields of cultural study.

Similarly valuable in the above regard has been the phenomenological impulse associated with the work of Edmund Husserl. In this connection I am not referring to Husserl's total program of philosophical reform or his full-scale attacks on historicism, psychologism, and sociologism, which seem to have promised more than they have (so far) delivered, but to the potent way in which he isolated, illuminated, and emphasized human intentionality on the one hand, and the unique character of the Western scientific tradition on the other. The cultural historian, I believe, has much to learn from Husserl's controversy with Dilthey, his view of the values and limitations of *Weltanschauung* research, and his persistent concern not for the "objective" sciences of nature but for the environing world (*Umwelt*) of the spiritual subject, as well as his demand for a complete transformation of attitude whereby the essentially intentional character of every act of consciousness is fully appreciated. Again I must hasten to add that I am not a Husserl scholar nor an historian of phenomenological thought; but I remain grateful for the ways in which this tradition has enriched the cultural disciplines and widened the scope of their inquiries. [12]

Husserl and certain aspects of his phenomenological program also provide a convenient modulation toward my concluding theme, which has to do with the ways in which cultural studies, and especially those with an historical dimension, are inescapably conditioned by the concerns and evidential artifacts of the present. This is apparent in the case of Husserl himself, whose sense of a crisis in modern philosophy drove him to an investigation of the origins of scientific thought in ancient Greece. The historical work of Ralph Barton Perry, which has been discussed above, also illustrates the inevitable pressures of time and circumstance on historical works. It was conceived during the great international crisis of the 1930s and early 1940s and published in 1944 while the United States was at war. The author's intention was clearly to enliven and deepen the national faith at a time when totalitarianism threatened the world. One of the early classics of the American Studies movement, Ralph Henry Gabriel's *The Course of American Democratic Thought* (1940), reflects many of these same interests and the same awareness of American democratic values at bay. So it is with all who undertake explorations of time past; there is no alternative but to use the canons of relevance and the explanatory theories that the day provides. This is to say that the past as we know it is best understood as an ideal construction. It is an extrapolation of the evidence at hand, including the memories of those alive, as shaped by the preoccupations of the investigator. The history that runs through human minds (even memories of yesteryear) is constantly changing—especially in a dynamic society like our own, whose parties, as Chesterton once observed, get later and later at night because we are trying to live tomorrow. We must, then, get used to the idea that the past is not "out there" to be scrutinized at our pleasure and compared with what we call historiography. It is rather a network of more or less plausible statements that cohere with each other in so far as we can make them do so, and which take account of the things in our world, like fading documents and crumbling buildings, which would be a frightfully anomalous part of our environment if we did not have a past in which they could have been written or built. For this reason the past is flexible. One rich archaeological find tomorrow might require the addition of tens or hundreds of thousands of years to the history of mankind on the American continents, just as the discovery of one detailed diary might force revisions of our interpretations of the Constitutional Convention.

These are bare statements, to be sure, unsupported here by extended arguments. Perhaps their most serious deficiency is that they do not account for the remarkable stability and coherence of the Western historiographical achievement as a whole, nor do they explain the West's passionate commitment to history.[13] Yet even these seemingly peremptory remarks may perhaps show, or at least suggest, that a view as to the nature and role of thoughts, decisions, hopes, and other acts of consciousness bears a very close relation to ways in which we understand the nature and role of our scholarly studies themselves. One, thus, may fittingly conclude by repeating Collingwood's provocative dictum: "Of everything other than thought, there can be no history."

NOTES

1. See Leon Festinger, *A Theory of Cognitive Dissonance* (Stanford, Calif.: Stanford University Press, 1957), and *Conflict, Decision, and Dissonance* (Stanford, Calif.: Stanford University Press, 1964). His *When Prophecy Fails* (New York: Harper Torchbook, 1964) is a remarkable account of the rise and fall of a contemporary religious movement.

2. Peter L. Berger, *The Sacred Canopy* (Garden City, N.Y.: Anchor Books, 1969), pp. 163ff.

3. The term "spiritual history," despite my wishes, will probably not gain favor in America because of many connotations that cling to it; but we need a more encompassing term than "intellectual history" to designate the full range of human subjectivity.

4. See Wilhelm Dilthey, *Pattern and Meaning in History*, ed. H. P. Rickman (New York: Harper Torchbook, 1962), *passim*, but especially chap. 4.

5. R. G. Collingwood, *The Idea of History* (New York: Oxford University Press, 1946), pp. 305, 304.

6. Sydney E. Ahlstrom, *Theology in America* (Indianapolis; Bobbs-Merrill, 1967), p. 168. The quotation is from Edwards's *Freedom of the Will*. There and elsewhere in his writings the same argument is set forth in great detail. It has weathered modern criticism rather well, though many others before and since have defended the position.

7. See the cautionary observations of Philip Pomper, "Problems of a Naturalistic Psychohistory," *History and Theory,* 12 (1973), 367-88.

8. One of the many places where Royce dwells on this theme is in *The Sources of Religious Insight* (New York: Charles Scribner's Sons, 1912), chap. 2, "Individual Experience and Social Experience."

9. Ralph Barton Perry, *Puritanism and Democracy* (New York: Vanguard Press, 1944), pp. 22-23.

10. William H. Goetzmann, *The American Hegelians: An Intellectual Episode in the History of Western America* (New York: Alfred A. Knopf, 1973). Other important works on the Hegelian tradition in the United States are Lloyd D. Easton, *Hegel's First American Followers: The Ohio Hegelians* (Athens: Ohio University Press, 1966), Henry A. Pochmann, *German Culture in America* (Madison: University of Wisconsin Press, 1957), and James Hastings Nichols, *Romanticism in American Theology* (Chicago: University of Chicago Press, 1961). See also the several major histories of American philosophy.

11. Josiah Royce, *The Spirit of Modern Philosophy* (Boston and New York: Houghton, Mifflin and Co., 1892), p. 852. See Findlay's essay in A. MacIntyre, ed., *Hegel* (Garden City, N.Y.: Anchor Books, 1972), pp. 3, 14.

12. In the writing of this paper I have not had the benefit of Maurice A. Natanson, *Edmund Husserl: Philosopher of Infinite Tasks* (Evanston, Ill.: Northwestern University Press, 1973); but see the work he edited: *Phenomenology and Social Reality* (New York: Humanities Press, 1971). Outstanding for its clarity is Quentin Lauer, ed., *Edmund Husserl: Phenomenology and the Crisis of Philosophy* (New York: Harper Torchbook, 1965). One also looks forward to Lauer's forthcoming commentary on Hegel's *Phenomenology of the Spirit*.

13. The Western historiographical tradition here referred to extends in its Graeco-Roman phase from Thucidides to Ammianus Marcellinus and, after a long interim, in its modern phase from the Renaissance through the likes of Gibbon, Ranke, and Mommsen to Bancroft and Henry Adams. Each of these, like all other historians, was finite and fallible, and each of them had distinctive beliefs and assumptions. Yet they shared a critical spirit, a concern for evidence and accuracy, and a commitment to broad public standards of plausibility. Because the stability and continuity of the tradition depend on these latter attributes, no compromise or deprecation of them is even faintly entertained or implied by the argument of the present essay.

The historical passion of the West has its origins in the biblical conception of history as a linear once-and-for-all movement from Creation to Consummation. In this view, even when it is ostensibly secularized by Enlightened or Marxian interpreters, all things move toward some end on which the meaning of life and the significance of all things depend. By the same token, however, the significance of a thing could be known only when its terminus were in sight—and even then only partially until the end of all things were known. Unless he be a prophet or a seer, therefore, the historian or any other interpreter of human affairs should make very modest claims to definitive results and let an interim ethic shape his efforts.

CHAPTER 5

Archaeology and Material History: A Personal Approach To Discovery of the Past

By John L. Cotter

JOHN L. COTTER, Adjunct Associate Professor of American Civilization at the University of Pennsylvania, is also Associate Curator of American Historical Archaeology at the University Museum, Philadelphia, and a retired career archaeologist with the National Park Service. Beginning in the 1930s, his special interests in Early Man in North America and the conservation of historical sites, and his many archaeological investigations and field projects have been reported in over eighty articles, reviews, and books, including his *Archeological Excavations at Jamestown, Virginia* (1959), *Bibliography of Historical Sites Archeology* (1966, 1968) and *Handbook for Historical Archaeology, Part I* (1968). He was co-founder, president, and editor of the Society for Historical Archaeology.

In the essay to follow, Professor Cotter encourages students to explore history by way of everyday artifacts, and to join in the conservation of our material heritage.

The following essay is devoted to two related purposes: to define archaeology and the new scope of its application in the recovery and conservation of the cultural heritage of America; and to demonstrate how one of its aspects, *Above Ground Archaeology,* can be offered to students as a path of personal discovery into the study of history.

Archaeology: Conservational Discovery

Archaeology may be defined as the retrieval and interpretation of the physical evidence of man's past. To this I would add, the application of historical and ethnographic models to the functional society involved, specifically those aspects of the society which existed at the site.

It is a curious and significant fact that ancient civilizations of the West and East alike gave little thought to traces in the earth of earlier peoples who were or were not their ancestors. It is true that in times of certain national crises, rulers or priests who led the ancient Mesopotamian, Palestinian and Nilotic civilizations sought by evoking and emulating the past to lend added respect to the material and spiritual achievements of new leaders. But Greece and Rome lived on mounds of potsherds with no recorded concern or speculation as to who created them or how long ago. When the poet-philosopher Lucretius in the first century B. C. wrote *Of the Nature of Things*, he speculated with amazing perception that man had progressed from his primordial use of hands, nails and teeth to wood and stone, and thence to the fashioning of copper, and finally, iron. (Book V, *Beginnings of Civilization*, lines 1009-1455.) But he cited no evidence in the earth.

Archaeology as a modern concept was conceived in the Renaissance of Italy and spread northward to Scandinavia and England from France in the 18th century. It burgeoned in the 19th century as a result of the revelations of ancient Egyptian civilization by Napoleon's conquests across the Mediterranean, and the spectacular discoveries at Pompeii. In America Thomas Jefferson was the first man of scientific bent to use modern archaeological techniques of excavation and observation in the investigation of an Indian mound in

Virginia. But it was not until the 20th century that archaeology was conceptualized in this country as *an extension of anthropological observation into the remote past*, and not until the end of the first half of the present century that the techniques and concepts of archaeological investigation were directed, except in sporadic instances, toward analyses of historical data.

Today much attention is focused on archaeological values and the conservation of archaeological resources throughout the world. The prime reason is that these resources are threatened more than ever before by the building and land disruption that have followed the human population explosion of the past century. Further, the attention to archaeological conservation is compounded by a world-wide compulsion to gain identity and perspective by understanding the past, both prehistoric and historic. In a fast-changing cultural and physical environment the realization is upon us that the pro tempora limits of human resources, cultural and physical, may be reached amid great stress in the near future. Thus there is obvious need to understand where we have been, in order to forecast where we may be going. The modern philosophical poet T. S. Eliot set our subject in perspective when he wrote in "Little Gidding" (1942) from the *Four Quartets:*

> We shall not cease from exploration
> And the end of all our exploring
> Will be to arrive where we started
> And know the place for the first time.
> Through the unknown, remembered gate
> When the last of earth left to discover
> Is that which was the beginning; . . .

The quest for man's identity is that elemental — and that profound: to know our beginnings with new and acute perception, perhaps for the first time.

Before we consider the comparative uses of written and artifactual remains for recovery of our origins and cultural heritage, let us take a look at an immediate and tangible aspect of archaeology—its conservational role in insuring that the record of the past survives as much as possible.

There are precious few policies, regulations or laws which are designed to insure the preservation of the documentary evidence of what has transpired in history. The conservation of archives is largely a matter of permission and not obligation. In our time of galloping technology, the control of written data by paper shredders is a social fact, and there is no law to guarantee even their legal use. Fortunately, there is an increasingly impressive bulwark of federal and state laws directed principally toward actions that may destroy in the land the physical evidence of the past which is of recognized value to the present and the future, although what the law has effectually preserved to date is comparable to a few documents rescued at random from the paper shredders. The record of the past in the land is with increasing speed erased by massive alterations due to urban development, subsoiling and land planning for agriculture, strip mining, industrial parks and airports; or it is buried under lakes of man's own making by the great water conservation dams. Charles R. McGimsey in his notable book on archaeological conservation, *Public Archaeology*, states that within the next twenty-five years the vast majority of the nation's archaeological resources will have been destroyed.

What the archaeologist is interested in are the man-made or man-altered objects that testify to the past, and also the intact context in which these occur. The exact location of the objects, and the soils and other objects with which they are associated, are as important as the objects themselves in our efforts to interpret and understand what has happened in the past. Careful investigation registers vitally important stratigraphy—the sequence in which the evidence occurs — and records the pollen, seeds, bones and other debris which contain clues to the ecology and lifeways which governed the inhabitants of a site. It is this contextual information that requires much of the archaeologist's interpretive efforts and ingenuity, since every site and every object is unique. What is found in a flood deposit laid down 5,000 years ago may rest four inches below a house floor dated in the 17th century A. D., and a glass bottle in the soil six inches above that floor may date from a picnic held on the spot in 1877. The meticulous work of archaeology requires knowledge of prior data, observation of the total environment of the site, and evaluation of the total information derived from it, together with designations of means for protection, relocation or study prior to unavoidable disturbance.

To an extent federal and certain state legislation has envisioned the importance and complexity of this scrutiny, although the fact remains that the National Register of Historic Sites and Buildings and the sites on state registers are no more than a minimal fraction of extant prehistoric and historic sites in the nation. To meet this need for conservation in some measure, guidance, organization and implementation are being provided through the government Corps of Engineers, the Department of Agriculture, the National Park Service's regional centers, and other government land development agencies. Usually contracts are funded with university, museum, or special research agencies to accomplish investigations as required. Some agencies such as the Bureau of Land Management and the National Forest Service also have begun to employ archaeologists to implement investigations on their lands, but the National Park Service is the keystone of the federal effort.

The major legal foundations of the push for environmental and cultural conservation have come roughly at thirty-year intervals. In 1876 the gathering movement to set aside national parks materialized in Yellowstone. In 1906 the *Antiquities Act* was passed calling for federal control of all archaeological resources on federally owned or controlled land and a permit system for implementing investigations. *The Historic Sites Act of 1935* directed the National Park Service to "make necessary investigations and researches in The United States relating to particular sites." This piece of legislation made possible the extensive river basin study and salvage operations which have continued to the present, while *The Reservoir Salvage Act of 1960* further defined the obligation of federal water control agencies to notify the Secretary of the Interior of intention to build a dam or license a private agency to do so. (Congress has recently

passed legislation amending this Act to allow every federal
agency to fund the preservation or investigation of archaeological sites threatened by the agency's construction program
through construction funds, a real watershed in funding,
since most costs heretofore have been supplied through
annual allotments to the National Park Service from con-
gressional appropriations.)

The Historic Preservation Act of 1966, as if following the
magic of the thirty-year interval of key legislation, provided a
major breakthrough in conservation legislation. It has set
forth an expanded National Register of districts, sites,
buildings, structures and objects significant in American
history, and provides matching funds to conduct statewide
surveys of sites for the Register. The Act instructs any agency
using public funds to recognize sites on this register and
protect them. *The National Environmental Policy Act of
1969* put the responsibility squarely on all agencies of the
government, or agencies using government funds or licensed
by the government, to submit an environmental impact
statement which considers the effect a project may have on
archaeological and historical sites as part of the cultural
environment, and alternatives to the project which might
prevent adverse impact. Furthermore, both the Department
of Transportation and the Department of Housing and Urban
Development are now charged by law to make efforts to
preserve historic sites and provide matching funds for doing
so.

Finally, *Executive Order 11593* initiates measures which,
in consultation with the President's Advisory Council on
Historic Preservation, assure that federal plans and programs
also contribute to the preservation and enhancement of
non-federally-owned sites, structures and objects of historical, archaeological, and architectural significance. This extension of benefits gives the full extra measure of reaching
potentially all sites short of invading the rights of private
owners to free use of their own property.

There are still two notable qualifications, however, on
machinery for conserving archaeological, historical, and
architectural sites of value: If the funds are not available, the

work cannot be implemented; and if the property is privately owned, the owner still has the sole choice of saving a site or not, unless his property is seized by right of eminent domain — a procedure traditionally not popular in this country. What can be salvaged on U. S. Government property, or on property affected by the expenditure of federal funds, is protected by various laws and regulations that make it possible for investigations to be made. But the vigilance of informed citizens of all ages and occupations is needed simply to alert conservation agencies such as the National Park Service, the National Forest Service, the Departments of Transportation, and of Housing and Urban Development, the Armed Services, and state archaeological agencies about particular sites that may be threatened. Federal and state archaeologists do what they can to implement the salvage necessary or protect sites from having to be salvaged, and they need all the cooperation and information they can get from the public.

A Word on Material History

Modern logicians and semanticists have been taking a new and critical look at the authority of the written word, and indeed a certain skepticism towards the recorded data of history is getting through to historians themselves. At best there is only a fraction of man's story that can be obtained from written records, which extend back only a little more than 5,000 years. The role of the historian is now appearing in a new light, and questions are being asked by social and cultural analysts of a new generation. Murray G. Murphey, Chairman of the American Civilization Department at the University of Pennsylvania, has just written a very different kind of book on history entitled *Our Knowledge of the Historical Past* (1973) in which he poses searching questions concerning the philosophical validity of our historical knowledge. Are there really any historical "facts," he asks, or are the "facts" of history only the recorded observations and conclusions of those who remember them—or, more likely, the conclusions of those who gather the surviving records of such observations and try to create from this evidence a model of factual events. The model itself will change from generation to generation, as every age rewrites history in terms of current needs, values, and social philosophy. At best, historical records are very imperfect artifacts with which to interpret the past.

Nonetheless, while what man says is not always the best record of what was, there are non-verbal artifacts, silent testaments with no opinions of their own to offer, which can be considered as historical evidence. Archaeology helps conquer the stereotypes of verbally-recorded history by offering an alternative source of data. The inanimate objects that man leaves behind him have the advantage of being able neither to dissemble nor distort the data they imply. Artifacts, in short, cannot lie; they can only be misinterpreted.

To paraphrase Ralph Waldo Emerson, the actions of the past and what the past created materially can speak so loudly we will not hear its words. A healthy, pluralistic view of the past is better insured by having the versatility of *documentation* extended to include the material remains of man's works as well as what is written about them. The keystone of Professor Murphey's inquiry into historical methodology and philosophy is his admonition: "... we can hardly rest content with the current state of our methods of confirmation in history. It is in this area that further work is most urgently needed. Whether such work takes a form which increases the similarity of history to the social sciences or whether it takes some other direction, the important thing is that we develop better ways of testing our statements about the past against the data which the past has left us." All the resources of statistical analysis, modern logic, and computerization are needed to sort out probabilities in documented history (written and material) and to formulate viable models of man's works and society both in history and prehistory.

Above Ground Archaeology: A Personal Approach to the Discovery of History (with Precaution) for Students of All Ages

But so much for theory. Effective education does not limit intellectual activity to the elite. It is a challenge to creativity by means of a very personal and individual learning experience through discovery. Discovery must be part of the environment of modern creative learning. Where the factor of competition prevalent in American education tends to make everyone alike, an individual search for identity and perception encourages each discoverer to be distinct; while a part of the pattern of human behavior, each personal and family history is unique in its own right. This recognition of the uniqueness of man and the commonality of mankind is the quest of anthropology.

Inasmuch as it gathers data on human society for the purpose of creating viable models of past life, archaeology is anthropology. The purpose of archaeology is to get a first-hand glimpse through the clues available to it of what it was like to live in past times and thus to get to know better who our predecessors were and how we became what we are today. Archaeology can be a voyage from the present time upstream through history toward its source which students, *with appropriate caution*, may take on their own initiative with resources they themselves discover. The goal is self-identity and the identity of the community in which one lives. Once an initial point of historical interest is reached, 1776 for example, there is no need to stop there. Rather, there will be a boundless invitation, and motive, to continue searching for evidence and references that lead the investigator further into his national and racial past, through Colonial history to the time of settlement and discovery, through history to prehistory, as far as personal initiative and intellect can go. Any community is a challenge to be discovered historically, and every family is a starting place, even if it is scattered and its data must be gathered by writing letters of inquiry to distant relatives. Those who have come recently to this country or their town have rich heritages to discover by researching information—memories and documents and objects the family has kept with them—from the place of origin. It may confidently be said that no individual in this country has less of a history to be discovered than any other. The more difficult the discovery, the greater the challenge to discover.

Archaeology in the historical context can illuminate past life in surprising ways. The archaeologist is not necessarily restricted, for example, to what is *below* the ground, prehistoric and buried. As James F. Deetz has very cogently pointed out in an article entitled "Archaeology as a Social Science": "A coherent and unified body of subject matter entirely appropriate to the archaeologist is the study of the material aspects of culture in their behavioral context, regardless of provenience." Deetz discovered, in fact, "a whole new world which wasn't even buried at all." It was all around him, in hub caps and the whole automobile, in modern houses, supermarkets, and cemeteries. Deetz's own work with colonial mortuary art led him to conclude, in his *Invitation to Archaeology*, that the ideal archaeological artifact for interpretation is probably the tombstone. Inscribed tombstones are demographic and cultural, stay reasonably put, represent a specific population, are well-dated, and may have artwork that is a whole key to cultural preference and change.

Clues to the past go unnoticed most of the time, and are not buried in the ground at all. In the attic, in the cellar, or in the storage room of the apartment or garage, things may be discovered that were used many years ago and have been put away and forgotten. At one time they were useful or valuable in everyday life to mothers and fathers, grandmothers and grandfathers, or to those so far back in family history they are only names dimly remembered or quite forgotten. Some intelligent information-gathering with these clues may create a picture of what it was like to live before automobiles, airplanes, motorcycles, dishwashers, electric dryers and clothes washers, television and radio, telephones and air conditioners, electric lights and all of the motorized equipment in the house. A feeling may be gained about how it was to cook without gadgets and gas or electric stoves, stitch without a sewing machine, drive a horse, or read by candlelight.

Clues to the past may also be in old letters, notes, diaries, newspapers, magazines, and in books of many kinds. For instance, an old textbook of 50 or 100 years ago or more is excellent evidence concerning what people in school were learning at that time, and how it compares with classwork today. An old children's book or a game or toy may tell much about familiar, everyday experiences of our ancestors. There is much interesting research that can be done to discover how old games, including baseball, football, basketball, and hockey were played many years ago under their original rules and field markings. The history of a school and its predecessor schools in the community often uncovers significant data long overlooked.

Archaeology, then, is not limited to the buried past of remote ages. It is a technique for discovering and conserving evidence of all times and places. It extends its inquiry both below and above ground. Shortly, I will describe how students may locate artifactual matter, primarily above ground, and put archaeological methods to work in a personal discovery of their history. First, however, a precautionary note must be sounded on the search for material remains.

Unique cultural objects and whole sites have been destroyed by uninformed diggers and deliberate looters alike. Often important objects, documents, and photographs disappear unnoticed into trash dumps because no one recognizes their value and significance. The challenge is to learn to recognize and discover evidence without destroying it. This takes knowledge of how to recover evidence carefully and under supervision, what to observe, what not to disturb, and what to do with what you find. Invariably sites are better left untouched than excavated by unskilled hands only to be badly damaged and their unique clues and environment destroyed. Archaeology requires many patiently acquired skills. *Below ground archaeology must be attempted only by trained and skilled people who work carefully and scientifically.* Archaeology should never be done simply for fun or simply to collect objects. The duty of the nation is to preserve the evidence of the past beneath the ground, or wherever it occurs, until it can be studied efficiently when it is necessary and beneficial to do so. Training for field archaeology, laboratory procedure, and report writing can only be acquired by working closely with, or under the instruction of, a trained and qualified archaeologist, whether professional or non-professional. Archaeology is no do-it-yourself hobby for the uninstructed. Because most high schools and many colleges do not have faculty members who are trained archaeologists or material historians, the program I propose is largely up to the individual student to implement on his own, with what help he can find among trained professionals in the community. But there are many teachers who *are* trained and enthusiastic conservators and researchers whose help can be of great value.

Organizing the Search for the Past

Looking into the evidence of the past does not mean disturbing what the family has stored away and then getting tired and leaving it disordered. That is a bad as digging up an ancient site with picks and shovels and looting whatever is found, while making no records of what you found and how you found it. As in archaeology, training and supervision are needed, but you can practice conserving data with some common-sense procedures.

Here is the first of the things you can do to start recording the past way of life in your community, or the activities in your own family: Set up a file of 3x5 or larger cards and type or print neatly the information needed to identify and describe the item you want to inventory and catalogue. For instance, you may wish to set up an *A* file for artifacts or objects, and a *D* file for documents. Thus, you would describe the first artifact as "A-1-1974" (for the date) at the top of the card. Next you would identify the object and list where it is to be found. Then write a sentence or two of description or other pertinent data—ownership by any particular individual, general topics to which it pertains, and like information. (Fig. 1.) Your *D* file for documents would be treated similarly.

If you wish to take on a real challenge in organization and data retrieval, you may try working up a more

```
                                    ARTIFACT

        Number                 Date
        Identity               Location

        Description
```

sophisticated card on which many classifications of things catalogued can be recorded. Key sorting cards can be sorted mechanically by running needles through holes along the edges. This method enables you to identify and find certain classes of associated objects and study them. For example: all objects of the 17th, 18th or 19th century; all objects of ceramics (earthenware, stoneware or procelain), glass, various metals, wood or other materials; objects by place, by owner, or by category of use, such as wood-working tools, embroiderers' tools; and so on. Or, in the case of documents, the owner, the date, the location, the subject category. You may even wish to put to use such a specific and all-inclusive guide as the Murdock classification of 999 subjects in the Cross-Cultural Index. (George P. Murdock, *Outline of Cultural Materials*, published by Human Relations Area Files, Inc. of Yale University. This reference is in most large libraries, civic and university.) But the main thing is to be orderly and as simple in organization as possible, so as to have a genuinely useful catalogue of your historical objects and references. By these means you will discover the basis of modern scientific

methods of keeping track of things, not only in your own
home but also in business and industry. Here is a sample of a
simple needle sort card prepared for recording grave findings.
(Fig. 2.) Beyond this, if you are prepared for computer
technology, you can devise a key punched card with 10 rows
of 80 units with a greater data storage potential, but first you
would do well to consult an experienced data researcher.

N NE E SE S SW W NW	N NE E SE S SW W NW	up down
Direction of Head	Facing Direction	

Name of Site _____

Site Location _____

Excavator _____

Reported in _____ p. ____

Burial number: _____

Flexed tight	Flexed loose	Extended	Bundle	Cremated	Grave goods	No Grave goods	Old Adult	Young Adult	Juvenile	Infant	Indeterminate	Male	Female	Pathology

You will want to label or otherwise identify any artifact
or document in your possession with the same key you used
on the card that described it. Again, use common sense and
ingenuity. Do not damage or deface any object. On a ceramic
or metal or wooden object you can apply a small rectangle of
liquid paper or white Hyplar with a fine brush in an
inconspicuous place, let it dry, and apply the label with pen
and black India ink ("A - the No. - the Year"). These
substances are removable with liquid paper thinner or
denatured alcohol, respectively. For objects that should not
be so labeled, such as documents, letters or fabrics, put the
label on the plastic envelope or other container, such as a
plastic box, you select to house and protect the material. In
all events, for rare or delicate objects seek the advice of a

trained conservator by consulting the directories of the American Association for State and Local History and the International Institute for Conservation of Historic and Prehistoric Works.

There is a very special type of historical document that, alas, is commonly neglected and ultimately lost to history through mere neglect. This is the photograph. First, as a conservator of history, you need to collect, inventory, and catalogue the *prints and negatives* that tell both family and community history. See that each print is either placed in a durable album with its identification, or filed together with a card or envelope identifying it in a file drawer or box. More important than the prints are the negatives that survive. Unhappily, negatives are commonly lost through carelessness and neglect, or ruined by improper storage where dampness or dirt and grime can reach them. Negatives are the source of future fresh prints to supply those which may be lost, and are therefore far more important than the prints.

Things to watch for are precious and rare glass negatives that may record persons, places and events of over 100 years ago. Remember also that color slides are prime historical documents that must, after 15 or 20 years, be duplicated because the dyes will eventually fade. The same may be said of motion picture film, if it is in color. And be sure color or black and white film is not ruined by too frequent showing. Be especially wary if you should discover any old 35 millimeter nitrate stock, that is, film manufactured out of inflammable plastic that in time will deteriorate into an unstable, highly inflammable jelly. If it has not deteriorated, it can be copied on modern acetate film stock. If it has, you should notify your fire department and ask for safe disposal of the film. Old still negatives similarly should not be exposed to fire or heat, and should be kept in individual envelopes, properly identified.

If you have a camera and have experience in photography, you may make a valuable historical record by making photographic studies of types of houses and buildings in your community that are representative of the history and development of the community, or are associated with notable people or events. Many times such buildings are destroyed by "progress" or by accident and their photographs are all that remain of them. Don't forget interior views are valuable, too. You will find valuable tips on this in Harley J. McKee's *Recording Historic Buildings* (National Park Service, 1970).

When you know what you can do and how to do it, you are ready to go to work to inventory, identify, classify and preserve the objects of the past, such as diaries, letters and other records of the history of your own family or of the community in which you live, or have lived. Some families, especially those that must move often, simply have not kept and stored away things that tell of the past. Nor are grandparents always around to talk about it. Get all the data you can from parents and other relatives from older generations, even if you have to set up extensive correspondence to do it. Clues from recent memories often can be developed into discoveries of data outside the family that can cast light on the setting of family history. For instance, your relatives may recall other persons who know a great deal about certain places, events, and objects of the past in your present or former community.

There are many other things to do: Make a historic base map of your community, town, township, or county. Begin with a topographic map, that is, one that shows the contours of the ground with elevations recorded on them, such as the U. S. Geological Survey can supply for almost every part of the country. Next, add overlays on translucent paper or plastic sheets on which you can draw (obtainable from drafting supply houses, photo-reproduction shops or through architects). These overlays can show the succession of prehistoric and historic periods, such as the earliest Indian (called Paleo-Indian) occupation, the Archaic and later prehistoric Indians, the period of discovery by people who came from Europe, and so on through periods of settlement and development into the 18th and 19th centuries.

You can seek information concerning the prehistoric occupation of the area in which your community is located by writing to your state archaeologist or the department of anthropology at your state university, consulting a volume of recent date on the prehistory of your state, if one has been published, or writing an inquiry to the state historical society. For references on the historic development of your community, consult the library resources of your county historical society, and local and state libraries. In this way the overlays will record the development of roads, farms, communities, towns, industries, and finally the modern city or countryside. Historical sites and buildings now appear in the proper sequence, and their identity and location are recorded. Should some of these sites and buildings still exist and be threatened by new development, you can be the first to sound the alarm bell in the community.

Finally, you can make a listing of theme subjects to be developed into reports for the record. You can think up dozens, but here are some for a start: the development of (1) Education in the community, (2) Crafts, (3) Industry, (4) Fire Protection, (5) Police Protection, (6) Sanitation, (7) Churches, (8) Retail Stores—dry goods, grocery stores, various specialty shops, from the beginning to department stores and supermarkets, (9) Public Transportation—trolley cars, buses, canals, highways, (10) Private Transportation from horses and buggies and wagons to automobiles and trucks. And so on. You can get much information for these theme studies from the libraries and historical societies of the area in which you live. But be wary, do not take for granted all you may find, because it may have been done by untrained and careless recorders of historical places and events. Be sure to list all of your references in footnotes so anyone reading your report will know where you got your information and can judge it for himself. (It is a good idea to discuss with your school or a local college or university library the possibility of turning over a copy of your work to them, even if it is not entirely finished. In that way the information you have developed will be available to others so that they may write an even more complete story.)

Now is the time, also, to record *Oral History* by talking to grandparents and older people of the community who may be willing to be interviewed. There is discovery in the memories of living people who may recall details of customs, technology and events, sentiments and attitudes which were inadequately recorded, or, in some cases, never recorded at all. (This, too, is represented in the concept of Above Ground Archaeology.) If you can manage a tape recorder competently and have one available, use it, but transcribe notes and quotations from the tapes immediately after they are made. By saving some of the choice tapes with their living speech you will establish wonderful archaeological records and testimonials for the future. You can develop a tape library of references for your project, and at the same time preserve the cherished voices of parents and grandparents while they still can tell their stories.

By now you will have begun to consider how you can cooperate with others to carry out projects in historical data retrieval and conservation. You may be able to help develop portions of such projects through action groups within history classes under the supervision of history teachers. Perhaps there is a junior historians group at your school or in your community or county which you could join and help promote such projects. If not, you could help start such an organization with the aid of your county or town historical society. But there is nothing to stop you from doing your own thing, alone, if need be. You can do a lot by yourself and on your own, learning as you go and developing your system for continuing the project with increasing skill.

Once you begin to get results from such a project you will find you have proved that history is not defined as a collection of recorded "facts," but rather something you can contribute to by becoming your own historian and researching clues to the past as you discover them. The "facts" of history are, upon analysis, merely the observations and interpretations of individuals whose responses are subject to change with time and custom. History is not dependent entirely upon those who describe what they and others have observed, but also upon the conservation and interpretation of objects and data which remain. Creative conservation holds out rich rewards for personal heritage and self-realization. By it you will come to realize that you are part of a living memory bank for all surviving information from the past. That is history and what a human being has always been.

BIBLIOGRAPHICAL NOTE

As if to return to the late 18th century pamphleteering, the American Revolution Bicentennial Commission has published a statement entitled *Above Ground Archaeology* (1974) by John L. Cotter and sponsored by The Society for American Archaeology. This statement (now reprinted in *American Quarterly*, August 1974, and available to conservation groups and educators from the Government Printing Office, Washington, D.C. 20402: Stock No. 2405-00528), constitutes the second part of this chapter, setting forth the premises for the conservation of historical sites and objects alike, and linking both to the understanding of historical data, beginning with the individual in his neighborhood. The pamphlet includes a complete listing of state liaison officers to the National Council on Historic Preservation and a list of state archaeological offices. Going from the layman's approach to conservation through personal involvement to the professional and legal aspects of the subject, Charles R. McGimsey's *Public Archaeology* (New York: Seminar Press, 1972) sets forth the complete legal premises and background of federal and state archaeological conservation legislation from the *Antiquities Act* of 1906 to the present, and details how conservation of sites is promoted by educational and research institutions.

Linking archaeology to historical research, Murray G. Murphey sets forth the premise that modern historical research must consider far more than the descriptive documentation in arriving at a viable model for *Our Knowledge of the Historical Past* (Indianapolis: Bobbs-Merrill Company, 1973). Professor Murphey, as an analytical logician, presents a very tough and challenging book that will leave most conventional-thinking historians stranded and dismayed on a beach of logical equations and some very uncomfortable concepts, among them skepticism regarding the "facts" of history.

Crucial to an insight into the meaning of historical archaeology as a facet of the study of human culture is the brief and readable *Invitation to Archaeology* (Garden City, N.Y.: Natural History Press [Doubleday & Co.], 1967), by James Deetz, and a compilation by Deetz of readings in the methods of archaeology entitled *Man's Imprint from the Past* (Boston: Little, Brown, 1971). From the standpoint of the museum curator and historian who uses archaeological techniques to gather illustrative artifacts and data, the staff archaeologist of Colonial Williamsburg, Ivor Noel Hume, has written the informative and highly entertaining *Historical Archaeology* (New York: Alfred A. Knopf, 1969), using Williamsburg and related Virginia sites as a reference.

Going into the broadened concept of archaeology as relative to the study of historical objects and documents and their conservation, Harley J. McKee's *Recording Historic Buildings* (Washington, D.C.: National Park Service, 1970) deals with architectural conservation by recording. And Clifford L. Lord's *Teaching History with Community Resources* (New York: Teachers College Press, 1967 [1964]), a brief but informative booklet, details what the historical data resources of a community are and how they can be used. The conservation of artifacts and historical records alike is the subject of the *Technical Leaflet Series* issued by the American Association for State and Local History.

For a knowledge of what has been published on historical archaeology in America the annual *Historical Archaeology* of The Society for Historical Archaeology, with its bibliographical cumulative notes, is a current reference—along with the Society's *Newsletter*, issued quarterly—for continuing summaries of the activities of historical sites archaeologists. The basic *Bibliography of Historical Archaeology* (1970) by John L. Cotter is available only as a printout or on microfilm from University Microfilms. A superb critical bibliography of technology with a directory of artifact collections is to be found in Brooks Hindle's *Technology in Early America* (Chapel Hill: University of North Carolina Press, 1966). This is a valuable contribution to "above ground archaeology."

Organizations which offer potential sources of help and

advice are: For archaeological sites, The Society for American Archaeology, 1703 New Hampshire Ave. N.W., Washington, D.C. 20009. For museum techniques and practices, The American Association of Museums, 2233 Wisconsin Ave. N.W., Washington, D.C. 20007. For historical sites, The National Trust for Historic Preservation, 740-748 Jackson Place, N.W., Washington, D.C. 20006. For historical object and data conservation, The American Association for State and Local History, 1315 Eighth Ave. South, Nashville, Tenn. 27203.

CHAPTER 6

Machines and Americans

By Roderick Nash

RODERICK W. NASH has become a national leader in conservation and environmental management as a teacher and scholar, a government consultant, and a veteran backpacker and whitewater boatman. A board member of many associations for wilderness preservation, he played a leading role in the response to the Santa Barbara oil spill in 1969, writing the internationally publicized *Santa Barbara Declaration of Environmental Rights*. His course in American Environmental History at the University of California, Santa Barbara, where he is Professor of History and Chairman of Environmental Studies, was the first of its kind. Professor Nash's interests in the American's relation to his land and technology, and in biographical interpretations of American history and American culture of the recent past are recorded in many essays and books, including *Wilderness and the American Mind* (1967, 1973); *The Nervous Generation: American Thought, 1917-1930* (1969); *The American Culture: The Call of the Wild, 1900-1916* (1970); *Environment and Americans: The Problem of Priorities* (1972); and *From These Beginnings: A Biographical Approach to American History* (1973).

Here, Roderick Nash reviews myth-making statements on "Machines and Americans" from literature, film, and popular lore, commenting on technology as an instrument of national mission.

Forced to be practical by the exigencies of civilizing a wilderness, Americans instinctively placed a large portion of their national faith in machines. It was not just a matter of using mechanical devices but of *believing* in them with an intensity approaching the religious. In Samuel Hays's fortuitous phrase, the United States has subscribed to a *gospel* of efficiency. The Conestoga wagon, steamboat, reaper, telephone, and more recently, the automobile and television, amounted to much more than material objects. The American mind seems to invest such machines with almost vital qualities. They have certainly been symbols of the way man could put his ingenuity to work on behalf of what seemed to be a better life. It followed that technology was inextricably bound up with the American dream. By the twentieth century Americans had placed heavy bets on technology as the main vehicle of national mission. We committed ourselves to the laboratory and factory in the way earlier generations rallied around the church or the republican concept. Yet beneath the apotheosis of the mechanical ran a darker undercurrent of doubt and fear. Occasionally a thoughtful American left the parade long enough to recognize that technology did not necessarily lead toward the millennium. The atomic bomb and the deterioration of environmental quality at the hands of a supertechnology have helped extend misgivings into wider cultural circles. Consequently a growing part of the American discussion of machines concerns the tension between their benefits and liabilities.

Mark Twain provides an excellent window through which to begin an examination of the relationship between men and machines in the American context. He was born on the fringes of Mississippi Valley settlement in 1835, at a time and in a place where technology was not a major force. Manual labor sufficed because there were few alternatives. Twain's fabled rafts, for example, utilized no outboard motors. When Twain died in 1910 the nation had been transformed, and machines were rapidly assuming a position of dominance in American life. His response to this change is instructive.

As a young man in a semi-frontier situation Twain glorified in mechanized power. Where he grew up, the steamboat symbolized that power, and Twain aspired to be a pilot. He got his chance in 1857 and, after a brief apprenticeship, enjoyed the thrill of piloting the big, black-stacked, triple-decked vessels. But men insisted on pushing machines to and beyond their limits. Disaster frequently resulted. For Twain it came in 1858 when the sleek new *Pennsylvania*, its boilers overheated in the interest of speed, exploded on the river below Memphis with a staggering loss of life. Twain was to have been on the *Pennsylvania*, but a quirk of fate in the form of an altercation with another pilot made him miss the trip. His brother, however, died horribly from scalding steam.

As Twain reflected on the explosion of the *Pennsylvania*, he began to understand that technology, assumed to be a vital part of the nineteenth-century American idea of progress, could betray its worshippers. Machines could turn on their makers. The lesson was there for those with the courage to read it: the best condition for man might well be the unmechanized past, not the technological future. Of course neither Twain nor America gave up on mechanization as a result of incidents like the *Pennsylvania* disaster. They could always be explained as aberrations, temporary problems that a more sophisticated technology would surely solve. On the other hand, there were seeds of a later and deeper disillusionment in Twain's discovery of the irony of technology along the Mississippi.

Putting his doubts aside after the Civil War, Twain plunged headlong into the great barbecue of technological exploitation. His zeal for machines, and his growing wealth as a successful author, made him an easy mark for inventors interested in raising capital. In the early 1880s Twain poured thousands of dollars into a steam generator, a steam pulley, a new kind of watch, a system of marine telegraphy, and a new engraving process. There were lesser projects, too, such as hinged pants buttons, self-pasting scrapbooks, and mechanical organs. Twain's most extensive and disastrous investment began innocuously enough when a Hartford jeweler cornered him in his billiard room and peddled $2000 worth of stock in a typesetting machine invented by James W. Paige. Twain paid the money sight unseen. A former printer, he knew the value of a device that could perform the most laborious task in that business. On seeing the typesetter in action, he immediately subscribed an additional $3000. The machine seemed almost human to Twain, a triumph of applied technology. Of Paige he wrote: "He is the Shakespeare of mechanical invention. In all the ages he has no peer." Understandably, when Paige came to Twain for more money, the writer obliged first with $30,000, then $80,000, and ultimately a total of almost $200,000. Twain fully expected to realize millions, but Paige proved to be a perfectionist who overrefined his inventions beyond the point of practicality. While Paige tinkered, simpler devices like the linotype captured the market. Finally, in 1894, the Paige typesetter was pronounced a failure and abandoned. Mark Twain never made a cent from his investment. In fact, the Paige affair dragged Twain into an ignominious bankruptcy.

Before the Paige debacle was played out to its bitter end, Twain began to perceive the liabilities of machines and an age of industrialization. Returning after an absence of twenty years to the Mississippi River of his youth, he was shocked at the changes technology had wrought. Towns and factories had replaced the forested shorelines in which Tom Sawyer and his friends delighted. Steamboating had degenerated from a romance to a business. The environment, in short, had deteriorated, and technology seemed to be a root cause. In the late 1880s Twain was prepared to render his judgement. As a vehicle he chose a novel entitled *A Connecticut Yankee in King Arthur's Court*. Twain opens the tale by transporting a nineteenth-century Yankee from Connecticut named Hank Morgan back to the sixth-century England of King Arthur. With a Yankee's flair for mechanics, Morgan proceeds to transform Arthurian England into a replica of America in the mid-nineteenth century.

For some chapters *A Connecticut Yankee* conceals its purpose. In the opening chapters Twain seems proud of the shining machines and towering edifices that Hank Morgan's leadership makes possible. Technological progress seems beneficial, just as it seemed to Mark Twain during the early part of his life. Ended at this juncture, *A Connecticut Yankee* would have taken its place among the optimistic utopian novels of the time, such as Edward Bellamy's *Looking Backward: 2000-1887*. Bellamy confidently predicted an America lifted to unprecedented heights by the application of technology. His message captured the enthusiasm of millions of Americans ambivalent about the sudden emergence of their nation into a machine age. But Mark Twain was writing primarily for himself, and at the very time he concluded *A Connecticut Yankee* he was starting to appreciate how misplaced was his confidence in James Paige, a figure comparable in many respects to Hank Morgan.

Twain prepared to give his own interpretation of the pursuit of technological progress. As the novel unwinds, Twain shows the reader the darker side of mechanization. Technological know-how not only produces schools, mines, factories and labor-saving devices, but also revolvers, rifles, cannons, and huge bombs. Moreover, Morgan's presence splits the modernized court of King Arthur into warring factions. In the concluding chapters, swarms of soldiers attack Morgan and his elite corps of fifty-two boys, who are armed with the latest in weaponry including dynamite, Gatling guns, and electrocuting fences. Their success in repelling the attack proves ironic. The stench from 25,000 rotting corpses pollutes Morgan's stronghold and kills all the victors. Because of the inherent baseness of human nature, technology has turned against its creators. Science is out of control. The machine is an enemy rather than a friend of man.

In Mark Twain's opinion *A Connecticut Yankee* was a scenario of how the world would end, and in industrializing, nineteenth-century America was on the fated track full speed ahead. Twain had come full circle from his youthful glorification of mechanics and machines. The final decades of his life were devoid of the sunny humor that characterized his early work. Man's potential for evil, magnified by the power of machines, at length prevailed.

Additional evidence about American attitudes toward technology can be found in surprising places. Especially in probing the dark seas of popular thought—man-on-the-street opinion—the historian must be imaginative in his search for documentation. Folklore, for instance, contains abundant information about the topic at hand. Consider the legend of John Henry. The year was 1873. The place, the Big Bend Tunnel of the Chesapeake and Ohio Railroad in West Virginia. To cut a passage through the hard rock, one drilling company utilized the labor of freedmen. With picks and sledge hammers the blacks drilled the holes for explosive charges. The champion of the work gang was John Henry, a giant of a man reputed to be able to drive a bit with a sledge hammer in each hand. The arc of his swing measured almost twenty feet.

One day in that summer of 1873 the Chesapeake and Ohio brought a new steam drill onto the job. Immediately sensing the threat to the human ego inherent in the machine, the crew arranged a drilling competition between John Henry and the mechanical drill. Twenty-five hundred observers were said to have witnessed the spectacle. At the conclusion of hours of furious effort, Henry had made two holes each seven feet deep. The steam drill made one but it was nine feet long. Whatever satisfaction John Henry and his colleagues could claim from these figures was wiped away by his death the subsequent night from a ruptured blood vessel. In the morning the steam drill was back on the job; John Henry was becoming a legend.

The reasons why workingmen both white and black talked and later sang about John Henry are not hard to discover. Here was a man who took on the machine and all it symbolized in head-to-head competition. True, he lost the battle, but there was existential dignity in facing the odds stoically—dying with one's hammer in his hand. And at least Henry had created an imposing symbol of man's fate in a mechanical age. There was a magnificence in his defeat that helped ease the pain. Remembering John Henry was a way of paying homage to every man who found his powers made puny by those of machines.

John Henry's response to mechanization was doomed to defeat. There was little balm for man's pride in a direct competition, but it seemed logical that a new field of heroism might open for those persons who controlled or drove machines. The power unleashed by technology would be, in a sense, absorbed and applied by the human operator. Yet problems remained. Mark Twain found out how quickly the glory of piloting a steamboat on the Mississippi could vanish when the craft exploded with staggering loss of life. The classic statement in American folklore of this man-machine situation stemmed from an incident that occurred April 30, 1900 on the Illinois Central Railroad's main line near Vaughan, Mississippi. The crack Chicago to New Orleans passenger train was late, and the engineer, one John Luther Jones, was determined to make up the time. Ignoring warning signals, he slammed into the end of a train that had not pulled sufficiently far onto a siding. At eighty miles per hour there wasn't much left, but rescue workers found "Casey" Jones, as he was called, still gripping the whistle and the throttle. Immortalized by a vaudeville song, Casey Jones illustrated the liabilities of linking man's ego too closely to the machine. After all, even in the event of success the victory belongs at least partly to technology.

It was an effort to reassert the purely human that produced the next major folk response to the machine. This entailed the creation in American popular thought of *super* men. Clear wish-fulfillment figures, these folk heroes had in common enormous power and a complete disdain of mechanical aids. Paul Bunyan is a case in point. The Bunyan legends first coalesced from the oral tradition of northwoods lumbermen about 1915. They concerned a colossus, Bunyan, who made lumber by ripping out giant trees by the handful and passing the trunks through the gaps between his teeth. Here was a creature, in short, to whom machines posed no threat, a response to the humiliation of a John Henry or a Casey Jones. Significantly, other industries developed their own super men. Around the steel plants they talked of Joe Magarac who held the molten metal in his cupped hands and rolled out the bars like clay.

The same human needs that produced the Bunyan legends gave rise later in the twentieth century to a new crop of larger-than-life human heroes. Superman, a 1930s comic

creation by two Jewish writers disturbed at the power of
Adolf Hitler, is the most obvious example, although Plastic-
man, Batman, and similar characters competed for public
attention. The point about Superman of greatest importance
here is that he spurned machines. If there was an onrushing
locomotive to be stopped, Superman simply put out his
hand. Here was the perfect answer to man's vulnerability
with respect to the machine and the anxieties it engendered.
It was significant, too, that Superman's real-life incarnation
was Clark Kent, a quiet, unassuming little man—the very kind
prone to being overwhelmed by technology. But after a
moment transforming himself in the legendary telephone
booth, Kent emerged with the perfect antidote to uncertainty about the human role in a technological age.

Turning from the semi- and purely imaginary to the real
in the panoply of American folk heroes, we must note the
significance of a man who in 1927 received what was quite
likely the greatest ovation in history for flying a single engine
plane nonstop from New York to Paris. As John W. Ward has
explained, Charles Lindbergh was so popular because he
spoke to some of his contemporaries' deepest anxieties. One
anxiety concerned the place of the human element in an age
increasingly dominated by technology. Lindbergh's flight
supplied evidence that man, as pilot, was still an indispensable part of a technological achievement such as the trans-
atlantic flight. Indeed Lindbergh underscored the point by invariably referring to "we," himself and the plane, in discussing
the achievement.

It might appear that the astronaut of the 1960s and
1970s succeeded to Lindbergh's role of restoring confidence
in man's importance in a technological age, but there were
qualitative differences between the aviators. The astronauts
did not stand out in the public mind as heroic individuals.
Within months of the first moon landing in 1969, surveys
revealed that the man on the street could not even recall the
names of the triumphant crew with the exception of Neil (or
was it Louis?) Armstrong. The problem was that the
astronauts were too much the organization men, too much
part of a technological team personified by the omnipresent

voice of Mission Control. In sharp contrast to Lindbergh who flew his plane alone, in complete isolation, spacemen worked as teams and were in constant contact with home base. One had the feeling that computers could return the spaceships to earth in the event of the failure of the human component. The conquest of space, in short, was a technological, not a human, triumph. It could not and did not assuage the anxieties that the man-machine tension generated.

Returning to the early twentieth century, we can find another real-life figure whose life and thought speak to the questions at hand. His name was Henry Ford, and his status was and is so legendary that he actually shades into the realm of folklore hero, joining the Bunyans and Supermen. "Ford" is inextricably linked with "car," and it was the automobile, more than any other machine, that heralded the new technological era for the average American. In 1896 Henry Ford built his first car. Within a few years he had it doing ninety miles per hour. It required more time to secure the financial backing necessary to launch the Ford Motor Company, but in 1908 the first Model T appeared. The rest is pure Horatio Alger. Ford sold six thousand Model T's that first year. Six years later, after the introduction of assembly-line production, the figure was 248,000. The total for 1921 was a million cars. In 1923, 57 per cent of all cars manufactured in the United States were Fords.

From the perspective of efficient production the Ford organization was also something of a miracle. Before 1913 it required twelve hours to make a car. Assembly line techniques reduced the time to ninety-three minutes. In 1920 Ford achieved his long-time dream of building one car for every minute of the working day. And still the technological genius was unsatisfied. On October 31, 1925, the Ford Motor Company manufactured 9,109 Model T's, one every ten seconds. By this time Ford was a living legend and, reputedly, the richest man who ever lived. Transcending the role of automobile manufacturer, he became an international symbol of the new industrial order. When the Germans sought a word to describe the mass production techniques that were revolutionizing industry, they settled on *Fordismus*. Ford

himself called machinery the "new Messiah," and he celebrated it as the panacea for mankind's problems.

   Yet there was another part of Henry Ford's thinking. The
old and the new mingled in his mind. On the one hand Ford
was indeed a builder and bulwark of modern, mechanized,
urbanized America. On the other he devoted an extraordinary amount of effort and expense to sustaining traditional, unmechanized America. This ambivalence produced
the curious effect of Ford, the nostalgic traditionalist,
repeatedly deploring the very conditions that Ford the
revolutionary industrialist did so much to bring about.

   This tension in Ford's thought between nostalgia and
progress is dramatically illustrated in his attitudes toward
farming and farmers. The forward-looking Ford stated his
belief that traditionally farm life was a ceaseless round of
inefficient drudgery. He supplied abundant evidence from his
Michigan boyhood. "I have traveled ten thousand miles
behind a plow," he remarked. "I hated the grueling grind of
farm work." With the incentive of sparing others the same
fate, Ford turned to the problem of industrializing agriculture. The farmer, in Ford's opinion, should become a
technician and a businessman. Tractors (Fords, of course)
should replace horses. Mechanization would make it possible
to produce in twenty-five working days what formerly
required an entire year. Fences would come down and vast
economies of scale take place. Agriculture would be revolu-
tionized by the same techniques of mass production that
transformed American industry. Ford's modern farmer would
not even live on his farm but instead commute from a city
home. To prove his point Ford bought and managed a 9000
acre farm near his boyhood home of Dearborn according to
the principles of mechanized agriculture.

   But Ford the father of modern farming was only part of
the man. He retained a strong streak of old-fashioned
horse-and-buggy agrarianism. Farming, from this perspective,
was more than a production challenge; it was a moral act. So
it was that even while Ford's cars made urbanization possible,
Ford lashed out at the emerging city as a "pestiferous
growth." Squarely in the Jeffersonian tradition, he con-

trasted the "unnatural," "twisted," and "cooped up" lives of city dwellers with the "wholesome" life of "independence" and "sterling honesty" that the rural environment offered. "What children and adults need," he told one reporter, "is a chance to breathe God's fresh air and to stretch their legs and have a little garden in the soil."

Understandably, contradictions regarding technology permeated Ford's thinking. The same man who envisaged fenceless bonanza farms could say, "I love to walk across country and jump fences." But the lover of trees could state in utmost seriousness that "better wood can be made than is grown." Similarly, the perfecter of the assembly line idealized village handicraft industries. He chose small towns for his branch factories believing that village life would permit Americans to reestablish a sense of community with nature and with each other that urbanization was destroying. At Greenfield Village near Dearborn, Ford balanced his bonanza farm and giant automobile plants with a model of old-fashioned, pre-technological society. "I am trying in a small way," he explained in 1926, "to help America take a step . . . toward the saner and sweeter idea of life that prevailed in pre-war days." Greenfield Village had gravel roads, gas street lamps, a grassy common, and an old country store. The automobile mogul permitted only horse-drawn vehicles on the premises. The backward-looking Ford engaged a glass blower, blacksmith, and cobbler to practice their crafts in the traditional manner, crafts that the forward-looking Ford and his assembly line had helped make obsolete. It was almost as if Ford were doing personal penance for his role in mechanizing America. If so, it was a ritual that many of his contemporaries understood and appreciated. Henry Ford was a national deity in the early decades of the twentieth century even if his senatorial and presidential bids fell short. As a plain old-fashioned billionaire, a technological genius who loved horses and buggies, he seemed to his countrymen to resolve the moral dilemmas of the age. Like Lindbergh, Ford seemed to testify to the nation's ability to move into a technological future without losing the values of an unmechanized past.

When the Model T enjoyed its golden age, the machine had yet to dominate American life. It was still possible to think in terms of a balance between human and technological values. Charles Lindbergh and Henry Ford expressed this balance in their respective ways during the 1920s. But with the passage of time the scales tipped increasingly toward the technological. An increase in American anxiety paralleled this shift. Faith in science and efficiency received a severe setback from the Great Depression. The spectacle of food being deliberately spoiled while people starved gave rise to a deep-rooted questioning of the wisdom of nationwide mechanizing of food production and distribution.

The greatest shock to American confidence in science can be dated precisely: August 6, 1945, at 8:15 A.M. At that instant an atomic bomb, the capstone of a heroic American effort in theoretical and applied physics, exploded over the Japanese city of Hiroshima killing about 80,000 persons instantly. Never in the known history of man had so many died at once. And the dead might be considered fortunate relative to some of the survivors. Many Japanese who lived through the blast suffered horrible radiation sickness, grotesque deformations of the body, and genetic dislocations that condemned their progeny to more of the same.

As the emotional impact of the first atomic bombs (another fell on Nagasaki August 9) rippled outward from the devastated cities, Americans had reason to question the beneficence of the whole scientific endeavor. The problem, and the incredible irony, of the advent of the atomic age, was that science in control was also science out of control. One of technological man's greatest achievements, something as important in the history of the race as the control of fire, had backfired colossally. Just as Mark Twain described in *A Connecticut Yankee*, scientific progress proved a liability, because while man had conquered a part of nature (the atom, in this case), he had not conquered himself. Ethics lagged behind technology. It was as if a three-year-old weighed 250 pounds. The child had the power to smash his playmates, but not the restraints that normally prevented such an occurrence. Inevitably, Americans wondered if man were better off as a

EXPLOSION AND BURNING OF THE OHIO RIVER STEAMER "MAGNOLIA," NEAR CINCINNATI, OHIO, MARCH 18, 1868.

Harper's Weekly, April 4, 1868. (Henry E. Huntington Library.)

John Luther "Casey" Jones at the Throttle of No. 638. Made famous by the Chicago Exposition.

Henry Ford in his first automobile, the Quadricycle, Detroit, 1896.
(Ford Archives, Dearborn, Michigan.)

Charles A. Lindberg and the *Spirit of St. Louis,* which he flew nonstop from New York to Paris, May 1927.

Paul Bunyan and "Babe."

Kirk Alyn in *Superman*. (Columbia Pictures, 1958.)

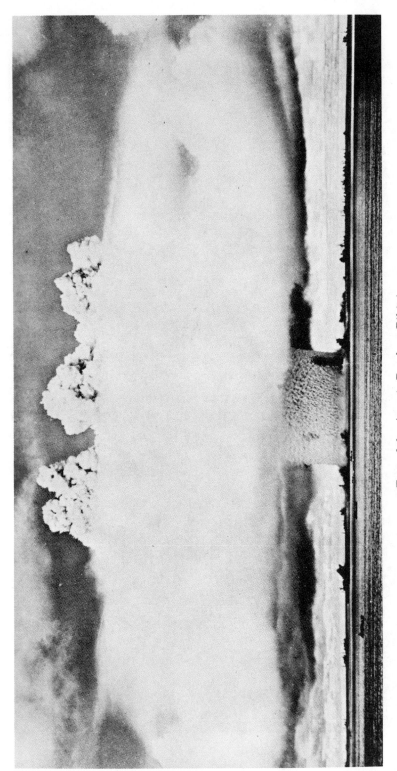

Test of the Atomic Bomb at Bikini.

Joan Weldon, James Arness, and Sean McClory in *Them*. (Warner Bros., 1954.)

result of the discovery and application of atomic energy. This thought led to a thoroughgoing questioning of the whole scientific endeavor.

The atomic bombing of 1945 was all the more shocking to the average American because of the cloak of secrecy with which the Manhattan Project had been draped. Since August 2, 1939, when Albert Einstein's warning to President Franklin D. Roosevelt produced an all-out campaign to beat the Nazis to the atomic bomb, the New Mexican deserts had kept the secret well hidden. Only a handful of scientists really knew the stakes of the game. Their attitude toward what they were doing is significant. At least some of the nuclear physicists and technologists approached the initial testing of an atomic explosive in New Mexico on July 16, 1945 with mixed emotions. It was far from certain that the device would actually release energy, but some of the scientists present profoundly hoped that their labor had been in vain. The consequences, they already suspected, were frightening. But when the detonator was pushed in the predawn desert quiet, according to an observer, "A pinprick of brilliant light punctured the darkness, spurted upward in a flaming jet, then spilled into a dazzling cloche of fire that bleached the desert to a ghastly white." The people present burrowed into the sand like ants. For a fraction of a second the light was greater than any ever produced before on earth. The temperature at the center of the fire-mass was four times that at the center of the sun. The pressure generated was more than 100 billion atmospheres, the most ever experienced at the earth's surface.

There was wonder as well as fear at the birth of the atomic era at the New Mexican test site: wonder at what man through his theoretical and applied scientific brilliance had wrought, and fear at how it might change the future. George Kistiakowsky, one of the principal architects of the first bomb, felt the moment of the explosion was "the nearest to Doomsday one could possibly imagine." It was what would be seen by "the last man in the last millisecond of the earth's existence." But to another observer, William Laurence, it was what the first man would have seen at the moment of

creation when God said "let there be light." Everyone sensed
that a Pandora's box had been opened. The Harvard physicist
Kenneth Bainbridge summed this feeling up best when he
turned after the July 16 blast to J. Robert Oppenheimer and
said softly, "Now we are all sons-of-bitches."

The events of the following month confirmed Bainbridge's fears. What might be considered the greatest accomplishment of science resulted in the greatest disaster of all
time. The atomic bomb confronted the scientific mind with
its traditional nemesis: morality. Physics was forced to meet
metaphysics. The scientists' fixation on "how" was obliged
to give way to the humanists' question "why?" The scientist
could no longer rest content with pushing back the frontiers
of knowledge as far as possible. He had to assume a
disquieting responsibility for the future of the race and the
dignity of the individual. C. P. Snow, the British philosopher
of science, summed it up this way: "The bomb . . . staggered
scientists with a moral shock from which the best and most
sensitive will not easily recover. Up to 1945 the climate of
science was optimistic. Now that unquestioning optimism
[has] drained away from most of the scientists I know." But
it was Albert Einstein, the man whose brilliance had been
instrumental in developing the bomb, who felt the hurt most
keenly. After World War II he predicted that unless man
banded together in world government, a nuclear holocaust
would wipe out most of the race. Two days before his death
in 1955, Einstein joined other famous scientists in signing a
plea for the prohibition of war. To a friend, Einstein
remarked that if he could relive his life he would not choose
to be a scientist, but rather, a carpenter.

On the popular level reaction to man's release of the
energy within the atom was uncertain. Initially the intellectual impact was lost in the euphoria of the end of the war.
Many Americans went along with President Harry Truman's
reasoning that the bomb was a military necessity for ending
war in the Pacific, but in the aftermath of the VJ Day
celebrations there were misgivings. Polls revealed that increasing numbers did not believe that the end justified the
means. In the bomb they saw confirmation that science had

gone out of control—man's technological skill had created a monster capable of destroying its creator. The machine, not man, held the key to the future of civilization. The ominous "button" that triggered atomic attack came to symbolize the situation. Cartoonist Jerry Doyle expressed a widespread feeling, in the *Philadelphia Record* late in 1945, when he drew a huge, muscular hand emerging from a turbulent bank of clouds. The hand was labelled "science." In its palm was a tiny ball. A closer look revealed it to be the world. Previously God or man had been thought of as controlling destiny; now machines were in the driver's seat, and Americans, as the discoverers of atomic energy, had to assume primary responsibility for their application. The initial use of this power was not encouraging. The mushroom-shaped cloud rising over Hiroshima and Nagasaki marked a distressing reversal of the American mission, a betrayal of the American faith in science and technology. Instead of leading the world toward the millennium, the United States seemed bent on its destruction.

Science fiction might be taken to be a folk literature of science. It offers a way of probing the American public's response to the spectacle of science going out of control. The 1930s marked the first flowering of science fiction in this country. Much of the writing in this genre was evangelical. Its purpose was to convince people of the glories of the scientific method, the capabilities of technology, the certainty of progress, and the beneficence of the post-Newtonian reign of reason. Real scientists were interested in science fiction at this time. They saw it as a way of building public faith in their profession and of explaining complicated scientific concepts to the layman. Consequently, publications such as *Astounding Science Fiction*, which John W. Campbell edited after 1937, occupied positions of some importance in the literature of the philosophy of science.

By the 1950s, however, one finds American science fiction greatly altered. The evangelical cheerleading is gone. Anxiety, caused by the spectacle of science going out of control, is a constant theme. In some cases a well-meaning scientist is overwhelmed by his creation. Robots or com-

puters or giant insects emerge from the laboratory to conquer
the race. In other instances, the scientist himself is the
monster. Having lost his humanity and his ethical perspective,
the mad scientist uses his superior powers to enslave or
otherwise terrify man. George Orwell's *1984* is a case in
point. The novel was as well known in the United States as it
was in Orwell's native England. Implicit in this kind of
writing was social criticism of science. The science fictionists
were, for the first time, frankly asking the "big" questions
that scientists usually avoid, such as: "What moves the
universe?" "Are physical laws constant?" And, "What good is
knowledge?" Frequently this writing emphasized the need
for values, for religion, for faith, and for humanism. One of
its constant themes was the disaster inherent in pursuit of the
present course of technological development. From booster
literature, science fiction had, in fact, become protest
literature.

Understandably, a large part of science fiction after 1945
concerned atomic energy and its consequences. Film figured
prominently as a medium for the discussion. Some motion
pictures simply portrayed the horror of nuclear war and its
consequences. *The Day the Earth Stood Still* (1951) employed an extraterrestrial visitor as the agent of the warning.
In *The Beast from 20,000 Fathoms* (1953) an atomic test in
the Arctic arouses a frozen monster which makes its way to
New York City (an ancestral breeding ground) and ravages
the human inhabitants. This theme of unexpected and
undesirable consequences of atomic experimentation was
extremely common in the 1950s. Obviously a by-product of
the uncertainties of entrance into the atomic era, it expressed
public fear that science had unleashed forces beyond scientific control. The classic expression of this theme occurred
in the film *Them* (1954). The threat in this case is from a
race of giant ants that evolved beneath the New Mexican
desert in the aftermath of the first atomic tests. Eventually
the ants make their way to the Los Angeles sewer system.
Just before they reproduce and overrun the city, a team of
scientists and soldiers locates the egg chamber and destroys
the ants. At the conclusion of the film the elderly professor

turns philosophical and reflects on the probability that man does not know what other changes he has wrought by altering the structure of atoms. The mood is pessimistic. The giant ants have been controlled, but the next danger could prove too much for man.

The recent past has added new chapters to the man-machine tension in the American experience. Atomic-related problems have declined as a popular theme, perhaps because it proved impossible to maintain the pitch of terror of the late 1950s and early 1960s. *On the Beach* (1959) was the last major film to utilize the nuclear-destruction theme, but other candidates for the subject of scientific nightmares arose. Following the lead of George Orwell, a number of writers considered the question of the uses of combined psychological and technological knowledge to control human behavior. The Harvard psychologist B. F. Skinner argued that the potential danger in this area was as great as that in atomic energy. Why not, he proposed in *Walden II*, develop beneficient forms of behavioral control. If men were to be mice, let them at least be happy mice. Many Americans, steeped in traditions of individual dignity, reacted violently against such proposals. Particularly suspect were developments in cybernetics, in eugenics, in computer technology, and in electronic surveillance of individual action popularly known as "bugging." If, as the Watergate tape recording controversy soon dramatized, it was possible to record even whispered conversation in an office over a span of years, what was the meaning of privacy, and, in a sense, of the sanctity of the individual? By this time, it was certain, communications technology had gone so far beyond the layman's capacity to understand that an undefined but disturbing fear was a part of American life. Orwell's "Big Brother," constantly watching the individual, had become a reality.

Still another basis for suspecting the machine came from the environmental movement that burgeoned late in the 1960s. Armed with machines, man had altered the face of the earth and interrupted the ecological process. Pesticides, for example, received wide publicity as agents capable of disrupting the delicate food chains on which all life depends. Technology permitted a rate of exploitation that threatened man with the prospect of running out of natural resources in the foreseeable future. To the average American it again appeared that man had gone too far in his effort to conquer nature. If pollution was the concommitant of advanced levels of civilization, then perhaps there was a point at which "progress" became self-defeating. For two centuries such reasoning was not easy for machine-worshipping Americans. The last hundred years have provided increasing evidence of the liabilities of mechanization, and, one hopes, increasing incentive to redress the balance between men and machines. President Dwight D. Eisenhower's farewell warning about a military-industrial complex and Ralph Nader's crusade against it, coupled with the related movements for "technology assessment" and environmental quality, give reason to hope that American civilization is capable of such self-control.

BIBLIOGRAPHICAL NOTE

Two anthologies of exceptional usefulness for the present purpose are John G. Burke, ed., *The New Technology and Human Values* (Belmont, Calif.: Wadsworth Pub. Co., 1966) and Carroll W. Pursell, Jr., ed., *Readings in Technology and American Life* (New York: Oxford University Press, 1969). Burke explores the conflicts between machines and human institutions such as democracy, education, individualism, religion, and government. Most of the statements he uses are from the years following World War II. The Pursell anthology takes an historical perspective beginning with colonial technology and the industrial revolution. Recent material includes such central commentaries as Dwight D. Eisenhower's 1961 farewell address to the American people and Congressman Emilio Daddario's discussion of the concept of technology assessment in 1967. Although not as suitable for classroom use, attention must be called to the comprehensive synthesis Professor Pursell compiled with Melvin Kranzberg entitled *Technology in Western Civilization* (2 vols.; New York: Oxford University Press, 1967). An extensive bibliography accompanies this work and offers an excellent source for research and lecturing purposes. Another edited collection with an emphasis on the significance of applied science in American life is David D. Van Tassel and Michael G. Hall, eds., *Science and Society in the United States* (Homewood, Ill.: Dorsey Press, 1966). John W. Oliver, *History of American Technology* (New York: Ronald Press, 1956) is largely a "nuts and bolts" survey and adopts an optimistic posture many modern readers would find naive. A relevant collection for the years since 1939 is James L. Penick, Jr., Carroll W. Pursell, Jr., Morgan B. Sherwood, and Donald C. Swain, eds., *The Politics of American Science* (Chicago: Rand, McNally, 1965).

No one interested in the interpretation of technology's impact on life in the United States should miss John A. Kouwenhoven's *Made in America: The Arts in Modern Civilization* (Garden City, N.Y.: Doubleday, 1948) and Leo Marx's *The Machine in the Garden: Technology and the Pastoral Ideal in America* (New York: Oxford University Press, 1964). Marx utilizes an American Studies approach with exceptional skill, finding the raw material for his discussion in 19th century literature. He extends parts of his analysis to the present in "American Institutions and Ecological Ideals," *Science*, 170 (1970), 945-52. This article should be read along with Carroll W. Pursell's article-length *The American View of Nature and Technology* (1972), which is a paper prepared for the Anthropology Case Materials Project sponsored by Indiana University and available at 914 Atwater, Bloomington, Indiana 47401.

A number of interpretative secondary studies exist to facilitate the task of the student and teacher of American attitudes toward the machine. Thomas Reed West, *Flesh of Steel: Literature and the Machine in American Culture* (Nashville: Vanderbilt University Press 1967) extends the analysis of Leo Marx into the recent period. Samuel Haber, *Efficiency and Uplift: Scientific Management in the Progressive Era, 1890-1920* (Chicago: University of Chicago

Press, 1964) and Samuel P. Hays, *Conservation and the Gospel of Efficiency: The Progressive Conservation Movement, 1890-1920* (Cambridge: Harvard University Press, 1959) concern a crucial period when technology and technological ways of thinking gained a major foothold in American culture. Roderick Nash's *Wilderness and the American Mind* (rev. ed.; New Haven: Yale University Press, 1973) treats a tension related to that between men and machines: the tension between wilderness and civilization. The social problems raised by modern technology are reviewed in Herbert J. Muller, *The Children of Frankenstein: A Primer on Modern Technology and Human Values* (Bloomington: Indiana University Press, 1970). Brilliant despite its shortness is John W. Ward's "The Meaning of Lindbergh's Flight," *American Quarterly*, 10 (Spring 1958), 3-16.

The automobile has figured so centrally in the American relationship to the machine that interested persons would do well to review John B. Rae's *The American Automobile* (Chicago: University of Chicago Press, 1965) and the three-volume study by Allan Nevins and F. E. Hill, *Ford: The Times, the Man, the Company; Ford: Expansion and Challenge, 1915-1932;* and *Ford: Decline and Rebirth, 1933-1962* (New York: Charles Scribner's Sons, 1954-1963). Additional discussion of the automobile as symbol and reality appears in Roderick Nash, ed., *The American Culture: The Call of the Wild, 1900-1916* (New York: George Braziller, 1970).

Mark Twain's importance in the American analysis of the effects and portents of technology is the subject of Henry Nash Smith's *Mark Twain's Fable of Progress: Political and Economic Ideas in "A Connecticut Yankee"* (New Brunswich, N.J.: Rutgers University Press, 1964). Automation has claimed increasing attention from writers. Ben B. Seligman, *Most Notorious Victory: Men in an Age of Automation* (New York: Free Press, 1966) offers one starting point to understanding. A considerable literature exists concerning the advent and initial applications of atomic energy. George O. Robinson, *And What of Tomorrow?* (New York: Comet Press, 1956) is a history of the Manhattan Project that created the bomb. Arthur Holly Compton, *Atomic Quest*

(New York: Oxford University Press, 1956) concerns the same subject from a different point of view.

The so-called "environment movement" that flowered in the 1960s contains many implications for the present subject of discussion. Along with Nash, *Wilderness* (above) see Nash's *Environment and Americans: The Problem of Priorities* (New York: Holt, Rinehart, and Winston, 1972) and Carroll Pursell's *From Conservation to Ecology* (New York: Thomas Y. Crowell, 1973). The significance of science fiction as a mirror of American attitudes toward actual scientific and technological developments is worth serious consideration. Start with Reginald Bretnor, ed., *Modern Science Fiction: Its Meaning and Its Future* (New York: Coward-McCann, 1953) and Sam Moskowitz, *The Immortal Storm: A History of Science Fiction Fandom* (Atlanta: Atlanta Science Fiction Organization Press, 1954). Donald Wollheim, *The Universe Makers* (New York: Harper & Row, 1971) updates the account.

CHAPTER 7

Some Paradox! Some Irony! Changing Images of American Woman, 1930-1974

By Betty E. Chmaj

BETTY E. CHMAJ, Professor of Humanities, American Studies, and Women's Studies at California State University, Sacramento, was founder and chairperson of the American Studies Association's National Commission on the Status of Women and his twice been a nominee for the presidency of the ASA. Her doctoral dissertation in American Culture at the University of Michigan was a study of American literature, painting, architecture, and music in their cultural context (1890-1917). She has published essays in these areas, directed conferences on protest movements, urbanism, jazz, and black/white interactions, and produced the radio series *Portrait of the Americans* (1965) for the National Association of Educational Broadcasters. Her investigations of the relation of American Studies to Women's Studies have resulted in two books: *American Women and American Studies,* Vol. I (ed. with the ASA Commission on Women, 1971) and *Image, Myth and Beyond: American Women and American Studies,* Vol. 2 (ed. with Judith Gustafson and Joseph Baunoch, 1973). These works and Professor Chmaj's frequent public lectures on women in film and American Studies have laid foundations for her chapter in this volume.

In her essay, Betty Chmaj examines female stereotypes in the popular and high arts, reconstructing images and ideas of woman in America since 1930.

When image collides with reality, when expectation defies result, when two sets of facts—each valid in its context— openly contradict one another, why not call it Paradox? Why not say it's Irony? With the subject of American Woman as a case in point, consider the following statements, which I offer as keynotes to this extended analysis of the ways the American woman has been viewed over the course of four and a half decades:

The experience of women during the 1940s thus presented a strange paradox. On the one hand, unprecedented numbers of females joined the labor force, substantially altering the existing distribution of economic roles. On the other hand, only minimal progress was made in the areas of greatest concern to women's rights. . . . Women's sphere had been significantly expanded, yet traditional attitudes toward woman's place remained largely unchanged.
    —William Chafe, in his chapter "The Paradox of Change,"
    The American Woman: Her Changing Social, Economic and Political Role, 1920-1970. Oxford University Press, 1972.

It is a paradox of our social history that motherhood has become a full-time occupation in precisely the era when objectively it could, and perhaps should, be a part-time occupation for a short phase of woman's life span.
    —Alice Rossi, "Equality Between the Sexes: An Immodest Proposal." In Robert Jay Lifton, ed., *The Woman in America.* Beacon Press, 1964.

It is paradoxical that Betty Friedan should look back nostalgically to the thirties which were, according to her, the years of female activity and initiative, in contrast to today's herd of consumers manipulated by hidden persuaders. In fact, the ratio of working women to housewives in 1930 was half that recorded today in the United States.
    —Evelyne Sullerot, *Woman, Society and Change* (translated by M. S. Archer). McGraw-Hill, 1971.

It is ironic that sixties' and seventies' women have seized on a more productive lifestyle than ever before, but the industry has turned its back on reflecting it. . . . (Rosen) One searches in vain in the contemporary cinema for a new perception of women which assumes their capacities and value. An international and rapidly developing women's movement has induced cinema to be only slightly more self-conscious about its patronizing and hostile portrayal of women. . . . (Mellen) The new liberated woman was nowhere in sight. . . . In every case we got [paradoxically] not only less than we might have expected and hoped for but less than ever before: women who were less intelligent, less sensual, less humorous, and altogether less extraordinary than women in the twenties, the thirties, the forties, or even the poor, pallid, uptight fifties. (Haskell)

—Three recent volumes on women in film: Marjorie Rosen,
Popcorn Venus: Women, Movies, and the American Dream.
Coward, McCann and Geoghegan, 1973. Joan Mellen, *Women
and Their Sexuality in the New Film.* Horizon, 1974. Molly
Haskell, *From Reverence to Rape: The Treatment of Women
in the Movies.* Holt, Rinehart and Winston, 1974.

The first four statements are by social historians, of differing
persuasions, on the eras of the forties, the fifties to the
mid-sixties, and the thirties compared to the present. The last
three are by film historians, all of whom have arrived
separately at the same conclusion about images of the present
day. What such voices have in common is a sensitivity to the
tension between image and reality, between events that did
not happen and those that did, between the way we might
have been and the way we were.

Is it not an implicit acknowledgement of how much we
still need to learn about the history of the American woman
that discussions of the subject rely heavily upon such words
as "paradox" and "irony," "mystery," "ambiguity,"
"curious contradiction," and "Her Infinite Variety"? Such
language should trigger the attention of the American Studies
scholar, for what looks like paradox or mystery to one whose
vision is bounded by a single discipline or set of disciplines
(such as the social sciences) may well be explained by the
interdisciplinary observer with additional data from other
areas (film, literature, the arts, advertising). The realm of
Women's Studies, which strikes me as easily the most
interesting and important area for research in American
Studies today, will not disappoint the scholar in this respect.
What it may eventually do, however, is evoke a retort from
the sympathetic: Paradox?! Irony?! What are they but names
to cloak failures in scholarship, reaches of innocent ig-
norance, hiding behind them innumerable tales of anonymous private tragedy in the lives of American women?!

The statements I have quoted are not, however, about
paradox in general, but about very particular kinds of
problems occurring during particular eras, when different
bodies of evidence offered conflicting views of who American
women were. The subject of the present essay is the
transformation of the image of woman from the thirties to

the present, a transformation that has been interpreted in different ways by conflicting schools of thought, each of which has been tempted to explain the conflict as "paradox" in some way. One of these schools might be labelled the Long-Way-Baby school, taking its name from the by now notorious slogan of the Virginia Slims ad campaign.[1] For my purposes here, William Chafe, from among those quoted above, can serve as spokesman for this view.[2] The other school of thought I shall call the Decline-of-Woman school, its members seeing decline at the very time those of the other school see advance and progress. Molly Haskell—as the title of her book, *From Reverence to Rape*, implies—can be taken as representative of this view.[3]

The era I have elected to examine is one about which relatively little has been known. The period from 1920 to 1970 had been "a *terra mythologica* populated by stereotype and misremembrance" until the appearance of Chafe's book, writes Carroll Smith-Rosenberg (she is quoted on the cover of the paperback version). Compared to the scholarly attention lavished on the nineteenth century, the twentieth century does indeed appear to have been ignored. The tendency in many histories and documentaries has been to tell the story of American women to about 1920—that is, up to the passage of the Nineteenth Amendment — and then to leap across the decades to the women's liberation movement of the sixties and seventies.[4]

Yet is is over eleven years since the appearance of Betty Friedan's pioneer volume, *The Feminine Mystique*, the work which virtually launched the women's movement by venturing alone into the "mythological" territory and advancing conclusions which outlined the basis for the Decline-of-Woman point of view. Friedan claimed that American women during the postwar era had retreated from the hard-won roles of independence they had formerly enjoyed into submissive roles and suburban homes, lured by a complex combination of motives she called a "mystique."

The fact is that mystiques and mythologies, images and stereotypes, are functioning during every era, making every age, in a sense, a *terra mythologica*—a territory ruled by "myth." The question is not how to rid ourselves of myths and stereotypes and substitute "the truth"—even if we could — but rather how to identify the dominant myths and images that have shaped our lives and told us who we are and ought to be, comparing these to the "social, political and economic" realities of that same time and place, seeking then to explain whatever disparities are found—however "paradoxical" or "ironic" such disparities may seem.

The discussion that follows consists of four sections. The first deals with certain problems of methodology that arise in the study of image and stereotype as found in different media. The second and third sections focus on two particular images, the Long-Suffering Lady and the Career Woman respectively, as case studies in image-reality relations, the one illustrating as well a continuity across two centuries, the other an instance of transformation across four decades. The fourth and longest section traces the transformation of American woman in several media, from the thirties to the present, through three stages.

I
PROBLEMS OF METHODOLOGY

My subject in this essay is the matter of stereotypes and images of the American women.[5] Of the several terms with overlapping meanings whose connotations, from negative to positive extremes, allow them to be ranged along a continuum—*cliche, stereotype, myth, image, archetype, role, role model*—I prefer to use the word *image* when the need is for the most neutral, least value-laden term and *stereotype* when the need is for greater accuracy in focusing upon a general type, identifying its element of caricature, and suggesting a point of view.

I am interested in images and stereotypes of women of different *ages* (and how American processes of socialization affect women at different ages), women of different *races* and *nationalities* and *religions* (and how they compare to each other and each other's contexts and values), women of different *classes* (upper, middle, lower), women of different *regions* and *regions of experience* (geographic, generational, rural or urban or suburban), women of different *eras*, different *occupations*, different *life styles*.

I am interested in the disparities between *male* and *female* responses to, and versions of, the same image or stereotype, between *positive* and *negative* types, between the images of *past* and *present*, between images that are *active* or *passive*. Sometimes the *absence* of any strong image or stereotype can be the most significant fact to observe (e.g., the "wipe-out phenomenon" affecting literature and film during the era from the fifties to the present); sometimes the *dominance* phenomenon will be the important one (e.g., "the cult of the apron" in children's literature, where most women who appear are mothers); sometimes the most interesting fact is a *conflict* phenomenon, one that pits two opposing or differing images of women against each other (e.g., Leslie Fiedler's distinction between Fair Maiden and Dark Lady in American literature; the observations of foreign visitors reported by Page Smith, pitting the status of free-spirited American daughters against that of entrapped American wives).[6] It is always a challenge to track down the *origins* of a stereotype or image, to classify its *manifestations* in different media and the arts, to trace its *tradition* over the course of history in one or more media—and from there, to piece out the degree of *continuity* as compared to the degree of *contrast* as an image undergoes transformation, obvious or subtle, over the course of time. Inevitably such efforts must lead to speculations over *causation*, both to explain the original birth and to account for change or continuity. In all this, the central question is always: what are the complex relationships between an image or stereotype and American cultural history—the major American myths and major

American realities of a given time?

That is to say, I am concerned to see scholars in both American Studies and Women's Studies move beyond the habit of simply identifying, listing, and defining stereotypes—important as these functions are—and beyond the

habit of evaluation by accusation: "I caught you stereo-
typing!" "Aha! subtle sexism!" "This exploits women!"
"This exposes a chauvinist in disguise!" And so on. It is time
for a host of scholars to begin to examine in greater depth
and with greater dispassion, using interdisciplinary methods if
possible, the relation of image to reality in ways that
acknowledge the presence of certain recurring problems and
themes that must be confronted if this important subject is
to be seriously and thoroughly explored. That is the central
appeal of this essay. By identifying some of these problems at
the outset, I hope to alert readers to their presence not only
in such discussion as follows, but beyond this, in the analyses
to be found in the proliferating volumes on American women
now coming off the presses. Among these problems and
issues, in addition to those I have already listed, four seem of
particular importance: how stereotypes function in the
culture, how they function in different media, how images in
different media function in the culture at different times, and
how images relate to realities in the different media at the
different times.

In the first instance, it is important to understand that
images and stereotypes found in the arts and popular culture
are not necessarily *reflections* of the society, *documents* of
its realities—the assumption one sometimes finds among
certain sociologically or anthropologically oriented scholars.
There are times when images and types do function in this
way, of course, but there are also times when they *illuminate*
reality heretofore unseen, or when they *shape* and *influence*
and *create* reality rather than serve as mirrors or echoes.
Sometimes images *prophesy* and anticipate, the artist becoming the culture's prophet; other times, they emerge after
the fact, lagging behind reality but serving to *summarize* what
has happened by giving it form. (Among my illustrations, de
Kooning's "Woman I" serves remarkably to summarize and
prophesy at the same time, as we shall see.) Some images
celebrate strengths or *criticize* weaknesses in the culture;
others act rather to *compensate* and provide relief through
escape when cultural realities seem too oppressive.

Some of the functions just described have been particularly (even perversely) evident in the treatment of American women. Haskell—and Freud—make this point, and their analysis extends to *all* media: "It is possible to see the movie myths and the attitudes toward women expressed by the movies not as an actual reflection of social and economic conditions but an inversion of them, and an inversion—to make matters more complicated—not of conditions obtaining at the time of the film, but either prior or subsequent to it. As Freud points out, in *Moses and Monotheism*, maternal deities were at their most powerful when the matriarchy was about to be toppled, and the same principle of compensation may account for the rise and fall of goddesses in cinema" (Haskell, p. 132).

Two illustrations are appropriate at this point. Here is Helen Waite Papashvily discussing the "domestic novel" ("sentimental novel") of the nineteeth century, seeking to explain its powerful influence:

> Yet just why readers, mostly women, took such morbid pleasure in crying over declines and deathbeds, sepulchers and cemeteries, no one attempted to explain.
> There are no "idle tears." The stylized horrors of Brown and his successors, the petty trials of Ellen Montgomery, but substituted for real and persistent grievances, and if a reader could not always give them name or form, nevertheless she wept like Ellen because "all the scattered causes of sorrow ... were gathered together and pressing upon her all at once."

Continuing her analysis of cause, Papashvily refers to an incident involving G. P. Putnam's mother, who insisted in tears he publish a book many others had rejected as trash:

> Catharine Putnam sensed *The Wide Wide World's* appeal because she and the author and the tremendous audience who wept over the pages for more than half a century shared a common lot. In a world made for men they were women. Law, custom, and theology told them they were inferior. Experience proved to them that they were not. Day after day, year after year, women lived within the frustrating confines of this contradiction, and gathered "scattered sorrows," reasons to weep, from injustices they could not understand and customs they could not change.[7]

Secondly, here is Marjorie Rosen discussing the realities for women of the 1930s as compared to their images in film:

> ... if one considers that by 1935 women's previously meager wages had dropped 20 percent, that in New York City alone females who five years earlier were earning $35 to $60 weekly wages now scraped by with

$25 to $35, Hollywood compounded its disservice by insulating feminine minds with a false, even obscene sense of well-being, suggesting possibilities which life, for the most part, did not. Perhaps because the Depression was treating its women so cruelly, the screen could afford to offer comfort in some small way. And constructive escapism, the kind Jean Arthur provided, is certainly not the worst of all evils.
Yet escapism it was. . . . (Rosen, pp. 137-38)

Like Papashvily, Rosen finds the imaginary life offered to women contradicting reality, compensating for a hard life, providing relief, but through escape rather than through not-so-idle tears. Like other film biographers, Rosen discovers that film images do not reflect reality (although she seems to feel they ought to), and at times she and others seem to subscribe—a point of importance to the study of methodology—to the devil or conspiracy theory of history to explain contradictions, with male villains of great power (abstract "Hollywood," industry moguls, directors) credited with the ability to conceive master plots to disguise the gap and keep women oppressed.

In the course of this study, the media from which I will be selecting examples include advertising, literature, the arts, comics, film above all, and on occasion such other examples as children's toys. That images function differently in each of these media is a truism that seems deceptively obvious.

Advertising aims at selling products, obviously; and obviously, if an image of woman will not increase sales (especially since over 75% of all advertising in America is directed at women), it will not be used. Conversely, an image that *will* sell products will surface again and again, even if no such woman exists until the advertisers "create" her. ("We've created a whole new woman," one ad agency executive said to me of the images of the 1970s, and his arrogant assumption served to remind me that in an affluent society, with more goods than needs, advertisers have long since learned to "create" new needs rather than respond to demands.) Although we do not *choose* to watch ads the way we choose other media, they affect us all whether we like it or not, and their influence is profound. Since Madison Avenue has been credited with a large role in the creation of the Feminine Mystique, my illustrations of this medium will appear in relation to the 1950s era.

For *literature and art,* the generalizations offered earlier are especially apt. They may reflect and/or illuminate the culture, giving literary and artistic form to the developments of an age in obvious (journalistic, documentary) or subtle (abstract, formal) ways. While they are more trustworthy at times in doing so than other media, they are under no obligation to report and reflect alone; they may also project counterforms and wish images. In the present case, male fantasies of women—the love of women, the fear of women— become especially important, and biographical data on the author or artist will be pertinent.

Comics are of special interest because they come closest to projecting a complete fantasy world that, if studied with care, may reveal the secret fears, expectations, values, and dream-images of a culture in more subtle (and more subtly accurate) ways than, say, literature, television, or the daily papers.

Film, it has been observed, occupies a kind of middle ground between literature and popular culture, and between fact and fantasy. How images of women have functioned in this medium will require my entire essay to demonstrate. I will be relying on film more than any other medium for a number of reasons, chief among which is its importance in shaping women's beliefs and lives during the era under discussion—one reason, perhaps, that an excellent body of new scholarship such as has not emerged for any other fictional medium is now available. [8]

As a single illustration to underline differences between media, consider the Barbie doll, a best seller in the toy industry since 1959. When Ruth Handler, president of Mattel, Inc., was asked about Barbie's relation to real life, she replied, "A doll and a toy reflect the world around a child," adding, "We can't reflect every facet of life—only some, the better facets." "Better" sounded as if Handler accepted a responsibility for guiding Barbie's destiny (even though the answer was intended, in 1970, to explain that Women's Liberation was not part of the world of most children). She saw Barbie, significantly, as "an 18-year-old dressed up to have a ball . . . every little girl's dream of what she wants to be." Thus Barbie is both reflection and wish-image. It is also significant that Barbie emerged during the 1960s, displacing the Betsy-Wetsy types of dolls to become top money-maker in the industry.

When Handler was asked why Barbie's "dream possibilities" limited her to roles as stewardess, tennis player, skier, fashion plate, health faddist, glamorous hostess, and the like, rather than as a woman who might accomplish through a career (as Handler herself did), she replied: "When there are enough women doctors around, Barbie will have a doctor outfit. When American girls go up in space, then we'll have a girl space doll." To which Alleen Pace Nilson, analyzing trends in children's literature for the same period, replied: "I don't think anyone in the field of children's literature would have answered a question about books that way. People have always recognized that books set standards of behavior, and publishers have looked on this as both an obligation and an opportunity—witness the recent flood of black books."[9] Yet toys too set standards, they too tell young girls and boys what we expect them to be and become. But the attitudes of toy-makers toward their social responsibilities are decidedly different from the attitudes of publishers, especially of textbooks and school books. Thus images of women in the latter medium are also different. It remains for us to decide whether the cult of the apron in the text (the housewife image) is either better or more influential than the cult of "plastic pretty" (sex-object image) Barbie is said to represent.

Finally, among the problems of methodology listed earlier, I included "the relation of image to reality," a phrase scarcely adequate to indicate a large and complex series of relationships and possibilities, only a few of which I can hope to demonstrate in the sections that follow. If I focus upon *economic* realities more than others to the same degree that I seem to focus on filmic images more than others, it is partly out of the need to limit scope, partly in response to the challenge of Chafe's volume, and partly because I find the pairing of filmic image and economic reality an excellent way to demonstrate contrast.

II

TUBERCULOSIS TO NEUROSIS:
TRIALS OF THE LONG-SUFFERING WOMAN

A capsule summary of the distance between nineteenth and twentieth century images of women which can serve to illustrate both the continuity of tradition and the contrasts during particular eras, as well as the relation of image to reality, may be obtained from the history of a single stereotype, that of the "Long-Suffering Woman." (Fig. 1.) Her history can be traced from the domestic novels of the nineteenth century (supplemented by the diaries and records of their authors and audiences), through the genre known as "women's films" of the 1930s and 1940s, to the television soap operas watched today by over 40 million people— mostly women, especially housewives.

Thanks to the writings of Papashvily and others, we know something of the Long-Suffering Woman's origins. [10] She was the dominant figure — the heroine, usually — of a genre of best-selling novels that appeared early in the nineteenth century, most of them by women authors—the group Hawthorne called "that damned mob of scribbling women." We also know the Long-Suffering Lady had an important impact upon millions of readers who wept through the chapters of these books at a time when their own lives were severely circumscribed, often stifled by efforts to live up to what Barbara Welter has called the Cult of True Womanhood. Papashvily, quoted earlier on this theme, feels these novels were as revolutionary in their way—and as influential, too—as the Seneca Falls Resolution that emerged about the same time. She does not find it accidental that the physical suffering actually endured by women of the period had its counterpart in the plots that appeared. As the century progressed, attention was focused on women's illnesses due to "increased scientific knowledge, better sanitation prac-tices, and more medical schools to train doctors."

The aches and pains of women were not imaginary and so they did not immediately disappear. Ill health, in any event, was too valuable a weapon to relinquish. Heroines in novels continued to contract smallpox, typhoid, tuberculosis and many mysterious and unnamed diseases that always necessitated cutting off their beautiful hair, which promptly grew back in masses of curls. There was no situation in a novel an attack of brain fever could not resolve, and determined young ladies even went so far as to die if they could prove their point in no other way. But the role of the confirmed invalid "enjoying ill health," the cheerful sufferer so common in the English domestic novels who spent a lifetime on the sofa, did not appeal to American women. They would be radiant, vigorous and active, fresh skinned, clear eyed, gay, daring and confident, perpetually young and always beautiful.[11]

In the later media, the women's films and soap operas, physical suffering also became a mainstay of the plots, but as a metaphor for general suffering more than a reflection of actual conditions. (Of late, television programs centered on doctors and hospitals have crept into evening hours as well.) In the two media of the twentieth century, the American sufferer was also a stronger, more radiant, more confident type than the clinging vines whose fainting spells and frailties have always been associated in the American mind with exotic foreigners. In film the long-suffering roles were played by the strong actresses — Garbo, Davis, Crawford, Irene Dunne, Greer Garson, Loretta Young, Susan Hayward — rather than fragile types unable to stand up to trouble. In all three media, the heroine emerged as a figure of stature, capable of withstanding every imaginable indignity and tragedy life handed her (despite any physical disabilities), towering over her satellites—friends, children, relatives—and putting to shame the men in her life—husbands, fathers, lovers, sons (sometimes weaklings or profligates)—who could never hold a candle to her shining moral superiority. In soap operas, some degree of change in this pattern is reported, but not much: "We still have the strong leading woman whom viewers like to identify with," says Doris Quinlan, producer of ABC's *One Life To Live*. "But we are writing men with more guts than we used to. Helen Trent had fourteen fiances, and none of them were worthy of her."[12]

The primary similarity of the three media is the function they served for their female audiences. "This is the big payoff—to end up with everyone watching in tears at the end," says Kitty Barsky, a writer on both *One Life To Live* and *All My Children*. Some films were advertised as "four-hanky productions" and the term "tear-jerker" was an apt one for the genre. Happy endings were not necessarily the rule. "The main thing is trouble," says Ruth Warwick, who plays Phoebe Tyler on *All My Children*. "Right here in River City. They say you get happy roles in a soap opera—forget it. If you're really a happy character, you're going to be fired or killed or something's going to happen."[13] The appeal of the contemporary soap opera remains the same as the appeal of the domestic novel Catharine Putnam read when "she and the author and the tremendous audience who wept over the pages for more than half a century shared a common lot." And happy roles, for this audience, are not reflections of that lot.

Comparing the images in these three media to the real lives of women during the two centuries is a fruitful area of investigation, about which much has been written in recent times (especially for the nineteenth century).[14] I shall be content here to summarize only the attitudes of the medical profession toward women's illnesses during this period, leaning on the report of Barbara Ehrenreich and Deirdre English to distinguish the continuities from the contrasts. The tendency during both centuries was to treat middle and upper-class women, who made up most of the audiences of the Long-Suffering Woman, as a client class of the medical profession, to encourage more women than men to be hospitalized, to treat pregnancy, childbirth, menopause, and menstruation as medical problems related to a pathological view of women, and to accommodate "profound class differences" in the medical system (upper-class women being treated as "congenitally sick," lower-class women as "potentially sickening"). But Ehrenreich and English are "struck even more by the differences" between centuries. Today the days of total leisure, even for upper-class women, are over, not only because so many women work but also because, without a servant group, women are expected to hold down both outside jobs and their jobs as housekeepers and mothers. They must be active and healthy for shopping, chauffeuring, managing the household, hostessing parties, and performing in bed. Doctors are scarcer, with less time for individual patients, so visits are short, efficient, impersonal. "Being sick is no longer consistent with our social roles nor is it a practical possibility, given the doctor shortage. Our medical image has come almost full circle from the days of female invalidism." [15] In fact, because women now live longer than men, health books advise them how to keep their *husbands* alive and well.

The most important change, however, already underway before the turn of the century, was the change in concern over physical illness to concern over psychological maladjustment—a new definition of being "sick." With it came one of the most terrifying of medical tendencies: the inclination to blame the victim for her "hysteria" (so-called because it was assumed that the "illness" was related to her womb, her feminine nature), or today, for her "psychosomatic" ailments. After summarizing the evidence, Ehrenreich and English arrive at a devastating conclusion: "The medical profession helped to create the popular notion of women as sickly in the first place; now it seems to have turned around and blamed the victim. Women patients are seen as silly, self-indulgent, and superstitious. Tranquilizers are used to keep us on the job when no quick medical fix can be found. How many times do we go to a doctor feeling sick and leave, after a diagnosis of 'psychosomatic,' feeling crazy?" [16] It is not accidental that some of the newest soap operas, daytime and nighttime, include psychiatrists in their casts — and doctors given to dispensing advice for emotional problems.

In 1944, a year that marks a turning point in the transformation theme, a film appeared that turned the basic formula of the Long-Suffering Woman's story on its head and became a premonition of things to come. Called *Lady in the Dark*, it was about a lady editor who is having headaches, accompanied by moments of terror so intense they interfere with her ability to make decisions, who then goes to a psychiatrist for help. The film was a musical, no less, billed as "the first Freudian musical" (based on a Moss Hart play), with Ginger Rogers playing the lead. (Note her "mannish" clothes in Fig. 1.) Hollywood could have her dance out the dream sequences in big extravaganza numbers while she is lying on the psychiatrist's couch. As the plot unfolds, the psychiatrist reveals her "problem" to be that she is "afraid to compete with women as a woman" (because she is jealous of her mother's beauty), that she compensates by dominating men, and that what she needs to cure her is a man to dominate *her*! Rogers promptly accepts the advice, prepares to step down as editor, and sets out to choose the right man.

What was unusual about this film was that the Long-Suffering types were not usually identified as professionals or career women—although one of the scandals in the medical practices of the nineteenth century was the use of punitive "medical" measures to discourage activism, especially feminism, among women patients. [17] Here, in the middle forties, it is the career woman who is on the couch, her "weak" housewife sister having survived to become the "fulfilled" and effective healthy Housewife Heroine described by Betty Friedan. Although it is an aberration among career woman films, as we shall see, *Lady in the Dark* documents *in extremis* the charges Friedan, Weisstein, Chesler and others have made against the use of psychotherapy and psychology in treating and defining women. [18]

III

TRANSFORMATION OF THE CAREER WOMAN:
AMERICAN FILM VERSUS AMERICAN ECONOMICS

My second case study is of the Career Woman as such, one of the strongest stereotypes in American film of the 1930s and 1940s. Again I wish to contrast image and reality during these crucial decades.

Although Ginger Rogers won an Academy award as Kitty Foyle four years before playing *Lady in the Dark*, she was less often associated with the Career Woman role than were such actresses as Jean Arthur, Claudette Colbert, Rosalind Russell, and, above all, Katharine Hepburn. Fig. 2 typifies the kind of image the screen projected of this type; it is Rosalind Russell in a still from *A Woman of Distinction* (1950). Just how stereotyped the genre was is wittily described by Russell, quoted in a volume dated 1970:

> I played—I think it was 23—career women. I've been every kind of executive and I've owned everything—factories and advertising agencies and pharmaceutical houses. Except for different leading men and a switch in title and pompadour, they were all stamped out of the same Alice-in-Careerland mold. The script always called for a leading lady somewhere in her thirties, tall, brittle, not too sexy. My wardrobe had a set pattern: a tan suit, a grey suit, a beige suit, and then a negligee for the seventh reel, near the end, when I would admit to my best friend on the telephone that what I really wanted was to become a dear little housewife. [19]

In 1973, while chairing the "Woman of the Year" ceremony for television, Russell expanded on the same theme. In her twenty-three films, she said, she had played the roles of reporter, insurance broker, soldier, newspaper woman, and parking lot owner, among others, and "at the end of every one of these films, I gave up all these jobs for the man I loved—Fred MacMurray! (Laughter.) If I had it to do over again, I'd hang on to Fred MacMurray—but I'd also hang on to the jobs! (Laughter and applause.)"

Beneath the disarming wit of Russell's statements is some awesome testimony to a number of facts about the changing image of American women. To begin with, the sheer number of films she played—especially after *His Girl Friday* (1940), still perhaps the best of the lot—astonishes. Add to this number the many films with Arthur, Colbert, Hepburn, Davis, Crawford, Garson, Dunne, Chatterton, Bergman, Stanwyck, Hayward and others in the Career Woman role, and the total becomes more astonishing still. The reason we are astonished, of course, is that we have scarcely known about the Career Woman genre at all; even on the Late-Late shows, very few of these films have been rerun, while films with other images of women have been repeated endlessly. *Lady in the Dark* is one of the few television has favored, while neither Russell's *Woman of Distinction* nor Hepburn's

Woman of the Year has appeared regularly—a telling clue to the way our contemporaries have preferred to visualize such women: as figures "in the dark," with neuroses unknown to the happily married, rather than as figures of distinction deserving to be honored in their own right.

The insidious endings of these films is a fact that has drawn the attention of every film critic and historian I know. Pauline Kael, June Sochen and Joyce Schrager, Haskell, Mellen, and Rosen have all remarked upon the phenomenon, as have I, in my "Who Put the Negligee in the Seventh Reel?"—a title borrowing from Rosalind Russell's testimony. It was part of the unwritten Hollywood code of the era—as totalitarian as the insistence that Crime Must Not Pay, and rising from the same simplistic moralism—that the Career Woman must be put in her place at the movie's end—which is to say, her place as a "dear little housewife." In an essay called "The Big Tease" (because the films merely tease women with false hope of independence and autonomy), Joyce Schrager and June Sochen survey six female movie stars—Hepburn, Russell, Davis, Lombard, Stanwyck, and Crawford—who played roles in four subtypes of "independent woman" films. In over eighty films studied, they found the woman giving up her independence at the end or becoming so atypical that she is shown to have departed from the cultural norm.

> The six women stars studied usually begin every film as whole women: that is, when they are *without* a man. ... The independent women films reverse the expected cultural scenario. Rather than man completing woman, at least in this category of film in the thirties, man fragments woman and turns her into a partial person.[20]

Rosen and Haskell place the career woman, first of all, in a larger genre of Working Women of the two decades. Writes Rosen: "Depression movies protrayed women working by their wits. Or at least by their wit. A curious conglomeration of detectives, spies, con artists, private secretaries, molls, and especially reporters and editors constituted a new genre, and the screen was—yes—graced with some of its breeziest comedies and gutsiest dramas" (Rosen, p. 134). Haskell agrees with the assessment and adds to the list the "nightclub hostesses" (production Code euphemism for prostitutes), department store salesgirls, the women of gold digger and show business genres, as well as the doctors and administrators played by "upper echelon women." "At Warner's, there were whole genres of working-women films, and if they look unusual today, it is only because there is nothing comparable in contemporary films" (Haskell, p. 141). Paradoxically, women who play such roles in real life today are not to be found on the screen at all. "The world cinema today," Joan Mellen has pointed out, seems totally "unable to provide an image of women who achieve *through* their drives instead of by an unnatural distortion of them" (Mellen, p. 17).

Among actresses who played career women, Hepburn deserves a special place. *Adam's Rib* (1949) is probably the high point of the entire genre, and almost the last as well. Even when the script required her to give up her career (or place in society) for her man, Hepburn was able to project a sense of intactness and independence that transcended the plot. Like Eleanor Roosevelt, Hepburn remained one of the few famous women to offer a role model of independence and autonomy while such images all but disappeared during the decades of the fifties and sixties. It is especially interesting, therefore, that a brilliant and memorable description by Pauline Kael of "the intelligent woman's primal post-coital scene" should emerge from a review that begins by recalling a 1933 Hepburn movie called *Christopher Strong*. The entire passage deserves to be quoted:

> Hepburn played a famous record-breaking aviatrix, obviously modelled on Amelia Earhart, who fell in love with a distinguished political figure, a married man (Colin Clive). He was drawn to her because, unlike his conventionally feminine wife (Billie Burke), she had audacity and independence; he said that was what he loved her for. But as soon as they went to bed together, he insisted, late on the very first night, that she not fly in the match she was entered in. There were many movies in the thirties in which women were professionals and the equals of men, but I don't know of any other scene that was so immediately

recognizable to women of a certain kind as *their* truth. It was clear that
the man wasn't a bastard, that he was doing this out of anxiety and
tenderness—out of *love*, in his own terms. Nevertheless, the heroine's
acquiescence destroyed her. There are probably few women who have
ever accomplished anything beyond the care of a family who haven't in
one way or another played that scene. Even those who were young girls
at the time recognized it, I think, if only in a premonitory sense. It is
the intelligent woman's primal post-coital scene, and it's on film;
probably it got there because the movie was written by a woman, Zoe
Atkins, and directed by a woman, Dorothy Arzner.[21]

Kael is probably right in arguing that "it was perfectly well
understood in 1933" that the woman's full possibilities as a
person were being destroyed by what the man did to her, and
that, by contrast, the "contrived, often sour endings" of
1940s films seemed phony. In the end, one is impressed more
by the *continuity* between the career women films of the
thirties and the forties than with the *contrast*. In general, the
history of the Career Woman in film may be seen to emerge
during the thirties (from roots in real lives of the twenties),
reach a peak during the early forties, become stereotyped by
the late forties, and disappear quite suddenly in the fifties.

During the same significant year that *Lady in the Dark*
anticipated trends of the age to come, 1944, Irene Dunne
played the mayor of a small town in a film called *Together
Again*. When she is advised by father-figure Charles Coburn
that she may lose her femininity in so exalted a position, in
which she is obviously effective and happy, she retorts (as
Ginger Rogers did not): "Women can live perfectly well
without men. But you're terrified of the idea that they can.
If you lose your emotional power over women, you're lost."
Although Dunne, too, gives up her mayoralty to go off with
Charles Boyer, there is in her speech a declaration of
independence that for a time defined the Career Woman as a
thoroughly liberated type.

By the fifties, however, it was clear that the negligee in
the seventh reel had done its work: the career woman, along
with other types of independent women and working
women, virtually disappeared from the screen. Actresses who
had played the roles found themselves suddenly out of work.
Jean Arthur gave up on the industry and went to teach at
Vassar; others too (like Irene Dunne) took on other work,

turned to legitimate theatre, or retreated into domesticity. Some learned to play new stereotypes, and of these, it is especially instructive to record the kinds of roles to which "strong" women seemed best suited — roles as kooks, 'characters,' and other marginal people, shrews and bitches who grow grotesque as they grow old. To ask *Whatever Happened to Baby Jane?* is a valid question, not only in terms of the career actresses in the film itself, who end up as spinsters surviving on sisterly envy as has-beens, but also in terms of the careers of Crawford and Davis, both of whom showed remarkable ability to adapt in order to survive. Another valid question might be: Who turned Mrs. Miniver into Mrs. Robinson? Rob the strong middle-class woman Mrs. Miniver represented of the purpose in life that the hardships of war provide and what else is she to do with her energies, once "dysfunctionalism" sets in? [22] Like Anne Bancroft as Mrs. Robinson in *The Graduate*, Rosalind Russell as Mrs. Harrington in *Five Finger Exercise* (1962) emerges as grotesque because of her sexual interest in a younger man. (Fig. 3.) In the play on which the film was based, her interest in her own son is also suspect. Her "smothering," almost lover-like attention having made him homosexual (it is implied), he protests becoming the object of his parents' terrible battles: "Is the war in this house never going to end? . . . The war you both declared when you married. The culture war with me as ammunition." It is a perceptive criticism of the cultural malaise of middle-class homes of the age. So is the wife's appeal to her husband in the midst of a quarrel: "My life was never meant to be like this—limited this way . . . . I'm just so frustrated I don't know what I'm doing half the time . . . . There are times I feel I'm being absolutely choked to death—suffocated. . . ." [23]

After her early role as the monster housewife in *Craig's Wife* (1936) — whom Mary McCarthy once called "the sort of woman who lives through her furniture" to the "point of inhumanity" — Russell was saved temporarily by her twenty-three Career Woman roles, but by the sixties she had come full circle again. She exemplifies the dilemma of real American women described by Jo Freeman: "The 1940's and

1950's witnessed the phenomenon of 'momism.' Everything was mom's fault — she was trying to run her husband and was ruining her children. No one noticed that this happened at the same time women are being encouraged to return to home and devote their lives to husband and family." [24] It would take another quarter century before everyone realized what Charlotte Perkins Gilman had warned, what Philip Wylie would contemptuously confirm (he is usually credited with making the term "momism" an epithet, in *Generation of Vipers*, 1942), that the occupations of homemaking and parenthood were insufficient outlets for people of drive and ability, unless they *did* carry the roles to extremes.

The filmic image of the career woman and the working woman, then, may be seen as reaching its glorious height in the thirties and continuing into the forties. But the forties were "the danger zone, the river of no return, when women, lured into jobs because of the war, didn't want to leave them when it was over" (Haskell, p. 145). So the film-makers "conspired" to drive them out by changing woman's image, eliminating the career woman entirely. "Women might have better jobs, largely as a result of the war, but they would pay more heavily for them in the movies. Naturally. They were more of a threat" (Haskell, p. 175). Rosen subscribes to the same conspiracy theory to explain the dramatic change: "Movies during the forties were no more reflective of the societal shift than those of the thirties. Movies, heretofore stressing female strength, now began to distort it." [25] Instead of the Career Girl in the breeziest comedies and gutsiest dramas, we now saw the emergence of the Evil Woman in the ambiguous melodramas of the forties and beyond.

If we turn abruptly, at just this point, to a different perspective on the thirties and forties—William Chafe's history of the "changing political, economic and social role" of the American woman—we will be strangely jarred. In that particular history, the decade of the thirties is not so glorious:

> As the new decade began, prospects for career women grew worse
> rather than better. . . . As the Depression swept the country, it became

less and less likely that women would enter male-dominated careers, and the proportion of female workers engaged in the professions fell from 14.2% in 1930 to 12.3% in 1940. (pp. 91-92)

And again:

The advent of the Depression provided the final blow to feminist hopes for economic equality. . . . Congresswoman Florence Kahn spoke for most of her colleagues when she declared that "woman's place is not out in the business world competing with men who have families to support," but in the home. (p. 107)

Then comes the decade of the forties, and suddenly a dawn:

Within five years, World War II had radically transformed the economic outlook of women. The eruption of hostilities generated an unprecedented demand for new workers, and, in response, over 6 million women took jobs, increasing the size of the female labor force by over 50 per cent. Wages leaped upward, the number of wives holding jobs doubled, and the unionization of women grew fourfold. Most important, public attitudes appeared to change. Instead of frowning on women who worked, government and the mass media embarked on an all-out effort to encourage them to enter the labor force. *The war marked a watershed in the history of women at work* and, temporarily at least, *caused a greater change in women's economic status than half a century of feminist rhetoric and agitation had been able to achieve.* (pp. 135-36, emphasis added.)

Remarkable. So radiant is the author over the (positive) transformation taking place that one scarcely catches the phrase, "temporarily at least," in the middle of the last sentence; nor does the enthusiastic Chafe seem dismayed that the change in attitude toward women who worked was not to last.

Here I would interrupt Chafe's analysis long enough to hear from other historians who traffic in historical realities. In an article that asks "Whatever Happened to Rosie the Riveter?" Sheila Tobias and Lisa Anderson dispel a number of myths. To begin with, the female war worker was not a "contented, middle-class housewife who entered the work force between 1942 and 1944 for patriotic reasons" but rather primarily a woman who had worked before the war "at a low-paying, insecure job in a service occupation (as waitress, laundress, or clerk)." Although she supported the resolutions of the UAW Women's Bureau (equal pay for equal work, postwar reemployment, wages, seniority) and Eleanor Roosevelt's expressed hope that women would not become "expendable home front soldiers," her pleas were in vain; she was forced out of the job market in staggering numbers in 1945 and 1946 through the combined efforts of business and unions. Not that she always minded the cutbacks as such, but she did resent not being rehired in accordance with her rightful seniority when a plant reconverted, and she was willing to file suits when jobs she had held were reclassified as men's work. She had worked because she needed to and wanted to, but she was forced out of the industrial sector of the economy without recourse, giving up "grudgingly" the jobs she had performed so well and the high income she had earned. The authors conclude that although impressive numbers of women today also work, "in terms of work, stature, and equity, the working woman of 1973 has a long way to go to catch Rosie the Riveter." [26]

Joan Hoff Wilson, meanwhile, portrays woman as "A Declining Force in American History," recalling that although the percentage of women in the labor force increased from 1920 to 1970, "the status of women within the ranks of labor actually declined." In the last fifteen years especially, "women have moved in but not up the labor scale in accordance with their increased levels of education." Median earnings of women workers as compared to men have declined "and this gap appears to be widening." [27] Sex-typing in jobs has increased, with the percentages of women in professional and technical work (the Career Women) declining at the very time the total percentage of workers increased. It is not that Wilson's facts are so different from Chafe's but rather that the two historians perceive them from almost diametrically opposed perspectives, reflecting in part their differing *expectations*.

Chafe is so struck by his findings that he is led to develop a full-blown behaviorist theory to answer the question "how does social change occur?" His answer: not by trying to change attitudes with "feminist rhetoric and agitation" but by changing behavior, as World War II changed behavior by putting women to work. It was that dramatic entry into the labor force that ultimately brought the rise of the new feminism of the sixties and seventies, he claims. What of the twenty intervening years described by Friedan, Rossi, and the others? Chafe speaks at length about "The Paradox of Change," but he still concludes: "There was nothing necessarily new about the feminine mystique, nor could it be said that women in the 1950's were more 'victimized' than they had been at other times in history. The feminists had simply given fresh expression to an old problem" (p. 232). Further, since "attitudes toward woman's place run too deep to be changed through direct conversion," our only alternative is to initiate a "new cycle which will undermine the structural basis for traditional views of male and female roles."

> It is just such a process which I believe has taken place in the years since 1940. With World War II as a catalyst, a dramatic change has occurred in women's economic role. . . . No one can claim that equality has been achieved as a result of these changes, but it may be that a foundation for seeking equality has been established. (pp. 253-54)

In his final sentence, Chafe looks forward to better relations between the sexes and the achievement of greater freedom for women "as the nation approaches the last quarter of the century." An altogether optimistic vision, and one to be applauded, but it leaves no place for image or attitude: the Economic Woman in Chafe's future is no less a stereotype than the Career Woman who was pushed out of films at the very time the real woman was beginning the long fight to reclaim her lost job and prestige.

IV
TRANSFORMATION ACROSS THE ARTS:
AN OUTLINE OF THREE STAGES

The Long-Suffering Woman and the Career Woman are, in a sense, opposite types—the one a figure of pity in a tragedy or lachrymose melodrama, the other inviting admiration in a wise-cracking happy comedy. Yet both belong to our larger

history of the American woman's image; in fact, it is
interesting that both reach the peak of their personal
histories at the same time, during the 1940s. For the
remainder of this essay, I wish to summarize the three stages
in the transformation of the American woman's image from
the 1930s to the present as found in various media. Allowing
for generous overlap, the three stages as I see them are: (1)
the era that included many strong, intact, independent
women, women who could hold their own vis-a-vis men and
problems (the thirties well into the forties); (2) the displace-
ment of these images of independence by two different kinds
of dependence and vulnerability during the era of the
Feminine Mystique (the fifties well into the sixties); and (3)
the degradation of women into images of female zombies,
grotesques, bitches and sex-object nymphets (from about the
mid-fifties to the present).

I should acknowledge here that "alternate" types might
also be found during each of the eras. This is especially true
of the first stage, when a great many more women (thus
many more varieties) were visible in the various media than
during the second and third stages. A better way of making
this point is to cite the force of the wipe-out phenomenon
that eliminated woman as image from many media during the
last two stages, so that the images of these periods represent
the leftovers after the decline.

At lectures, the question is regularly put to me about the
possibility of a fourth stage, one coinciding with the new
images of women emerging with the woman's movement
today. My answer has been that there have been to date very
few effective *positive* expressions of the new mood and the
new woman in media reaching a substantial audience.
Documentaries abound, and gestures of fierce rejection of old
images are made in many media *by* women. The dominant
image in literature and film as of this writing is that of
Woman as Victim, while a few examples I will mention later
show the woman breaking out of her past only to confront
the future as a question-mark. But none of these has the
force of the movement captured in the image. *Television*
roles by Mary Tyler Moore, Bea Arthur, Lily Tomlin, and

others may mark the beginnings of a trend, but it is too early to say. To date, the single most positive image expressive of a potential "fourth stage" (apart from the three-act drama of 1973, featuring Billy Jean King over Bobby Riggs: 6-4, 6-3, 6-3) is Helen Reddy's award-winning and forceful song, "I Am Woman."

First Stage: Images of Independence

In 1932, the immigrant sculptor Gaston Lachaise completed one of his "Standing Women" (Fig. 4) that seems, in fact, to be a bronze incarnation of the Helen Reddy song. Because she has so long dominated the sculpture court of New York's Museum of Modern Art with her commanding presence, she may well be the most famous of the Lachaise women. Large in size—large-breasted, large-bellied, muscular, standing strong upon the earth with hands on hips—she does indeed seem to be saying: "I am strong! I am invincible! If I have to, I can do anything . . . I am Woman!" Lachaise was moved to portray Woman as he did for a number of reasons, chief among which was his adoration of his model—the woman he followed to America and later married, his lifelong inspiration. He associated woman with her sexuality; she symbolized strong primitive forces of passion. To a few detractors of a later age, she might appear "grotesquely swollen, like some prehistoric fertility symbol";[28] but for our purposes, "Standing Woman" stands as a joyous celebration of independent womanhood, the Earth Mother, the Nature Principle incarnate, unabashed and all up front. As such, she serves marvelously to represent the images of strength and independence affirmatively portrayed during the thirties and early forties.

Among these images, that of the Strong Mother stands out: the pioneer mother, the immigrant Ma, the black Mammy, the middle-class Mrs. Miniver, the working-class and lower-class and surrogate mothers and moms. The Jewish mother flourished with Yiddish theatre; the Irish mother was a favorite, as were mothers of Southern and Eastern European nations, and rural mothers of every nationality. They appeared in plays of Elmer Rice and Clifford Odets, among others; Hemingway's Pilar in *For Whom the Bell Tolls* belongs to the type, as does Ma Joad of Steinbeck's *Grapes of Wrath*, the quintessentially 1930s novel. But so does Mammy of *Gone with the Wind*, a more popular novel and film than the proletarian works the era has become known for. (Mammy and Scarlett O'Hara *both* belong, despite the latter's image as a scarlet version of the Southern belle. Together, they rebuild Tara and learn to cope with the postbellum age in a way remarkably similar to that described by Anne Scott in *The Southern Lady*, 1970: a triumph of womanly strength in a difficult time.) Include also the images of Tugboat Annie, Stella Dallas, Aunt Jemima, *Sergeant York's* ma, and Carl Sandburg's mothers:

> The strong men keep coming on,
> The strong mothers pulling them on . . . .

Here is how Bessie Berger and her husband Myron are described in the stage directions to a typical thirties drama, Odets's *Awake and Sing* (1933):

> BESSIE BERGER, as she herself states, is not only the mother in this home but also the father. She is constantly arranging and taking care of her family. She loves life, likes to laugh, has great resourcefulness and enjoys living from day to day. A high degree of energy accounts for her quick exasperation at ineptitude. . . .
>
> MYRON BERGER, her husband, is a born follower. He would like to be a leader. He would like to make a million dollars. He is not sad or even depressed. Life is an even sweet event to him, but the "old days" were sweeter yet. He has a dignified sense of himself. . . . But he is heartbroken without being aware of it.[29]

And in the famous passage towards the end of *Grapes of Wrath*, Ma Joad speaks for a part of the culture when she answers Pa's complaint that he has "lost his place" and that women were taking over the family — "Woman sayin' we'll do this here, an' we'll go there, an' I don' even care":

> "Woman can change better'n a man," Ma said soothingly. "Woman got all her life in her arms. Man got it all in his head. . . . Man, he lives in jerks—baby born an' a man dies, an' that's a jerk—gets a farm an' loses his farm, an' that's a jerk. Woman, it's all one flow, like a stream,

little eddies, little waterfalls, but the river, it goes right on. Woman
looks at it like that. We ain't gonna die out. People is goin' on—changin'
a little, maybe, but goin' right on."[30]

So forceful are such mother images during the age that
one is led to wonder whether women had displaced men as
focal points of interest during the Depression and war years.
Page Smith has speculated over the phenomenon of mother-
worship in America during the nineteenth century, particularly toward its end. It was one way of "neutralizing
women," Smith postulated, to "deify her as The Mother,
'key figure of civilization, holy being of total virtue, calm and
elevated substance, and perfect comprehension of her children.' " Charlotte Perkins Gilman in 1898 might rail against
mother-worship as a form of pathology—"morbid, defective,
irregular, diseased"—that prevented woman from achieving
full potential as a person, but Gilman was speaking to an
audience not yet ready to hear. At the end of the nineteenth
century, Smith concludes, the exaltation of motherhood was
encouraged on the one hand by the general sentimentality of
the period and on the other hand by the feeling that
American men were failures ("as foreign travellers so frequently charged") and that their failures, especially as fathers
to their sons, "created a kind of emotional vacuum filled by
the figure of Mother who became, in a more cynical age, that
monstrous caricature — omnivorous, insatiable, merciless
Mom."[31]

Can we not transfer part of Smith's agrument to explain
the strong mothers of the thirties, as well as the Moms they
would later become? The 1930s was also a period when the
failures of men were everywhere apparent, a period of
sentimentalism, and a period when the search for eternal
verities at a time of crisis might again make Mother a center
of interest. She might even compensate for the fact that
women were so rudely forced out of the job market,
"neutralizing" their anger by being deified as a key figure of
civilization. Could not Ma Joad as well as Jean Arthur offer
"constructive escapism"?

Except that women of the era *were* displaying unusual
strengths. Support for the belief in woman's superior strength

can be obtained by comparing the fictional statements by and about Bessie Berger and Ma Joad with the factual declarations of Eleanor Roosevelt, especially in her first book, *It's Up to the Women* (1933). The theme of the volume was that women must assume responsibility for reforming the nation if America were to survive the crisis of Depression. According to Mrs. Roosevelt, the new order coming into being would require both "the ability and brains of our men" and "the understanding heart of women" because "especially in times of crisis women had more strength of a certain kind than men." "Perhaps it is better described as a certain kind of vitality which gives them a reserve which at times of absolute necessity they can call upon." When it came to the most important issue, abolishing war and bringing about peace, Mrs. Roosevelt did not seem to have much faith in men at all, not even for "ability and brains." "Only the women and youth of any country can initiate this change. They will have the men to help them later on in the fight but they will meet some of the same unbelief and lethargy that they have come up against in the past."[32] Although Mrs. Roosevelt was not a radical feminist, such sentiments, borrowed from feminists before her, were not to be heard again for nearly forty years.

As Eleanor Roosevelt's advocacy that women and youth take the initiative for cultural reform prophesied a public aspect of present feminist thought, so Amelia Earhart's moving letter to her fiance on the eve of their marriage anticipated, on the private level, the idea of the contract marriage. Here is what she wrote to George Putnam:

> You must know again my reluctance to marry, my feeling that I shatter thereby chances in work which means so much to me. . . .
> In our life together I shall not hold you to any medieval code of faithfulness to me, nor shall I consider myself bound to you similarly. If we can be honest, I think the differences which arise may best be avoided. . . .
> Please let us not interfere with each other's work or play, nor let the world see private joys or disagreements. In this connection I may have to keep some place where I can go to be by myself now and then, for I cannot guarantee to endure at all times the confinements of even an attractive cage.

1.
Three Images of the Long-Suffering Woman. A) "Not only were women seen as sickly — sickness was seen as feminine" [Barbara Ehrenreich and Deirdre English. *Complaints and Disorders: The Sexual Politics of Sickness*] B) Ginger Rogers and Mary Phillips in *Lady in the Dark* [Paramount, 1944]. C) Sickness and sorrow in ABC soap opera *One Life to Live* [Time Magazine].

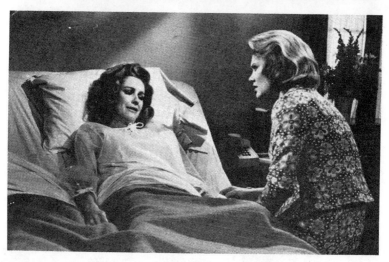

2.
Rosalind Russell in *Woman of Distinction*. (Columbia Pictures, 1950.)

3.
Rosalind Russell and Richard Beymer in *Five Finger Exercise*. (Columbia Pictures, 1962.)

4.
Gaston Lachaise. *Standing Woman*. 1932. (Collection, The Museum of
Modern Art, New York. Mrs. Simon Guggenheim Fund.)

5.
Willem de Kooning. *Woman, I*. 1950-52. (Collection, The Museum of
Modern Art, New York.)

6.
Advertising Defines the Feminine Mystique.

7.
Transformation of the Movie Sex Goddess. Top: Mae West, Marlene Dietrich. Left center: Jean Harlow. Lower left: Greta Garbo. (Publicity photos courtesy of Filmex Co.) Center right: Marilyn Monroe in *Bus Stop*. (20th Century Fox, 1956.)

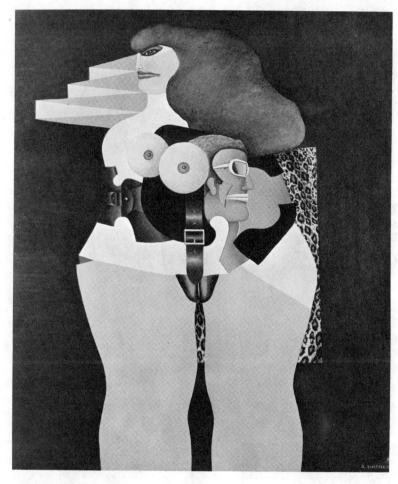

8.
Richard Lindner. *Leopard Lily*. 1966. (Galerie Rudolf Zwirner, Cologne, Germany.)

9.
The Transformation of Bette Davis: "Who Turned the Young American Girl into the Great American Bitch?" Clockwise: Davis in the early thirties, and the sixties — *Dead Ringer* (Warner Bros., 1964); *The Anniversary* (20th Century Fox, 1968); and, on the following page, with Joan Crawford in *Whatever Happened to Baby Jane* (Warner Bros., 1962).

10.
Mel Ramos. *Hippopotamus.* 1967. (Courtesy of the Louis K. Meisel Gallery, New York.)

11.
Early Valkyrie: *Avengers* #83, 1968. (The *Avengers* is a registered
trademark of the Marvel Comics Group. Copyright© 1974.)

12.
Current Valkyrie: *Defenders* #5, 1973. (The *Defenders* is a registered trademark of the Marvel Comics Group. Copyright© 1974.)

I must exact a cruel promise, and this is that you will let me go in
a year if we find no happiness together. . . . [33]

Between them, Eleanor Roosevelt and Amelia Earhart represented to the public images of women as extraordinary
people, real-life models Americans could read about and
compare to the images in literature, the arts, and especially
popular culture.

But it was the movies, more than any other medium of
the time, that established the image of the strong, independent woman. To begin with, the importance of film in the life
of the nation during "the Golden Age of Hollywood" (1930
to 1945) can hardly be overstressed. It is of special interest
that "the heyday of Hollywood coincided with the one and
only time when there was a heyday for women in the West
Coast Dream Factory." [34] The movies functioned primarily
to provide escape from the terrible realities of the day, and
offered roles with which troubled men and women could
identify, if only in their fantasy lives.

The actresses revered as screen "goddesses" — Garbo,
Dietrich, Harlow, and West especially—expressed independence in their own ways. That they dominated men shame-
lessly has often been noted; so has the fact that men
presumably loved every minute of it. The tart, wise-cracking
directness of Harlow and the sense of mystery Garbo
projected (making love, in Rosen's phrase, "as if her partner
were invisible") were built on feelings of strong self-identity.
Recently Kenneth Tynan, reviewing Dietrich's solo show,
remarked: "She knows where all the flowers went—buried in
the mud of Passchendaele, blasted to ash at Hiroshima,
napalmed to a crisp in Vietnam—and she carries the knowledge in her voice. She once assured me that she could play
Bertolt Brecht's 'Mother Courage,' and I expect she was
right." [35] In a remarkable chapter called "The Mae West
Nobody Knows," Mellen presents her subject as an unexpected forerunner of the modern liberated woman. There
were two sides to West, Mellen argues, the one who reduced
herself to sex object and the one who was, simultaneously,
"defiant and self-sufficient, seeking mastery over her life."

It is the latter aspect of the West personality that is revolutionary. It projects a uniquely free image of woman rare for Hollywood during the 1930's, or now. . . . It is true that Mae West, no social revolutionary, does not project new values. But within the existing structure of attitudes defining the appropriate responses of men and women, West turns the tables. It is she who is superior and achieved, she for whom sexual command affirms feminine strength. . . . West looks over the field, reduces and discards, takes lovers at will, but never surrenders freedom or control. . . . she arrogates to herself all the insolent privilege, haughtiness and self-esteem which our culture had until her time in the film granted the male alone.

   Mae West thus deploys her own brand of sexism to create an image of a liberated woman—and Hollywood is her vehicle. (Mellen, pp. 229-32)

In her autobiography West herself confirmed such an interpretation: a striking image of the sex goddess as independent woman. These are images of strength that contrast sharply to the vulnerability and innocence of the sex goddesses of a later age, particularly of Marilyn Monroe. (See Fig. 7.)

   There was a sense of inner security shared by both sexes in thirties movies that stood in rude contrast to the doubts of the real world. "The movies seemed to be saying that because men are secure, women can outsmart them without unsexing them, and because women are secure, they can act smart without fearing reprisals, or the loss of femininity. The security was largely mythic—in real life, things were bleak— but the breezy confidence compensated for a powerlessness that afflicted society as a whole" (Haskell, pp. 129-30). The key word again is "compensated," and the theory advanced by four different film historians is that the confidence exuded by goddesses, the great ones, in their relations with men was intended to counterbalance the failures of the society as a whole.

   The sense of security and intactness of the goddesses was possessed as well by other film women. The kind of elegant but sharp-witted wife-partner played by Myrna Loy in the *Thin Man* series is a case in point; another is the Showgirl role that can be traced from Ruby Keeler through Alice Faye and Betty Grable, a genre which, like the Actress genre, permitted the woman to achieve success herself, rising from chorus girl to star, rather than merely supporting or symbolizing male success. (But even the Showgirl and the Actress often had to give it all up for her man in the seventh reel; in later films both would be punished for success interpreted as "maladjustment"—e.g., *Sunset Boulevard, The Star, All About Eve, The Goddess, Whatever Happened to Baby Jane?*) There was evidence of security in sexual identity, Haskell adds, in the penchant for male impersonation—songs by Dietrich in top hat and suits, dances by Eleanor Powell and Keeler in top hat and tails, Garbo playing the lesbian Christina, Hepburn as a "Peter Pan-like Sylvia Scarlett: all introducing tantalizing notes of sexual ambiguity," evidence that "they can afford to play with their roles, reverse them, stray, with the confidence of being able to return to home base" (Haskell, p. 129). Other genres told the same story. Heiresses and playgirls abounded (Colbert in *It Happened One Night* was typical), their upper-crust independence making them the true precursors of the forties career women (Rosen, p. 180). Gold-digger films allowed a remarkable degree of sisterly affection and ingenuity to be displayed in the cooperative hunt for rich men. Dance teams, like Astaire and Rogers, projected equality of relationship. And not even the Heiress, Gun Moll, Detective-Wife, or Career Woman—all of whom could hold their own against the men they bandied words and wits with—quite matched the "banter" of large, strong Marie Dressler, especially when she slugged it out with Wallace Beery in *Min and Bill.*

Lastly, the child stars of the era—Shirley Temple especially (reigning box-office star, male or female, from 1935 to 1939), Jane Withers, Judy Garland, Elizabeth Taylor, Margaret O'Brien, Peggy Ann Garner, and others—may well have been the most independent of all. The impact of the child-oracle roles played by Temple was profound; one critic says "her opinions *counted* in areas where no adult woman would dare venture, much less be heeded" (Rosen, p. 183). Continuing a tradition begun by Mary Pickford in the twenties—that of the sausage-curled and dimpled but shrewd and enterprising child, capable of telling off the elders under cover of innocence—Temple improved the times wonderfully with the wisdom of the child. Meanwhile, *The Wizard of Oz* (1939), with Garland's Dorothy as its star, emerged to become the most beloved film of the age.

There were parallels in comics, children's literature, and radio not only to child stars but other women's roles of the time: Orphan Annie, begun in 1924, dispensed her wisdom through the thirties and forties; Nancy Drew mysteries from 1930 on offered another version of the girl detective; Baby Snooks was the original funny girl of the air waves; Brenda Starr, Reporter was allowed to remain an unmarried career woman and the star reporter for her newspaper. As for Blondie and Dagwood, Maggie and Jiggs, the strength of woman was less impressive than the ineptness of the man, with his eagerness to escape from wife and duties either to the local bistro or the living-room couch.

Thus far, I have treated the era of the forties primarily as an extension of the thirties, which to a degree it was, in terms of continuing images of strong independent women. The continuity can be explained partly by the war and the sudden need for women as war workers at all economic levels. For a few years, images in fiction and fact seemed to coincide as the media and the society alike supported all women patriotically involved in the war effort. Rosie the Riveter was a cultural heroine in reality as well as myth. Wacs, Waves, nurses in white, and waiting war wives playing long-suffering roles were applauded. The positive images of working women and professional women in newspaper stories, popular magazines, even the *Reader's Digest* (as well as the movies) stand witness to the respect for woman's strength and independence during the forties.

But when other images are examined, including that of the Evil Woman (e.g., Barbara Stanwyck in *Double Indemnity*, Mary Astor in *The Maltese Falcon*), and when we turn our attention to the years 1944 to 1950, the era becomes more difficult to describe. It is a transitional period, but also a peak period for many women's genres, a perfect era for "ambiguity." Is it any wonder that different scholars looking at the same era see it so differently? Chafe and

Haskell define the extremes, the one exulting over woman's new freedom, the other mourning her terrible decline; but Barbara Deming may be closer to capturing the ambiguity in her book *Running Away from Myself: A Dream Portrait of America Drawn from the Films of the Forties* (written in 1950 but published much later). Interpreting films of the forties as dream images through which "we can read with a peculiar accuracy the fears and confusions that assail us," Deming announces in her opening sentences: " 'Abandon all hope, you who enter here!' Dante found these words written above the entrance to Hell. I should give the same warning to anyone about to enter the world through which this book will lead him": a world in which Americans run away from themselves, through film, into one kind of hell or another, toward suicide, renunciation, or death. [36]

A better illustration of the ambiguity in attitude toward women at this point in American history is Willem de Kooning's "Woman I" (Fig. 5), the most famous woman in modern American painting. The artist worked on the painting for two years and all but gave it up. Both the artist and his critics have speculated over his effort to produce her, their explanations ranging from de Kooning's struggle to make a statement using semi-abstract methods to the role of the artist's mother in arousing resentments. The first explanation emerges from an interview in which the artist explained to David Sylvester:

> It had to do with the female painted through all the ages, all those idols. .... it became compulsive in the sense of not being able to get a hold of it and the idea that it really is very funny, you know, to get stuck with a woman's knees, for instance. .... When I look at them now, they look vociferous and ferocious, and I think it had to do with the idea of the idol, the oracle, and, above all, the hilariousness of it. I do think that if I don't look upon life that way, I won't know how to keep on being around. [37]

As in Deming's case, the artist sees his own survival involved in the creation of his ambiguous image; to portray "the hilariousness" is a way of looking upon life and avoiding a personal hell. But the artist's leading biographer, Thomas

Hess, implies that the Woman's power to intimidate and the
artist's struggle against creating her are alike attributable to
de Kooning's mother. When de Kooning was five years old,
Hess points out, his parents were divorced, the court
assigning him to his father, "probably because of the
extremely warm relationship between them." The mother
"fought the decision, at first simply by grabbing up the child
and taking him home with her, later through a successful
appeal to the court." To which Hess adds:

> I touch on these details because, as will be indicated, they supply
> possible clues to de Kooning's magisterial Woman of the early
> 1950's—an image which has become a totem and an icon of the times.

Hess then identifies "Woman I" as a representative of the
Black Goddess, "the mother who betrays the son, gets rid of
the father, destroys the home." Perhaps that was one reason
the son "took so many months to finish 'Woman I,' and
why it was immediately afterward destroyed, only to be
resurrected." Even the humor in the painting, so important
to de Kooning's own ability to survive, is conceived by Hess
as the son's means of compensating ("balancing") the sin
committed by the mother, who is basically "to blame." [38]
      Of many possible interpretations of causality behind the
work, I cite these as illustrating different kinds of approaches
to explaining a given image of woman in a given art form. But
for the immediate purpose of illustrating a point in time for
the transformation in attitude toward the strong, large,
queenly, formidably sexual woman, "Woman I" is not to be
matched in the annals of art. Hess is right in saying of de
Kooning's entire "Woman" series of the fifties that they
made "a traumatic impression on the public—to date, they
have been the last modern paintings to do so." Like the
Lachaise woman (Fig. 4), "Woman I" is vibrant and alive and
passionate, but exaggeration has made these qualities lu-
dicrous; she is a subject of savage satire rather than reverence.
Her grin mocks and her eyes peer; her outsized breasts are
almost as threatening as her teeth. Instead of standing firm
upon the landscape, she engulfs it, but the landscape also
threatens to absorb her. (De Kooning later said, speaking of

the abstract landscapes he also painted, "The landscape is in the Woman, the Woman is in the landscape.") Is she victim or victimizer of man and society? The answer is she is both, she is ambiguous, and she summarizes the past as she foretells the future. It is as if the large, strong, sexual women celebrated for their optimism and force during such periods of stress as the Depression and the war had suddenly become objects of ridicule, once the culture's need for their strength disappeared. Now they must convert to roles as overdressed shoppers of the affluent society, with little more to do with their excess energies than spend money on clothes, attend bridge parties, and smile incessantly at men, at the public, at the camera. De Kooning called it "the American smile" and he found it on billboard images of women everywhere. It was soon to become the hallmark of the age—and he painted it as a leer.

Second Stage: Era of the Feminine Mystique

If the images of independence of the thirties and forties I have thus far described represented a first stage in the transformation process, what caused them to disappear? Why did they give way to a second stage dominated by images of dependence, vulnerability, emptiness, and softness during the "poor, pallid uptight fifties"? A full analysis of causal factors would include some facts already cited and some not yet mentioned: the effects of World War II on the economy; the insistence of servicemen on having their jobs back after the war and getting college educations at government expense (no comparable reward to women for their part in the war effort); the rise of the affluent culture and the advertising that accompanied it, turning women into America's consumers (as men were the producers); the segregation of male and female realms of activity with the growth of the suburbs and their separation from the city; the effects of a new psychology deriving from Freudian precepts upon interpretations of sex and family roles; the disillusionment that follows every war—in this case, a disillusionment with two decades of privation in succession—leading easily to a hungry embrace of affluence as a means to freedom from such fears.

The keyword now was "security,"—meaning both economic and psychological security, security to free men and women alike from the need to be strong in the face of hardships.

The 1960 census revealed the dramatic changes that had taken place the decade before. Americans were marrying younger and oftener, the marriage rate rising to an unprecedented 97%. One woman of every three was married by the age of 19. Young couples were leaving their parents' homes earlier to establish their own, having children earlier and having larger families. The pressures on young girls to marry or be ostracized, and once married, to have children or a good explanation, were very real. Women retreated from the professions in dramatic numbers, and the percentages obtaining college degrees, especially advanced degrees, drastically declined. Since the whole story of the twenty-year retreat, along with supporting statistics and elements of the rationale, was first told in Friedan's landmark book (whose interdisciplinary approach still makes it one of the most useful for American Studies), "the era of the Feminine Mystique" provides the best label for the second stage of the transformation process.

According to the mystique, the wedding day was the most important day in a woman's life, and the advertisers soon discovered (see Fig. 6) that weddings could sell anything, including the tires for the honeymoon car. As homemaking was proposed to women as a full-time occupation, consumer goods were defined as extensions of the love mystique, and women were promised "a love affair with Dan River sheets," orgiastic bliss from the experience of waxing floors, Thrill and Joy and Cheer from soap products; even appliances were offered as sex substitutes: "A Good Washer is Like a Good Man." After marriage and homemaking came the rituals of motherhood: beginning with the baby shower, and afterwards Happy Mom in immaculate gloves and suit driving an automobile with Happy Infant at her side. In such a role, the American Fair Maiden was expected to find total fulfillment; if something went wrong, if Baby spit up or cried, if Mom ever felt cheated or bored, it must be her own fault.

Friedan called the central figure in the drama of the Feminine Mystique "the Happy Housewife Heroine," and it is her image that deserves our attention first, for she has quite an ancestry! It dates back to the Cult of True Womanhood described by Welter for the period 1820-1860; to the cult of the Good-Good Girl as Fair Maiden in nineteenth century American literature described by Leslie Fiedler (who, disliking the type, also calls her ice maiden, monster of virtue, blue iceberg, and other such epithets); to the image of the Young American Girl who appeared in novels of writers from James Fenimore Cooper to Henry James (who gave her the most flattering title: "Heiress of All the Ages"); and to the paintings of James's contemporaries, Winslow Homer, John Singer Sargent, even Mary Cassatt. Miss America, the True Woman, Fair Maiden of ancient myth, Heiress of the Ages — the Breck Girl (Fig. 6, top) defines the type today: blonde and blue-eyed, clean and wholesome, contented, confident, innocent. Comparing her to a very early Bette Davis (Fig. 9) will make the point that this image of the American Girl had never really disappeared from the American imagination. This bland maiden, as in the case of Davis, was simply suspended for the two decades when the more interesting, and independent alternatives became available.

In film, the rise of Doris Day marked the most obvious expression of the new type. June Allyson, emerging as Sweet and Lovely in her roles of the forties, played the perfect wife of the fifties. Many new versions of the girl-next-door type emerged: Debbie Reynolds, Audrey Hepburn, Leslie Caron, Sandra Dee (the rest are by now forgotten). The primary point that magazine fiction, advertising, movies, and other media had to make about this type was that she was happy in her subservience to man, eager to play the supportive role, "fulfilled." The role was described as requiring ingenuity and a variety of talents to meet the variety of problems she must solve—one shibboleth was that wife and mother were occupation enough to use up a whole college education—but her aptitudes did not make her any the less dependent: submission to her role was, in Freudian terms, her "destiny" as a woman.

The Good-Good Girl was the first of two primary types
who displaced the independent women of the era before. The
second was the Good-Bad Girl—especially, in film, Marilyn
Monroe (followed by "Monroe imitations" like Jayne Mans-
field, Anita Ekberg, Kim Novak, Mamie Van Doren, Diana
Dors, and from abroad, Lollobrigida, Loren, and Bardot). [39]
"The two innovations, or rather, important changes in films
of the fifties were, paradoxically, contradictory. . . . We saw
on the screen two types of women: the sex symbols and the
clean and wholesome Mrs. Americas. In between was, with
rare exceptions, a great big void." Thus was the history of the
era summarized for *Movie Digest* in 1972. [40] And thus was
the bifurcation of the American woman into two simplistic
stereotyped figures accomplished, as unnoticed as the irony
in the habit of "blaming mom" at the same time women were
told to return to the home and devote their lives to husbands
and families.

But there was more in common between the two
"paradoxical" types of the era than was at first apparent.
Unlike the self-assured goddesses of a previous era, Monroe
projected a kind of innocence, vulnerability, and dependency
on men that her famous predecessors did not share. (See Fig.
7.) It was just this kind of natural and childlike innocence
perversely combined with voluptuousness that made the
image of Monroe so forceful during her time. It was easy
enough to see the dimension of dependency and submission
in the Doris Day women whose identity came through
husband and family. But submission was also expected of the
sex-object women, as any girl who grew up during the era of
the Monroe mystique can testify—as Alix Shulman, among
others, testifies in her *Memoirs of an Ex-Prom Queen*
(1973); as a former student of mine testified when she
summed up the prevailing attitude of college men toward the
girls they dated as: "Before you couldn't; now you'd better."

That her kind of innocence was ultimately fatal is the
tragedy of Monroe's personal life, now a subject of strong
contemporary interest. It was fatal not only because she was
forced by the studios to keep repeating the stereotyped
Dumb Blonde roles she came to perform with consummate

comedic skill, but also because she herself was an innocent ("needing to be loved," the biographers repeat) who felt compelled to live by the sex goddess role her public applauded while at the same time she struggled to fulfill the alternate roles of wife and mother, and somehow become a real person as well. Her suicide, like Sylvia Plath's, has left still shaken a generation that believed in her.

As long as American women could choose between the two roles, at least they knew where they stood; but more and more, by the sixties, they were expected to be *both* kinds of women to their men. Since both were dependency roles — subservient or helpless or vulnerable—the result was, conversely, greater demands upon the men, economically and sexually. "A good wife knows how to be an expensive mistress," read the headline to a fur coat ad in the *New York Sunday Times*, and the explanatory copy revealed much about the emergent tensions in American homes (by now, the divorce rate was skyrocketing) as women looked to husbands to fulfill their needs for "attention" and husbands inclined to look elsewhere for escape:

> Are you so busy being devoted to your husband that you never make reckless demands? That's a mistake. Try acting spoiled now and then. Simply *have* to have some wildly beautiful extravagance. This magnificent Swakara Broadtail should fill the bill admirably. How will your husband feel about suddenly having an expensive mistress? He'll complain about the cost of maintenance. And be a lot more attentive.

It was also the era of the Barbie doll, who managed to project the duality: a teenage Marilyn Monroe and Doris Day combined in a single image. The bosomy doll had a figure worthy of a Playmate of the Month (note the emergence of *Playboy*, Playboy Clubs, and Playboy bunnies during this same era); her dimensions have been computed as equivalent to 40"-24"-30", with legs a fourth longer than average. She is not just a body, a sex object; she is also fastidiously groomed, a Fair Maiden in face and feature. Her real function—an important index to woman's role in an age of affluence—was to be a Consumer, consuming the clothes, cars, bathtubs, beauty accessories, girlfriends and boyfriends that were purchased for her. When Ruth Handler identified the

18-year-old Barbie as "every little girl's dream of what she wants to be," she provided a glimpse of the terrors facing women both before and beyond this "penultimate" age of woman's being—the fears of being too fat, too flat, too plain, too poor, too sexless, and—finally—too old (over 18!).

More important than either of the two images of dependency that emerged during the postwar era was the fact that with dependency came invisibility: the decline of woman as such, her disappearance from images in textbooks, children's media, literature, and film. All-male casts became common in all these media, or casts with males in starring roles, whose interest in each other was more important than their relation to their women. Since it was difficult in any event to make the life of the typical American girl interesting, authors and screen-writers turned to the marginal women—the neurotics, the spinsters, the alcoholics, the prostitutes. (Pauline Kael once asked: "How many kinds of prostitute could Shirley MacLaine play?") It was the era of Tennessee Williams. The same Vivien Leigh who had played Scarlett O'Hara with such defiance now withered and became insane as another Southern belle, Blanche DuBois, in *A Streetcar Named Desire*. Some of the best actresses appeared in the roles of frustrated or hopelessly idiosyncratic women who did *not* make it into the marriage-and-family scene (the spinsters, the Women Alone), or became Devouring Moms and Madwomen if they did. Hepburn played four spinster roles—in *African Queen, Desk Set, Summertime,* and *The Rainmaker* — as well as the terrible mother in Williams's *Suddenly Last Summer* and the poignant deranged figures in *Madwoman of Chaillot* and *Long Day's Journey into Night*. Russell played in *Picnic, Mame, Gypsy, Five Finger Exercise,* and other roles that are cases in point; Davis's and Crawford's roles might be added. Not included are the names of those who disappeared from sight entirely unless, like Doris Day, they managed to make the story of the virginal type interesting or, like Lucille Ball in *I Love Lucy*, managed to combine housewifery with idiosyncracy.

Third Stage: Emergence of the Female Zombie and the

Great American Bitch

It is difficult to draw a line of demarcation between the second and third stages of the transformation process, but it is not difficult to identify the differences in the end results. The Good-Good Girls and Good-Bad Girls (transferring Fiedler's language to film) were offered as positive types; they usually appeared in bright comedies. The Women Alone, neurotics and spinsters and has-beens, during the earlier era were at least portrayed with tenderness; they inspired deep sympathy. Not so the types who followed in their wake, extending their tradition through the sixties into the seventies.

In his volume *Man in Modern Fiction* of 1958, Edmund Fuller included a chapter called "The Female Zombies" to describe a then new trend in American literature. "Distorted images of woman, and confusions about her sexual bond with men, are particularly conspicuous in current literature," he wrote, and he speculated over the cause: "Some novelists, consciously or otherwise, are avenging themselves upon women, degrading and humiliating them vicariously, triumphing over them in a fictional domination, sexual and otherwise, that is lost from their life reality." Others, "less disturbed, cling nevertheless to the picture of woman as an appendage to man and a sexual object." [41] From the passages he quotes to illustrate the degradation, the worst offenders among novelists appeared at that time to be James Jones and Norman Mailer, but many other images have since emerged to fit the title Fuller provided. Another apt term to describe the images that emerged during the third stage of the transformation was coined by Delores Barracano Schmidt, also in a discussion of literature — the term "Great American Bitch." [42] The Bitch's origins, Schmidt argues, were in the fantasy projections of male writers of the 1920s, but her domination of the "literary suburbias" of a later era now seems much more obvious to us — women in the works of Philip Roth, John Cheever, John Updike, Herbert Gold, and Edward Albee, as well as Mailer and Jones.

Since a preeminent version of the Zombie or Bitch is the

voracious image of the sexually predatory, castrating, man-
eating woman, it is appropriate to represent this third stage
with Richard Lindner's "Leopard Lily." (Fig. 8.) Heavily
painted and sexually aggressive in aspect—with her strapped
and delineated vagina, her size and threatening thighs (all
Lindner women are large in thigh), her leopard-skin-rug
emblem implying stereotyped animal passion, she is portrayed with cold objectivity as both predator and victim of
modern American urban culture. It was an attitude Lindner
displayed toward all his women, most of whom are girdled
and armored against a culture that required them to be
armored. Note the Organization Man she has "eaten" in her
belly. Lindner's post-Pop Art paintings, like the plays of
Edward Albee and the novels of the black humorists, belong
to a generation with a sensitivity to the grotesque and the
cruel emptiness in American life. By now, the Elizabeth
Taylor of *National Velvet* and *Father of the Bride* has passed
beyond the stage of playing Cleopatra or Maggie the Cat
(serving, during the Monroe era, as sex symbol) to playing
Martha in *Who's Afraid of Virginia Woolf?* and the Zombie
Woman in a succession of films that followed. Bette Davis has
turned into Baby Jane, having earned for herself the title
"First Lady of Fright" for her campy horror films of the
sixties. (Fig. 9 asks the question: Who turned the Young
American Girl into the Great American Bitch?) Lolita and
the teeny-bopper (who appear in such Lindner works as
"Disneyland" and "Ice") have joined the Barbie doll and
"Baby Doll" to lower the sexual age of women still further.
Housewives who had lived by the Feminine Mystique are
beginning, in the late sixties, to tell of what it was really like
(as in Sue Kaufmann's *Diary of a Mad Housewife*, 1967), and
literature is populated with images of disintegration and
death. Norman Mailer's hero kills his wife and goes scot-free:
it's called *An American Dream*. It is a terrifying image of
themselves that American women see; and Lindner's harsh,
uncompromising portraits of women shrieked out a warning
to them in the sixties. [43]

The wipe-out phenomenon continuing, the women who
remain in literature and film are marginal people, worthy of

attention only as mutations or *misfits* (it is interesting that
Monroe's last film bore that title), whether comic or tragic.
Diana Trilling's survey of American literature revealed images
to confirm Lindner's vision. Woman in literature had become
"something far more insidious than a mere scold," as the
Moms had been at first; she was being used to represent the
society man hated, the force in life that robbed him "of his
last shred of purpose and dignity." "Sexually she is all hunger
and depredation. In terms other than those of sexual desire
she is an empty shell, as empty and meaningless as the
society." So she is discarded. The "image that has been
suggested by art," Trilling concluded, "is virtually that of a
mutation of the species." 44 Summarizing what has happened
in film in the ten years from 1962 to 1973 ("from a
women's point of view, the most disheartening in screen
history"), Molly Haskell indicates that the most memorable
women's performances of this period provide a dazzling list:
"whores, quasi-whores, jilted mistresses, emotional cripples,
drunks. Daffy ingenues, Lolitas, kooks, sex-starved spinsters,
psychotics. Icebergs, zombies, and ballbreakers" (Haskell, pp.
327-28). No wonder Marsha Mason, who was singled out as
the "one celluloid Cinderella of 1973," complained: "I'm
tired of seeing—and *being*—the neurotic hooker. I've had my
fill of empty-headed women's roles which give you one of
three alternatives: You fail . . . you love . . . you die. God, if
only they'd let a woman *grow* once in a while!" 45

While the misfits and mutations, zombies and bitches and
ballbreakers, are haunting the realms of art, literature, and
films, the most striking development in popular culture is the
spread of what was once called pornography and is now
permitted everywhere (*not* X-rated) in the name of freedom
from censorship. From out of the *Playboy* centerfold comes
the mindlessly smiling full-length nude female cutie. The
blatancy and ubiquity of her image is the particular point Mel
Ramos succeeds in making when he paints her perched on a
hamburger, a pile of French fries, or a hippopotamus. (Fig.
10.) She still adorns the magazines displayed on drugstore
stands. (*Playboy*, by now merely "bourgeois," has had to
make way for the new pornography of *Penthouse* and *Oui*.)

But her enticing (if strangely bland) nudity now appears in still more conventional places—in magazine ads and television ads, where she is often seen caressing herself to sell towels and soap and bath oil beads; on posters sold in bookstores and 'head shops' (I have seen them adorning the bedrooms of ten-year-old boys and the office walls of college professors). She invites without threatening, unlike her sisters in the higher arts, and in her own way she assures the men and the male-dominated culture that everything is really okay.

Perhaps the most telling evidence of the degradation of women is the new preoccupation with rape. The number of actual rapes has increased nationally to one every twelve minutes, and rapes in fiction are more and more approved. At least twenty films within two years featured rape, Aljean Harmetz reported in October of 1973, and almost none of them served as anything more than a "plot point." "Once the woman has been raped, the film no longer concerns her"; the rest of the script focuses on the central male figure or figures, even if she has not died from the ordeal, which she sometimes does.

> Rape is the new Hollywood game. There is supernatural rape ("The Legend of Hell House," "The Exorcist"); incestuous rape ("The Damned"); multiple violations of one woman's body ("Man of La Mancha," "Lolly Madonna XXX," . . . "The Little Sparrow"); rape ardently enjoyed by the victims ("The Getaway," "Blume in Love," "Straw Dogs"). There is stylized rape ("Pat Garrett and Billy the Kid," "Clockwork Orange"); strongly implied rape ("Frenzy"); and even, in one old-fashioned instance, rape as a fate worse than death ("Enter the Dragon").

Interviewing male directors, producers, and vice presidents of film companies to seek explanations, Harmetz was told that rape is "extremely successful at the box office," that rape "turns men on," that one producer even believes it turns women on too, and that rapes "have something to do with the fantasy life of the men who make movies. They seem to want to believe that at some point the woman stops struggling and starts moaning, that *all* women really love it, *really want to be raped*." [46] There seems little hope that men of such minds will produce films about real women that "allow them to *grow* once in a while."

Male fantasy projection seems to be the most popular explanation for all of the images of degradation. Such theories must of course undergo thorough scrutiny before they can be accepted, but the one medium that is ready-made to accommodate fantasy projection is the comic book. On the cover of Marvel Comics issue #83 of the *Avengers* series (Fig. 11) will be found as good an example as the contemporary popular media have to offer of the interpretation that many men have had of women's liberation and its implications — its implications, that is, for *them*. The cover presents a new character called Valkyrie as the triumphant liberationist leader of the group of voluptuous Marvel superheroines who appear to have defeated the superheroes stretched out upon the ground. Actually, the story in the comic book itself acts to dispel male fears of being thus overthrown by the likes of Black Widow, Medusa, the Wasp and Scarlet Witch (significant names), for at the penultimate moment, Valkyrie reveals herself to be a well-known female villain in disguise—one who has, to revenge a broken romance, *pretended* to believe in women's liberation in order to win the unwitting sisters to her side and achieve her ulterior goal. The liberationist is unveiled as a fraud, a force of evil, and thereupon destroyed. Such a "happy ending" ought to banish male fears. Or so it seemed in 1970.

Mellen, however, carries the analysis of what has happened in recent years an important step beyond the assumption of male fantasy projection. Once "the image of woman as prim, sexless domestic" gave way, she writes, *all* women began to be assimilated into images of "loose women." "The facade of protection has been withdrawn and the real, unconscious feelings toward women emerge." These feelings, we discover with dismay, are decidedly negative. The rape images become ways of getting even with the women's movement. "It is society's own vengeance upon women. It enslaves those it protects and it rapes and mutilates those who escape its inhibiting norms. . . ."

This then is why the current cinema, seemingly so adult and sexually

free, is degenerate in its image of women. The collapse of the sweet
housewife has not occurred in the context of a new social order in
which a repressive family is not essential. . . . On the contrary, the
deterioration of bourgeois values has brought panic, and a vision of a
humane alternative goes unperceived. (Mellen, pp. 26-27)

One need not accept Mellen's view of family as repressive to
agree that something very like panic *has* set in, producing
images of degradation contemptuously conceived at the very
time that a powerful women's movement is challenging the
entire social order.

At the level of abstraction where writers analyze the
social order, the importance of the women's movement in the
history of Western culture is being acknowledged. For
example, Philip Slater in *Earthwalk* sees the movement
challenging the entire apparatus of our culture. The way the
culture treats women has been an index to its internal
pathologies. "The women's movement emerged in the West
when the social significance of women in the culture had
reached its lowest point in history—when women were
excluded from valued occupations, isolated from each other,
frequently uprooted by their mobile spouses, and even had
their domestic tasks reduced to triviality by technology."
The movement inevitably has come to challenge the apparatus of the family, whether its individual members agreed
that the family was oppressive or not; it challenges the way
the family has worked to produce the individuals who run
the "free enterprise" system. [47] Given the *total* conditions of
American culture, the women's movement is both an
inevitable outcome of the past and a promise of reforming, or
at least changing, that culture's future. There is simply, at
this point, no way of turning back to "the way we were."

At the level of personal experience, however, new images
in the arts and the media, as well as personal testimony, are
now offering a pattern a good deal more upsetting. Perhaps
the most honest but unnerving images to emerge during the
past years are the images of uncertainty and paralysis that
have come in the wake of women's liberation—stories of
women who have broken out of the past and cannot turn
back, yet face question-marks in their futures. The decision

of Marvel Comics to bring Valkyrie back as just such a figure of uncertainty was a brilliant one. (It is striking that a medium that trades in fantasy should this time have outstripped the others in illuminating cultural fact.) After Valkyrie was "reborn" from villain to superheroine, she became one of a new Marvel group called "The Defenders," and used her powers like the best of the individualistic, detached heroes in the comic book world. But now she is forever asking who she is, reflecting on her uncertain identity. (Fig. 12.) Confessional works by women in other media are beginning to present similar images of uncertainty— as in stories and articles appearing in *Ms.* Magazine since 1973, new novels by women, the question-mark ending to the television drama *I Love You, Good By,* and the book by Pat Loud of the series *An American Family.* "I've changed for good, like it or not," Pat Loud writes; yet she also says, "I'm not sure I've progressed much since the days when I was ninety percent Big Mama and nobody cared what I thought about anything. In other words, I'm still trying to find out just who I am." A reviewer who complained that Pat Loud's story "cheats the reader of the resolution of the crisis" was oblivious, as Susan Lester rightly notes, to the degree to which Pat Loud's story is the story of all of us. [48] These inconclusive images, these question-mark endings, these images of paralysis may well be an index to the uncertainty— the *panic*, indeed—of a society that is rejecting one kind of social order before it has agreed upon an alternative.

In Summary—One Last Paradox

Here, then, in the contrast between present-day images and present realities emerges the final "paradox." On the one hand are the popular Barbie doll, the sex object perched on the hippo and smiling down from bookstore walls, the Virginia Slims slogans assuring women they have come a long way, the television ads portraying life in the middle-class family Nirvana as endless contentment. At the same time, the women's movement is celebrated in some quarters for promising to liberate women and men alike. Chafe proposes a vision of economic revolution that is succeeding not only in liberating women but through its "ripple effects" revolutionizing home life and child-rearing as well. Feminist Gerda Lerner offers a vision of "unparalleled opportunity" for the young American woman today: "Her opportunities for fulfillment have never been greater; and, paradoxically, her dilemma has never been more profound. The multiplicity of choices of necessity means conflicts and doubts, uncertainty and the potential for error. But that is the price that must be paid for freedom." [49]

On the other hand are reports from women of their despair, images of entrapment, fear, and disintegration. Let a poem by Marge Piercy appropriately titled "Barbie Doll" tell the story of contrast:

Barbie Doll

This girlchild was born as usual
and presented dolls that did pee-pee
and miniature GE stoves and irons
and wee lipsticks the color of cherry candy.
Then in the magic of puberty, a classmate said:
You have a great big nose and fat legs.

She was healthy, tested intelligent,
possessed strong arms and back,
abundant sexual drive and manual dexterity.
She went to and fro apologizing.
Everyone saw a fat nose on thick legs.

She was advised to play coy,
exhorted to come on hearty,
exercise, diet, smile and wheedle.
Her good nature wore out
like a fan belt.
So she cut off her nose and her legs
and offered them up.

In the casket displayed on satin she lay
with the undertaker's cosmetics painted on,
a turned-up putty nose,
dressed in a pink and white nightie.
Doesn't she look pretty? everyone said.
Consummation at last.
To every woman a happy ending. [50]

The poem summarizes the elements of woman's image

and stereotype with which this essay has been concerned, and the irony of the final line makes my point. Some irony. The women's movement emerged when it did to protest the chasm that divided image from reality, to assure that Piercy's conclusion would not be the "happy ending" for the American woman. Now the movement is over a decade old, and irreversible, but instead of images of liberation, we are surrounded by evidence of male backlash, counter-revolt, images of degradation, female zombies, poster cuties, instances of rape, images of paralysis. "Paradoxically, her dilemma has never been more profound." Some paradox.

NOTES

1. The dust jacket to Molly Haskell's book begins its description of the contents: "You've come a long way baby . . . and it's all been downhill." To take but one more example from a myriad of angry retorts, a UAW Poster was headlined: "That Stupid Commercial That Says 'YOU'VE COME A LONG WAY, BABY' is a Lie." The slogan is seen everywhere in literature of the women's movement, but it is still aggressively in use by Virginia Slims.

2. A distinction should be made between the traditional version of the Long-Way-Baby interpretation of women's history, which is found in most college texts prior to the 1960s and typifies nearly all interpretations of feminism prior to Betty Friedan's *The Feminine Mystique*, and the newer versions of the same attitude represented by Chafe. Several of the essays in R. J. Lifton's *The Woman in America*, originally published in 1964 as an issue of *Daedalus*, take this view, Rossi excepted. David Riesman seems to. Gerda Lerner at times seems more optimistic than most, as in the Epilogue to *The Woman in American History* (Reading, Mass.: Addison-Wesley, 1971). The documentary "Social Change and the American Woman" (Encyclopedia Britannica, distributed by Wolper Productions) is a good example of the view.

3. For convenience, I will paginate within the text references or quotations from the works cited in my epigraphs. Besides Haskell, Rosen, and Mellen, these also accept the Decline-of-Woman view (as do I): Betty Friedan, *The Feminine Mystique* (New York: W. W. Norton & Co., 1963); Alice Rossi, cited in the epigraphs; Joan Hoff Wilson, "Woman as a Declining Force in American History," in Betty E. Chmaj, ed., *Image, Myth and Beyond: American Women and American Studies, II* (Pittsburgh: KNOW, Inc., 1973); Page Smith in "The Great Withdrawal" chapter of *Daughters of the Promised Land* (Boston: Little Brown, and Company, 1970); and many others who have followed Friedan's interpretation.

4. Eleanor Flexner, *Century of Struggle: The Women's Rights Movement in the United States* (Cambridge, Mass.: Harvard University Press, 1959), the most widely used text on feminism, is typical. William O'Neill, *Everyone Was Brave* (Chicago: Quadrangle, 1969), offers a pessimistic but more complete view in

suggesting the death of feminism in the twenties and spending slightly more time than most on the following decades. Two recent documentaries illustrate the leap across the *terra mythologica* especially well: "Women's Rights in the United States" (Altana Productions, 1973), Barbara Welter, general editor; and "We the Women," narrated for television by Mary Tyler Moore (CBS, 1974). Aileen Kraditor, *The Ideas of the Woman Suffrage Movement, 1890-1920* (New York: Columbia University Press, 1965) simply stops at 1920.

5. I have approached the topic of the present essay previously in public lectures, a videotape entitled "Who Put the Negligee in the Seventh Reel: Stereotypes of American Woman," and Chapter 9, "Stereotypes of Women in Comic Books," and Chapter 11, "Images of Woman in Twentieth Century American Art," of my collection *Image, Myth and Beyond*.

6. Leslie Fiedler, *Love and Death in the American Novel* (New York: Stein & Day, 1966); Smith, Chapter 5 of *Daughters of the Promised Land*.

7. Helen Papashvily, *All the Happy Endings: The Domestic Novel in America* (1956; rpt. Port Washington, N.Y.: Kennikat Press, 1971), pp. 10-11.

8. In addition to the major works by Haskell, Rosen, and Mellen cited at the beginning, note the following: Rosen wrote a shortened version of her analysis for *Ms.* Magazine, April 1974, called "Popcorn Venus, or How the Movies Have Made Women Smaller Than Life," pp. 41-47, 84-88. June Sochen is coming out with a book on film. See also the paper by Joyce S. Schrager and June Sochen, fn. 34; Estelle Changas, "Slut-Bitch-Virgin-Mother: The Role of Women in Some Recent Films," *Cinema*, 6 (Spring 1971), 43-45; Janice Law Trecker, "Sex, Marriage, & the Movies," *Take One*, 3 (May-June 1971), 12-15; Joseph W. Baunoch, "Film Stereotypes of American Women," in Chmaj, ed., *Image, Myth and Beyond*

9. Handler is quoted in "Women's Liberation vs. Barbie," *New Vistas*, 13 June 1970. Nilson, "Women in Children's Literature," *College English*, 32 (May 1971), 921.

10. See Barbara Welter, "The Cult of True Womanhood, 1820-1860," *American Quarterly*, 18 (Summer 1966); Ann Wood, "The 'Scribbling Women' and Fanny Fern: Why Women Wrote," *American Quarterly*, 23 (Spring 1971); Fiedler, *Love and Death in the American Novel*; Frederick Lewis Pattee, *The Feminine Fifties* (New York: D. Appleton-Century, 1940), on the 1850s; Herbert R. Brown, *The Sentimental Novel in America, 1789-1860* (1940; rpt. New York: Octagon, 1972).

11. Papashvily, *All the Happy Endings*, p. 128.

12. "The Code of Sudsville," *Time* magazine, 20 March 1972, pp. 93-94.

13. *Ibid.*

14. Beyond the titles already mentioned, see Nancy F. Cott, ed., *Roots of Bitterness: Documents of the Social History of American Women* (New York: E.

P. Dutton, 1972), and Martha Vicinus, ed., *Suffer and Be Still: Women in the Victorian Age* (Bloomington: Indiana University Press, 1972), as a start. A bibliography of relevant works appears in Ehrenreich and English, cited below, pp. 90-94.

15. Barbara Ehrenreich and Deirdre English, *Complaints and Disorders: The Sexual Politics of Sickness*, Glass Mountain Pamphlet No. 2 (Old Westbury, N.Y.: The Feminist Press, 1973), p. 75 *et passim*.

16. *Ibid.*, p. 79.

17. *Ibid.*, pp. 32-37. With reference to the entire discussion in this section should be mentioned Carroll Smith-Rosenberg, "The Hysterical Woman: Sex Roles in Nineteenth Century America, *Social Research* 39 (Winter 1972).

18. Friedan, *The Feminine Mystique*; Phyllis Chesler, *Women and Madness* (Garden City, N.Y.: Doubleday, 1972); Chesler, "Patient and Patriarch: Women in the Psychotherapeutic Relationship," and Naomi Weisstein, "Psychology Constructs the Female," in Vivian Gornick and Barbara K. Moran, eds., *Woman in Sexist Society* (New York: Basic Books, 1971). See also Thomas S. Szasz, *The Myth of Mental Illness* (New York: Dell, 1961).

19. Quoted in David Shipman, *The Great Movie Stars: The Golden Years* (New York: Crown Publishers, 1970), p. 483.

20. Joyce S. Schrager and June Sochen, "The Big Tease: Women in Films, 1930-1945," a paper presented to the American Studies Association, San Francisco, 20 Oct. 1973. Pagination refers to the memeographed version, which is available from the authors at Northeastern Illinois University, Chicago.

21. Pauline Kael, "The Plight of Movie Women," *New Yorker*, 27 Nov. 1971, p. 1. Later in this essay I will also draw on Kael's "Marilyn Monroe and Contemporary Sex Goddesses," in *I Lost It At The Movies* (Boston: Little, Brown, and Company, 1965).

22. "I think that it can be argued that in general upper-class women in the western world have gradually increased dysfunctionalism since the Middle Ages. ... more and more women today are educated to do literally nothing except 'love' within the confines of the nuclear family," writes Joan Hoff Wilson, "Woman as a Declining Force in American History," pp. 1, 3. The dysfunctionalism she finds most acute among middle-class American women today.

23. Peter Shaffer, *Five Finger Exercise: A Play in Two Acts and Four Scenes* (New York: Harcourt, Brace and Co., 1958), pp. 106, 88. The preface to this edition is by Frederick Brisson, Rosalind Russell's husband, who brought the play to America for the 1960-61 season. The turning point in the relationship between Mrs. Harrington and Walter (Maximillian Schell) comes when, after a tender exchange about the possibility of being "friends" despite the "difference in our ages" (her line), Walter at last asks: "Mrs. Harrington, forgive me for asking this, but do you think it's possible for someone to find a new mother?" She "sits very still" as her "expression of eagerness fades, and its remnant hardens on her

face." Becoming distant and cold she arranges to have Walter sent away. Clearly, she was not thinking their "relationship" would be one that would cast her as a *mother*!

24. Jo Freeman, "Women on the Move: The Roots of Revolt," in Alice S. Rossi and Ann Calderwood, eds., *Academic Women on the Move* (New York: Russell Sage Foundation, 1973), p. 1.

25. Rosen in *Ms.* Magazine, p. 46.

26. "Whatever Happened to Rosie the Riveter?" *Ms.* Magazine, June 1973, pp. 92-94. See also Frieda Miller, "What's Become of Rosie the Riveter," *New York Times Magazine*, 5 May 1946.

27. Wilson, "Woman as a Declining Force in American History," p. 312.

28. Sam Hunter, *Modern American Painting and Sculpture* (New York: Dell, 1959), p. 164. His statement in context reads: "In the twenties and thirties Lachaise's full-blooded female figures grew more distorted and expansive, afflicted by a curiously inflated tropism, until they became grotesquely swollen, like some prehistoric fertility symbol." Such assessments, written well after the strong women had been replaced in the public imagination by the fastidious Sego-slenderized images of women, may, of course, tell us as much about the interpreter's image of women as about the artist's. That is one point of the present essay. For a recent sympathetic analysis of Lachaise's intent and results, see Gerald Nordland, *Gaston Lachaise: The Man and His Work* (New York: George Braziller, 1974).

29. In *Three Plays by Clifford Odets* (New York: Random House, 1935), pp. 15-16.

30. John Steinbeck, *The Grapes of Wrath* (New York: The Viking Press, 1939), p. 577.

31. Smith, *Daughters of the Promised Land*, pp. 210-14.

32. See Joseph Lash, *Eleanor and Franklin* (New York: Signet Books, 1973), pp. 505, 516-17.

33. In George Palmer Putnam, *Soaring Wings: A Biography of Amelia Earhart* (New York: Harcourt, Brace and Company, 1939), p. 76.

34. Schrager and Sochen, "The Big Tease," p. 1.

35. Tynan quoted in "Dietrich—A Real Blue Angel," *Sacramento Bee*, 2 June 1974.

36. Barbara Deming, *Running Away from Myself: A Dream Portrait of America Drawn from the Films of the Forties* (New York: Grossman, 1969), p. 1.

37. David Sylvester, ed., "De Kooning's Women," *Ramparts*, 7 (4 April 1969), p. 24.

38. Thomas Hess, *Willem de Kooning* (New York: Museum of Modern Art, 1968), p. 12. Hess has also written an essay in *Willem de Kooning* (New York: George Brazillier, 1959), from which I have derived some of these generalizations.

39. Simone de Beauvoir's interpretation of Bardot's impact is a startling one, to say the least. She feels Bardot's free naturalness and aggressiveness in the game of love make her an example of liberation unappreciated in her own country. "She has a kind of spontaneous dignity, something of the gravity of childhood. The difference between Brigitte's reception in the United States and in France is due partly to the fact that the American male does not have the Frenchman's taste for broad humor. He tends to display a certain respect for women. The sexual equality that Bardot's behavior affirms wordlessly has been recognized in America for a long time." De Beauvoir, *Brigitte Bardot and the Lolita Syndrome* (1960; rpt. New York: Arno Press, 1972), p. 22.

40. Marjorie Rosen, "Goodbye Sweet and Lovely: Movies that Women's Lib Would Like to Burn," *Movie Digest*, July 1972.

41. Edmund Fuller, *Man in Modern Fiction* (New York: Random House, 1958), pp. 95, 115. As its title implies, *Man in Modern Fiction* deals more with Man than Woman, so it should not be too surprising that the chapter on Female Zombies talks more about males—those who write about sex, those who experience sex with women, and how they feel about it—than it does about females as portrayed by themselves. See also Fuller, "How Movies Portray Women," *Wall Street Journal*, 19 March 1974.

42. Delores Barracano Schmidt, "The Great American Bitch," in Betty E. Chmaj, ed., *American Women and American Studies* (Pittsburgh: KNOW, Inc., 1971), pp. 254-58. See also Judith A. Gustafson, "Will the Real Great American Bitch Please Stand Up? Stereotypes of Women in American Literature," in Chmaj, ed., *Image, Myth and Beyond*.

43. See my discussion in Chapter 11 of *Image, Myth and Beyond*, which focuses on Lindner at length. See also Dore Ashton, *Richard Lindner* (New York: Harry N. Abrams, 1970).

44. Diana Trilling, "The Image of Women in Contemporary Literature," in R. J. Lifton, ed., *The Women in America* (Boston: Beacon Press, 1964), pp. 52-71 *passim*.

45. Marcia Borie quotes Marsha Mason in "How Men Dominate Stardom in the New Hollywood—Why Women No Longer Reign," *Modern Screen*, June 1974, p. 63. The article draws heavily on Haskell's book, documenting her conclusions with interviews.

46. Aljean Harmetz, "Rape: New Hollywood Game—An Ugly Movie Trend," *Datebook,* 23 Oct. 1973.

47. Philip Slater's book *Earthwalk* (New York: Doubleday, 1974) is reviewed and quoted by Albert Schwartz, *New Republic*, 25 May 1974, pp. 24-26.

48. Pat Loud with Nora Johnson, *Pat Loud: A Woman's Story* (New York: Coward, McCann and Geoghegan, 1974), commented on by Susan Lester, "Pat Loud Has Something to Tell Us," *Ms.* Magazine, July 1974, p. 91.

49. Gerda Lerner, *The Woman in American History*, p. 190. Although I greatly admire Lerner and her scholarship, I personally found this emphasis on the last page of an otherwise usefully short volume disappointing.

50. "Barbie Doll" in Marge Piercy, *To Be of Use* (Garden City, N.Y.: Doubleday & Company, 1973), p. 26.

CHAPTER 8

Literary Formulas and Their Cultural Significance

By John G. Cawelti

JOHN G. CAWELTI, a Board member of the Popular Culture Association, is a principal commentator on the interrelations of literature and history with popular culture. In writings on such diverse figures and topics as Mickey Spillane and Herman Melville, Horatio Alger and Henry James, World's Fairs and Westerns he has used a wide assortment of cultural materials to expose the underlying patterns of our nation's faith, fantasy, and behavior. His longer works include *Apostles of the Self-Made Man* (1965), *The Six-Gun Mystique* (1970), and a forthcoming book on popular literary formulas tentatively entitled *Adventure, Mystery and Romance.* Dr. Cawelti is Professor of English and Humanities and Chairman of the Committee on General Studies in the Humanities at the University of Chicago.

John Cawelti discusses in his essay the problems of placing popular literature in formulaic and generic patterns that will show the extent to which it reveals and is shaped by culture.

Our earliest experiences of literature involve us in the different pleasures and uses of novelty and familiarity. As children we learn new things about the world and ourselves from stories. By hearing about creatures and events that transcend the limits of space and time allotted to us we widen the range of our imaginations and are prepared to deal with new situations and experiences. However, children also clutch for the security of the familiar: how often a child rejects a new story, preferring to hear one he has already been told a hundred times. As he hears again the often-heard, his eyes glaze over with pleasure, his tense body relaxes, and the story ends in peaceful slumber. The recurrent outlines of a familiar experience have returned. In that well-known and controlled landscape of the imagination the tensions, ambiguities and frustrations of ordinary experience are painted over by magic pigments of adventure, romance, and mystery. The world takes on for a time the shape of our heart's deepest desires.

Older children and adults continue to find a special delight in familiar stories, though in place of the child's pleasure in the identical tale, they tend to substitute an interest in certain types of stories which have highly predictable structures that guarantee the fulfillment of conventional expectations: the detective story, the western, the romance, the spy story and many other such types. For many persons such formulaic types are the greater portion of their experience of literature. Even scholars and critics professionally dedicated to the serious study of artistic masterpieces often spend their off-hours following a detective's ritual pursuit of a murderer, or watching one of television's spy teams carry through its dangerous mission. An enormous number of books, magazines, films and television dramas depend on such formulaic structures. Thus, these formulaic stories are artistic and cultural phenomena of tremendous importance. However, because of their association with the off-hours, the times of relaxation, entertainment and escape, this type of narrative and dramatic construction has been largely ignored by literary scholars and historians, or left to the tender mercies of sociologists, psychologists and analysts of mass culture. Because of their orientation, these disciplines have tended to treat formula stories as ideological rationalizations, psychological stratagems, or opiates for the masses. Such approaches oversimplify the problem by translating or reducing an artistic phenomenon into other terms. To fully understand and interpret the phenomenon of formulaic stores we must treat them as what they are: artistic constructions created for the purpose of enjoyment and pleasure. To come to some insight into their cultural significance we must arrive at some understanding of them as a form of artistic behavior. However, because formula stories represent a widely-shared kind of artistic behavior — a form of collective artistic behavior — we must also deal with the phenomenon in relation to the cultural patterns it reveals and is shaped by.

Formulas, Genres, Symbols, Myths, and Archetypes

In general, a literary formula is a structure of narrative and dramatic conventions which is employed in a great number of individual works. Because it is a pattern of conventional elements and relations, a formula is generally understood by both creators and audiences. We must now go further and explore just what sort of a pattern we are dealing with. There are two common usages of the term *formula* which are closely related to the conception I wish to set forth. In fact, if we put these two conceptions together, I think we will have an adequate definition of literary formulas. The first usage simply denotes a conventional way of treating some specific thing or person. Homer's epithets — swift-footed Achilles, cloud-gathering Zeus, etc. — are commonly referred to as formulas as are a number of his standard similes and metaphors — "his head fell speaking into the dust" — which are assumed to be conventional bardic formulas for filling in a dactylic hexamater line. By extension, any form of cultural stereotype commonly found in literature — red-headed hot-tempered Irishmen, brilliantly analytical and eccentric detectives, virginal blondes and sexy brunettes — is frequently referred to as formulaic. The important thing to note about this usage is that it refers to

patterns of convention which are usually quite specific to a
particular culture and period, and do not mean the same
outside of this specific context. Thus the nineteenth century
formulaic relation between blondness and sexual purity gave
way in the twentieth century to a very different formula for
blondes. The formula of the Irishman's hot temper was
particularly characteristic of English and American culture at
a time when the Irish were perceived as lower-class social
intruders.

The second common literary usage of the term *formula*
refers to larger plot types. This is the conception of formula
commonly found in those manuals for aspiring writers which
give the recipes for twenty-one sure fire plots: boy meets girl,
boy and girl have a misunderstanding, boy gets girl.
These general plot patterns are not, like the first usage of
formula, specifically cultural. Instead, they seem to represent
types of story which, if not universal in their appeal, have
certainly been popular in many different cultures at many
different times. In fact, they are examples of what some
scholars have called archetypes, or patterns which appeal to
many different cultures.

Actually, if we look at a popular story type such as the
western, the detective story, or the spy adventure, we find
that it combines these two sorts of literary phenomena.
These popular story patterns are embodiments of archetypal
story forms in sets of cultural conventions. To create a
western involves not only some understanding of how to
construct an exciting adventure plot, but also how to clothe
this plot in certain nineteenth and twentieth century stereotypical images and symbols such as cowboys, pioneers,
outlaws, frontier towns, saloons, etc. and how to use
appropriate cultural themes or myths — such as nature vs.
civilization, the code of the west, or law and order vs.
outlawry — to support and give significance to the action.
Thus, formulas are literary patterns in which specific cultural
stereotypes become embodied in more universal story patterns.

The reason why such formulas develop is, I think, fairly
straightforward. There are certain kinds of story patterns

which particularly fulfill man's needs for enjoyment and escape. But in order for these patterns to work, they must be presented in relation to figures, settings, and situations that have particular kinds of meaning in the culture which produces them. One cannot write a successful adventure story about a social character type that the culture cannot conceive in heroic terms; this is why we have so few adventure stories about plumbers, janitors, or streetsweepers. It is conceivable that a culture might emerge which placed a different sort of valuation or interpretation on these tasks, in which case we might expect to see the evolution of adventure story formulas about them. Certainly one can see signs of somewhat analogous developments in the popular literature of Soviet Russia and Maoist China.

Thus, a formula is a combination or synthesis of a number of specific cultural conventions with a more universal story form or archetype. With this definition in mind, we can list some of the most important elements that go into the construction of a formula:

1. Image – any object or person represented in words (or in the case of other media, sounds or shapes and colors).
2. Idea – any concept or attitude represented in words (or sounds, shapes or colors).
3. Symbol – an image used in such a way that it implies ideas, feelings, or other images. The line between image and symbol is a vague one, since even the barest of images will have some kind of connotative qualities for most people. In general, an image becomes a symbol when it tends to force its implications on our attention by virtue of its connection with conventional systems of meaning. A picture of a man riding a horse may be only an image, but if his costume or setting makes us see him as a cowboy, we are involved with a symbol. If he turns out to be John Wayne, the symbolism becomes still more precise and specific. The term *icon* is often used to differentiate visual from verbal symbols. Symbols can also be ranged along another continuum from the

collective to the personal. Our interpretation of the
symbol "cowboy" depends on a whole set of conventional forms in the context of which we have
experienced that symbol. On the other hand, a
symbol in a symbolist poem may have to be
interpreted solely in terms of its unique use in that
particular poem, or in relation to the personal
symbolism of the poet. Formulas, of course, tend to
involve fairly straightforward collective symbolism.

4. Theme — an idea used in such a way that it implies
    symbols, feelings, or other ideas. In much literary
    discussion the terms "symbol" and "theme" are often
    used interchangeably. The line between them is
    certainly not a sharp one, but it is sometimes useful
    to distinguish between a charged image ("symbol")
    and a charged idea ("theme").

5. Myth — symbols or themes represented as involved in
    some form of action. It may seem a bit churlish to
    reduce a term that has assumed such a complexity of
    meanings to a definition at once so terse and vague.
    However, this formulation does seem to state the two
    essential conditions of most things that have been
    commonly referred to as myths: 1) a myth is a
    pattern of some sort and not a single symbol or
    theme; rather, it involves the setting of one or more
    symbols in some larger context that can best be
    defined as an action; 2) a myth has some sort of
    special meaning; it tells of an action or complex of
    actions charged with basic significance for those who
    use it; therefore we can best understand it as a
    pattern made up of charged elements (symbols and/or
    themes). A myth may be a story of some sort, like
    the myth of Oedipus, or a fragment of a story, like
    the myth of the shootout, or something that is only
    by implication a story, like the myth of success or of
    the master race, but at its most basic level a myth
    places a symbol or theme in the context of some sort
    of direct or implied activity. The concept of myth has
    become an enormously important one in the twen-

tieth century through the work of scholars like Frazer and Eliade who have made cultural, psychological and religious interpretations of mythical patterns. However, despite the brilliance of many of these studies, the concept of myth has remained rather vague and ambiguous. Perhaps, one might say that myth has itself become mythical for the twentieth century. Because of this vagueness, I have chosen to deal with story patterns largely in terms of what I feel to be the more precise concept of formulas. I will largely use the term myth as a convenient designation of the many levels of subsidiary patterns which can be discerned as elements of a particular formula.

6. Archetype — a mythical pattern which can be discerned in many different cultures.

7. Formula — an embodiment of archetypal story patterns in terms of specific cultural symbols, themes, and myths.

8. Genres — There is bound to be a good deal of confusion about the terms formula and genre since they are occasionally used to designate the same thing. For example, many film scholars and critics use the term popular genre to denote literary types like the western or the detective story which are clearly the same thing that I have called formulas. On the other hand, the term is often used to describe the broadest sort of literary type such as drama, prose fiction, lyric poetry, etc. This is clearly a very different sort of classification from that of western, detective story, spy story, etc. Still another usage of genre involves concepts like tragedy, comedy, romance, and satire. Insofar as concepts of genre refer to particular sorts of story patterns and effects, they do bear some resemblance to the kind of classification involved in the definition of popular genres. However, when such conceptions clearly imply universal or trans-cultural conceptions of literary structure, they are examples of what I have called archetypes. I don't think it makes a great deal of

difference whether we refer to something as a formula or as a popular genre, if we are clear as to what we are talking about and why. In the interests of such clarification let me offer one distinction which I have found useful.

In defining literary classes, it seems to me that we commonly have two related but distinguishable purposes. First of all, we may be interested simply in constructing effective generalizations about large groups of literary works for the purpose of tracing historical trends or relating literary production to other cultural patterns. In such cases we are not primarily interested in the artistic qualities of individual works, but in the degree to which particular works share common characteristics which may be indicative of important cultural tendencies. On the other hand, we use literary classes as a means of defining and evaluating the unique qualities of individual works. In such instances, we tend to think of genres not simply as generalized descriptions of a number of individual works, but as a set of artistic limitations and potentials. With such a conception in mind, we can measure the quality of individual works in at least two different ways: 1) By the way in which they fulfill or fail to fulfill the ideal potentials inherent in the genre and thereby achieve or fail to achieve the full artistic effect of that particular type of construction. These are the terms in which Aristotle treats tragedy. 2) By the way in which the individual work deviates from the flat standard of the genre to accomplish some unique individual expression or effect. Popular genres are often treated in this fashion, as when a critic shows how a particular western transcends the limitations of the genre or how a particular film director, working within the limitations of popular genres, nonetheless achieves a distinctive individual statement. This is the approach implicit in much *auteur* criticism of the movies, where the personal qualities of individual directors are measured against some conception of the standard characteristics of popular genres.

The concept of a formula as I have defined it is a means

of generalizing the characteristics of large groups of individual works from certain combinations of cultural materials and archetypal story patterns. It is useful primarily as a means of making historical and cultural inferences about the collective fantasies shared by large groups of people, and of identifying differences in these fantasies from one culture or one period to another. However, when we turn from the cultural or historical use of the concept of formula to a consideration of the artistic limitations and possibilities of particular formulaic patterns, we are treating these formulas as a basis for aesthetic judgments of various sorts. In these cases, we might say that our generalized definition of a formula has become a conception of a genre. Thus, formula and genre might be best understood not as terms denoting two different things, but as reflecting two phases or aspects of a complex process of literary analysis. This way of looking at the relation between formula and genre is borne out by the way in which popular genres develop. In most cases, a formulaic pattern will be in existence for a considerable period of time before it is conceived of by its creators and audience as a genre. For example, the western formula was already clearly defined in the nineteenth century, yet it was probably well into the twentieth century before the western was consciously conceived of as a distinctive literary and cinematic genre. Similarly, though Poe created the formula for the detective story in the 1840s and there were many stories and novels which made some use of this pattern throughout the later nineteenth century, it was probably not until after Conan Doyle that the detective story became widely understood as a specific genre with its own special limitations and potentialities. There are even instances where genres are conceived only retrospectively after the formulaic patterns have largely ceased to be popular. This is the case with the film genre referred to by recent critics as *film noir*. I'm not sure that what is called *film noir* actually constitutes a genre, but if we assume for the moment that it does, then it is a generic conception which is distinctly the creation of later critics.

If we conceive of genre as a conception of literary classes which views certain typical patterns in relation to their artistic limitations and potentials, it will help us in making a further useful clarification. Because the conception of genre involves an aesthetic approach to literary structures, it can be conceived either in terms of a specific formula of a particular culture or in relation to larger, more universal literary archetypes: there are times when we might wish to evaluate a particular western in relation to other westerns. In this case we would be using a conception of a formula-genre, or what is sometimes more vaguely called a popular genre. However, we might also wish to relate this same western to some more universal generic conception such as tragedy or romance. Here we would be employing an archetype-genre.

These, then, are some major terms which can be employed in the study of formulaic literature. As I have indicated, I hold no special brief for this particular terminology, but I do believe that the implied distinctions between the descriptive and the aesthetic modes of generalization and between the cultural and universal conceptions of types of stories are crucial, and must be understood in the way we use whatever terms we choose for this sort of analysis. I will now deal with what can be said in a general way about the cultural analysis of formulaic structures.

Formulas and Culture

Formulas are cultural products and in turn presumably have some sort of influence on culture because through many repetitions they become the conventional way of representing and relating certain images, symbols, themes, and myths. The process through which formulas develop, change, and are superseded by other formulas is a kind of cultural evolution with survival through audience selection.

Many different sorts of stories are written about a great diversity of subjects, but only a few become clearly established as formulas. For instance, out of the vast potential of story possibilities associated with the rise of urban industrialism in the nineteenth century, only a very few major formulaic structures have developed, such as the detective story, the gangster saga, the doctor drama, and various science-fiction formulas. Other story types have been re-peated often enough to become partly formulaic, such as the story of the newspaper reporter and the scoop, or the story of the failure of success as represented in the figure of the great tycoon; but these two types have never had the widespread appeal of the western, the detective story, or the gangster saga. Still other potential story topics have never become popular at all. There is no formula for the story of the union leader — despite the best efforts of "proletarian" critics and novelists in the 1930s. There is no formula with a political leader as protagonist though he is a figure of major importance on the urban scene. In formula stories he plays at most an important minor role in the gangster saga. Farmers, businessmen, engineers, architects, teachers, have all been treated in a number of individual novels, but have never become central figures in a major formulaic structure.

What is the basis on which this process of cultural selection of formulas takes place? Why do some sorts of stories become widely popular formulas while others do not? How do we account for the pattern of change within formulas, or why one story formula supersedes another in popularity? What does popularity itself mean? Can we infer from the popularity of a work that it reflects public attitudes and motives or is it impossible to go beyond the circular observation that a story is successful with the public because the public finds it a good story?

First of all, we can distinguish, I think, between the problem of the popularity of an individual work and the popularity of a formula. Determining why a particular novel or film becomes a best-seller is especially problematic because it is difficult to be sure what elements or combination of elements the public is responding to. For example, in the case of the enormously successful novel *The Godfather* is it the topic of crime and the portrayal of violence that made the book popular? Probably not, since there are many other novels dealing with crime in a violent way that have not been equally successful. Thus, it must be something about the way in which crime and violence are treated. Only if we can find other books or films which treat the topic of crime in a

similar way and also gain a considerable measure of popularity can we feel some confidence that we have come closer
to isolating the aspects of *The Godfather* which are responsible for its public success. Clearly, we can only explain the
success of individual works by means of analogy and
comparison with other successful works, through the process
of defining those elements or patterns which are common to
a number of best-sellers.

A formula is one such pattern. Thus, when we have
successfully defined a formula we have isolated at least one
basis for the popularity of a large number of works. Of
course, some formulaic writers are more successful than
others and their unique popularity remains a problem that
must be explored in its own right. During his heyday, Mickey
Spillane's hard-boiled detective stories sold far better than
those of any other writer in the formula, and Spillane's
success was certainly one main reason why other writers
continued to create this type of story. Yet quite apart from
Spillane's own personal popularity, the hard-boiled detective
formula in the hands of writers as diverse as Dashiell
Hammett, Raymond Chandler, Carter Brown, Shell Scott,
Brett Halliday, and many others, in hard-boiled detective
films by directors like Howard Hawks, John Huston, and
Donald Siegel, and in TV series like *Cannon, Mannix,* and
Barnaby Jones, has been continually successful with the
public since the late 1920s. When it becomes such a widely
successful formula, a story pattern clearly has some special
appeal and significance to many people in the culture. It
becomes a matter of cultural behavior which calls for
explanation along with other cultural patterns.

Unfortunately, to construct such an explanation requires
us to have some notion of the relation between literature and
other aspects of culture, and this remains an awfully murky
area. Are literary works to be treated primarily as causes or
symptoms of other modes of behavior? Do they have any
relation to other kinds of behavior at all, or is literature an
integral and autonomous area of human experience without
significant effects on political, economic, or other forms of
social behavior? Do works of literature become popular

primarily because they contain a good story artistically told or because they embody values and attitudes which their audience wishes to see affirmed? Or does popularity imply some kind of psychological wish-fulfillment, the most popular works being those which most effectively help people to identify imaginatively with actions they would like to perform, but cannot, in the ordinary course of events? These and many other assumptions have influenced the way in which different scholars have treated the cultural significance of literature. We certainly do not know at present which, if any, of these assumptions about the cultural significance of literature is correct. Persuasive arguments can be made for each one. Before attempting to develop a tentative theory to explore the cultural meaning of literary formulas, let us look briefly at what can be said for and against some of the principal approaches that have been used to explore the relation between literature and other aspects of human behavior.

Three main approaches have been widely applied to explain the cultural functions or significance of literature. These may be loosely characterized as 1) impact or effect theories; 2) deterministic theories; and 3) symbolic or reflective theories.

1) Impact theories are the oldest, simplest, and most widespread way in which men have defined the cultural significance of literature. Such theories assume basically that literary forms and/or contents have some direct influence on human behavior. Naturally, the tendency of this approach is to treat literature as a moral or political problem and to be interested in determining what literary patterns have desirable effects on human conduct and which have bad effects, in order to support the former and suppress or censor the latter. Socrates suggests in *The Republic* that it may be necessary to escort the poet to the gates of the city since his works stimulate weakening and corrupting emotions in his audience. Over the centuries, men of varying religious and political commitments have followed this advice, seeking to censor various kinds of literary expression on the ground that they would corrupt the people's morals or subvert the state.

Today, many psychologists are seeking to determine what kind of effect the representation of violence has on the behavior of children. Presumably, if they are able to demonstrate some connection between represented violence and aggressive behavior, the widespread clamor against film and television violence will increase and laws will be passed regulating the content of these media.

The impact approach also dominated mass communications research in its earlier years, when sociologists were primarily interested in propaganda and its impact. Propaganda research sought to show just how and in what ways a literary message could have an effect on attitudes and behavior and it discovered, for the most part, that insofar as any effect could be isolated, propaganda simply caused people to believe and act in ways they were already predisposed towards. It became evident to most researchers in this area that their original quest for a direct link between communication and behavior oversimplified a more complex social process. Much of the more interesting recent research has tended to focus on the process of communication rather than its impact, showing the ways in which mass communications are mediated by the social groups to which the recipient belongs, or by the different uses to which communications are put. However, the more complex our view of the process of communication becomes, the less meaningful it is to speak of it in terms of cause and effect.

Another basic weakness of impact theories is that they tend to treat literary or artistic experience like any other kind of experience. Since most of our experience does have an immediate and direct effect on our behavior, however trivial, the impact theorists assume that the same must be true of literature. The difficulty with this view is that our experience of literature is not like any other form of behavior because it is an experience not of reality but of something imagined and created. Reading about something is obviously not the same thing as doing it. Nor are the very strong emotions generated in us by stories identical with those emotions in real life. A story about a monster can arouse fear and horror in me, but this is certainly a different emotion from the one I feel when confronted by some actual danger or threat, because I know that the monster exists only in the world of the story and cannot actually harm me. This does not mean that my emotion will necessarily be less strong than it would be in reality. Paradoxically, feelings experienced through literature may sometimes be stronger and deeper than those aroused by analogous life situations. For instance, I am inclined to believe that the fear and pity evoked by literature is likely to be stronger for most people than that generated in any real life circumstance. That literature can give us such intensified emotions may be one of the reasons we need stories. However, no matter how strong the feeling aroused by a work of literature, we do not generally confuse it with reality, and therefore it does not affect us as such. There are probably some important exceptions to this generalization. Unsophisticated or disturbed people do apparently sometimes confuse art and reality. Many people treat characters in a soap opera as if they were real people, sending them gifts on their birthdays, grieving when they are in difficulties, asking their advice and help. Some of this behavior is simply an unsophisticated way of expressing one's great pleasure and interest in a story, but some of it may well indicate that a person has lost the capacity to make our ordinary differentiation between imagination and reality. On such people, literature may well have a direct and immediate behavioral impact. I suspect that this is particularly the case among relatively disturbed children. Not surprisingly, it is here that recent studies may indicate a causal connection between represented violence and violent behavior. However, for most people in most situations, the impact approach assumes much too simple a relationship between literature and other behavior to provide a satisfactory basis for interpreting the cultural significance of any literary phenomenon.

If such reflections lead us to question the idea that literature has a direct causal effect on behavior, this does not mean that we must take the position that literature causes nothing and is only a reflection of reality without further consequence than the evocation of some temporary state of feeling. Such a view seems just as implausible as the notion that art directly and immediately changes attitudes and behavior. One of my colleagues has often remarked that all of us carry a collection of story plots around in our heads and that we tend to see and shape life according to these plots. Something like this seems to me to be the basic kernel of truth in the impact theory. Our artistic experiences over a period of time work on the structure of our imaginations and feelings and thereby have long-term effects on the way in which we understand and respond to reality. Unfortunately, no one has ever managed to define and demonstrate the existence of such long-term effects in any convincing way, in part because we have never been able to define with any precision just what are the most common and wide-spread patterns of literary experience. The analysis of formulas may be a promising method of beginning to study long-term effects, for formulas do shape the greater part of the literary experiences of a culture. If we can clearly define all the major formulas of a particular culture, we will at least know what patterns are being widely experienced. It may then be possible to construct empirical studies of the relation between these formulas and the attitudes and values which individuals and groups manifest in other forms of behavior. David McClelland and his associates managed to isolate a pattern of action in stories which they correlated with a basic cultural motive for achievement. In cross-cultural studies reported in *The Achieving Society*, McClelland suggests that the presence of this pattern of action in the stories of a particular culture or period is correlated with a definite emphasis on achievement in that culture or in a succeeding period. Some of the cases McClelland cites could be instances where the stories heard most often by children did have a long-term impact on their behavior as adults; it is, of course, difficult to determine the extent to which these story patterns were causes or symptoms, but this, I feel, is a problem that can never be solved. Insofar as we can establish correlations between literary patterns and other forms of behavior, we will have done all we can expect to do by way of establishing the long-term impact of literature. The reason for this can be best understood by turning to the second major approach that has bene employed to explain the cultural significance of literature: the various theories of social or psychological determinism.

2) Deterministic theories. These approaches — the most striking being various applications of Marxian or Freudian ideas to the explanation of literature—assume that art is essentially a contingent and dependent form of behavior which is generated and shaped by some underlying social or psychological dynamic. In effect, literature becomes a kind of stratagem to cope with the needs of a social group or of the psyche. These needs become the determinants of literary expression, and the process of explanation consists in showing how literary forms and contents are derived from these other processes.

The deterministic approach has been widely applied to the interpretation of all sorts of literature with interesting if controversial results, ranging from the Oedipal interpretation of *Hamlet* to interpretations of the novel as a literary reflection of the bourgeois world-view. When used in conjunction with individual masterpieces, the deterministic approach has been widely rejected and criticized by literary scholars and historians for its tendencies toward over-simplification and reductionism. However, the method has gained much wider acceptance as a means of dealing with formulaic structures like the western, the detective story, and the formula romance. Thus some scholars see the whole range of formulaic literature as an opiate for the masses, a ruling-class stratagem for keeping the majority of the people content with a daily ration of pleasant distractions. Others have interpreted particular formulas in deterministic terms: thus the detective story is seen as a dramatization of the ideology of bourgeois rationalism or as an expression of the psychological need to resolve in fantasy the repressed childhood memories of the primal scene.

All such explanations have two fundamental weaknesses. 1) They depend on the *a priori* assumption that a particular social or psychological dynamic is the basic cause of all kinds of human behavior. If it is the case that, for example,

unresolved childhood sexual conflicts are the basic cause of
most forms of adult behavior, then it doesn't really explain
anything to show that the reading of detective stories is an
instance of such behavior. The interpretation does not
explain anything beyond the original assumption, except to
show how the form of the detective story can be interpreted
in this way, and the only means of proving that the form of
the detective story should be interpreted in this way is
through the original assumption. Because of this circular
relationship between assumption and interpretation, neither
can provide proof for the other. That the detective story has
a certain form does not prove the original assumption about
how it should be interpreted, and the original assumption
does not prove that the form should be interpreted in a
particular way unless the assumption can be demonstrated by
other means. However, even then, there remains the problem
of showing that the experience of literature is the same as
other kinds of human activity. 2) This brings us to the second
weakness of most deterministic approaches: their tendency
to reduce literary experience to other forms of behavior. For
example, most Freudian interpretations treat literary experience as if it could be completely analogized with free
association or dream. Even if we grant that psychoanalysis
has proved to be a successful approach to the explanation of
dream symbolism, it does not follow that literature is the
same or even analogous. Indeed, there seems to me to be as
much reason to believe that the making and enjoying of art
works is an autonomous mode of experience as there is to
assume it is dependent or contingent or a mere reflection of
other more basic social or psychological processes. Certainly
many people act as if watching television, going to the
movies, or reading a book were one of the prime ends of life
rather than a means to something else. There are even
statistics which might suggest that people spend far more
time telling and enjoying stories than they do in sexual
activity. Of course, the psychological determinist would
claim that listening to a story is in fact a form of sexual
behavior, though stated in this way, the claim seems extreme.
    Though there are many problems connected with the

psychoanalytic interpretation of literature, it is difficult to dismiss altogether the compelling idea that in literature as in dreams unconscious or latent impulses find some disguised form of expression. One senses that this is particularly true of formula stories as distinguished from mimetic literature. Formula stories may well be one important way in which the individuals in a culture act out unconscious or repressed needs, or express in a disguised symbolic fashion latent motives which they must give expression to, but cannot face openly. Perhaps one important distinction between the mimetic and escapist impulses in literature is that mimetic literature tends toward the bringing of latent or hidden motives into the light of consciousness while escapist literature tends to construct new disguises or to confirm existing defenses against the confrontation of latent desires. Such a view might be substantiated by the comparison between Sophocles's play *Oedipus the King* and a detective story. In Sophocles's play the process of detection leads to a revelation of hidden guilts in the life of the protagonist, while in the detective story the inquirer-protagonist and the hidden guilt are conveniently split into two separate characters — the detective and the criminal — thereby enabling us to imagine terrible crimes without also having to recognize our own hidden impulses toward them. Unfortunately, it is easy to generate a great deal of pseudopsychoanalytic theorizing of this sort without being able to substantiate it convincingly. Nevertheless, I think we cannot ignore the possibility that this is one important factor that underlies the appeal of literary formulas.

Thus, though we may feel that most contemporary deterministic approaches oversimplify the significance of literary works by explaining them in terms of other modes of experience, I think we cannot deny that stories, like other forms of behavior, are determined in some fashion. Though artistic experience may have an autonomy which present theories of social and psychological determinism are not sufficiently complex to allow for, I presume that, as human behavior in general is more fully understood, we will also be better able to generalize about how social and psychological factors play a role in the process by which stories and other imaginative forms are created and enjoyed. In the present state of our knowledge, it seems more reasonable to treat social and psychological factors not as single determinant causes of literary expression, but as elements in a complex process which limits in various ways the complete autonomy of art. In making cultural interpretations of literary patterns, we should consider them not as simple reflections of social ideologies or psychological needs, but as instances of a relatively autonomous mode of behavior which is involved in a complex dialectic with other aspects of human life. If, on the basis of convincing historical or social evidence, we are persuaded that a particular group is characterized by certain basic attitudes, it is reasonable to see these attitudes entering into the artistic works created and enjoyed by that group as one kind of limit on what is likely to be represented in a story and how it is likely to be treated. If it appears that these attitudes are rejected or not dealt with in a particular work, then it would be wise to consider whether a) we have misinterpreted the work, b) we are dealing with an individual creation that transcends the prevailing attitudes, or c) we are encountering early signs of a large-scale change in attitude. What we must avoid is an automatic reading into a story of what we take to be the prevailing cultural attitudes, or psychological needs. This has been too often the path taken by the deterministic approach and in its circularity it tells us nothing about either the literary work or the culture.

3) Symbol, Myth and Formula. A third approach to the cultural explanation of literary experience reacts against the more extreme forms of reductive determinism by granting a special kind of autonomy to artistic expression. According to this approach, the work of art consists of a complex of symbols or myths which are imaginative orderings of experience. These symbols or myths are defined as images or patterns of images charged with a complex of feeling and meaning, and they become, therefore, modes of perception as well as simple reflections of reality. According to this approach, symbols and myths are means by which a culture expresses the complex of feelings, values, and ideas it

attaches to a thing or idea. Because of their power of ordering feelings and attitudes, symbols and myths shape the perceptions and motivations of those who share them. The flag is a relatively simple example of a symbol. Though nothing but a piece of cloth made in a certain pattern of colors and shapes, the flag has come to imply an attitude of love and dedication to the service of one's country that has even, in many instances, motivated individuals literally to die in an attempt to protect the piece of cloth from desecration. In recent years this symbol has in turn become a counter-symbol for some groups of an unreasoning and destructive patriotism, and this implication has motivated other individuals to risk danger and even imprisonment to desecrate the piece of cloth. The first use of the flag illustrates one class of symbolism which poses relatively few problems of analysis and interpretation since the meaning of the symbol is more or less established by some specific enactment, in this case laws designating a specific design as the national emblem. In this sense the flag, like other symbols of this sort, has an official status with a specifically designated set of meanings. This is indicated by the fact that it is against the law to treat the flag in certain ways. The second use of the flag as counter-symbol of regressive or false patriotism is of a different sort altogether. This symbolism was not created by specific enactment and has no official status. It emerged as one means of focusing and representing the animosity of certain groups toward actions and attitudes being taken in the name of the country and defended by traditional claims of patriotism. I don't know whether it is possible to determine who first conceived of using the flag as a symbol of this sort, but it is clear that throughout the 1960s, particularly in connection with the agitation against the Vietnam War, this new symbolism of the flag became a powerful force generating strong feelings and even violent actions both in support of and in opposition to this new form of symbolism.

These two types of symbolism indicate the great significance which symbols have for culture and psychology. In fact, the concept of symbolism seems to resolve some of the problems we have noted in connection with the impact and deterministic approaches to explaining the cultural significance of literary experience, for the symbolism of the flag suggests how it is possible for an image both to reflect culture and to have some role in shaping it. Not surprisingly, some of the most influential studies of American culture in the past two decades have been analyses of symbols and myths primarily as these are expressed in various forms of literature. However, there remain a number of problems about this approach, many of which have been effectively articulated in a critique of the myth-symbol approach by Bruce Kuklick in his essay "Myth and Symbol in American Studies" in the October 1972 issue of *American Quarterly*. Kuklick defines two kinds of objections: the first concerns certain confusions in the theoretical formulations of the leading myth-symbol interpreters, while the second involves a number of problems of definition and method. Since the formula approach which I am using in this study is essentially a variation of the myth-symbol method of interpretation, I feel we must examine the most important of Mr. Kuklick's objections to it.

Essentially, Kuklick argues that certain theoretical confusions in the myth-symbol approach prevent it from being a meaningful way of connecting literary expression with other forms of behavior. He points out that the myth-symbol critics assume the existence of a collective mind (in which the images, myths, and symbols exist) which is separated from an external reality (of which the images and symbols are some form of mental transmutation). This separation is necessary, he suggests, in order for the interpreter to determine which images are real and which are fantastic, or distortions, or value-laden. Unfortunately, this separation of internal mind from external reality leads the method right into the philosophical trap of the mind-body problem, as exemplified in what Kuklick calls crude Cartesiansim. The result is as follows:

> A crude Cartesian has two options. First, he can maintain his dualism but then must give up any talk about the external world. How can he know that any image refers to the external world? Once he stipulates that they are on different planes, it is impossible to bring them into any

meaningful relation; in fact, it is not even clear what a relationship could conceivably be like. Descartes resorted to the pineal gland as the source and agent of mind-body interaction, but this does not appear to be an out for the [myth-symbol interpreters]. Second, the Cartesian can assimilate what we normally take to be facts about the external world – for example, my seeing the man on the corner – to entities like images, symbols and myths. ... Facts and images both become states of consciousness. If the Cartesian does this, he is committed to a form of idealism. Of course, this maneuver will never be open to ... Marxists, but it also provides problems for the [myth-symbol interpreters] : they have no immediate way of determining which states of consciousness are "imaginative" or "fantastic" or "distorted" or even "value-laden" for there is no standard to which the varying states of consciousness may be referred. In either of these two options some resort to Platonism is not strange. A world of suprapersonal ideas which we all share and which we may use to order our experiences is a reasonable supposition under the circumstances. But this position, although by no means absurd, is not one to which we wish to be driven if we are setting out a straightforward theory to explain past American behavior. (p. 438)

According to Kuklick, the only solution to this dilemma is to give up the idea of using symbols and myths to explain all kinds of behavior. Instead, it is reasonable to postulate mental constructs like images and symbols only as a means of describing a disposition to write in a certain way. In other words, a symbol or a myth is simply a generalizing concept for summarizing certain recurrent patterns in writing and other forms of expression. Insofar as it explains anything, the myth-symbol approach simply indicates that a group of people has a tendency to express itself in patterns:

Suppose we define an idea not as some entity existing "in the mind" but as a disposition to behave in a certain way under appropriate circumstances. Similarly, to say that an author has a particular image of the man on the corner (or uses the man on the corner as a symbol) is to say that in appropriate parts of his work, he writes of a man on the corner in a certain way. When he simply writes of the man to refer to him, let's say, as the chap wearing the blue coat, we can speak of the image of the man, although the use of "image" seems to obfuscate matters. If the man is glorified in poem and song as Lincolnesque, we might speak of the author as using the man as a symbol, and here the word "symbol" seems entirely appropriate. For images and symbols to become collective is simply for certain kinds of writing (or painting) to occur with relative frequency in the work of many authors. (p. 440)

I think we must accept Mr. Kuklick's contention that insofar as the myth-symbol approach depends upon our making a direct connection between literary symbols and other forms of behavior, such as specific political or social actions, it is highly questionable. In fact, this is simply a more sophisticated form of impact theory. To explain the American course of action in Vietnam as the effect of the American myth of the redeemer nation, or to say that the shoot-out in the western symbolized the Korean war, is to indulge in speculations about causal connections which can never be demonstrated or substantiated, and which probably assume an oversimplified view of the relations between art and other kinds of experience. However, to take the further step of insisting that the myths and symbols found in written (and other forms of expressive) behavior can only be understood as a generalization about that specific kind of behavior seems contradictory to experience, for we can all think of many ways in which our lives have been shaped by the symbolic or mythical patterns we have encountered in various forms of literature. The problem is to arrive at some better and more complex understanding of the way in which literature interacts with other aspects of life, for I think we can grant, with one possible exception (i.e., those forms of literature with a clearly didactic or rhetorical purpose), that written symbols do not have a direct and immediate causal effect on other forms of behavior. Otherwise the impact approach to interpreting the cultural significance of literature would long since have proved more fruitful.

As we have seen, all imaginative works contain some mixture of conventions and inventions, and I think that we can assume that this mixture reflects two basic cultural functions performed by imaginative literature. Conventions represent familiar shared images and meanings and they assert an ongoing continuity of values; inventions confront us with a new perception or meaning which we have not realized before. Both of these functions are important to culture. Conventions help maintain a culture's stability while inventions help it respond to changing circumstances and provide new information about the world. The same thing is true on the individual level. If the individual does not encounter a large number of conventionalized experiences and situations, the strain on his sense of continuity and identity will lead to great tensions and even to neurotic breakdowns. On the other hand, without new information about his world, the individual will be increasingly unable to cope with it and will withdraw behind a barrier of conventions as some people withdraw from life into compulsive reading of detective stories.

The dialectic between culture and imaginative inventions is a very complex and difficult one and I have no intention of trying to deal with it here. In part, the difficulty arises because of the unique quality of such inventions. Therefore each case requires a separate treatment and is very difficult to generalize, except through the use of such problematic summarizing conventions as symbol and myth. Fortunately, I am concerned here with only the more conventional forms of imaginative literature. Here, I think it is possible to arrive at a tentative general theory about the cultural significance of this type of story which can aid us in making specific cultural interpretations of particular patterns.

The basic assumption of this theory is that conventional story patterns work because they bring into an effective conventional order a large variety of existing cultural and artistic interests and concerns. This approach is different from traditional forms of social or psychological determinism in that it rejects the concept of a single fundamental social or psychological dynamic in favor of viewing the appeal of a conventional literary pattern as the result of its bringing into play a variety of cultural, artistic, and psychological interests. Successful story patterns like the western persist, according to this view, not because they embody some particular ideology or psychological dynamic, but because they maximize a great many such dynamics. Thus, in analyzing the cultural significance of such a pattern, we cannot expect to arrive at a single key interpretation. Instead, we must show how a large number of interests and concerns are brought into an effective order or unity. One important way of looking at this process is through the dialectic of cultural and artistic interests. In order to create an effective story, certain archetypal patterns are essential, the nature of which can be determined by looking at many different sorts of stories.

However, these story patterns must be embodied in specific images, themes, and symbols which are current in particular cultures and periods. To explain the way in which cultural imagery and conventional story patterns are fitted together constitutes a partial interpretation of the cultural significance of these formulaic combinations. This process of interpretation reveals both certain basic concerns that dominate a particular culture and also something about the way in which that culture is predisposed to order or deal with those concerns. We must remember, however, that since artistic experience has a certain degree of autonomy from other forms of behavior, we must always distinguish between the way symbols are ordered in stories and the way they may be ordered in other forms of behavior. To this extent, I think Kuklick is correct in suggesting that the existence of symbols and myths in art cannot be taken as a demonstration that these symbols are somehow directly related to other forms of behavior and belief. Yet there are certainly cultural limits on the way in which symbols can be manipulated for artistic purposes. Thus, our examination of the dialectic between artistic forms and cultural materials should reveal something about the way in which people in a given culture are predisposed to think about their lives, and thus, should provide us with useful hypotheses about motivation which can be explored in relation to other forms of behavior.

As an example of the complex relationship between literary symbols and attitudes and beliefs which motivate other forms of behavior, we might look at the role of political and social ideologies in the spy story. Because of its setting, the spy story almost inevitably brings political or social attitudes into play since conflicting political forces are an indispensible background for the antagonism between the spy-hero and his enemy. Thus, in the espionage adventures written by John Buchan and other popular writers of the period between World Wars I and II — "Sapper," Dornford Yates, E. Phillips Oppenheim and Saxe Rohmer, for instance — one dominant theme is that of the threat of racial subversion. The British empire and its white, Christian civilization are constantly in danger of subversion by villains who represent other races or racial mixtures. Saxe Rohmer's Fu Manchu and his hordes of little yellow and brown conspirators against the safety and purity of English society are only an extreme example of the pervasive racial symbolism of this period. It is tempting to interpret these stories as reflections of a virulent racism on the part of the British and American publics. There is no doubt some truth in this hypothesis, especially since we can find all kinds of other evidence which reveals the power of racist assumptions in the political attitudes and actions of these publics. Yet few readers who enjoyed the works of Buchan and Rohmer were actually motivated to embark on racist crusades, and it was in Germany rather than England and America that racism became a dominant political dogma. Even in Buchan's case, many of the attitudes expressed in his novels are far more extreme than those we find in his non-fiction and autobiographical works, or in his public life and statements. It is a little difficult to know just what to make of this. Was Buchan concealing his more extreme racist views behind the moderate stance of a politician? Or is the racial symbolism in his novels less a reflection of his actual views than a means of intensifying and dramatizing conflicts? Umberto Eco in a brilliant essay on the narrative structure of the James Bond novels suggests that something like this may well be the case with Ian Fleming's "racism":

> Fleming intends, with the cynicism of the disillusioned, to build an effective narrative apparatus. To do so he decides to rely upon the most secure and universal principles, and puts into play archetypal elements which are precisely those that have proved successful in traditional tales. . . . [Therefore] Fleming is a racialist in the sense that any artist is one, if, to represent the devil, he depicts him with oblique eyes; in the sense that a nurse is one who, wishing to frighten children with the bogey-man, suggest that he is black . . . . Fleming seeks elementary opposition: to personify primitive and universal forces he has recourse to popular opinion. . . . A man who chooses to write in this way is neither Fascist nor racialist; he is only a cynic, a deviser of tales for general consumption. (*The Bond Affair* [London: Macdonald, Co., 1966], pp. 59-60.)

As in the case of Fleming, many of the apparently ideological attitudes in Buchan may arise more from dramatic than propagandistic aims. Therefore we must exercise some caution in our inferences about the social and political views which the author and audience of such stories actually believe in. Most audiences would appear to be capable of temporarily tolerating a wide range of political and social ideologies for the sake of enjoying a good yarn. As Raymond Durgnat has suggested by his article "Spies and Ideologies" in *Cinema* magazine for March 1969, recent spy films with ideological implications ranging from reactionary to liberal have been highly successful. Or to take a different example of the same sort of phenomenon, a number of recent black detective films and westerns, which portray whites as predominantly evil, corrupt, or helpless, have been quite successful with substantial segments of the white as well as black publics.

But even if we grant that the melodramatic imperatives of formula stories tend to call forth more extreme expressions of political and moral values than either author or audience fully believes in, there still remains a need for author and audience to share certain basic feelings about the world. If this sharing does not occur at some fundamental level, the audience's enjoyment of the story will be impeded by its inability to accept the structure of probability, to feel the appropriate emotional responses, and to be fascinated by the primary interests on which the author depends. Thus, an audience can enjoy two different stories which imply quite different political and social ideologies, and even to some extent moral values, so long as certain fundamental attitudes are involved. Durgnat puts the point rather well in explaining why the same public might enjoy *Our Man Flint*, a spy film with very conservative political overtones, and *The Silencers*, which is far more liberal in its ideology:

> The political overtones of the movies appear only if you extrapolate from the personal sphere to the political, which most audiences don't. The distinct moral patterns would be more likely to become conscious, although neither film pushed itself to a crunch. In other words, the two moral patterns can coexist; both films can be enjoyed by the same spectator, could have been written by the same writer. Both exploit the same network of assumptions. (p. 8)

This "network of assumptions" is probably an expression, first, of the basic values of a culture, and on another level, of the dominant moods and concerns of a particular era, or of a particular subculture. That Buchan is still enjoyed with pleasure by some contemporary readers indicates that there are enough continuities between British culture at the time of World War I and the present day to make it possible for some persons to reconstruct Buchan's system of probabilities and values. That Buchan is no longer widely popular, however, is presumably an indication that much of the network of assumptions on which his stories rest is no longer shared.

These considerations suggest the importance of differentiating literary imperatives from the expression of cultural attitudes. In order to define the basic network of assumptions which is a reflection of cultural values we cannot simply take individual symbols and myths at their face value, but must uncover those basic patterns which recur in many different individual works and even in many different formulas. If we can isolate those patterns of symbol and theme which appear in a number of different formulas popular in a certain period, we will be on firmer ground in making a cultural interpretation, since those patterns characteristic of a number of different formulas presumably reflect basic concerns and valuations which influence the way people of a particular period prefer to fantasize. In addition, the concept of formula as a synthesis of cultural symbols, themes, and myths with more universal story archetypes should help us to see where a literary pattern has been shaped by the needs of a particular archetyped story form, and to differentiate this from those elements which are expressions of the network of assumptions of a particular culture. Thus the spy story as a formula which depends on the archetype of heroic adventure requires a basic antagonism between hero and villain. The specific symbols or ideological themes used to dramatize this antagonism reflect the network of assumptions of a particular culture at a particular time. However, the creation of a truly intense antagonism may well involve pushing some of these cultural assumptions to extremes which would not be accepted by most people in areas of life other than fantasy.

Most of Mr. Kuklick's other criticisms of the myth-symbol approach come down to an attack on the way in which myths and symbols have been defined and interpreted. He argues that most myth-symbol interpreters have defined the central myths of the American past in terms of concerns of the present and argues that they have thereby committed the historical fallacy of "presentism." He also points out that they have based their analysis almost entirely on printed literary materials that can be said to relate to only a minority of the population. Indeed, some scholars have based their interpretations on a small number of masterpieces which, despite the argument that great writers have a unique capacity to articulate central cultural myths, cannot really be said to reflect more than the interests and attitudes of the elite audiences who read them. Whether or not these criticisms apply to some of the myth-symbol interpreters, and I must confess that they do in a number of instances, I think that they are largely obviated by the method of formula analysis. First of all, a formula is by definition a pattern characteristic of the widest possible range of literature and other media. Therefore it does not involve drawing cultural inferences from a few select masterpieces in a medium that does not cover the entire culture. The major formulas are basic structural patterns in mass media like the movies and television as well as in printed literature. Therefore, they are understood and enjoyed by the great majority of the population at one time or another. In addition, while the concept of a symbol or myth is vague enough that it can be interpreted in many different ways, the study of formulas has a built-in defense against presentism for it forces us not just to explain the meaning of a single symbol or myth, but to account for the relationship between many different myths and symbols. In doing this, I feel we are inevitably forced to come closer to the original intention. While it may well be possible for us to treat the symbolic figure of Cooper's Leatherstocking in such a way as to lose track of the original meaning he had for Cooper, I think that if we insist upon reading about Leatherstocking in the context of all the various characters and situations that

Cooper places him in, and then comparing this with other later embodiments of the western formula, we will certainly find it far more difficult to misread Leatherstocking's original meaning for Cooper. The analysis of a formula always involves us in the exploration of a literary whole, while themes, symbols, or myths are usually only parts of larger patterns. To select a theme or symbol out of a larger whole invariably has an arbitrary aspect that the analysis of formulas avoids.

To understand more fully the relation between artistic and cultural interests involved in the creation of formulas, we need to know more about the range of cultural functions which formulas fulfill. I think we can assume that formulas become collective cultural products because they successfully articulate a pattern of fantasy which is at least acceptable to if not preferred by the cultural groups who enjoy them. Thus, formulas enable the members of a group to share the same fantasies. Literary patterns which do not perform this function do not become formulas. When a group's attitudes undergo some change, new formulas arise and existing formulas develop new themes and symbols. Because formula stories are created and distributed almost entirely in terms of commercial exploitation, if a particular formula loses its popularity with its audience, the producers will soon turn to experimenting with new formulas or with changes in existing formulas until they discover one that sells. Therefore, allowing for a certain degree of inertia in the process, the production of formulas is largely dependent on audience response. Existing formulas commonly evolve in response to new audience interests. A good example of this process is the recent success with urban audiences of a new kind of black-oriented action-adventure film. The great majority of these new black films are simply versions of traditional formulas like the western, the hard-boiled detective story, and the gangster saga with an urban black setting and protagonists. These formulas enable the new black self-consciousness to find expression in conventional forms of fantasy which are not significantly different in their assumptions and value structures from the sort of adventure stories

which have been enjoyed by American audiences for several
decades. The new black cowboy or gangster or detective hero
is the same basic hero type in the same kind of action. Thus,
in this case, the evolution of formulas has assimilated black
needs for some sort of distinctive artistic expression into the
shapes of conventional fantasies. It would appear, then, that
the basic cultural impetus of formulaic literature is toward
the maintenance of conventional patterns of imaginative
expression. Indeed, the very fact that a formula is an
often-repeated narrative or dramatic pattern implies the
function of cultural stability. Formulaic evolution and
change are one process by which new interests and values can
be assimilated into conventional imaginative structures. This
sort of process is probably of particular importance in a
discontinuous, pluralistic culture like that of modern industrial societies. Therefore, literary formulas tend to flourish in such societies.

I would like to suggest four interrelated hypotheses about
the dialectic between formulaic literature and the culture
which produces and uses it:

1) Formula stories affirm existing interests and attitudes
   by presenting an imaginary world that is aligned with
   these interests and attitudes. Thus westerns and
   hard-boiled detective stories affirm the view that true
   justice depends on the individual rather than the law
   by showing the helplessness and inefficiency of the
   machinery of the law when confronted with evil and
   lawless men. By confirming existing definitions of the
   world, literary formulas help to maintain a culture's
   ongoing consensus about the nature of reality and
   morality. We assume, therefore, that one aspect of
   the structure of a formula is this process of confirming some strongly held conventional view.

2) Formulas resolve tensions and ambiguities resulting
   from the conflicting interests of different groups
   within the culture or from ambiguous attitudes
   toward particular values. The action of a formula
   story will tend to move from an expression of tension

of this sort to a harmonization of these conflicts. To use the example of the western again, the action of legitimated violence not only affirms the ideology of individualism, but also resolves tensions between the anarchy of individualistic impulses and the communal ideals of law and order by making the individual's violent action a defense of the community against the threat of anarchy.

3) Formulas enable the audience to explore in fantasy the boundary between the permitted and the forbidden and to experience in a carefully controlled way the possibility of stepping across this boundary. This seems to be preeminently the function of villains in formulaic structures: to express, explore, and finally to reject those actions which are forbidden, but which, because of certain other cultural patterns, are strongly tempting. For example, nineteenth century American culture generally treated racial mixtures as taboo, particularly between whites, orientals, blacks and Indians. There were even deep feelings against intermarriage between certain white groups. Yet at the same time, there were many things which made such mixtures strongly tempting, not least the universal pleasure of forbidden fruits. Thus we find a number of formulaic structures in which the villain embodies explicitly or implicitly the threat of racial mixture. Another favorite kind of villain, the grasping tycoon, suggests the temptation actually acceded to by many Americans to take forbidden and illicit routes to wealth. Certainly the twentieth century American interest in the gangster suggests a similar temptation. Formula stories permit the individual to indulge his curiosity about these actions without endangering the cultural patterns which reject them.

4) Finally, literary formulas assist in the process of assimilating changes in values to traditional imaginative constructs. I have already given the example of the new black action films as an instance of this process. The western has undergone almost a reversal

in values over the past fifty years with respect to the representation of Indians and pioneers, but much of the basic structure of the formula and its imaginative vision of the meaning of the West has remained substantially unchanged. By their capacity to assimilate new meanings like this, literary formulas ease the transition between older and new ways of expressing things and thus contribute to cultural continuity.

This analysis of the major ways in which literary formulas relate to the processes of culture is necessarily speculative. However, it does provide us with some explanatory hypotheses which can be tested both in the analysis of formulaic literature and in investigations of the ways in which creators and audiences relate to these formulas. I think we can further assume that the more successful and persistent a formula is, the more it has been able to accomplish in some unified way the various cultural functions I have outlined. Thus, in interpreting the patterns of a formula, we must discover how a particular synthesis of archeptypal narrative structures with cultural themes and symbols makes possible the accomplishment of a range of artistic and cultural functions. In other words, we must treat the various formulaic structures as means of ordering into a unified imaginative experience a complex of artistic and cultural interests. Of course, for the moment, we cannot completely demonstrate or substantiate interpretations based on speculative theory of artistic and cultural functions; but even if we had more complete "empirical" information about the psychology of artistic experience, that would in turn be based on some general theory or paradigm of explanation. Lacking precise demonstration, the test of the value of a theory is a) whether it seems true to human experience as we know it, and b) whether it provides a means of accounting for the different elements in the phenomenon under study. Thus the real test of this approach will be in the specific analyses it produces. However, in addition to isolated analyses of particular formulas, the method does allow for a number of comparisons between different formulas and different cul-

tural contexts which can, I think, provide further sub-
stantiation for the cultural interpretations we ascribe to
individual formulas:

1. The comparison of basic story patterns with the
    cultural symbols and myths embodied in those
    patterns can show us the various ways in which
    groups choose to understand and value certain
    symbolic characters and actions. These modes of
    valuation and perception *may* be reflected in other
    forms of behavior. If so, these ways of setting
    symbols and myths into stories probably reflect basic
    attitudes of the groups that create and enjoy the
    formula.

2. We can determine what the most popular formulas
    are for a particular group, and thereby generate
    hypotheses about the range and variety of a group's
    imaginative concerns. Formulas used by one group
    can be compared with those used by others; for
    instance, formulas primarily used by men with those
    catering to women.

3. We can compare the different formulas used by a
    particular group in order to discover patterns which
    are present in more than one formula. If a symbol or
    theme appears in a number of the formulas used in a
    particular culture or period, this should indicate some
    interest, concern, or attitude of unusual importance.

4. The way in which different cultures or periods make
    use of the same basic formula can be compared; for
    instance, French detective stories can be compared to
    those of England, or the westerns of 1900 compared
    with those of 1970. Significant changes in the
    valuations or relations ascribed to elements in the
    formula probably indicate significant differences in
    attitudes and values.

5. We can analyze the way in which the same basic
    cultural symbolism or mythology is used in a variety
    of formulas; as, for example, the symbolism of crime
    as used in such different formulas as the gangster

story, the classical detective story, the hard-boiled detective story, and the crime caper story. The presence of different formulas centering on the same mythology probably suggests a variety of attitudes toward that set of phenomena; the growth and decline of different formulas involving the same symbols suggests shifts in attitude toward the social phenomenon.

6. We can trace the evolution of a particular formula over a substantial period of time. Shifts in emphasis, valuation of symbolic characters, plot types, and themes probably express changes in attitude and motive on the part of the formula's public.

No doubt there are other ways in which the comparative analysis of formulas and of the inner relations within formulas may generate hypotheses about the interests, concerns, and values of the groups which create and enjoy various types of formulaic literature. These problems should be enough to keep us busy for a while, particularly if we supplement our tentative analysis of the formulas with the necessary testing of our hypotheses in relation to other forms of behavior, and with the necessary studies to establish with greater precision just which groups use which formulas in which circumstances.

I would not wish to claim that in the method of formula analysis we have described there lies the ultimate key for interpreting either literature or culture. Clearly it is a useful method for defining collective literary patterns, and it may help to shed more light on the problem of widely shared public attitudes and how and why the change. In addition, the exploration of formulas may give us some additional insight into the complex nature of the psychology of art, the principles underlying the way in which people respond to imaginative experiences, and how this relates to the rest of their lives. The possibility of gaining even a little knowledge of these matters surely justifies the method.

BIBLIOGRAPHICAL NOTE

The study of popular formulas derives from the age-old tradition of the study of literary genres. It is not certain whether Aristotle invented this conception, but his *Poetics* was surely a basic formulation of this approach to literary analysis, which has never been superseded. The student of modern literary formulas can do no better by way of clarifying his approach to the definition of literary types than by familiarizing himself with this fundamental theoretical work. Aristotle has been often commented on throughout the ages; some idea of the scope and variety of the tradition of generic criticism can be gleaned from the anthology *Critics and Criticism*, edited by R. S. Crane (Chicago: University of Chicago Press, 1952). A recent attempt to apply and expand the Aristotelian conception of genre can be found in the work of Elder Olson, especially *Tragedy and the Theory of Drama* (Detroit: Wayne State University Press, 1961) and *The Theory of Comedy* (Bloomington: Indiana University Press, 1968).

The method of analysis proposed in this paper has also been strongly influenced by the tradition of mythical and archetypal analysis which springs especially from Frazer's *The Golden Bough*, further developed by the psychoanalyst Carl Jung and by contemporary post-Jungian scholars like Mircea Eliade and Joseph Campbell. For a compelling application of this mode of thought to literary analysis see the work of Northrop Frye, especially the section on "Archetypal Criticism: Theory of Myths" from *Anatomy of Criticism* (Princeton, N. J.: Princeton University Press, 1957). Though I find myself largely persuaded by Frye's general approach to the treatment of archetypes, I have found it necessary to define a different set of archetypes to deal adequately with the problem of popular literature. A tentative attempt in this direction can be found in my essay "Notes toward a Typology of Literary Formulas" in *Indiana Social Studies Quarterly*, 26 (Winter 1973-74), 21-34.

The analysis of American culture through the study of its

dominant myths and symbols has been a major preoccu-
pation of American studies for at least two decades, from
Henry Nash Smith's brilliant and profoundly influential
Virgin Land (Cambridge, Mass.: Harvard University Press,
1950) to Richard Slotkin's recent study *Regeneration Through
Violence* (Middletown, Conn.: Wesleyan University Press,
1973). Other useful works in this tradition are R.W.B. Lewis,
The American Adam (Chicago: University of Chicago Press,
1965), Ernest Tuveson, *The Redeemer Nation* (Chicago:
University of Chicago Press, 1968), Leslie Fiedler, *Love and
Death in the American Novel* (New York: Criterion Books,
1960) and *The Return of the Vanishing American* (New
York: Stein and Day, 1968), Edwin Fussell, *Frontier:
American Literature and the American West* (Princeton, N.
J.: Princeton University Press, 1968), John Ward, *Andrew
Jackson: Symbol For an Age* (New York: Oxford University
Press, 1955), John Cawelti, *Apostles of the Self-Made Man*
(Chicago: University of Chicago Press, 1965), Irvin Wyllie,
The Self-Made Man in America (New Brunswick, N.J.:
Rutgers University Press, 1954), and Cords and Gerster, *Myth
and the American Experience* (New York: Glencoe Press,
1972).

Mass communications research has added greatly to our
culture, though this research sometimes seems to me to be
based on questionable assumptions about the relation be-
tween artistic experiences and other forms of behavior. A
useful sampling of this research can be consulted in the two
Rosenberg and White anthologies, *Mass Culture* (Glencoe,
Ill.: The Free Press, 1957) and *Mass Culture Revisited* (New
York: Litton Educational Publishing, 1971). Cf. also Joseph
Klapper, *The Effects of Mass Communication* (Glencoe, Ill.;
The Free Press, 1961), Erik Barnouw, *Mass Communication*
(New York: Rinehart, 1957), and Harold Mendelsohn, *Mass
Entertainment* (New Haven, Conn.: College and University
Press, 1966).

For analyses of popular genres and formulas from various
points of view, the following works are recommended: Russel
B. Nye, *The Unembarrassed Muse* (New York: The Dial Press,
1970), a remarkable general history of the popular arts with a

very useful annotated bibliography; Reuel Denney, *The Astonished Muse* (Chicago: University of Chicago Press, 1957), a pioneering analysis of popular culture by a sociologist; Robert Warshow, *The Immediate Experience* (Garden City, N.Y.: Doubleday, 1964), a collection of essays by a remarkably perceptive literary critic which includes basic analyses of the two major popular genres of the western and the gangster film; Carl Bode, *The Anatomy of American Popular Culture, 1840-1860* (Berkeley: University of California Press, 1960), a study of the popular arts in a particular period; James D. Hart, *The Popular Book* (New York: Oxford University Press, 1950), a study of major types of best-selling books over the course of American history; John Cawelti, *The Six-Gun Mystique* (Bowling Green, Ohio: Bowling Green University Press, 1970), a theoretical treatment of popular formulas using the western as an example. The reader should also turn to a new work on popular film genres by Stuart Kaminsky, *American Film Genres* (Dayton, Ohio: Pflaum-Standard, 1974).

Individual popular formulas have received increasing attention in the last decade. A few of the important works in this area are:

1. The Detective Story

Jacques Barzun and Wendell Taylor, *A Catalog of Crime* (New York: Harper and Row, 1971), and O. A. Hagen, *Who Done It?* (New York: R. R. Bowker, 1969). Two massive bibliographies of detective literature including secondary books and articles. Barzun and Taylor is extensively annotated.

Howard Haycraft, ed., *The Art of the Mystery Story* (New York: Simon and Schuster, 1946), and F. M. Nevins, Jr., *The Mystery Writer's Art* (Bowling Green, Ohio: Bowling Green University Popular Press, 1970). Two excellent anthologies of essays on the detective story, including a number of important practitioners of the genre.

Howard Haycraft, *Murder for Pleasure* (New York: Appleton-Century, 1941), Julian Symons, *Mortal Con-*

sequences (New York: Harper and Row, 1972), Colin Watson, *Snobbery with Violence* (London: Eyre and Spottiswoode, 1971), and Boileau-Narcejac, *Le Roman Policier* (Paris: Payot, 1964). Important general histories of the detective story genre.

2. *The Thriller*

Ralph Harper, *The World of the Thriller* (Cleveland: Case-Western Reserve University, 1969). A philosophical analysis of the thriller formula.

Brian Davis, *The Thriller* (New York: E. P. Dutton, 1973). A discussion of the thriller as a genre of film.

Kingsley Amis, *The James Bond Dossier* (New York: New American Library, 1965). A brilliant study of one of the major contemporary thriller creations, Ian Fleming's saga of James Bond. The reader should also watch for the forthcoming work on the thriller by George Grella.

3. *The Western*

George Fenin and William Everson, *The Western: From Silents to Cinerama* (New York: Orion Press, 1962), Jean-Louis Rieupeyrout, *La Grande Adventure du Western* (Paris: Editions du Cerf, 1964), Jim Kitses, *Horizons West* (Bloomington: Indiana University Press, 1969). Three major studies of the film western. For further bibliography in this area the reader should consult Cawelti, *The Six-Gun Mystique*, and Jack Nachbar, "A Checklist of Published Materials on the Western Film," *Journal of Popular Film*, 2 (Fall 1973), 411-28.

4. *Science-Fiction*

Kingsley Amis, *New Maps of Hell* (New York: Harcourt Brace, 1960). A very personal but insightful study of science-fiction.

Samuel Moscowitz, *Explorers of the Infinite* (Cleveland: World Publishing Co., 1963) and *Seekers of Tomorrow* (Cleveland: World Publishing Co., 1966). The closest thing to a thorough history of science-fiction.

Robert Plank, *The Emotional Significance of Imaginary Beings* (Springfield, III.: Thomas, 1968). A brilliant study of some of the psychological factors underlying the popularity of science-fiction.

Thomas Clareson, ed., *SF: The Other Side of Realism* (Bowling Green, Ohio: Bowling Green University Popular Press, 1971). The best anthology of critical essays on science-fiction.

CHAPTER 9

National Development and Ethnic Poetics: The Function of Literature In the Liberation Of Peoples

By Jay Martin

JAY MARTIN is a pioneer in the application of comparativist approaches to the study of American culture. A former director of undergraduate American Studies at Yale University, he oversaw the creation of the Comparative Cultures Program at the University of California, Irvine, where he is currently Research Critic of American Literature and Language. He has been President of the Southern California American Studies Association, a member of the ASA Executive Council, and a Guggenheim Fellow. Among his writings are *Conrad Aiken: A Life of His Art* (1962), *Harvests of Change: American Literature 1865-1914* (1967), *Nathanael West: The Art of His Life* (1970), *Robert Lowell* (1970), and *A Singer in the Dawn: Reinterpretations of Paul Laurence Dunbar* (1975). Professor Martin's biography of Henry Miller will appear in 1976. As a Rockefeller Foundation Fellow during 1975-76, he is at work on a volume of literary history, *Into the Teeth of Dragons: American Literature 1900-1950.*

Comparing American literary nationalism to the "Ethnic Poetics" of Black America and a revolutionary Latin American culture, Professor Martin argues the thesis that national aesthetics develop in the gap between political and economic independence.

219

Asked by Hoyt Fuller in January of 1969, "Do you see any future at all for the school of black writers which seeks to establish a black aesthetic?"—the great black critic Saunders Redding answered succinctly: "No. Not in America. Besides, aesthetics has no racial, national or geographic boundaries. Beauty and truth, the principal components of aesthetics, are universal." [1] Many would agree with Redding, who has also argued that black culture, including its literature, must be studied in the context of American civilization. Certainly, such later nineteenth-century black writers as Dunbar and Chesnutt complained not that white Americans judged them by non-black aesthetics, but that they drew a color line *against* them. More recently, the black writers of the Harlem Renaissance and of the 1930s—from Arna Bontemps through Richard Wright — were likely to strive to seek (as Wright put it) "unity with all the progressive ideas of our day," [2] in *avant garde* writing or in revolutionary politics. Ishmael Reed, as recently as 1970, has urged critics to treat black writing as a rich vein *in* the Western tradition. [3]

It is difficult to disagree with all of these authoritative men; yet there is no denying, I believe, that in the last three or four years a well-defined black aesthetic has emerged, which not only has a "future," but a series of parallels in the past, and also a clear cultural function. It also has a group of spokesmen, an organ, and an editor. Adumbrated first in symposia in Hoyt Fuller's *Negro Digest* (later, *Black World*), the critical approaches to the black aesthetic were organized into Addison Gayle's 1971 volume, which offers a program both for the production and the judgment of literature. Though it is true that some of the critics printed in this volume deny that the black aesthetic can be talked about at all (for instance, Don L. Lee: "The Black Aesthetic cannot be defined in any definite way" [4]), most of the critics in Gayle's book tend to choose sides and to propose oppositions from which a composite picture of a black aesthetic program does emerge. Perhaps, for the sake of clarity, one should really call what is being proposed here a "poetics" rather than an "aesthetics"—since it combines a view of the function of life with a sense of the nature of art, but in deference to Gayle's title, I will keep to the word "aesthetics" in the discussion that follows.

The crucial battle line is drawn by Hoyt Fuller's statement of "the doctrine of revolution to which so many of the brighter black intellectuals are committed, that philosophy articulated by the late Frantz Fanon which holds that, in the time of revolutionary struggle, the traditional Western ideals are not merely irrelevant, they must be assiduously opposed." [5] Larry Neal puts this most boldly: "It is the opinion of many black writers, I among them, that the western aesthetic has run its course; it is impossible to construct anything meaningful within its decaying structure"—and he proposes, alternately, that black writers turn toward "the usable elements of Third World Culture." [6] From these remarks flows the series of associations, assertions, and oppositions which comprise the Black Aesthetic:

Against		For	
1.	The West, European Nations, Colonizers	1.	The Third World, The Colonized
2.	America	2.	Africa
3.	Past, Tradition	3.	Present, Change
4.	Established Myths, Symbols, etc.	4.	"New Myths"
5.	Cultural Universals, Common Humanity	5.	Environmental Uniqueness of Black experience, Pluralism
6.	The Individual	6.	The Community
7.	The "Elite"	7.	The People
8.	Pure poetry, beauty	8.	"Applied" poetry, functionality
9.	Negative Protest, Reform	9.	Anger and Affirmation, Revolution
10.	White sterility	10.	Black fertility
11.	Separation of Art and Politics	11.	Connection between Art and Politics
12.	A Vision of Racial Cooperation	12.	A Vision of Separate Nation Building

In general, we have suggested here a vivid contrast between states of cultural health. On the most playful level the contrast is sexual, an inversion of the old racist accusation that blacks are more naturally sensual than whites—an accusation which, in this post-D. H. Lawrence age, can be turned into an argument that sexual power is a sign of

moral purity and intellectual health. Writers like Neal and
John Killens like to blast Updike and Salinger and the "crop
of literary nit pickers . . . without testicles." [7] More seriously,
as Gayle puts it, the "black artist of today is at war with the
American society," and looks forward to what Gerald
McWorter calls a "post American future." [8] He will be
revolutionary in a number of ways, then—artistically, he will
be bent on "destroying those images and myths that have
crippled and degraded black people, and [on instituting] . . .
new images and myths that will liberate them"—and he will
also play a political role. [9] With missionary clarity Ron
Karenga has set forth the connections between art, the black
community, and black cultural nationalism. Art, he has said,
"is not sufficient. What completes the picture is the social
criteria for judging art. . . . For all art must reflect and
support the Black Revolution, and any art that does not
discuss and contribute to the revolution is invalid. . . . Black
art must expose the enemy, praise the people and support the
Revolution." As a corollary, individuality must also be
repudiated. Karenga is very clear about this: "We say that
individualism is a luxury that we cannot afford." It is merely
"useless isolation" from the community which each man
must serve. Literature must be applied, which is to say that it
must have an immediate and predictible social use; this is
what Ameer Baraka desires in demanding poems that kill,
that "wrassle cops into alleys, taking their weapons, leaving
them dead, with tongues pulled out and sent to Ireland." [10]

What is the function and goal of the Black Aesthetic?—
criticism should ask, rather than asking how defensible this
one or that of its tenets may be. I regard them all as
defensible, and from a certain point of view—I have in mind
the phenomenological—as true. Anthony F. C. Wallace has
shown in *Culture and Personality* that no single personality
contains all the responses or shows all the ranges of
assumption which describe the whole culture. No two
personalities are identical, as no two life experiences can be.
Very likely, the difference between one individual and
another is greater than the difference between classes,
families, or subsocieties. The individual is the only

ineluctably unique entity in society, yet there are numerous commonalities in experience. Certainly, race is likely to play an important part in the acquisition of experience since race has been in America one of the social determinants of behavior. This is only to say that an ethnic subsociety is one of the predictable categories for association and for experiential commonality, and anyone who reflects on the squabbles of families even over fundamental issues will recognize several truths at once—of which three are basic: Each person must have a different experience and therefore a slightly different set of moral, social, and political perceptions. Nothing can alter this fact. Nonetheless, civilization has been created through mental devices making the leap from experience to knowledge. On the family level, these devices are summed up in the word *love*; on the ethnic, by the word *community*; on the social, economic, and political by *empathy, class, status, arbitration,* and *negotiation*; on the regional level by designations like *New Yorker* or *Hoosier*; and on the national by *citizen*; and so forth.

Such terms, it is clear, describe nothing actual—rather, they recommend that we think of our unique responses as part of a *class* of responses. They are part of a phenomenology which holds our world together. The assertion of black uniqueness and the Black Aesthetic which flows from it is the same device: it recommends, and emphasizes, an alternate phenomenology—a way of looking at the world, a mode of surviving in it. "Every Negro baby in America is born . . .," Cecil Brown has very perceptively said, "into a world of white values, and if he is to survive that world, he has to *achieve* blackness."[11] The doctrines of the Black Aesthetic provide a means by which blackness may be achieved. They are fundamentally assertions that hitherto black men and women have sought identities—which is to say, have described their commonalities with others—in contexts which have denied validity to their personal dignity, and they insist that alternate contexts are better suited to the achievement of self-understanding and self-regard. "Third-World," "African," "New Myth," "Black Revolution," "Community," "Black is Beautiful," "Black Fertility," and finally, "Uniqueness of the Black Experience"—these are all phrases designed to propose a way of understanding experience and thus one's own place and status in it. The first function of the Black Aesthetic, then, is psychological; it does not describe anything actual, it recommends an actuality: blackness, a sense of personal worth judged on its own terms instead of through white values. It is not appropriate, for this reason, to ask what status in being the claims of the Black Aesthetic have, but, what are the functions and uses of such claims, phenomenologically considered?

It is, I have said, first of all psychological, forming the context for the five stages of identity formation which Charles Thomas describes in *Boys No More*, and which William Cross and others have discussed. [12] I will assume that the psychological benefits are obvious and that Thomas's arguments are familiar and, in general, unarguable. Let me just give, in brief, Thomas's model. Prior to the black-identity movement, blacks, he argues, were endangered by a confusion of self-worth due to dependency on white social values for self-definition. He then describes five stages of psychic development. The *first* is *withdrawal* from non-black society and social values; *second, testifying* to (and so objectifying) the pain endured in denials of one's own personal worth; the *third* he calls the stage of *information processing* of the dignity of the black cultural heritage; the *fourth* is *activity*, in which a person works through a group to find links to a larger black experience: *finally*, in the *transcendent* stage one loses his hangups about race, age, sex, and class and renegotiates his relationships with other racial and ethnic groups. The stages of identity formation described by Cross, though differing in terminology, are very similar: Pre-encounter, Encounter, Immersion, and Internalization. It is clear that the first function of the Black Aesthetic, then, is to provide justifications for *withdrawal*, opportunities for *testifying, commentary* on the greatness of the black heritage, and reasons for *activity*, as well as a visible group of intellectual activists.

The primary psychological benefits are perfectly obvious,

then, when the Black Aesthetic provides an organized, identifiable and articulated body of material whose distinct aids in identity formation are evident. So I will pass on to speak of what I regard as the final goal of the Black Aesthetic—which is, I believe, economic rather than psychic; or, more precisely, uses a psychological perspective as an instrument in achieving economic viability. In what follows I will describe the purpose of such an aesthetic as an instrument of national development. To the Black Aesthetic I will compare, *first*, the "American Aesthetic" (or "Poetic") which had a powerful influence on life in the United States during the period, roughly, from 1776 to the mid-1840s; and *second*, the "Americanidad Aesthetic" whose influence on the life of Latin Americans began in the 1830s and continues to the present day.

The history and purpose of a nationalist aesthetics is clear. It originates when a formerly colonized people begin to achieve political equality with their former oppressors. Its function resembles magical thinking—it is to persuade the newly liberated group that the former oppressor is decadent and powerless and that the new nation has replaced the old on the historic stage— that a new race of men has appeared to redeem the world. It is, in short, an expression of the new nation's sense of its own value while it is still vulnerable. Its function ends when the nation is no longer vulnerable—that is, when it achieves economic independence from its colonizer, and the colonized move from stress upon (to use Max Weber's terms) "status," or *ethnos*, to stress upon "class," the *ethos* of economic association groups.[13] In the case of the republic of the United States, national aesthetics became influential at the time of the Revolution and continued until economic independence was achieved in the mid-1840s. In the case of Latin America, the Americanidad Aesthetics began, similarly, with political revolt. However, as economic independence from Spain, France, and Portugal became foreseeable, North America made Latin America dependent on Northern economic development. Thus, since the goal of economic independence has been only partially achieved, the assertion of a nationalist aesthetics in Latin

America has not only continued with the same urgency, it has also tended more to stress all that stands counter to economic life—the mystique of the inner man, of soul and spirit. We must see the Black Aesthetic in this context of a nationalist aesthetics. Beginning with some faint stirrings in the 1930s but really originating with the political advances of the civil rights movement of the 1960s when political equity was achieved in the courts, the Black Aesthetic is now at a stage of development comparable to that of American Aesthetics around 1800. It will remain an ideological force in America until the Black man achieves economic independence. At that point it will have served its purpose and will disappear—though not before permanently influencing American life and letters. If, on the other hand, economic equity is made impossible, we can expect Black ideology to stress "race memory," "soul," and a variety of doctrines of outer unintelligibility. National aesthetics exist in the gap between political and economic independence, and continue as long as the gap does. So much for my thesis. Let us look at the process in operation.[14]

The American Aesthetic was decidedly defensive. Cultivated Britons, after all, Hugh Henry Brackenridge wailed in 1779 in the *United States Magazine*, were likely to imply that Americans were "so many Ouran-Outans of the woods" in cultural matters. Well into the 30s (and even the 40s), debate in England raged over whether an American literary culture could exist since so few institutions of culture could be found "in these woods." When Americans could find the (in James's phrase) "elements of high civilization" only in England, how, Britons mocked, could Americans write an *American* literature? As the poet Eaglesfield Smith complained, the "son of Columbia" who attempted "to cultivate a natively poetical soul" met jeers "on every side."

The task of American criticism, then, became the designation of the elements of experience which gave Americans a perspective on reality different from that of Europeans. Little by little these were named—the American landscape, the influence of American ideas, the impact of the lusty "barbarism and materialism" (Emerson's phrase) of

Americans, the freedom of the American mind; these and other features of American life were offered as requiring the production, based on an American Aesthetic, of a literature different from that of Europe. Beginning in the late eighteenth century, a large number of magazines were founded to sponsor American literature—whatever that might be. Their first issue, the editors of the *Boston Magazine* claimed in 1783, had one-third of its contents written by Americans. Mathew Carey, one of the most influential American editors, founded the *American Museum* with the expressed intention of aiding the cause of American letters. "American publications," he declared, "shall always meet a preference" in the pages of his journal. By 1891 the *Massachusetts Magazine* claimed that "a decided majority of our present magazine is at least American." It was not long before Americans started to anthologize themselves, since they were commonly ignored by British editors. An issue of Carey's *American Museum* contained a selection of poets under the heading of the "Columbian Parnassiad." But with Elihu Smith's *American Poems* (1793), *The Columbia Muse* (1794), and Caleb Bingham's *The Columbian Orator* (1797), the business of publishing distinctive American collections began. It would not be long, then, before Americans would refuse to wait upon the judgment of the *Edinburgh Review*, but would review their own works. Americans would not tolerate, as T. G. Fessenden said, a condition in which "Columbian genius lies, prostrated, / Because its fairest fruit are rated / By hearts of flint and heads of block." The climax to these critical thrusts came in 1814 with the founding of the *North American Review*, whose avowed purpose was "to foster American genius," and, by independent criticism, to instruct and guide the public taste.

But from what did American distinctiveness derive? The American landscape provided an early answer. David Humphreys observed no "piles of rubbish" such as "ruin'd statues" or "crumbling" walls and arches to deface the grandeur of the American scene; those wrecks of "high civilization" were fortunately absent. Perhaps, alternately, Americanness resided more largely in the ability of

Americans to "examine things on the plan of nature and
evidence, and laugh at the grey-bearded decisions of doting
authority," as one who called himself "The Friend" urged in
the *American Museum* for 1789. This view, that American
uniqueness was located in the distinctive ideas held by
Americans, was generally preferred. What were these ideas?
There were various answers. American ideas being the
product of youth, Noah Webster argued in 1783, it "would
be to stamp the wrinkles of decrepit age upon the bloom of
youth," or to attempt to erect "a durable and stately edifice
... upon mouldering pillars of antiquity," to oblige
Americans to follow the hoary traditions of Europe, which
had "grown old in folly, corruption and tyranny." Thus, as
Judith Murray told her readers in *The Gleaner* (1798),
Americans must "radically throw off every foreign yoke."
This included non-American literature. Joel Barlow went so
far as to declare *The Iliad* a "serious misfortune to the human
race in a view of philanthropy." Convinced that traditional
ideas had "degraded the species in other countries," he urged
his fellow Americans to write a poetry based on the
American love of liberty, so "that true and useful ideas of
glory may be implanted in the minds of men." Thus urged,
writers set out to comply. "Hail Columbia," its author,
Francis Hopkinson, admitted, was written "to get up an
American Spirit. . . . It was truly American and nothing else."
Most propagandists of the theory that "American ideas" were
the distinctive feature of this new culture argued that
Americans were reasonable—but most, too, specifically
denied that Americans were rationalistic. Somehow, Americans were judged to move between the irrationality of
authority and the pagan rationalism of the Deists, Hume, and
Voltaire; their science and morals were based on "God's own
work," as Timothy Dwight told his students at Yale. More
inclined to define American thought by its relation to the
frontier, Timothy Flint saw the American as "more ardent,
quicker in movement, more misled by his imagination, more
figurative and impassioned in his diction," than the Briton. In
either case, Americans expressed genius, "spirit," the "flood
tide of the soul" (Alcott), or "passion, enthusiasm and

impulse" (Simms).

In due course, a rather clear set of aesthetic principles began to emerge, along with a sense of what Americans opposed:

Against	For
The Old World, the Colonizers	The New World, the Colonized
Europe	America
The Past, Tradition	The Present
Corruption, sterility, decadence	Vitality, potency, power
Hierarchies	Individuals
Authority and Tradition	Liberty and Change
Deism	God's Design
Aristocracies and Elites	Masses, the "People"
English language	American speech
Belief in Universals	Belief in National Experience
Classical Mythology	Native Themes & Symbols
The Past	The Future
Separation of Literature & Politics	An "America . . . as independent in literature as she is in politics" (Noah Webster).
The Polished	The "voice of aboriginal nations" (Emerson)

American critics were quite ready to defend their aesthetic with the same militancy that American soldiers had defended their political independence (indeed, many of the earlier theorists had fought in the Revolution), for they regarded their literary work as not only revolutionary but as a fulfillment of the impetus of the Revolution. Even Washington Irving, though he was probably the greatest stylist writing in English around 1810, announced his conviction that Americans should prefer rude native efforts over polished British works: "We would rather hear our victories celebrated in the merest doggerel that sprang from native invention, than beg, borrow or steal from others, the thoughts and words in which to express our exaltation." Irving was convinced that Americans must simply give up all contact with British literature; for, "by tasking our own powers, and relying entirely on ourselves, we shall gradually improve and rise to poetical independence." Sophisticated Britons might scorn such critical jingoism; but Americans were certain that Irving was right, and whether foreign

authors were skillful or not, their influence was judged by
William Gilmore Simms and others to be "pernicious." James
Fenimore Cooper dedicated his entire work to removing,
through literature, any "craven and dependent feeling"
toward England by portraying (and perhaps helping to
create) the "manly, independent" spirit of Americans. For
his part, Herman Melville argued that "this matter of a
national literature has come to such a pass . . . we must turn
bullies, else the day is lost, or superiority so far beyond us,
that we can hardly say it will ever be ours." He advised
America to "first praise mediocrity even, in her children,
before she praises . . . the best excellence in the children of
any other land." He himself was ready to be a bully and to
defend Richard Emmons's *The Fredoniad* against *The Iliad*.
This was nationalistic militance with a vengeance, but
Melville was left behind by John Neal who, editing *Brother
Jonathan* in 1843, called for "Authors . . . American to the
back bone—American in speech—American in feeling—
American through life, and all the changes of life—and
American, if it must be so . . . in death." Like Melville, Neal
preferred a "bad original" by an American to a "good copy"
from a foreign author. Poe, too, announced a "Declaration of
War" against English letters, the "British Yoke" or "the sin
of colonialism." Freed from colonization, true Americanism,
he said, "defends our own literature, sustains our own men of
letters, upholds our own dignity, and depends upon our own
resources." Not only Neal and Poe but also the editors of the
*Analectic, Niles' Weekly Register, The Portico, The Spirit of
the Times* and many other magazines programmatically
ignored "the higher, more refined" classes and dedicated
themselves to "the people at large, who constitute the
nation"—as Paulding saw it; or to "the unschooled classes of
people," "the deep, rich soil at the bottom of society," as
Parkman wrote. The proper language for such a literature
must catch, as Neal wrote, the speech of men as they "talk
. . . every day, in the street," avoiding the sentence "daintily
put together" and stressing the colloquial, the fresh idiom.
Americans were not persuaded by Lord Kames's classical
insistence that "general rules" and "certain inflexible laws"

"governed by principles common to all men" should prevail in literature. As the *Monthly Anthology* flatly stated in 1810, "If there be principles of taste which should be common to all nations, it is almost impossible to ascertain them." The fact was obvious. Even the young Thoreau, asked by his Harvard professor to say how a native author could be universal, replied at once: "He must look through a national glass."

By the end of the 1840s the needs which only aesthetics could once satisfy were being met by economic advance. In 1840 N. P. Willis marked the culmination of American Aesthetics by the development of Atlantic steam navigation and the increase in international trade: "In literature," he said, "we are no longer a distinct nation." When, somewhat later, Howells could speak of American literature as a "condition of English literature," the quest for an American Aesthetic was over. It is certainly true, as scholars of American literature well know, that the materials of the quest for an American poetics continued to fascinate American writers, from Whitman to William Carlos Williams; but for these writers, that was a *subject*, like the "Matter of Troy" out of which medieval writers composed their epics— though the battles were won and lost, and all the battling was long over.

The same process, very much extended, may be seen at work in the creation of the Americanidad Aesthetic of Latin America. The first explicit arguments that a national litera-ture must exist followed shortly after the first stirrings of political nationhood. Perhaps we should look to an Argentinean, Andres Bello, for the first influential announce-ment of an American literature. In 1810 he had gone to England with Bolivar on behalf of the Venezuelan patriots. In a magazine, *Biblioteca Americana*, which he edited with Juan Garcia del Rio in 1823, he printed the first of his great "silvas Americanas," *Call to Poetry*. The six-line invocation strikes at once the American note. Here, Bello calls for men to leave Europe, "land of . . . misery," and to "fly to the great scene of the world of Columbus," where "earth still wears her primitive dress."[15] Bello went hardly further than this *ufanismo*, but others inevitably did. In his preface to *Los Consuelos* of 1836, for instance, Estaban Echeverria, one of the leaders of the anti-Rosas movement, acknowledged that poetry in America enjoyed less influence than in Europe. "If it wishes to gain influence," he said, "it must have an original character of its own, reflecting the colors of the physical nature which surrounds us, and be the most elevated expression of our predominant ideas and of the sentiments and passions which spring from the shock of our social interests. Only thus, free from the bonds of all foreign influence, will our poetry come to be as sublime as the Andes, strange, beautiful and varied as the fertile earth, which produces it."[16] Following upon the initial announcements of Americanidad by Bello and Echeverria, the aesthetic unfolded in much the same manner as I have previously described with the Black and American aesthetics. It spilled out of the *Justa Literaria* between Rafael Obligado and Calixto Oyeula, which Carlos Guido y Spano judged with the comment: "The guitar is worth as much as the lyre. For a new world, new songs."[17] It emerged in the remark of the Peruvian Jose Santos Chocano in his sonnet "Blason": "I am the singer of America, aboriginal and wild"; in Ruben Dario's description of himself as "a Spaniard of America and an American of Spain," or his search for what was "poetical in the Americas" in "the old things, in Palenque and Utallan, in the legendary Indian, in the refined and sensual Inca, in the great Monteczuma of the Golden Throne";[18] in the great debate between D. F. Sarmiento and Bello and his disciples in the pages of the *Mercury* and the *Literary Weekly* on the relative merits of classicism and romanticisi.ı. It was announced decisively in 1846 at Valpariso, when Juan Maria Gutierrez published the first systematic anthology of Spanish American verse, in three volumes, with Bello's *silva* as his dedication. In Brazil it was heralded by the abolitionist Joaquin Nabuco, who told the Academy of Letters: "The truth is, that although they speak the same language, Portugal and Brazil will have, in the future, literary destinies as profoundly distinct as their national destinies. ... The formation of the Academy of Letters is an affirmation of the fact that, in literature, as in politics, we are a nation with a destiny and a character of its own—a nation that can be directed only by itself, developing its originality through its own resources and wishing only that glory which can come from its own glories." [19] In due course, his countryman the great Euclides da Cunha would seek to write, "with the rude pen of the Cabolco,"[20] an epic work about the new man—*o homen novo, el nueve indigina*—with the sense, very much like Whitman's, that a new Adam was being born in Hispanic America.

I do not intend to catalog the history of the Americanidad Aesthetic—for it passed through Rodo's *Ariel* into the *ultraista* movement—into, for instance, Borges's prefaces to his first volume of poetry, *Fervor de Buenos Aires* (1923), and his anthology of war verse, *Indice de la Nueva Poesia Americana* (1926), or into the journal which Borges co-edited: *Martin Fierro*, the name of the gaucho in Hernandez's national epic. And it is vividly present in the recent essay, "A Literature of Foundations," by Octavio Paz in *Tri-Quarterly*.[21] Why has the Americanidad Aesthetic survived instead of declining as the American Aesthetic did? The Mexican philosopher Leopoldo Zea puts the matter clearly: "As for the Spanish American, he has resigned himself to feeling inferior not only to the European but also to the American of the United States."[22] Perhaps the matter is put even more neatly in two poems by Dario. In the first, "A Roosevelt," he condemned "the colossus of the North" for its materialism:

> The United States are rich; they're powerful and great;
> They join the cult of Mammon to that of Hercules,
> And when they stir and rear, the very Andes shake . . .
> But our America, which since the ancient times
> Has had its native poets; which lives on fire and light,
> On perfumes and on love; our vast America,
> The land of Monteczuma, the Inca's mighty realm,
> Of Christopher Columbus the fair America,
> America the Spanish, the Roman Catholic,
> O men of Saxon eyes and fierce barbaric soul,
> This land still lives and dreams, still loves and stirs!
> Take care!
> The daughter of the Sun, the Spanish land doth live!

And from the Spanish lion a thousand whelps have sprung!
'Tis need, O Roosevelt, that you be God himself . . .
Before you hold us fast in your grasping iron claws.
And though you count on all, one thing is lacking,–God![23]

But in his poem of 1906, "Salutacion al Aguila," he welcomed the delegates from North America to the Pan American Congress for Economic Development in Brazil, prayed for the secret of the northern republic's political and material success and reminded it that the Eagle existed with his brother, the Condor, on lofty heights.[24] Though a Venezuelan critic declared that rather than utter such sentiments he would have cut his hand off, Dario was responding instinctively to the easing of conflict in economic advance. But, as Vasconcellos much later concluded, "the extraordinary breed to the North . . . has beaten us at every game in the material struggle," and for that reason "we cover [them] with insult."[25] For that reason, too, the aesthetics of Americanidad have increasingly emphasized the non-political, non-economic, non-practical, non-logical aspects of existence as the true centers of being. In particular, a special emphasis on race thinking and racial cliches, which Cesar Grana has analyzed, came to replace economic expectation. Condemnations of pragmatism, materialism, and bourgeois stability abound in the literature of the South. Chocano succinctly expressed the limited position which he and his fellows defended in this aphorism: "Walt Whitman has the North, but I have the South."[26]

What Spanish, Portuguese and, later, North American culture is for Americanidad Aesthetics; what English and Old World culture was for American Aesthetics; the United States is for the Black Aesthetic. In each case, nationalist aesthetics is a defense, a weapon, consisting of the creation of its political and economic oppressor in the magical terms by which the oppressor's defeat may be imagined. It suggests that the oppressor is decadent—he has power, but no internal resources. Against a vividly imagined European corruption, Americans asserted the value of the new Adamic man; against European tyranny and Yankee materialism, the Latin Americans urged the power of a "distinct race"; against

United States racism and economic discrimination, American Blacks urge the virtues of soul and racial memory, embodied in a new Third World man, unique in history and incomprehensible to non-blacks.

My subject here has precisely been the Black Aesthetic and its function at the present time. The model I have been trying to set up and to illustrate runs as follows:

1. A national aesthetics (or poetics) comes into being coincidentally with the real or potential liberation of a people from a former oppressor.
2. Its function is to strengthen the resolve and energies of the new group or nation in the pursuit of equality at all levels, on the world stage, with the former oppressor.
3. The aesthetic, then, will stress the virtues of the new group and the vices of the old in fairly predictable terms. It has elements of race supremacy and political messianism in it.
4. If economic equality is achieved, the aesthetic will lose its force as an instrument in liberation and disappear—or rather, become the "matter" or subject material for subsequent writers.
5. If economic oppression continues, then the aesthetic will, at some point, begin to alter its function and to provide a way of dismissing the importance of economic achievement by stressing the racial, personalistic and messianistic elements present from the first in nationalist aesthetics, as ends in themselves.

I wish to go on to try to make a few more points concerning the use of the methods of American Studies in the analysis of minority life. It is, after all, the fate of this most recent version of nationalist aesthetics in the United States which must concern us—which is to say, the future of economic development for the black man, and minorities in general in America; or, more generally still, for the underdeveloped peoples of the Third World. It is precisely this future which we cannot predict, but can only help to make. The question is, which phenomenology shall we will? For we

should be under no illusion about whether or not we can
choose. The two possibilities of the fate of black nationalist
aesthetics are well put in two quotations which which I shall
make toward an ending. The first is from an American
Muslim, Askia Muhammad Toure, who styles himself the
"Magi of the Black Nation." His announcement of the black
national mission imaginatively brings together elements of
biblical revelation, ecology, history, African-style chants,
community psychology, and Marxist evangelism, in one
poetic evocation:

> "Calling Mankind, calling Third World Brothers, calling
> Mankind, calling Third World Brothers, calling Mankind,
> calling Black people, calling Black people, calling Brown
> people, calling Yellow people, calling Yellow people,
> calling Third World Brothers, calling Third World Brothers:
> > The Sun Is Rising In The West!
> > The Sun Is Rising In The West!
> > The Black Nation Is Rising/The Black Nation Is Rising
> > The Black Nation in the Dead/Cracker/West is Rising
> > shaking the foundations of the Evil Cracker Empire
> > (GOG & MAGOG)!
> "We are its voices, WE are its magic singers, shamans,
> prophets, beyond this limited evil Now, we work Spiritual
> JuJu upon his twisted soul (GOG & MAGOG): singing his
> children into hippies, singing him to CANCERHEARTDISEASE
> ASHES & HONKIEDEATH.
> "We conjure up a future, reaching into our Afro-Souls,
> into the spiritual realms of our Afro-Manity, calling forth
> the blood & spiritual energies of departed Ancestors: lost
> African Souls screeeeaaaaming in Middle Passage Death, Slave-
> revolt leaders, castrated warriors, raped mothers, lynch-
> rope victims of "liberty." From our Towers in the West,
> WE invoke the Whirlwind of Revolution, causing the planet
> to shake upon its moorings. WE invoke Apocalypse to purge
> this plant of Evil & the White Lie. But beyond this,
> beyond the blood & flames of Armageddon, WE invoke new
> visions of ORIGINAL MAN/SPIRITUAL MAN/COMMUNAL MAN,
> evolved to harmony with his brothers & the Universe,
> Master of Nature, Lover of Peace. New Visions of full
> bellies/hope-filled eyes/disease-free bodies/liberated
> minds & spirits. It will be—yes! WE WILL do it here/now—
> yes! Beyond cracker-ism and white magic in the alienated-
> presentevilNOW — yes! BlackMusicMagicVision here/now — yes!
> CitiesBurningHonkies dyingEvilFading here/now—yes! WE
> WILL WIN/WE WILL WIN/WE WILL WIN/WE WILL WIN/WE WILL WIN
> WE WILL WIN/WE WILL WIN—YES! Calling Mankind, Calling
> Third World Brothers, Calling Mankind, Calling Third
> World Brothers, Calling Mankind. . . ."[27]

The second is by the eighteenth-century Brazilian poet
Castro Alvres who, better than any other poet I know, saw
very precisely the connections between political liberation,
economic assimilation, and a universalist aesthetics of human,
rather than national development:

> The world an enormous tent for all humanity,
> With space for roof, the earth itself for hearth
> Where happy dwells the universal family.
> From the African Sahara, from frozen Siberia,
> From the Caucasus, from unhappy Iberian fields,
> From the hallowed marbles of Homeric land,
> From pampas and savannas of our great,
> Our proud America, there shall burst forth
> The hymn of freedom which is labor's own!
> And with the worker's song, accompanied by
> The hammer's audacious orchestra, shall mingle
> The noise of printing presses and ideas,
> As each out of freedom forges epic poems,
> Callused the hands of all, bathing their foreheads
> In freedom's sun above the horizon breaking.[28]

The first quotation has the splendid grandeur of
apocalyptic collisions; needless to say, I prefer the latter
vision. Yet it is a vision which most black people do not yet
have the luxury to choose themselves, and however we wish
it, none of us may have it until all of us do.

It is possible, I have been trying to say, that the kinds of
methods of cultural analysis developed by the American
Studies programs and scholars in the last thirty years —
building upon the work of anthropologists, literary critics,
political scientists, historians and economists—can be used to
illuminate some of the conditions of the culture of minority
groups and of developing nations, particularly as comparative
culture analysis is called into play. A fuller analysis of my
subject, indeed, could be done and would include some
discussion of the relation of nationalist aesthetics to the
romantic movement; observations on the circumstances
under which history is novel and when the notion of
repetition in history may be misleading; a discussion of the
difference between my analysis of the political and economic
function of nationalist poetics and the arguments of
orthodox Marxist critics, such as Frantz Fanon;[29] and some

commentary on the relation of scholarship to political and social change.

Such further studies might be undertaken and they would confirm, I think, the analysis I have given, as well as expanding it in interesting directions. They would show, in any event, that literature has often had clear (and clearly felt) uses in achieving national missions. It should be clear as well that American Studies, too, has a particular mission beyond analysis, and it is precisely this: to aid in the development of the national resource of mind, to bring about the widening of consciousness in America, and to aid, therefore, in the evolution of America itself.

NOTES

1. Redding, quoted by Adam David Miller, "Some Observations on a Black Aesthetic," *The Black Aesthetic*, ed. Addison Gayle, Jr. (Garden City, N.Y.: Doubleday & Co., 1971), p. 380.

2. Wright, "Introduction: Blueprint for Negro Writing," *The Black Aesthetic*, p. 325.

3. Reed, *19 Necromancers from Now* (Garden City, N.Y.: Doubleday & Co, 1970), p. 11.

4. Lee, "Toward a Definition: Black Poetry of the Sixties (After LeRoi Jones)," *The Black Aesthetic*, p. 232.

5. Fuller, "Towards a Black Aesthetic," *The Black Aesthetic*, p. 8.

6. Neal, "The Black Arts Movement," *The Black Aesthetic*, p. 258.

7. Killens, "The Black Writer Vis-a-Vis His Country," *The Black Aesthetic*, pp. 359-60; Neal speaks of the main preoccupation of the contemporary American theatre as "sick white lives in a homosexual hell hole," in "The Black Arts Movement," p. 263.

8. Gayle, "Introduction," *The Black Aesthetic*, p. xviii; McWorter, quoted by James A. Emanuel, "Blackness Can: A Quest for Aesthetics," *The Black Aesthetic*, p. 208.

9. Fuller, "The New Black Literature: Protest or Affirmation," *The Black Aesthetic*, p. 327.

10. Karenga, "Black Cultural Nationalism," *The Black Aesthetic*, pp. 31-37; Karenga quotes Jones on p. 32.

11. Brown, quoted by James A. Emanuel, "Blackness Can: A Quest for Aesthetics," p. 187.

12. Charles W. Thomas, *Boys No More* (Beverly Hills, Calif.: Glencoe Press, 1971); William S. Hall, William E. Cross, Jr., and Roy Freedle, "Stages in the Development of Black Awareness," *Black Psychology*, ed. Reginald L. Jones (New York: Harper & Row, 1972), pp. 156-65.

13. Weber, *Economy and Society: An Outline of Interpretative Sociology*, ed. Guenther Roth and Claus Wittich, Vol. I (New York: Bedminster Press, 1968).

14. In my rapid survey I am entirely indebted to the materials in Benjamin T. Spencer's *The Quest for Nationality: An American Literary Campaign* (Syracuse: Syracuse University Press, 1957), *passim*. Unless otherwise indicated, the quotations in the following account may be found in this useful book.

15. Bello quoted in Pedro Henriquez-Urena, *Literary Currents in Hispanic America* (New York: Russell & Russell, 1963), pp. 99-100.

16. Echeverria quoted in Alfred Coester, *The Literary History of Spanish America*, 2nd ed. (New York: Macmillan, 1941), pp. 109-10.

17. Coester, *Literary History*, pp. 150-51.

18. "When I feel myself an Inca," Chocano writes, "I render homage to the Sun. . . . When I feel my Spanish blood I evoke colonial days." Quoted in Coester, *Literary History*, pp. 472-73. Dario quoted in Henriquez-Urena, *Literary Currents*, pp. 41, 171.

19. Coester, *Literary History*, pp. 198-99; Henriquez-Urena, *Literary Currents*, p. 135; and Arturo Torres-Rioseco, *New World Literature: Tradition and Revolt in Latin America*, Berkeley and Los Angeles: University of California Press, 1949), P. 107, summarize this debate.

20. Quoted in Isaac Goldberg, *Studies in Spanish-American Literature* (Port Washington, N.Y.: Kennikat Press, 1968 [1920]), p. 98.

21. *The Tri-Quarterly Anthology of Contemporary Latin American Literature* (New York: E. P. Dutton & Co., 1969), especially the conclusion: "Spanish American literature . . . is rootless and cosmopolitan, is both a return and a search for tradition. In searching for it, it invents it. But invention and discovery are not its purest creations. A desire for incarnation, a literature of foundations" (p. 8).

22. Zea, "Concerning an American Philosophy," *The Modern Mexican Essay*, ed. Jose Luis Martinez, trans. H. W. Hillborn (Toronto: University of Toronto Press, 1968 [1958]), p. 430.

23. Translated by Alfred Coester, *Literary History*, pp. 464-65.

24. The text of this poem is in Coester, *Literary History*, p. 465

25. Quoted by Cesar Grana, "Cultural Dreams and Historical Frustrations in Spanish American Literature," *Fact and Symbol: Essays in the Sociology of Art and Literature* (New York: Oxford University Press, 1971), pp. 196-97.

26. Quoted in Arturo Torres-Riosico, *The Epic of Latin American Literature* (Berkeley and Los Angeles: University of California Press, 1967 [1942]), p. 115.

27. *Natural Process: An Anthology of New Black Poetry*, ed. Ted Wilentz and Tom Weatherly (New York: Hill & Wang, 1970), pp. 141-42.

28. Quoted in John Nist, *The Modernist Movement in Brazil: A Literary Study* (Austin, Texas: University of Texas Press, 1967), p. 9.

29. The theory that a nationalist aesthetics appears coincidentally with the achievement of a political right and the promise of an economic opportunity is very clearly in opposition to the thinking of Frantz Fanon on this matter. Combining Jung's theories with Adler's assumption that all neuroses involve some sort of goal for which the neurotic is doomed unsuccessfully to strive, Fanon saw the dilemma of Caribbean blacks as psychological. "The neurotic structure of an individual," he wrote in *Black Skin, White Masks*, "is simply the elaboration, the formation, the eruption within the ego of conflictual clusters, arising in part out of the environment and in part out of the purely personal way the individual reacts to these influences", (New York: Grove Press, 1967), p. 81. The neurosis of the black man, Fanon argued, was that he could not exist in himself, but only in his impossible attempt to become white. Thus blacks collectively reinforced a cultural inferiority complex. In his speech before the Congress of Black Writers and Artists in September 1956, he continued his anatomy of colonialism. "Having judged, condemned, abandoned his cultural forms, his food habits, his sexual behavior ... the oppressed *flings himself* upon the imposed culture with the desperation of a drowning man." But the colonist will not accept him. The result is psychic retrogression: "This [precolonial] culture, abandoned, sloughed off, rejected, despised, becomes for the inferiorized an object of passionate attachment. There is a very marked kind of overvaluation. ... Having formerly emigrated from his culture, the native today explores it with ardor. It is a continual honeymoon." (This speech is reprinted in *Toward the African Revolution* [New York: Grove Press, 1969], pp. 31-44.) For Fanon, in short, the basis of the Black Aesthetics is in collective neuroses. This is not only far from the truth and the conclusions of such black psychologists as Joseph L. White and C. W. Thomas, but also damaging to a just understanding of the historical role of nationalist aesthetics. For Fanon the search for cultural identity is the endpoint of neurotic retrogression. For me it is a stage in the political and economic independence in the growth of a formerly colonized and oppressed group. Since Fanon was so clear that colonialism had an economic base, it is surprising that he let his own profession of psychiatry blind him to the economic function of nationalist aesthetics. As a revolutionary, too, he could allow himself to see nothing good in the development of a cultural nationalism.

CHAPTER 10

In Search of an
American Ethnophysics

By Jay Mechling

JAY MECHLING, Assistant Professor of American Studies at
the University of California, Davis, is one of the third
generation of whom he writes, having received all of his
degrees in American Studies (Stetson and the University of
Pennsylvania). He pays particular attention in his teaching
and writing to "problems of knowledge" in culture study,
applying his methodological inquiry to substantive problems
such as the history of the family, the history of the
behavioral sciences, and the connections between American
science and other belief systems in the culture. He is
co-author of "American Culture Studies: The Discipline and
the Curriculum" (winner of the 1973 *American Quarterly*
Award) and chairs the Bibliography Committee of the
American Studies Association. His latest project in American
Studies is a book-length treatment of The Politics Of
Boyology in the Progressive Era.

Jay Mechling inquires here whether a paradigm revolution
in the "third generation" of American Studies is about to
replace the Myth/Symbol/Image school of criticism with a
more satisfactory methodology derived from cognitive
anthropology.

American Studies is now fully into its third generation of
practitioners.* The import of this fact is not merely that
American Studies has now been around long enough to be
considered a permanent fixture in the university curriculum,
nor only that it is mature enough to have its own professional
association, its own journals, and its own drama of professional allegiances and jealousies (even feuds). Far more
important in the sociology of the American Studies community is the fact that many, perhaps most, of the third
generation — that is, those who earned American Studies
degrees as both undergraduate and graduate students in the
1960s — have never or only briefly identified themselves with
an established discipline. This generation of American Studies
graduates has joined a vocal minority in the second generation to press once again for the community to consider on
what grounds it can call itself a discipline. [1]

The unique biographical commitment to interdisciplinarity of this third generation, combined no doubt with
the simultaneous biographical fact of having been students in
American universities during the politically and intellectually
tumultuous 1960s, makes the recent call for methodological
coherence qualitatively different from previous manifestos.[2]
I do not intend here to write a sociology of the American
Studies community, though such an undertaking is tempting;
but I find that I cannot begin to write about the goal of this
essay without at least referring to some of the more salient
aspects of the American Studies community in 1974. I take
our community to be in a stage which Thomas Kuhn calls a
"transition to maturity" in paradigm revolution, a stage
during which alternative exemplars are competing for adherents. [3] Depending upon how one applies Kuhn's criteria, the
myth/symbol/image school of American Studies has been the
closest thing which the community has had to a paradigm,
and a great deal of American Studies scholarship in the 1950s
and well into the 1960s can be understood as "normal
science" under this paradigm. Thus, I recall in my own

*This is a substantially revised version of an essay presented to the Northern
California Chapter of the American Studies Association, May 1973. I wish to
thank Robert Merideth, David Wilson, Alan M. Smith, Murray G. Murphey, and
John L. Caughey for careful reading and cogent critiques of earlier drafts.

undergraduate American Studies education at Stetson University in the mid-1960s that, after reading Smith, Lewis, and Ward, [4] part of my learning "how to do American Studies" was to take the myth/symbol/image formula and apply it to a new problem. In one case, I took Ward's treatment of Jackson and used it to make sense of the cultural artifacts surrounding the career of Sergeant Alvin York.

The point of this example is not that I was "clever" (in Kuhn's sense of "the clever practitioner," I was), but that the Ward exemplar provided a clear model of (1) the sort of problem which I considered an "appropriate" American Studies problem, (2) the sorts of materials which I was to study, and (3) the theoretical vocabulary and methodological apparatus which I was to apply to those materials in order to come up with an *explanation* of verbal and non-verbal artifacts which survived from the America of a Sergeant York or an Andrew Jackson. Gradually, my American Studies education at Stetson, and later at the University of Pennsylvania, equipped me with other vocabularies and other models of explanation, all of which seemed designed to prove that the puzzles in the myth/symbol/image paradigm were really anomalies, after all. Subsequent developments in the discipline, such as the recent attacks by Bruce Kuklick and Thomas Krueger upon myth/symbol/image assumptions, appear to have completed this process. [5]

Kuhn points out that an old paradigm, no matter what its state of disarray, is never completely abandoned until an alternative is present to take its place. And this, it seems to me, is the present status of the American Studies community. Our current disarray and confusion is symptomatic of the transitional period between paradigms, a period which is made all the more confusing by a seemingly open marketplace of theories and methods. It is against this background that I wish to consider seriously one important candidate for a new paradigm for American Studies—namely, the New Ethnography, or "cognitive anthropology."

I wish to make one final observation before directly considering the New Ethnography as a possible paradigm for American Studies. The matter of the American Studies community's selection of an exemplar from among several candidates is the "how shall we do American Studies?" question, but it is not really the first question which ought to be asked. In his important "Postscript—1969" to his original argument, Kuhn wisely remedies his previously inconsistent use of the word *paradigm* and begins to talk of a community's *disciplinary matrix*, which includes not only the exemplars but the symbolic generalizations, the values, and the models which a given scientific community shares as well. The importance of the shared *values* of the community is that the practitioners share a common goal for their activity and that they agree to certain criteria by which exemplars are to be judged as consistent or inconsistent with attaining that goal. [6] Thus, the *"how* shall we do American Studies?" question must presume that the *"why* shall we do American Studies?" question has been answered already. Otherwise, we would not have criteria by which to judge competing exemplars.

I very much regret to say that we in American Studies have not yet agreed to make the goal of American Studies a problem to be debated. There are sub-groups within the American Studies community who do share values and criteria by which to judge scholarship as fulfilling the "why?" question, but these sub-groups are not communicating with one another. Rather, they are making disastrous assumptions that doing American Studies *naturally* presumes their set of values and criteria. Not only are the humanists and social scientists (to take one basic split in this interdisciplinary enterprise) persuaded by very different sorts of explanations, but surely even subsets of these two groups would differ on the sorts of explanations and generalizations about American life that would satisfy them.

I wish to warn the reader, therefore, that the remainder of this essay addresses the "how shall we do American Studies?" question without really resolving the necessarily antecedent "why?" question. At the same time, I recognize that other disciplines also have struggled with the "how?" question without consensus on the "why?"; historians, for example, can argue historical epistemology without often inquiring into the purpose and usefulness of historical knowledge. My evasive tactic, for the time being, will be to substitute a "pseudo-why?" question for the authentic one and proceed to evaluate the New Ethnography as a potential paradigm for American Studies. I shall assume for the purposes of this essay, in other words, that the goal of doing American Studies is to unmask the deep-structure rules which Americans use to give meaning to their environment and which they use to generate appropriate or acceptable behavior within that environment. I consider this a "pseudo-why?" question because it masks a deeper reason for wanting to understand the origins and dynamics of Americans' deep-structure rules. [7] Nonetheless, I believe that there are enough practitioners in the community who would accept my answer to my "pseudo-why?" question (for whatever divergent motives) for me to proceed with my analysis of the New Ethnography.

The New Ethnography

The motive which animates the New Ethnography (perhaps the old ethnography, as well) is the desire to explain a paradox with which both humanists and social scientists have traditionally struggled—that is, in the words of anthropologist Anthony F. C. Wallace, the paradox

> that cultures do exist and societies do survive, despite the diversity of the interests and motivations of their members, the practical impossibility of complete interpersonal understanding and communication, and the unavoidable residuum of loneliness that dwells in every man. [8]

To put the matter differently, it is the "organization of diversity" more than the "replication of uniformity" in human society that fascinates Wallace and his fellow cognitive anthropologists. [9] Recognizing diversity as the most salient characteristic of human beings, cognitive anthropologists aim to determine the *minimal* sharedness which still allows people to live together in organized social groups. The practical politics of choosing to study the organization of diversity rather than the replication of uniformity, therefore, is that there is *both* the potential for a maximal "meaningfulness of experience" within human society *and* a minimal "psychic unity of human groups." [10]

What the humans in a social organization minimally share, according to cognitive anthropologists, are mediating schemata (structures or processes) in the brain which organize incoming stimuli and select a behavioral response. [11] *Culture*, then, is "those sets of equivalent or identical learned meanings by which the members of a society do in fact define stimuli." [12] Explicitly borrowing their model from linguistics (as we shall see below), the cognitive anthropologists have come to identify as the loci of such meanings the *rules* which are inferred from the observation of stimulus and response sequences in a society of persons. The task of the New Ethnography, then, is the ethnographic description of "the rules which the actors are presumably employing, or attempting to employ, in the execution and mutual organization of [social] behavior," recognizing that "a set of such related rules forms a calculus which describes cognitive process." [13]

The importance of recent linguistic models as analogies for cognitive anthropology warrants a brief sketch of these origins. The clearest case of borrowing is from the generative and transformational grammar models presented by Chomsky first in 1957 and later modified in 1965. Of the three sorts of components—that is, the syntactic, the phonological, and the semantic—which contribute to a person's ability to generate an almost infinite number of meaningful sentences in a language, Chomsky is most interested in the syntactic component of a generative grammar. [14] Chomsky's goal, in other words, is to infer from actual linguistic behavior the system of rules which an "ideal speaker-hearer" must master in order to be able to converse in his or her native tongue. An important distinction in the study of generative grammar is that between *competence* ("the speaker-hearer's knowledge of his language") and *performance* ("the actual use of language in concrete situations"). [15] Chomsky is prepared only to say that a generative grammar is a model of competence, not performance, but that studies in the more difficult matter of performance must certainly be a by-product of the study of competence. What Chomsky ultimately wishes for, but which he recognizes will be extremely difficult to achieve, is a theory of performance to parallel his theory of competence. Obviously, there are many "acceptable utterances" which make perfect sense to speaker-hearers in a language community, and "grammaticalness" (a matter of the theory of competence) is only one of many factors which contribute to the acceptability of a given utterance. Although Chomsky only presents the barest outline of a future theory of performance, his notion of "acceptable utterances" and his assertion that acceptability is a matter of *degree* are important elements which are picked up later by the cognitive anthropologists.

The New Ethnography originated in the recognition by several linguistic anthropologists that the syntactic, structural rules which generate meaningful sentences in a language must have some direct relationship to the rules which generate other sorts of meaningful social behavior in human groups. Levi-Strauss has perhaps been the most explicit in drawing the analogy between language and social structure, but the principle that all symbolic systems (e.g., kinship, political institutions, cuisine) are *codes* seems to be shared by cognitive anthropologists of all sorts. [16] Thus, the New Ethnography echoes the linguistic model not only in its search for underlying rules but in its parallel notion of competence, as well. Following a precedent established earlier by Goodenough, Frake proposes that

> a description of cultural behavior is attained by a formulation of what one must know in order to respond in a culturally appropriate manner in a given socio-ecological context. Such a description, like a linguist's grammar, is productive in that it can generate new acts which will be considered appropriate responses by the members of the society being described. [17]

As Frake emphasizes elsewhere, the ethnographer's task is not to predict behavior (i.e., performance) but "to state rules of culturally appropriate behavior" (i.e., competence). [18] Like Chomsky, however, the cognitive anthropologists wish to recognize that not all possible utterances or acts by a competent member of a society are equally probable in a specific context. Just as the acceptability of utterances is a matter of degree for Chomsky, so acceptability (or appropriateness) is also a quality upon which, presumably, culturally possible acts can be rank-ordered on the basis of their relative desirability. At least one anthropologist, in fact, has constructed such rank-orders. [19]

The acknowledgement that there may be significant intracultural variations in the ways in which rules generate appropriate behavior is simply another way of affirming the view that the study of culture is the study of the organization of diversity. Some variations can be attributed to idiosyncrasies, some to the shared statuses and roles of people, and some to the differences in contexts. [20] This much other anthropologists have acknowledged. What makes the view of the cognitive anthropologists so extraordinary, however, is their insistence that the variants "are not mere deviations from some assumed basic organization; with their rules of occurrence *they are the organization.*" [21] If the reality of cultures, therefore, is that they cannot be described by only one set of rules, then it follows that a unitary description of the culture of a whole society is possible *only* for the anthropologist and is *real* only as his construct. "It is highly unlikely," writes Tyler,

> that the members of a culture ever see their culture as *this kind of* unitary phenomenon. Each individual may have a unique, unitary model of his culture, but it is not necessarily cognizant of all the unique, unitary models held by other members of his culture. He will be aware of and use some, but it is only the anthropologist who completely transcends these particular models and constructs a single, unitary model. This cognitive organization exists solely in the mind of the anthropologist (cf. Bateson 1958:294). Yet, to the extent that it will generate conceptual models used by the people of a particular culture, it is a model of their cognitive systems. [22]

In fact, Wallace argues that the individual models (the "mazeways") of members of a society need overlap only very little in order for a social system to be maintained. Theoretically, societies could be ranged on a continuous scale from the most simple (that is, the one in which there is the least amount of specialized knowledge and almost all members of the society share essentially the same set of cognitive rules) to the most complex (that is, the society in which social knowledge is most specialized and the sharing of cognitive rules is at an absolute minimum). Wallace has demonstrated that the sharing of identical cognitive maps is *not* a functional prerequisite for ongoing social interaction. It is sufficient that the cognitive maps be only *equivalent* in the sense that "the behavior of other people under various circumstances is predictable, irrespective of knowledge of their motivation, and thus is capable of being predictably related to one's own actions." [23] More importantly, however, Wallace argues that not only is it *not* necessary that all members of a society share all cognitive maps, it is not even necessary that they share at least one common to all. "Indeed," writes Wallace,

> we now suggest that human societies may characteristically *require* the nonsharing of cognitive maps among participants in a variety of institutional arrangements. Many a social system will not "work" if all participants share common knowledge of the system. It would seem therefore that cognitive *non*-uniformity may be a functional desideratum of society . . . . [24]

Wallace sees two important functions of cognitive *non*-sharing. First, non-sharing allows the building of large, complex institutions which would be beyond the cognitive comprehension of any one human brain. Second, cognitive non-sharing "liberates" a person from having to learn the cognitions of everyone else in his society. Culture, then, is based on a complementarity, not a sharing, of cognitive rules, and "culture may be conceived as an invention that makes possible the maximal organization of motivational and cognitive diversity." [25]

The chief methodological problem for the cognitive anthropologist is to discover a procedure which would unmask the deep-structure, cognitive rules employed by people in generating socially acceptable acts. In one sense, of course, this is the phenomenologist's problem of understanding "other men's minds," but it should not be thought that the cognitive anthropologists' notion of the locus of reality of culture reduces their method to some sort of dead-end solipsism. After all, people are born into societies which already "hang together," as Berger and Luckmann would say, so it must be that children and even adult neophytes *acquire* from other people (as opposed to invent)

most of the cognitive rules by which they organize perceptions and generate appropriate behavior. And if it is true that
the cognitive structures in one's brain are learned from the
brains of others, then it must be that those cognitive
structures can be embodied in signs and symbols and can be
communicated as a coded message from one mind to another.
Hence, embedded somewhere in the symbolic behavior of
human beings are the cognitive structures which we have
called culture. [26]

The use of symbolic behavior as "access data" into men's
minds is not a revolutionary method in anthropology, or in
any of the social sciences or humanities, for that matter.
What is rather new as a method of the cognitive anthropologists is their interest in *everyday conversation* as the
symbolic behavior which most richly reveals the deep
cognitive structures in the minds of the conversants. It is the
"folk knowledge" of conversation, of naming things in the
socio-ecological environment, and of talking about the
relationships between those things that the New Ethnography
wishes to tap. [27]

From among the several sorts of folk-knowledge which
are embodied in everyday conversation, cognitive anthropologists have chosen to focus upon only a few semantic fields,
mostly those which are characterized by taxonomic relationships. [28] Examples of taxonomic semantic fields are kinship
terminology, the terminology of cuisine, the terminology of
material artifacts, and the terminology of the ethnosciences
which name and organize the plants, animals, physical
objects, and physical events in the environment. [29] (Included
in this latter category would be *ethnophysics*, to which I
want to turn shortly.) The premier method of the New
Ethnography for analyzing the rules and logic of these
taxonomies is componential analysis, a rather sophisticated
technique for isolating the dimensions on which the meaning
of a term is assigned. [30]

Presuming, then, that the anthropologist has a procedure
for specifying the rules by which, say, a native decides what
to call a kinsman who is presented to him and described in
terms of generation, lineage, and gender, there is the final

problem of *psychological* versus *structural validity*. Romney and D'Andrade, for instance, have discovered that they could construct two different componential analyses to account for the same set of American English consanguineal core terms. Both analyses are structurally valid in that an anthropologist could use either model to generate the appropriate term for a given kin-person. [31] The question is, which of these models is "psychologically real" to the members of the society who address kin-persons daily?

Although Wallace and some of his colleagues have developed additional research strategies to distinguish between the mere structural and the psychological reality of kin-term models, [32] the ultimate dilemma of this distinction will remain until anthropologists develop a theory of performance as sophisticated as their theory of competence. Certainly there is more than one psychologically valid schema being used by the members of a society at any given time, and it is probable that even an individual learns and uses alternate (but equally psychologically real) schemata in generating appropriate behavior in different settings. Clearly, the most important task before the cognitive anthropologists is to construct a theory of performance which explains on what external cues is one or another set of cognitive rules employed by an actor.[33] Lacking such a theory of performance at the moment, the best the cognitive anthropologist can do is specify the structurally valid models and attempt to rank-order them on their "degree of acceptability."

American Studies and American Culture Studies

With this sketch of the New Ethnography now behind us, I want to inquire whether or not the New Ethnography can or should become paradigmatic for the American Studies community. My raising this question may seem foolish to the few American Studies scholars who are already experimenting with the method and pointless to the large segment of American Studies people who see cognitive anthropology as alien to their humanistic activity. I think the question is neither foolish nor pointless. It is not foolish because it forces us to consider the distinctions (if any) between anthropology and American Studies. For some, this distinction is more apparent than real. The response of one of my colleagues to my assertion that the New Ethnography has never really been applied to a complex, industrial society such as the twentieth-century United States was to cite a half-dozen studies on American semantic domains. Similarly, an anthropologist-acquaintance of mine from a nearby university told me not so long ago: "I do American Studies—I have just completed a study of Sacramento's Chinatown!"

The point is that the New Ethnography is still just another anthropological method when it is being used to study the cognitive rules of *other* people! James P. Spradley is not a tramp and my anthropologist-acquaintance is not an Asian-American. Except for the before-mentioned analyses of American English kin-terms, the New Ethnography has never been put to the test on a culture which is to some degree shared (even complementarily) by the anthropologist. The emics/etics debate now raging in anthropology thus assumes a whole new dimension when the object and the subject of culture-study become one-and-the-same in the person of the American Studies scholar, and the resolution of the paradigmatic struggle for anthropology may not necessarily solve the unique epistemological problems inherent in reflexive culture-study.[34] In the offing, therefore, is not merely a cross-disciplinary borrowing by American Studies of a whole-cloth anthropological paradigm but a genuinely distinct intellectual activity—call it American Culture Studies—which is duplicated only when, say, the Navajo study the Navajo, Asian-Americans study Asian-Americans, or anthropologists study anthropologists.[35]

For us in American Culture Studies, the crucial question is whether the methods of the New Ethnography do yield, in fact, the deep cognitive structures which, in their patterns of occurrence, constitute modern American culture. There is no reason why the American Studies uses of the New Ethnography cannot be tested, just as the methods of the myth/symbol/image paradigm were tested decades ago. It is only by using the New Ethnography to generate explanations of the data of American experience that the American Culture Studies community will be able to choose the most persuasive and most satisfying method for our discipline.

The above explanation of why a test of the adequacy of the New Ethnography as an American Culture Studies paradigm is not foolish also suggests why it is not pointless. A paradigm born in linguistics, cultivated in anthropology, and modified for American Culture Studies need not be antagonistic to the traditional, humanistic interests of large numbers of people in American Studies. The very fact that cognitive anthropology looks to symbolic behavior as its source of external evidence for internal rules seems completely compatible with the humanities. The major change which the New Ethnography would effect in American Culture Studies would be a new focus upon the symbolic behavior of everyday conversation and folk knowledge. This change in focus is already underway in the growing interest in Popular Culture Studies, and there is no reason why the New Ethnography cannot become a paradigm for Popular Culture Studies and fill the vacuum created by the decreasing popularity of the myth/symbol/image paradigm. Indeed, the current interest in structuralism expressed by some Popular Culture Studies people is evidence of the compatibility of cognitive anthropology and Popular Culture Studies. [36] Thus, for social scientists and humanists alike, a great deal is at stake in the question of whether the New Ethnography can become paradigmatic for American Studies.

An American Ethnophysics?

Which brings us, finally, to a possible test of the New Ethnography as a method particularly suited not only for the study of others' cognitive rules but for reflexive culture-study as well. I am proposing as a test the task of describing a twentieth-century American ethnophysics. While I am not now prepared to describe such an ethnophysics, I am prepared to outline the basic problems to be faced and strategies to be tried in making problematic modern American cognitions. I hope the title of this essay conveys the sense in which this is still a "search" for an American ethnophysics, which, I believe, eventually can be found.

What the anthropologist means by the term "ethnophysics" can best be explained by comparing it with the
ethnoscience in which most of the New Ethnography has
been done—that is, ethnobiology. The goal of ethnobiologies
—ethnobotany, ethnozoology, enthnoentomology, and eth-
noichthyology, to name a few[37]—is to infer the criteria
which a native informant uses to classify the biological world
by examining the hierarchic semantic structure the informant
uses to name the things in that world. The general procedure
for studying ethnobiology is for the anthropologist to
accompany one or more native informants into the field,
eliciting from the informant the name of a plant or animal,
its relation to other life forms, and its relation to man (e.g.,
medicinal, tabooed, religious, cosmetic, culinary). The ethnologist almost always supplements this information with his
own observations of the customary uses of the biological
item, including its use in artwork, magic, ritual, and the like.
The attitude of most ethnologists in this work is appropriately tolerant. The Navajo or Hopi are not seen as
"wrong" when they call two different plants (by our Linnean
taxonomy) by the same name. Rather, they are merely seen
as using different criteria, such as the *use* of the plants by
man, than we to classify their flora. A proper sense of
cultural relativism is preserved in these ethnobiological
monographs.

It is at this point that a strange double-standard enters
the New Ethnography. There are almost no studies of
ethnophysics in the literature. If we accept the Human
Relations Area Files (HRAF) description of *ethnophysics*, we
discover that only in the area of color terminology (not even
a physical theory of color and light) and native conceptions
of time and space do we find anything even remotely
resembling the ethnophysics of a culture.[38]

How can we account for an apparent absence of the
study of ethnophysics (or ethnochemistry or ethnomathematics, for that matter) in the study of cognitive systems?
Certainly not for a lack of evidence. The HRAF code
numbers for ethnophysical materials are present in the HRAF
Outline of Cultural Materials, and both the HRAF files and

Garvan's Index of American Cultures[39] contain cultural materials (secondary materials in HRAF, primary in the Index) which are scored "822" for ethnophysics.

A survey of both the *Outline of Cultural Materials* and the sorts of items scored "822" in both files reveals, however, the extent to which theoretical indecision about an ethnophysics has created a methodological muddle. Thus, in the *Outline* there is some suggestion that certain sciences are not "ethnosciences" in that they represent more abstract and theoretically pure thought. The placement of subcategories in the *Outline* leaves this quite ambiguous.[40] Furthermore, that ambiguity in the coding manual seems to have created confusion for the graduate students who originally coded both the HRAF and Index materials. Beyond the most explicit mention of Newtonian principles in Puritan documents in the Index of American Cultures, for example, the naive reader is at a loss to account for the "822" coding of many of the materials.

Assuming that the idea of an ethnophysics has occurred to anthropologists in the past (certainly it occurred to Murdock and his colleagues and has occurred to any graduate student who had to score ethnographic materials with category 822), there are two theoretically-based reasons why ethnophysics may have been neglected in favor of ethnobiology: either (1) culture does not intrude upon human perceptions and conceptions of physical phenomena, whereas it does intrude upon human perceptions and conceptions of the biosphere; or (2) physics (and related sciences) are culture-specific, but in a much more complex way than are the biological sciences. Let us consider each of these possibilities in turn.

First, the double-standard notion that the physical sciences are culture-free, while the biological sciences are not, is simply not persuasive. There is no obvious reason why the behaviors of physical bodies are any more or less ambiguous stimuli than are entities and behaviors in the biological world. Thomas Kuhn's seminal work on scientific paradigms as cognitive paradigms is as persuasive in his examples from the physical sciences as it is in his examples from the biological

sciences. Furthermore, historians of science have demonstrated in the case of Ptolemaic and Copernican models of
the universe, and most especially in the case of the
Newtonian universe, how those paradigms defined physical
reality, necessitated certain patterns of "normal" science, and
became general models of causation for their cultures.

If we are reasonably convinced by Kuhn and others that
physics is ethnophysics, on some level at least, then we must
conclude that anthropologists have neglected ethnophysics
because, in their view, its essential nature makes it a cognitive
system quite unlike ethnobiology. Indeed, this appears to be
the assumption being made very informally by the anthropological community. While the New Ethnography views *all*
cognitive, symbolic systems of classification as devices the
human organism employs to bring order to the apparent
chaos in the behavioral environment, clearly not all ordering
systems are considered equal. Sturtevant sees the sciences on
a continuous scale, asserting that "ethnoscience differs from
Simpson's 'theoretical science' in that it refers to the
'reduction of chaos' achieved by a particular culture, rather
than to the 'highest possible and conscious degree' to which
chaos may be reduced."[41] This theoretical distinction
between ethnosciences and abstract sciences helps account
for the before-mentioned ambiguities in the HRAF codes.

The net effect of this distinction has been for the
anthropologist to surrender the study of ethnophysics to
historians of ideas and philosophers of science. This vol-
untary surrender of American ethnophysics to historians of
ideas (or, at best, to intellectual historians)[42] pretty much
characterizes the way in which Relativity Theory and
quantum mechanics have been handled by American Studies.
Despite Kuhn's insistence that scientific revolutions, including that represented by Einstein, are changes in world
view, the questions being asked by the problem's historian-
captors are framed in the same old ways familiar to us all.
Thus, since physics, and especially Relativity Theory, is
conceived as being a highly theoretical matter which can only
be understood by a very small cluster of world scientists, the
study of this revolution becomes a kind of genealogical tree

in which the forebears and descendents of the "idea" of Relativity are traced in either direction.

The questions stemming from this definition of the problem are quite standard, such as, "How are American ideas about Relativity connected with European ideas of Relativity?" or "How is the idea of Relativity related to parallel ideas in other American belief systems?" One commonly-used anthology on Relativity Theory as a scientific revolution orders its materials along these predictable questions: "The Origins of the Special Theory of Relativity," "The Nature of Relativity Theory," "How Was Relativity Theory Born?," "The Impact of Relativity Theory," and "The Lay Reaction."[43] The primary source readings under each of these headings are excerpts from men like Newton, Mach, Lorentz, Poincare, Eddington, and, of course, Einstein himself. Even the readings which represent "lay reaction" are from two British professors, an art critic, a psychologist, and a Spanish philosopher (no less than Ortega y Gasset), hardly the sort of "lay persons" with whom most Americans could easily identify. If Relativity Theory was a cognitive revolution, as Kuhn supposes, then it must have been one of the smallest and most elite revolutions on record.

The difficulty encountered in trying to establish Relativity Theory as a cognitive map for the community of American scientists is increased once the historians push their analysis beyond the scientific subculture to ask whether or not there was a larger, American cognitive community created by Relativity physics. The usual ploy in trying to prove cultural convergence is to survey the other belief systems in American culture in order to discover ideas parallel with or derivative from the scientific idea. Accordingly, Relativity physics, the modern revolution in painting (represented by the European schools, such as Cubism), music (represented by Schoenberg and Stravinsky), and literature (represented by the poetry of Gertrude Stein, the drama of Pirandello, or the stream-of-consciousness fiction of Faulkner) are all viewed as part of the same cultural revolution. Gestalt psychology was proclaimed a new psychology "after the manner of Einstein," and it did not take historians long to trace relativity ethics to Relativity physics. [44]

The case the art historians, intellectual historians, and historians of philosophy make for the interconnectedness of modern physics and modern belief systems is a very fragile one, held together (I suspect) only by our instinctive certainty that cultures must, somehow, "hang together." Perhaps we should make this instinct problematic, for it is not at all obvious that the seemingly similar developments are connected in any necessary way, nor is it obvious that the core they share is Relativity physics. Since the model of inquiry for this analysis has been the history of ideas, rather than the anthropological study of art styles as cognitive maps, studies in cultural convergence have become embarrassing exercises aimed at proving that artists and writers really did read scientific periodicals and that their art styles embody ideas about the nature of matter, time, and space. Art historian John Richardson has demolished the link between Cubism and Relativity Theory, [45] and other critics have noted that point-of-view existed in literature far earlier than Faulkner. Evidence from other cultural subsystems, in short, does not persuasively show that Relativity Theory was a cognitive paradigm for any large community of Americans.

Is there, then, a way to "rescue" Relativity ethnophysics from its history-of-ideas captors? The drive to unmask the cognitive rules of American cultures with the same ease with which we have unmasked the cognitive rules of the Navajo, for instance, urges us to invent some way in which the methods of cognitive anthropology can become the methods of an American Culture Studies. Let me suggest in the remaining pages of this essay the sorts of questions we are going to have to start asking if we are ever to make modern American physical science — especially Relativity physics — an American ethnophysics.

The primary justification for studying the ethnosciences of a society is that the rules and cognitions associated with the natural environment are usually more central to the overall "world view" of the society than are the cognitive structures associated with other subsystems. The notion that science and art are what James Boon might call "privileged operational zones of culture" permeates the structuralism of Levi-Strauss, and the cognitive anthropologists who have done work in ethnoscience seem to agree that the basic structures and patterns found in ethnoscientific knowledge are likely to recur in other cognitive subsystems. It is in this sense, the degree to which rules and understandings in the ethnosciences are generalized by people and applied to other subsystems of human behavior, that we can speak of a society's ethnosciences being "central."[46]

But cultural knowledge is socially distributed among roles and institutions, so that in even the simplest societies there is no one person who knows all the rules.[47] In relatively simple societies the overlap of role-specific subsystems of cultural knowledge is usually quite large. Thus, although there may be a certain level of specialization of ethnoscientific knowledge in Navajo culture—that is, there is a medicine man who "specializes" in knowing which combinations of plant and animal parts cure which diseases—most of the ethnobiological knowledge in Navajo culture is shared by all adult members of the society, so that it matters little whether an ethnologist picks a medicine man or a "lay person" as his informant on Navajo ethnobotany.[48] The "special" knowledge which the medicine man may have in these cases is "recipe knowledge" of how, when, and under what conditions to prepare the potions, salves, and the like derived from plants and animals in the society's environment.

For simple societies, then, in which role specialization is minimal, the ethnographic description of the cognitive structures of the ethnosciences of those societies may be an activity equivalent to describing general, deep-structure, cognitive structures of the society as a whole. In this instance, Kuhn's thesis concerning the cognitive nature of scientific paradigms can be extended into generalizations about the cognitive paradigm of a whole society. Not only can it be done; it has been done. It has been an easy step in American Studies for intellectual historians, for historians of arts, and a host of other scholars to move, say, from a description of Newton's physical science paradigm to seventeenth and eighteenth-century cognitive maps in theology, literature, social thought, and the arts.[49] Indeed, a great deal of what we call "interdisciplinary study" has come out of the work connecting Newton's physics with Pope's poetry, or the Great Chain of Being with Jefferson's architecture, or literary Naturalism with Darwin's biological paradigm. We in American Studies have a great investment in the proposition that cultures do hang together and can be studied holistically.

Note that, in all of the scholarly research aimed at "connecting" the cognitive structures of science with the cognitive structures in the other subsystems of seventeenth, eighteenth, and nineteenth-century American and European cultures, these scholars make *exactly* the same assumption as do the ethnologists who study Navajo or Hopi ethnobotany. That is, they assume that the scientific knowledge of the society under study is not a subsystem of specialized knowledge but is knowledge which is accessible to most members of the society. More importantly, this accessible knowledge is said to be generalized into other cognitive subsystems. It is assumed, for example, that the literate, eighteenth-century American could internalize the rules of Newtonian physics to the degree that those rules governed the style of garden he built with his house, the style of architecture he preferred for the house itself, his ideas about the political nature of man, and the ethics he derived from his Christian Natural Theology. Similarly, it is assumed that a nineteenth-century American could internalize the cognitive rules of Darwinism sufficiently to guide his taste in literature, art, religion, politics, law, and (most especially) the business world.

These assumptions may very well be unwarranted. The assumption certainly is never questioned by the persons making the connections between scientific paradigms and general cognitive paradigms for a society. The fact is, of course, that not all societies are simple. Certainly the United States is a relatively complex society with an elaborate social distribution of specialized knowledge. What this means for American Culture Studies is that the assumption that American science *must* connect in some way with American art, American religion, American law, and so on, can no longer be an *a priori* tenet in interdisciplinary culture studies. These connections are now hypothetical and, as such, they are subject to empirical verification. Is it a fact that modernism in the American arts or relativism in American law and social thought are manifestations of the same deep-structure codes created by Relativity and quantum physics?

To say that we must make the homology between two American phenomena an empirical question presupposes that we have a clear idea of *similarity*. In other words, just how are we to know when we come across identical or homologous patterns in subsystems as seemingly dissimilar as, say, painting and physics? For traditional American Studies, the *metaphor* has been the key analytical element for proving connections between disparate systems. The "survival of the fittest" (not even Darwin's phrase) becomes a metaphor for social relations and is worked-out symbolically by Jack London in *The Sea Wolf*; non-Euclidean geometries are seen as a metaphor used by Boasian anthropologists to argue for ethical relativism; and, of course, Einstein's Special Theory of Relativity becomes the 'obvious' source of experiments with time and space in the stream-of-consciousness fiction of William Faulkner. The consummate use of the metaphor as an analytical tool to discover similarities and even deep-structure meanings (covert culture) between different symbolic systems in America is Leo Marx's *The Machine in the Garden*, the contribution of the myth/symbol/image school which has made most explicit its model of culture and its operationalization of empirical similarity. [50]

I believe that the myth/symbol/image school has been tried and has failed to prove itself as a satisfactory paradigm for explaining the way in which American sciences are ethnosciences. I do not wish to belabor the anomalies in that paradigm, but I do want to add to the critiques by Berkhofer, Kuklick, and Krueger one important point: it is not so much the use of metaphors which has sabotaged the myth/symbol/-image paradigm as it is its very limited definition of the sorts of American symbolic behavior which embody the codes and

metaphors. Semantic structures are really a great deal more
rich and complex than this school's notions of "metaphor,"
"myth," and "image" imply. True homologies between
different cognitive subsystems are a great deal more subtle
than Wolf Larsen's fighting a storm or Cezanne's dissolution
of *a priori* space.

What cognitive anthropology provides as a paradigm,
then, is an operational definition of similarity. In Wallace's
terms, the empirical question is now whether the cognitive
structures employed by American Relativity physicists are
identical, merely *equivalent*, or actually *nonequivalent* to the
cognitive structures employed by American painters, American legal scholars, American mothers, American pulp novelists, or any other category of persons in contemporary
American society. [51] If the cognitive structures in these
cultures are not identical (as Wallace would expect, given the
view that the problem of a complex society like the United
States is "the organization of diversity"), then to what extent
are they equivalent? That is to say, to what extent are the
perceptions and conceptions of a specialized paradigm
community of American physicists learned and generalized
by non-physicists in the society and used to shape cognitions
and generate appropriate behavior in settings other than the
science laboratory? If we can answer these questions, then we
will have finally begun to work out the details of an
explanatory paradigm uniquely appropriate to the reflexive
activity we call American Culture Studies.

Our search for an American ethnophysics for the late
nineteenth and early twentieth centuries becomes, accordingly, an inquiry into the social distribution of scientific
knowledge for that American society. We cannot assume, as
have some of our colleagues in anthropology or eighteenth-
century intellectual history, that a description of the cognitive rules of Relativity physics will constitute a description
of trans-situational American cognitive rules. Rather, we
must separate the question into at least two stages. The first
stage is entirely Kuhnian, determining what sort of cognitive
map Relativity Theory (or any physics theory, for that
matter) represented for the *scientific community* which

shared that paradigm. The second stage of our inquiry would be to determine whether and how the cognitive rules associated with the scientific paradigm *may be* learned by non-scientists and come to be employed in the generation of appropriate (or acceptable) behavior in non-scientific settings in American society. In short, we would ask the empirical question: what, exactly, was the social distribution of the knowledge and cognitive rules of a community of physicists? Further, were the cognitive rules of American physicists equivalent to those of other American scientists or university students or businessmen or litterateurs?

In initially focusing upon the community of American physicists, our analysis would be much like that of the historian of ideas or, better, the cognitive anthropologist. That is, we would first want to describe precisely the sort of cognitive rules which Relativity Theory might have represented to that community of scientists. The kinship term and folk taxonomy examples from the New Ethnography would suggest that the psychological reality of an ethnophysics would lie in the language—i.e., the symbol system—which is learned and manipulated by the community of physicists; but the parallel between the taxonomic ordering of botanical knowledge and the taxonomic ordering of knowledge in Relativity physics is unclear. Oswald Werner does graph hypothetical taxonomies for Ptolemaic and Copernican cosmologies, in which the ordered items are heavenly bodies, but what exactly are the terms (lexemes) ordered by Relativity Theory?

Our examples from cognitive anthropology fail us here because the terms of the new physics assume radically new relationships which are not easily rendered into taxonomies or tree-structures. Newton's single term "mass," to take only one example, becomes in Relativity physics at least two sets of terms: a "rest mass" plus a "mass" which is related to velocity by the Lorentz Transformations. [52] In short, Einstein largely retains the language of Newton but assigns wholly new meanings to the familiar words, a chronic problem in scientific revolutions. [53] It may be likely, therefore, that the semantic structure of the lexicon of Relativity

physics is a nontaxonomic arrangement for which eth-
nosemanticists do not yet have perfected methods of
analysis. [54]

More important is the likelihood that a physics should
not at all be analyzed as a static semantic structure. The
"meaning" of Relativity Theory lies not exclusively in its
individual lexemes but in sentences which assert that there
are certain relationships among the terms. This is, in part, the
distinction which Tyler wishes to make between *perceptual*
and *conceptual* knowledge. Wallace, too, has recognized that
semantic structures are probably only a very small portion of
available cognitive schemata, and he lists examples of two
other sorts of structures—"relations" and "processes." [55]

What these distinctions mean for an analysis of Relativity
Theory as a cognitive paradigm for a community of scientists,
therefore, is that it is probable that Relativity Theory
represents a sort of cognitive map for which the New
Ethnography *does not yet have satisfactory methods of
analysis*. Cognitive anthropologists are the first to recognize
this temporary impasse (Tyler outlines seven "Problems and
Prospects" in his introduction to the best available anthology
of the New Ethnography), and I see no reason why American
Culture Studies scholars cannot join forces with the cognitive
anthropologists in solving the puzzles which are currently
preventing the New Ethnography from becoming paradigmatic for the American Studies community. [56]

The second stage of this inquiry into an American
ethnophysics awaits the solution to the first. We can begin
work on empirical verification of identical or equivalent
cognitive maps only when we have a clear model of the
cognitive processes and relations represented by modern
physics. It is difficult to imagine the precise sort of cognitive
structure which Relativity physics or quantum physics may
prove to be, but a few homologies seem at least plausible.
David Bohm's work on the relationship between modern
physics and human perception may be the basis for some
future work on equivalent maps in physics and phenomenological psychology, both of which (says Bohm) are sciences
concerned with "what is *relatively invariant* in the ever-

changing movements that are to be observed in the world." [57] It may be also that the meaning of propositions about causality in physics recur in causal propositions from bodies of non-physics knowledge. [58] At any rate, we shall be able to confirm or disconfirm these possible connections once we have cognitive models similar to the semantic trees which have proven to be so useful in the study of ethnobiologies.

There is, of course, the possibility that even a thorough search for homologies between the sciences and other subsystems in twentieth-century American culture will yield no equivalence at all. But it should not be thought that such an empirical disconfirmation would constitute "negative results." On the contrary, our possible failure to demonstrate that Relativity physics is an American ethnophysics could be as valuable a discovery as the wished-for connectedness of American cognitive subsystems. From this point of view, the general phenomenon under study would be the extreme multiplication of subuniverses of meaning in modern American culture, a situation created by an interconnected web of forces (e.g., industrialization, bureaucratization, pluralism, specialization, professionalization) which themselves can be subjected to an American Culture Studies analysis. Our particular interest in a community of American physicists could be an entree into the structure and dynamics of this phenomenon. The argument might go something like this. The scientific community's definition of the reality of the physical world becomes, in the twentieth century, a body of highly specialized knowledge which is held only by an elite group of scientists. American physicists in the early twentieth century were able to establish themselves (albeit unconsciously) as an "esoteric enclave" whose specialized knowledge of physical reality was inaccessible to other Americans. Besides the normal institutional devices for maintaining this segregation, the language (and, hence, the subuniverse of meanings) of the physicists became largely unintelligible to outsiders. The lifting of physical theories out of mechanical models into mathematical models represents an extreme example of the way in which a subculture retreats into its own language system. [59]

This perspective on the influence of Relativity physics upon other "subuniverses of meaning" in the culture now implies a very different sort of interconnectedness between, say, modern art and science than has been argued by historians. Although art historian John Richardson's argument that Cubism is linked not to Relativity but to modern logics ("for they too separate the mode of representation from the thing represented") is a convincing shift in the history-of-ideas in art, we should study not the manifest content and style of that art so much as the implications of the fact of that development for our study in the social distribution of knowledge in twentieth-century American culture. For while European artists, like Relativity physicists, tended to make their shared perceptions and knowledge more inaccessible to the general culture, that development was much less common in American art. Despite a handful of American imitators of elite European styles, American art even after the 1913 Armory Show evidenced a social realism which was eminently accessible to the nonartist American. This phenomenon, as well as the function of the popular arts in an increasingly specialized culture, must be explained as part of the holistic study of an American ethnophysics. The question of accessibility to shared meanings in music, literature, religion, medicine, and other cognitive systems in American culture awaits the integration American Culture Studies can bring to this inquiry. [60] 9-0566

I have briefly sketched only some of the ways in which the study of Relativity theory *as an American non-ethnophysics* can illuminate important elements in early twentieth-century American culture. Many more aspects of this study are possible from the Berger and Luckmann model, and there is no reason why we need to be limited to that model. The point is that, once we pose the question in the language of cognitive anthropology, the inadequacy of disciplinary or even multi-disciplinary methods for this inquiry becomes evident. The search for an American ethnophysics reveals, in fact, the very unique theoretical and methodological problems which cannot be solved by borrowing willy-nilly from anthropology or history but which must be engaged with a convergent-disciplinary model of culture. It is in this sense that the search for an American ethnophysics is part of a holistic study of modern American culture, and the so-called "holism" of cultural historians turns out to be a narrow definition of interdisciplinarity. It is the extreme difficulty of this action, of making one's own culture and one's own cognitive map problematic, that is at once the most frustrating and most exhilarating aspect of American Culture Studies.

NOTES

1. A sociology of the American Studies "community" is being written in bits and pieces. The generational analysis which I mention in my opening sentence is suggested by David S. Wilson's "An Outline Cultural Analysis, Descriptive and Tendentious, of the American Studies Establishment in California: From Society to Community, from Protodiscipline to Discipline," unpublished dittoed paper, November 6, 1972. Equally helpful perspectives are Robert Merideth's "Introduction" to *American Studies: Essays on Theory and Method*, ed. Robert Merideth (Columbus, Ohio: Charles E. Merrill Publishing Company, 1968), pp. v-xiv, and Gene Wise's "Seven Strategies for American Studies," unpublished paper presented to the third biennial meeting of the American Studies Association in Washington, D.C., in October 1971. I realize that for me to refer to the American Studies group as a "community" is more than slightly ironic in light of its lack of a sense of shared values.

2. Compare Henry Nash Smith, "Can 'American Studies' Develop a Method?," *American Quarterly*, 9 (Summer 1957), 197-208; Richard E. Sykes, "American Studies and the Concept of Culture: A Theory and Method," *American Quarterly* 15 (Summer 1963), 253-270; and Jay Mechling, Robert Merideth, and David Wilson, "American Culture Studies: The Discipline and the Curriculum," *American Quarterly*, 25 (Oct. 1973), 363-389.

3. Thomas S. Kuhn, *The Structure of Scientific Revolutions* (2nd. ed. rev.; Chicago: University of Chicago Press, 1970).

4. Henry Nash Smith, *Virgin Land: The American West as Symbol and Myth* (Cambridge, Mass.: Harvard University Press, 1950), R.W.B. Lewis, *The American Adam: Innocence, Tragedy, and Tradition in the Nineteenth Century* (Chicago: University of Chicago Press, 1955), and John Ward, *Andrew Jackson: Symbol for an Age* (New York: Oxford University Press, 1955).

5. Bruce Kuklick, "Myth and Symbol in American Studies," *American Quarterly*, 24 (Oct. 1972), 435-450; and Thomas A. Krueger, "The Historians and the Edenic Myth: A Critique," *Canadian Review of American Studies*, 4 (Spring 1973), 3-18.

268 Jay Mechling

6. A great deal of work has been done on the values of scientific communities. The best of this work is still Robert K. Merton, "Priorities in Scientific Discovery: A Chapter in the Sociology of Science," in *The Sociology of Science*, ed. Bernard Barber and Walter Hirsch (New York: Free Press of Glencoe, 1962), pp. 447-485; and Warren O. Hagstrom, *The Scientific Community* (New York: Basic Books, 1965). To these definitive statements about the values of the scientific community, and to his own statements about those values (pp. 152-159, 185), Kuhn adds two important qualifications: "First, shared values can be important determinants of group behavior even though the members of the group do not all apply them in the same way .... Second, individual variability in the application of shared values may serve functions essential to science," Kuhn, p. 186.

7. To understand the rules which I and persons in my behavioral environment employ to organize our perceptions and generate acceptable behavior is a necessary but not sufficient condition for me to reaffirm the "man-madeness" of most of those rules and processes. My study of the cognitive maps of others as well as my own forces me to consider what in my "mazeway" is humanly *given* by my biology (especially my brain, the product of human evolution) and what is man-made and *variable*. This clarifies for me the limits of humanly possible acts and introduces into my cultural and behavioral repertoire possibilities alternative to those I have come to believe represent "the world *tout court*." Simply put, I view understanding the cognitive rules of everyday life as the precondition which enables me to de-reify and de-mystify the world which is presented to me as objective fact.

Unfortunately, this sort of knowledge is as much a prelude to the manipulation of others' behavior as it is to the "irrevocably revolutionary act" of which Ivan Illich speaks (See the epigraph to Robert Merideth's essay in this volume). This implies, for me and for others, the need for an ethic which guarantees the good and human use of knowledge obtained in the process of doing American Studies. We do not yet have this ethic and are significantly less sophisticated in this matter than are many of our colleagues in sociology and anthropology.

8. Anthony F. C. Wallace, "The Psychic Unity of Human Groups," in *Studying Personality Cross-Culturally*, ed. Bert Kaplan (Evanston, Ill.: Row, Peterson and Company, 1961), p. 131. For a similar attempt to explain how it is that institutions "hang together" despite the lack of any *a priori* reason for assuming that they should, see Peter L. Berger and Thomas Luckmann, *The Social Construction of Reality: A Treatise in the Sociology of Knowledge* (Garden City, N.Y.: Anchor Books, 1966), esp. pp. 63-65, 82-92.

9. Anthony F. C. Wallace, *Culture and Personality* (New York: Random House, 1970 [1961]), pp. 22-24. It is plausible that the increased interest of anthropologists and sociologists in the paradox of "the organization of diversity" is, itself, a product of a society which seems to its members impossibly diverse and characterized more and more by alienation and failures in communication. Hans Peter Dreitzel suggests as much in his "Introduction" to *Recent Sociology No. 2*, ed. Hans Peter Dreitzel (New York: The Macmillan Company, 1970), esp. pp. viii-x.

10. Wallace, "The Psychic Unity of Human Groups," p. 141; and Wallace, *Culture and Personality*, pp. 24-36. The search for the elements of a pancultural human mind is a common theme in the Structuralism of Claude Levi-Strauss, and more than one cognitive anthropologist believes in cultural universals. See Claude Levi-Strauss, *The Savage Mind* (Chicago: University of Chicago Press, 1966) and Tyler's "Introduction" to *Cognitive Anthropology*, ed. Stephen A. Tyler (New York: Holt, Rinehart and Winston, 1969), esp. fn. 11, pp. 21-22. This confidence in cultural universals is encouraged by Noam Chomsky's identification of linguistic universals in his *Aspects of the Theory of Syntax* (Cambridge, Mass.: M.I.T. Press, 1965), pp. 27-30, and by similar speculations in his *Problems of Knowledge and Freedom*, (New York: Vintage Books, 1971), pp. 23, 43-45.

11. Wallace, *Culture and Personality*, pp. 75-79.

12. Wallace, "The Psychic Unity of Human Groups," p. 132.

13. Anthony F. C. Wallace, "Culture and Cognition," *Science*, 135 (Feb. 2, 1962), 1.

14. Chomsky discusses the syntactic component, as well as his notions of the deep structure and surface structure of a sentence, in *Aspects of the Theory of Snytax*, pp. 3, 16-18.

15. *Ibid.*, p. 4.

16. Claude Levi-Strauss first posited the analogy between language and other cultural phenomena in the essays collected as *Structural Anthropology* (Garden City, N.Y.: Doubleday and Company, 1963). He subsequently has proceeded with his analysis of cultural systems as "codes" in his multivolume "Introduction to a Science of Mythology," of which *The Raw and the Cooked* (New York: Harper and Row, 1964) and *From Honey to Ashes* (New York: Harper and Row, 1973) are in English translation. An interesting, if overly cute, critique of Levi-Strauss and French structuralism is Marvin Harris's *The Rise of Anthropological Theory: A History of Theories of Culture* (New York: Thomas Y. Crowell Company, 1968), pp. 464-513. Later in his history, Harris labels the cognitive anthropologists' analogy between linguistic codes and higher-order codes in non-verbal behavior a "patently false analogy." Harris, pp. 582-583.

17. Charles O. Frake, "Cultural Ecology and Ethnography," *American Anthropologist*, 64 (1962), 54.

18. Charles O. Frake, "Notes on Queries in Ethnography," in *Transcultural Studies in Cognition*, ed. A. K. Romney and R. G. D'Andrade, in a special issue of the *American Anthropologist*, 66 (1964), 133.

19. Tyler, pp. 4-5, suggests that there may be a hierarchical order of responses, ranked on their relative desirability. Ward H. Goodenough has actually designed Guttman scales of this sort. See his "Rethinking 'Status' and 'Role': Toward a General Model of the Cultural Organization of Social Relationships," in *The Relevance of Models for Social Anthropology*, ed. Michael Banton (New York: Frederick A. Praeger, Publishers, 1965), pp. 1-24, and his "Some

Applications of Guttman Scale Analysis to Ethnography and Culture Theory,"
Southwestern Journal of Anthropology, 19 (Autumn 1963), 235-250.

20. Tyler, p. 4. Intracultural variations in which people organize phenomena in ways characteristic of their shared roles imply a "social distribution of
knowledge," and Berger and Luckmann develop a useful vocabulary for talking
about this phenomenon. People also vary their behavior according to context, as
Tyler says, and Milton Rokeach's situational analysis of beliefs, attitudes, and
values provides a framework for this sort of intracultural variation. See Milton
Rokeach, *Beliefs, Attitudes, and Values: A Theory of Organization and Change*
(San Francisco: Jossey-Bass, 1968).

21. Tyler, p. 5. It is for this reason that statistical generalizations about
personalities ("mazeways") are of very limited value in talking about shared
psychological characteristics. See Wallace, "The Psychic Unity of Human
Groups," pp. 147-149.

22. Tyler, p. 5. Responding to this same paragraph, historian Robert
Berkhofer has delimited the peculiar problems faced by historians who must try
to aggregate folk cultures into the sort of meta-description mentioned by Tyler.
See Robert F. Berkhofer, Jr., "Clio and the Culture Concept: Some Impressions
of a Changing Relationship in American Historiography," *Social Science
Quarterly*, 53 (Sept. 1972), esp. pp. 313-314.

23. Wallace, *Culture and Personality*, p. 35.

24. *Ibid*.

25. *Ibid*., pp. 35-36.

26. Frake, "Notes on Queries in Ethnography," p. 133.

27. Both Frake and Hymes have called for "an ethnography of speaking,"
and it is on this matter of using everyday conversation as evidence of cultural
meaning that the cognitive anthropologists and the cognitive (phenomenological)
sociologists converge. Compare Dell H. Hymes, "The Ethnography of Speaking,"
in *Anthropology and Human Behavior*, ed. Thomas Gladwin and William C.
Sturtevant (Washington, D. C.: Anthropological Society of Washington, 1962),
pp. 13-53; and Aaron V. Cicourel, "The Acquisition of Social Structure: Toward
a Developmental Sociology of Language and Meaning," in *Understanding
Everyday Life*, ed. Jack D. Douglas (Chicago: Aldine Publishing Company, 1970),
pp. 136-168.

28. William C. Sturtevant, "Studies in Ethnoscience," in *Transcultural
Studies in Cognition*, ed. A. K. Romney and R. G. D'Andrade, in a special issue of
the *American Anthropologist*, 66 (1964), 99-131, describes the distinctive
characteristics of a taxonomic relationship. It was Sturtevant who gave cognitive
anthropology the appellation "The New Ethnography." One problem in terminology must be resolved before we can proceed. Although Sturtevant proposes the
use of "Ethnoscience" to describe the New Ethnography, including the study of
all folk taxonomies, Wallace uses "ethnoscience" in its more limited meaning of
sciences (i.e., ideas about Nature and Man). I prefer Wallace's usage of the term

and shall hereafter use "ethnoscience" to mean culturally-specific sciences, such as ethnobotany, ethnozoology, ethnopsychology, and so on.

29. Some examples of this varied literature are: Brent Berlin, Dennis E. Breedlove, and Peter H. Raven, "Covert Categories and Folk Taxonomies," *American Anthropologist*, 70 (1968), 290-299; Brent Berlin, Dennis E. Breedlove and Peter H. Raven, "General Principles of Classification and Nomenclature in Folk Biology," *American Anthropologist*, 75 (1973), 214-242; Norma Perchonock and Oswald Werner, "Navaho Systems of Classification: Some Implications for Ethnoscience," *Ethnology*, 8 (1969), 229-242; and Oswald Werner, "Semantics of Navaho Medical Terms," *International Journal of American Linguistics* 31 (Jan. 1965), 1-17. Two contributions to American Studies are John L. Caughey, "Simulating the Past: A Method for Using Ethnosemantics in Historical Research," *American Quarterly* 24 (Dec. 1972), 626-642; and Richard P. Horwitz, "Architecture and Culture: The Meaning of the Lowell Boarding House," *American Quarterly*, 25 (March 1973), 64-82..

30. Ward H. Goodenough, "Componential Analysis and the Study of Meaning," *Language*, 32 (1956), 195-216.

31. A. Kimball Romney and Roy Goodwin D'Andrade, "Cognitive Aspects of English Kin Terms," in *Transcultural Studies in Cognition*, ed. A. K. Romney and R. G. D'Andrade, in a special issue of the *American Anthropologist*, 66 (1964), 146-170. The distinction between *structural validity* and *psychological validity* was first made by Anthony F. C. Wallace and John Atkins in "The Meaning of Kinship Terms," *American Anthropologist*, 62 (1960), 58-79, and is elaborated by Wallace in "The Problem of the Psychological Validity of Componential Analyses," *American Anthropologist*, 67 (1965), 229-248.

32. In addition to the Wallace articles above, see Peggy R. Sanday, "The 'Psychological Reality' of American-English Kinship Terms: An Information-Processing Approach," *American Anthropologist*, 70 (1968), 508-523; and Peggy R. Sanday, "Analysis of the Psychological Reality of American-English Kin Terms in an Urban Poverty Environment," *American Anthropologist*, 73 (1971), 555-570.

33. Romney and D'Andrade, p. 154. Such a theory of performance might achieve the synthesis of emic and etic analyses which Berkhofer is calling for in "Clio and the Culture Concept," pp. 319-320.

34. Spradley's *You Owe Yourself a Drunk: An Ethnography of Urban Nomads* (Boston: Little, Brown & Company, 1970) is the best known and, in some ways, the most successful ethnosemantic study of an American semantic domain.

"Emic" statements describe the perceptual and conceptual paradigms of a culture in the terms which are meaningful or "real" to the actors themselves, while "etic" statements describe persons' perceptual and conceptual paradigms with terms and models agreed upon by a community of scientific observers. Unfortunately, cases of clear-cut emic or etic descriptions are rare. Harris's is an extensive treatment of these distinctions and ambiguities, though I disagree with several of his conclusions. Also useful is Berkhofer's "Clio and the Culture Concept," pp. 311-320. Cognitive sociologist and methodologist Aaron V.

Cicourel is acutely sensitive to the problem of "performing like a native," and his discussion of the emic/etic problem is first-rate. See Cicourel, esp. pp. 159-166. Also first-rate is Murphey on Quine's notion of "ontological relativity." See Murray G. Murphey, *Our Knowledge of the Historical Past* (Indianapolis: Bobbs-Merrill Company, 1973), esp. pp. 33-37. What goes unsaid in most of these discussions is that the distinction between emic and etic categories becomes considerably complex when the informant is *also* a member of the community of scientists, as when an American Culture Studies scholar undertakes the unmasking of modern American perceptual and conceptual cognitive calculi.

35. I shall call the discipline American Culture Studies, adopting the usage advocated by me, Robert Merideth, and David Wilson in our essay "American Culture Studies: The Discipline and the Curriculum," *American Quarterly*, 25 (Oct. 1973), 363-389. I use the phrase "American Studies" in an historical sense, referring primarily (but not exclusively) to the model of inquiry represented by the myth/symbol/image school. Of course, American Studies has always been "reflexive" in the sense that the movement's founders realized that they were studying their own values, beliefs, and institutions; but the false nature of that sort of "reflexive" stance is proven in its unaltered export overseas. That is, American Studies in Japan, in Italy, in England, or wherever, is still pretty much in the style of 1940s and 1950s American Studies in the United States, though clearly an American student's studying American culture is not the same activity as a Japanese student's studying American culture, nor is it likely that a given method of culture-study would yield the same data and understandings in those two dissimilar situations.

In another sense, American Studies is embarrassingly late in formulating the theory and method of "reflexive" culture-study. Radical caucuses from the major professional associations responded to the Vietnam War and domestic crises of the 1960s by turning their respective social sciences and humanities "back upon America." Journals such as *Critical Anthropology*, the *Insurgent Sociologist, Red Buffalo*, and American Studies's *Connections* represent an attempt to achieve what C. Wright Mills ten years earlier called "the sociological imagination." Good examples of this parallel movement in several disciplines are: Dell Hymes, ed., *Reinventing Anthropology* (New York: Vintage Books, 1972), John O'Neill, *Sociology as a Skin Trade: Essays towards a Reflexive Sociology* (New York; Harper and Row, 1972), Alvin W. Gouldner, *The Coming Crisis of Western Sociology* (London: Heinemann Educational Books, 1971), and, of course, C. Wright Mills, *The Sociological Imagination* (New York: Oxford University Press, 1959).

36. This is an impression gleaned from discussions at a workshop on "Structuralism and American Studies" which I co-chaired with Mary G. Land at the fourth biennial convention of the American Studies Association, October 18-20, 1973, in San Francisco.

37. For a sample of ethnobiological monographs, see Francis H. Elmore, *Ethnobotany of the Navajo* (Santa Fe: University of New Mexico Press, 1944), Borys Malkin, *Seri Ethnozoology* (Pocatello, Idaho: Idaho State College Museum, 1962), Alfred F. Whiting, *Ethnobotany of the Hopi* (Flagstaff: Museum of Northern Arizona, 1966), and Leland C. Wyman and Flora L. Bailey, *Navaho Indian Ethnoentomology*, University of New Mexico Publications in Anthropology, Number 12 (Albuquerque: University of New Mexico Press, 1964).

38. George Murdock, *et al.*, *Outline of Cultural Materials* (New Haven: Human Relations Area Files, 1967) defines Category 822, Ethnophysics, as "popular conceptions of matter, energy, and their properties; notions about space, time and gravitation; ideas about form, color, and sound (e.g., color symbolism, patterned use of color); beliefs about shadows, reflections, and echoes; notions about electricity, magnetism, chemical properties (e.g., alchemy); etc." Thirteen cross-references are also listed. See p. 129 of the *Outline*. Missing in the explicit definition of "ethnophysics" is a theory of causation–part of the "object orientation" which Hallowell says every society provides its members– but ideas about the causes of events are coded in separate belief and behavioral systems, as in 753, "Theory of Disease," or 777, "Luck and Chance." See A. Irving Hallowell, *Culture and Experience* (New York: Schocken Books, 1955), esp. pp. 91-92. For examples from the color terminology research, see Sturtevant, pp. 117-119. Hallowell's chapters on spatio-temporal orientations in culture *(Culture and Experience,* pp. 92-100, 184-202) and Emiko Ohuki-Tierney's "Spatial Concepts of the Ainu of the Northwest Coast of Southern Sakhalin," *American Anthropologist,* 74 (June 1972), 426-457, are about the only research available on space and time in primitive cultures. An ethnosemantic analysis of Ptolemaic and Copernican cosmologies is Oswald Werner's "Cultural Knowledge, Language, and World View," in *Cognition: A Multiple View,* ed. Paul L. Garvin (New York: Spartan Books, 1970), pp. 155-175.

39. Anthony N. B. Garvan, "Historical Depth in Comparative Culture Study," *American Quarterly*, 14 (Summer 1962), 260-274.

40. The 810 categories, "Exact Knowledge," are separate from the 820 categories, "Ideas about Nature and Man." While the former categories include logic (811), philosophy (812), pure science (815), and applied science (816), the latter include ethnometerorology (821), ethnophysics (822), several ethno-biologies, ethnopsychology (828), and ethnosociology (829). Mathematics, for some unexplained reason, is included as category 803 (under "80. Numbers and Measures") rather than as "Ethnomathematics" among the 820s. In fact, it is not at all clear whether that location of mathematics represents some theoretical decision that math is qualitatively different from physics. It may be that math was excluded from the ethnosciences as an artifact of the numbering system: the *Outline* can only accomodate nine sub-categories and "ethnomathematics" would have been a tenth ethnoscience!

41. Sturtevant, p. 100.

42. For the distinction between "intellectual history" and "the history of ideas" see Rush Welter, "The History of Ideas in America: An Essay in Redefinition," *Journal of American History*, 51 (March 1965), 599-614.

43. L. Pearce Williams, ed., *Relativity Theory: Its Origins and Impact on Modern Thought* (New York: John Wiley and Sons, 1968).

44. In fact, the whole artistic revolution called "Modernism" is almost always linked with Einstein and Relativity Theory, but the "proof" of this association is almost always an unarticulated assumption that trends and styles which coexist in time and space (no matter how tortured the family resemblance)

must be related. This attempt to put the burden of proof upon those who may claim that coexisting cultural revolutions might not necessarily be connected is a clever debating strategy; but I do not think it is necessary for those advocates to avoid that burden. Actually, there is some theoretical justification for positing a connection between a culture's ethnosciences and its arts. Sturtevant supports Simpson's assertion that man's ordering of his external world "is most conspicuous in the two most exclusively human and in some sense highest of all our activities: the arts and sciences" (Simpson, quoted in Sturtevant, p. 99). The closest thing ethnoscience has to a cultural theory of art is that developed by Levi-Strauss in *The Savage Mind*. In his view, folk taxonomies have an important aesthetic function which lies halfway between science and mythology. Moreover, art is, for Levi-Strauss, not merely a passive homologue of the objects ordered by science but a real *experiment* by which the artist "proceeds from a set (object + event) to the *discovery* of its structure" (Levi-Strauss, *The Savage Mind*, pp. 22-26). Unfortunately, intellectual history formulations of the relation between modern art and Relativity Theory never quite reach this level of structural analysis, most often relying upon crude similarities between styles.

45. John Adkins Richardson, *Modern Art and Scientific Thought* (Urbana: University of Illinois Press, 1971), pp. 104-111.

46. Levi-Strauss explicitly connects science with magic and art in his opening chapter, "The Science of the Concrete," of *The Savage Mind*, pp. 1-33. Boon makes the same point in wholly different terms, including the "privileged operational zones" which represent the intersection of several codes in a culture. Clearly, science is in such a zone. See James A. Boon, "Further Operations of 'Culture' in Anthropology: A Synthesis of and for Debate," *Social Science Quarterly*, 53 (Sept. 1972), esp. 227-232.
    What I am suggesting, following Wallace's lead (*Culture and Personality*, p. 76), is that the human learning phenomena of "stimulus equivalence" and "response equivalence" make it possible for people to apply to other cognitive domains the rules learned in the more "central" domains like science. Not only is such generalization possible, people actually generalize their rules, as demonstrated by Paul E. Breer and Edwin A. Locke in their *Task Experience as a Source of Attitudes* (Homewood, Ill.: Dorsey Press, 1965).

47. Berger and Luckmann, pp. 77-92.

48. Alfred Whiting's informants on Hopi ethnobotany, for example, included a basket-maker, a storekeeper, a medicine man, an old woman, a village chief, and a museum assistant. See Whiting, p. 59.

49. See Basil Willey, *The Eighteenth Century Background* (Boston: Beacon Press, 1940), Frank O. Lovejoy, *The Great Chain of Being* (Cambridge, Mass.: Harvard University Press, 1936), and Daniel Boorstin, *The Lost World of Thomas Jefferson* (Boston: Beacon Press, 1948).

50. Leo Marx, *The Machine in the Garden: Technology and the Pastoral Ideal in America* (New York: Oxford University Press, 1967). Of theoretical interest in connection with this exemplar is Bernard Bowron, Leo Marx, and Arnold Rose, "Literature and Covert Culture," *American Quarterly*, 9 (Winter 1957), 377-386.

51. "Equivalence" is a term from symbolic logic; two propositions are equivalent "when the truth of either one implies the truth of the other." For a complete discussion of the notion of equivalent cognitive maps, see Wallace, "The Psychic Unity of Human Groups," pp. 147-153.

52. For those readers who have no knowledge whatsoever of Relativity physics, Lincoln Barnett's *The Universe and Dr. Einstein* (New York: Bantam Books, 1957) is a short, well-written book for the lay audience. Leopold Infeld's *Albert Einstein* (New York: Charles Scribner's Sons, 1950) is also very readable, if a bit more technical than Barnett's book, and its main attraction is Infeld's intimate knowledge of Einstein as friend and colleague. Einstein's own populariza- tion of his theory, *Relativity: The Special and General Theory* (New York: Crown Publishers, 1961), is useful, as is Ronald W. Clark's massive biography, *Einstein: The Life and Times* (New York: World Publishing Company, 1971).

53. Kuhn, pp. 200-202, discusses the problem of vocabulary and translation in paradigm revolution.

54. Tyler, pp. 15-16, mentions some of the possible non-taxonomic semantic arrangements of lexemes from a belief system. Wallace (*Culture and Personality*, pp. 88-93) describes a few lexical domains which may be beyond componential analysis.

55. See Tyler, p. 16, on the possibilities of analyzing linguistic units larger than a lexeme—e.g., discourse analysis or propositional analysis. Compare this with Wallace's discussion (*Culture and Personality*, pp. 94-109) of "relations" and "processes."

56. One problem with the history-of-ideas approach for American Culture Studies is the fact that Relativity Theory was an almost exclusively European idea in its origins. Thus, it cannot be said to be an American folk science in the sense of emerging from the American people, their customs, or their institutions. Relativity Theory could be regarded as a folk-physics, however, to the extent that we can prove that it was accepted by a substantial number of American scientists as a way of knowing the physical world.

Sociologist Bernard Barber has suggested that a useful way to study the sources of acceptance of a scientific discovery or paradigm is to study the *resistance* to those paradigms. So far, this is an untried approach to the American acceptance of European physics, but one which might be well worth pursuing. The running confrontation between opponents and proponents over the "twin- paradox" is only the most obvious of the patterns of resistance which can be studied in the popular literature of the first few decades of this century. Patterns of religious, social, and political sources of resistance to the new physics might also emerge from the study of those American scientists who never accepted Relativity Theory. Physicist Dayton C. Miller (1866-1941) is the only resister I have been able to locate so far among the scientists; there is no biography of him. There must have been other resisters, both within science and without; we need to locate them to discover on what idiosyncratic and shared grounds they could not believe in Relativity Theory. That search will take some digging, for just as Kuhn predicted (pp. 136-143 of "The Invisibility of Revolutions"), the scientific community buries its mistakes, so that those scientists who were not part of the mainstream of scientific "progress" are forever lost to the history of science. Bernard Barber, "Resistance by Scientists to Scientific Discovery," in *The Sociology of Science,* ed. Bernard Barber and Walter Hirsch (Glencoe, Ill.: Free Press, 1962), pp. 539-556. See the brief discussion of Miller in Isaac Asimov's *Asimov's Biographical Encyclopedia of Science and Technology* (Garden City, N.Y.: Doubleday and Company, 1964), 368a.

57. See the Appendix, "Physics and Perception," in David Bohm's *The Special Theory of Relativity* (New York: W. A. Benjamin, 1965), pp. 185-230. Bohm argues that "scientific investigation is basically a mode of extending our *perception* of the world, and not mainly a mode of obtaining *knowledge* about it" (p. 219). Thus, for Bohm, the similarity between Relativity Theory and the perceptual theories of Piaget is not accidental but reflects the fact that science is a mode of perception. Bohm would agree with Infeld that it will be possible for people to learn to perceive the world in such a way that the Special Theory of Relativity will seem as "natural" and "intuitive" to them as does Newton's mechanical model of the universe. This entire Appendix is provocative reading, as is Marshall H. Segall, Donald T. Campbell, and Melville J. Herskovits's *The Influence of Culture on Visual Perception* (Indianapolis: Bobbs-Merrill Company, 1966).

58. This is a complicated matter made more so by the possibility that the causal models of people like Kuhn and Wallace may stem in part from the very scientific revolution which we want to explain. Without raising the spectre, let me merely refer the reader to three excellent treatments of the causality issue: Werner Heisenberg, *Physics and Philosophy: The Revolution in Modern Science* (New York: Harper and Row, 1958), Ernst Cassirer, *Determinism and Indeterminism in Modern Physics: Historical and Systematic Studies of the Problem of Causality* (New Haven: Yale University Press, 1956), and David Bohm, *Causality and Chance in Modern Physics* (London: Routledge and Kegan Paul, 1957).

59. Berger and Luckmann, pp. 87-88. The loss of intelligibility of the nature of the physical universe is only part of a larger theme which often appears in radical critiques of modern culture. Ortega y Gasset's critique of the modern arts reflects this theme and was written largely in reaction to early twentieth-century physics. See his *The Dehumanization of Art, and Other Writings on Art and Culture* (Garden City, N.Y.: Doubleday, 1950). More recent critiques of the ways in which professionalization and specialization in modern culture have made the world "opaque" for most men are Ivan Illich's *Deschooling Society* (New York: Harper and Row, 1970) and Paul Goodman's *People or Personnel; and, Like a Conquered Province* (New York: Vintage Books, 1968). A great many readers of earlier drafts of this essay have raised the question whether this phenomenon of the unintelligibility of theoretical science to most members of a culture is really unique to modern physics. Americans of the eighteenth century, runs the argument, may not have had any more understanding of Newtonian physics than twentieth-century Americans have of Einsteinian and quantum physics. In both cases, my friends continue, the lay public learns just enough of the jargon of the science to apply or misapply it to common experience. Furthermore, doesn't the learning of just a little of the jargon and main concepts of a theoretical science make it an ethnoscience, on some level at least? My response to this possibility is twofold. First, I completely agree that intellectual historians have not *proven* that eighteenth-century models of the physical and

biological world were internalized beyond the level of easy jargon and surface symbolizing. Second, however, I believe there is a *qualitative* difference between the possible internalization of a mechanical model (such as Newton's) and a mathematical model (such as Einstein's) of the physical universe. Popularizations of Einstein's Special and General Theories of Relativity, beginning with Einstein's entry in 1916 on up to Ronald Clark's biography of Einstein, attempt to translate the mathematical model into analogies which the average reader can understand, and these popularizations would make excellent data for the study of an American ethnophysics.

60. While Richardson is to be commended for his cogent attack on the specious link between Cubism and Relativity Theory, he goes on merely to substitute one idea for another, never really freeing the inquiry from the history-of-ideas formula. His explanation of modern art—especially Cubism—as a counterpart of the Intuitionist, Formalist, and Logicist modern logics has structural validity, but Richardson offers no evidence that the new epistemology was psychologically real to any other cognitive community (i.e., museum patrons) beyond a small group of European artists. Hence, like the physicists, these artists were maintaining their segregation (not cognitive sharing) from a larger cultural community by purposely falling back into a formalist symbolic system which had meaning only within that specialized culture—in this case, the Cubists. One important research task which American Culture Studies can establish for itself is a set of principles by which the symbols in one cultural system (e.g., art, music, literature, science) can be transformed into the symbols of another system. See, for example, William Bright's "Language and Music: Areas for Cooperation," *Ethnomusicology*, 7 (1963), 26-32, an attempt to establish an equivalent vocabulary for dealing with meaning in language and music.

CHAPTER 11

"It's a Small World": High School, American Culture Studies, And Cultural Revolution

By Robert Merideth

ROBERT MERIDETH's special interest is in formulating theories of American culture and American Culture Studies that are both comprehensive and politically transforming. He has paid particular attention in earlier writings to the human consequences of schooling institutions and practices at the university level. An avowed communitarian anarchist, he acknowledges the influence of Ivan Illich, the Humanist psychologists, and Paul Goodman, about whom he is now writing a book. Professor Merideth is a co-founder of the Radical Caucus of the American Studies Association, an editorial member of the National *Connections II* American Studies Collective, and Chairman of American Studies at the University of California, Davis. He has written *The Politics of the Universe* (1968), edited Edward Beecher's *Narrative of Riots at Alton* (1965) and the anthology *American Studies: Essays on Theory and Method* (1968), and contributed some forty essays on aesthetics, literature, education, and politics to a variety of periodicals ranging from the *Journal of Aesthetics and Art Criticism* to *The Nation.*

In his essay Robert Merideth applies a radical philosophy of education and American Studies to case studies in high school teaching, advocating both *disciplinarity* and *cultural revolution.*

"I call an act 'revolutionary' only when its appearance within a culture establishes irrevocably a (significantly) new possibility: a trespass of cultural boundaries which beats a new path. A revolutionary act is the unexpected proof of a new social fact . . ."[1]

1. Disneyland and High School

The personal and political contradictions for me of a pre-Institute visit to Disneyland were collapsed momentarily in favor of my kids' beautiful hopes. You do get your money's worth there. The place is kept tidy. Things are orderly. A good-sized coke costs only 15¢; boys in white with dustpans swarm the streets; you get a map and the tickets are carefully graded from A - E, as in school. It's easy to move from Frontierland to Tomorrowland, from fatigued pack-mules and fake steamboats to submarines and simulated moonshots. And Matterhorn, a paper mache challenge, looms over everything. Nothing surpasses 'It's a Small World,' though, and to start there, as Amy, Anne, Emily, and I did, meant giving myself away however briefly to Disney's vision. We rode through the animated representation of the joy and loveliness of the planet's children in a plastic caricature of Henry Thoreau's boat floating the Concord and Merrimack Rivers. The kids were wide-eyed while I quietly cried. I was crying in response to my kids' wonder, the fine craftsmanship and noveau art, and the appeal of Disney's utopian imagination, as well as in anger at the ease by which I was moved by the sentimentality of the scene. I was had, I thought then, my hard earned subversive politics and understandings notwithstanding. But it would not be' until well into the middle of the Institute's final week — when Roderick Nash showed a slide of Matterhorn during one of his lectures on the environment — that the puzzling experience of the day began to find many of its meanings, and not till the end of the summer that I made all of it I could. In between, there would be a whole series of lectures and workshops on American culture and on teaching American Studies in the schools. Somehow my experience at Disneyland was connected to what I wanted to say in my own workshop on American Culture Studies [2] and high school. Eventually I would make the connection.

As late as the next night, just before the beginning of the Institute and after my kids had left Los Angeles, I was still uncertain that I was the person to lead the workshop, however. The uncertainty had a number of sources. I have not taught in high school and I like to make abstracted arguments; neither of those facts was likely to endear me to my students, if my past experience with high school teachers was to be taken as a guide. My notions about education are best articulated by radical reformers like Ivan Illich and Paul Goodman, another fact not likely to make me popular. Perhaps most importantly, my general attitude toward high school is still pervaded by the guilty hostility I felt as a high school sophomore over twenty years ago when my classmates and I one by one, out loud in class, read Dickens's *A Tale of Two Cities*. The boredom and the tedium overwhelmed me then (secretly I read ahead) and the memory of it still does.

Dreary fascination. The oxymoron that compelled me was the simultaneous dreariness and fascination of the subject, on many levels. The characteristic American Studies subjects as they were to be articulated by the lecturers at the Institute — art and architecture, cultural anthropology and material history and above-ground archaeology, religion and philosophy, literature, environmental studies, minority studies, women's studies, popular culture — have their own attractive, compelling fascination; but revealing that fascination to high school students often becomes a dreary exercise in games-playing, frustration, cross-purposes, and oppressive socialization. Again, high school itself is a fascinating American institution like the two-party system and freeways, but often it represents a long, dreary experience for adolescents, replete with guards, hall passes, requirements, moralisms, and antiseptic institutional smells. The students would be better off doing some of what attracts them — making love, learning about a real world, playing games seriously, or playfully working at useful tasks. Again, high school undoubtedly represents for many teachers their fascination with meaningful work, learning, and teaching. Surely, like me, they aspire to pass on what it means to be human as they see it, to recreate the excitements of their discipline, to transmit their respect for intelligent thinking and acting, but the job encourages the dreary, controlling authoritarian in everyone. Finally, the problems of teaching fascinate teachers; but they are always the same, repeated at conferences and meetings like motifs in an endless, repetitive, dreary popular song — the students, the administration, the subjects, no experiment, the community, what to do.

As I thought about it Sunday night, in short, in the high schools students tune out, though they may struggle hard to get good grades so that they can make it to a good university where they will again struggle hard to get good grades so that they can make it into professional school, which is all the more reason for thinking about de-grading education. Teachers are diminished by a slow attrition. The interaction of students and teachers in such a situation produces on the whole either a devastating, neurosis-inducing boredom, or frustration and repressed rage. The situation may seem not quite that bad all the time, and as I learned from my teacher-students it does not to many within it. The predictable protest against my view and the ameliorations people mention nevertheless still seem to me to testify either to the lengths people will go to legitimate habitual behavior patterns or to human resilience, not to the glory of high school as a place to work and make a revolution. At best, some people have an amazing capacity to make liberated space in the interstitial gaps all but the most totalistic institutional systems leave.

The view I had of high school as the Institute began seemed to me not only possibly true but plausible, even unexceptional. The picture I conjured up was bleak, but surely no bleaker than what is found in popular books like *Blackboard Jungle* and *Up the Down Staircase* or what emerges from an inferential reading of the stiff, cardboard sententiousness of James Conant's studies. John Anthony Scott, whose *Teaching for a Change* (New York, 1972) I have found useful, draws a similar picture. Most recently, the 188 page report by the National Commission on the Reform of Secondary Education (December 1973) proposes lowering the compulsory attendance age to 14, in part because school simply is not working. The point I decided to try to make early in the workshop was that such a description of so pivotal an institution as the high school — through which nearly every American passes for three or four years — should lead us to reconsider as a whole the condition and nature of the civilization that generated and tolerates it. While we spend our time and energies paying fascinated attention to the details of our dreary subject, would we not do well simultaneously to make problematic the civilization that is the source of such dreariness — of such dullness, regimentation, repression, frustration, seemingly insoluble problems, and contained rage? Does it not make sense, as the workshop deals with the problem of translating the methods and understandings of American Culture Studies into high school courses and curriculums, to pay attention to ourselves in the context of the debilitating quality of everyday life in Los Angeles, which is better characterized by its freeway system and neon plasticity (what were we to make of that 'Felix' Chevrolet sign at the corner of Figueroa and Jefferson Boulevard near the USC campus?) than by the scattered, lovely, elite architectural structures (the Wright and Neutra houses, the Gamble House, the Schindler furniture) we spent the third day of the Institute on a bus seeking out? It seems to me to make all the more sense to do that because one of the chief methodological processes of American Culture Studies, as I understand it, is to make problematic all cultural givens (the environment, lifeways, systems, language, beliefs), particularly those that bear heavily and burdensomely on the human potential for grace, excitement, growth, peak experience, health, friendship, community, a good sexual life, and useful work. Even in a self-conscious civilization like the contemporary United States, characterized by rapid technological and moral change, culture is taken by the masses of people as if given, as if its elements had the quality of natural law. To show it problematic, to understand fully how the human world is socially constructed,[3] is only to do one of the major jobs of a teacher at any level. To be sure, doing that job is to risk provoking in oneself and in students considerable anxiety, even metaphysical anxiety. Taken as natural law, culture functions as a support system, and very few human beings can survive without some such support, even if the support itself paradoxically generates neurosis. But if the high school is to be any more than a crude socializing institution, shaping young people so that they fit into a Procrustean and dehumanized world, and if doing American Culture Studies in high school is to contribute to a cultural revolution, surely it is exactly that risk that teachers must be willing to take.

I did say some of all that the first week of the Institute. On the whole I felt myself in a position somewhat like that of Paul Goodman when, giving a taped lecture to a class of graduate students in elementary education, he remarked that he would be no real help to them. They wanted to hear about ways to improve the schools, but he had come to suppose not that the schools *had* problems so much as they *were* the problem, or at least a major component of the problem. I would go further, to the proposition not that American culture *has* problems — any American can list them by culling the week's newspaper stories — but that it *is* the problem. Its most basic and permanent elements — the works of engineering and architecture through which Americans move in their daily lives, the transportation system that moves them, the very nature of the centralized, hierarchical, presumably representative political system, the structure of the business system, the style in which the work needed for social survival is done (and the style in which most work in America, not needed for social survival, is also done), the way science is translated into a wasteful and controlling technology, the nature of Western science itself, the health delivery system (better characterized as an illness-rectification system), the communication media and their manipulations, the mass arts, the racial and sexual order — all these and more tend by their very nature, not by their accidental distortions, to dehumanize the population. What help would that observation be to high school teachers who find themselves obliged to do their daily work in a regular way? From my point of view, to persist in more of the same is no solution to the problems of teaching American Culture Studies in the high school, yet what alternatives to more of the same were there?

2. Toward Cultural Revolution

Four forthright alternative lines of action suggest themselves, at least on the theoretical level. I list them in an order of plausibility and desirability, the least plausible and the most desirable first.

(1) Contribute to the making of an immediate cultural revolution, a transformation of the cultural order, so that the institutions and lifeways into which children are socialized are liberating ones. In such a recreated world as I imagine, either there would not be school as we know it (thus solving the problem of teaching American Culture Studies in the high school by bypassing it) or school would be a very different institution from what we are familiar with. School at all levels would be (let us say) a community resource. Citizens would enter and study for a period of time when they need formal knowledge. They would learn from a community of facilitators, masters, and scholars, as in Illich's vision, or perhaps as in Goodman's *The Community of Scholars* or even Hesse's *Magister Ludi.* Ideally teachers would be masters very much in but not wholly of the world, and by that contribute to it.

(2) Act to deschool society *before* such a cultural revolution occurs or is visibly in process, on the assumption that school is a linchpin institution holding the present cultural order together and that such an act would contribute to the coming of a revolution. To deschool is thus revolutionary *praxis,* an action growing out of a cultural analysis that sees school in the United States as an essential institution of cultural maintainence. School is so important to the cultural support system, however, that deschooling requires some kind of alternative before it can serve as a viable political program. Ivan Illich describes at length one set of technically workable alternatives in his *Deschooling Society.* Such self-generating learning networks or "opportunity webs" as he advocates would, if adopted, themselves contain the seeds of cultural revolution. They imply a massive reallocation of resources, effort, and value. The

vested interests resisting such an alternative are enormous. Add up all the schooling budgets in the United States and the total surpasses the military budget of one of the most militaristic nations the world has known, the United States in the 1960s and 1970s.

(3) Re-conceive and reconstruct the High School — its purposes, procedures, curriculums, and courses. This line of action assumes that not all schooling is to be de-institution-alized — that the primary schools (where at its best the teaching is directed toward growth) will remain basically the same, and that the university, though with far fewer students feeling forced by cultural compulsions to attend, has a kind of basic formal soundness. The high school is the anomaly, having neither the babysitting, literacy, socialization justifications of the primary grades nor the disciplinary, body of knowledge, realm of intellect, scholarly justifications of the university. Thus, to imitate experiments in Philadelphia and Boston where members of the community have substantial control over the high school and where students learn by engaging the world with the assistance of tutors and counselors is to begin to construct nationwide a new concept: High School Without Walls. Such a reconstruction could move in one of at least two directions: toward an exaggeration of work/learn programs, where the learning is adaptive to the social order, or toward critical perception and analysis, where the learning is transformative and in the end revolutionary. An appropriate contribution to the latter might be made by American Culture Studies and I shall return to it specifically in discussing a proposal for teaching "culture-victims" and in general in discussing the survival theme.

(4) Redo the courses once more, intensely aware that the crucial function of teaching in this time and dehumanizing civilization is to contribute to cultural revolution through nurturing the growth of human beings. Education "always deals in socialization," as Becca Livingston argues in a fine essay on American Studies and high school. Conventionally, as she says, the aim is to reproduce and reinforce internally in students "assumed meanings and values which legitimate and

maintain the world-as-is." The sense of roles, norms, limits, and connections and of alternative ways of being in the world more productively, peacefully, and humanly is diminished. Creative energies are routed toward adjusting, maintaining, enlarging, and perfecting established institutions and social relations. What would happen if high school teachers were to see their work in American Culture Studies as contributing to "counter-socialization"? Like Becca Livingston, I mean by this not the imposition or inculcation of new values to replace the old ones, but the construction of a new frame of reference, value-laden perhaps but not itself a value. Such reference points as "for a human being to suffer unjustly is intolerable" are not by themselves values. Nor are they tautological, though "in a more decent society" they might "appear to be." They are, "in effect, an assertion that values are called for .... [In] contemporary society, as it now is, the adoption of this particular reference point would have a genuinely revolutionary impact on education, for what it asserts is the human obligation to make moral judgments from the standpoint of humanity." [4]

Becca Livingston sees the adoption of such a frame of reference as "subversive." I agree and it is within the context of such a subversive, revolutionary frame of reference that the redoing of courses once again is, in my view, obliged to go on. To put the matter differently, redoing courses ought to be engaged in as, progressively, a contribution to reconceiving the high school, deschooling society, and ultimately making a cultural revolution. Besides, redoing courses is something that high school teachers can *do*. It has possibilities, whereas the first three alternatives are pie in a theoretical revolutionary sky. It is to such a redoing, therefore, that the high school workshop paid most attention during the three weeks of the Institute, though the third alternative — reconceiving the high school — got its due also.

3. "There Must be a Better Way"

The kind of learning I advocate for high school I have elsewhere described as "reflexive." [5] By "reflexive learning" I mean a turning or bending backwards on oneself, as with a reflexive verb or mirror, though often the mirror may distort as in a fun-house at a carnival. The study of one's own culture can be a reflexive learning situation. Culture is, after all, the most encompassing term available to describe the environment through time of which each of us is a dialectical product. Studying it necessarily means that we approach the source of our being and experience, just as in earlier centuries men sought to pierce the veil that hid from them the inscrutable God, source of all good and woe. The study of one's own culture, making what was before opaque now problematic, can be a therapeutic activity. Fortunately, culture works in ways less mysterious than God and can be comprehended without special revelation. But how exactly is one to construct a course or curriculum in American Culture Studies that is reflexive and that will survive and flourish in high school? As Paul Goodman remarked, there are three basic ways to teach: teach the child directly, teach him indirectly through the subject, or teach the subject. Kindergarten teachers tend to teach the child. University professors tend to teach their subject. In dealing with the high school, do we not find ourselves in that no-man's land where we are to teach the person *through* the subject? Surely "there must be a better way," as participants in the workshop variously remarked, "to teach American literature," "to make American history interesting," "to integrate courses," and in general "to get [high] school in touch with reality." Just as surely, that better way is *not* that implied by the design of the Institute. Various experts lecturing on their understanding of aspects of a decade urges by implication a kind of synthetic but unconceptualized *translation* of a number of bodies of knowledge into an organized, relatively conventional high school course of study. Nothing could be less useful, in my view, despite what were often brilliant, penetrating, knowledgeable lectures. It is not by multiplying bodies of knowledge or by multi-disciplinary teaching that American Culture Studies in high school will be liberatingly reflexive.

Presumably it was my sense of the conceptual and

educational flaws in Classic American Studies, as well as my strong political resistance to the putatively objective academic liberalism of most of the lectures, that led to my discomfort at the Institute, though I almost always get restless at lectures. (Lecturing is not a powerful mode of teaching.) Certainly in discussing my discomfort here I risk being unfair to the lecturers, who after all were only doing what they do well and were asked to do; but there was a great deal I disagreed with and my resistant discomfort was strongly felt, enough to drive me to *ad hominem* poems. Rereading my poems, I find that I felt most strongly about the sterility of the lecture/classroom scene, the subtle denigration of revolutionary visions, using the mind to report, more than to analyze and guide, and the celebration of skepticism and objectivity. I note particularly a poem I wrote in response to Daniel Aaron's lecture praising what I summarized as Edmund Wilson's complexity, skepticism, curiosity, historicism, detachment, objectivity, fidelity, and aloofness — which as I see it are not altogether desirable ways to be in the world. I imagine I wrote about Daniel Aaron particularly because he was President of the American Studies Association and therefore represented somehow in his person the style of a legitimated American Studies. Indeed, the Institute itself — its form, content, style — was coming to represent for me legitimated American Studies in the United States *at its best.* Thus to involve myself in its details and to see where I stood in relation to it was to locate myself concretely in relation to legitimated American Studies in the United States as a whole.

Let me summarize my disagreement under four headings: historicism, multiple explanation, culture, and politics.

Historicism: The lecturers characteristically "explained" cultural phenomena by ordering them sequentially through time, as if engaged in an unstated collective conspiracy aimed at refuting by ignoring the *post hoc ergo propter hoc* fallacy. The chronological mode was implicitly and explicitly justified in a number of ways. John Cotter, for example, talked about a "world-wide compulsion to gain perspective and identity" through understanding the past. Sydney Ahlstrom mentioned how we explain by "telling a story" and argued for historicism as "an outlook on life, a pervasive way of being in the world." Surely here we have an important element in legitimated American Studies scholarship. Historicism implies a perspective and a form of objectivity. It provides a way not only to order but to organize experience. Strictly speaking, in dictionary terms, it suggests (a) a belief that processes are at work in history that man can do little to alter, (b) a theory that the historian must avoid all value judgments, and (c) a veneration of the past or of tradition. Emphatically I do not want to argue that all the lecturers consciously hold historicist views. My point here is only that all were operating as historians of one kind or another, that putting the present (or the 1930s, or whatever time is to be explained) in historical sequence and thus context, whether for historicist reasons or not, seemed to lecturers and audience alike a wholly acceptable and predictable way to go about doing American Studies, and that this agreement between lecturers and audience was seldom articulated. Mostly it was a matter of unstated consensus.

When I tried in the high school workshop to make problematic the historicism characteristic of legitimated American Studies, the discussion was sharp and the resistance was strong. Obviously, it seemed to me, not only university scholars but high school teachers as well were operating according to an unarticulated agreement about the nature of explanation in American Studies: American Studies for them was a form of history. A key element in its loose paradigmatic design was chronology. Chronology implied a category of understanding, a way of seeing the world somehow appropriate to the educational system. Students understood when they knew sequences. Courses, therefore, were to be chronologically ordered and chronology had some special status as an ordering principle. The ordering is the meaning. As I say, the resistance was considerable, and I came away from the workshop feeling I had persuaded no one not already persuaded to doubt chronology as a way to organize American Culture Studies in high school. Nevertheless, I persist in the argument. If the learning in high schools is to be reflexive, if we are to teach high school students through or by means of the subject, then attending to the pastness of the past, or even (excessively) to the presentness of the past or the pastness of the present, is educationally pernicious. The past does not explain the present. I propose that we consider (1) abandoning the generally accepted notion that the job of American Culture Studies teachers is to interest students in the past (in resistance to the intense interest they feel in the present, in which after all they live and must act), and (2) making articulate the historicist assumptions of legitimated American Studies, so that they might be submitted to criticism and, if necessary, revision. It is self-evident neither that the past is a Good Thing for students to know nor that historicism is the best or only mode in which to do American Culture Studies, in or out of high school.

Multiple Explanation: Consider Basil Willey's straight-forward response to the question: what is explanation?

> Dictionary definitions will not help us much here. 'To explain,' we learn, means to 'make clear,' to 'render intelligible.' But wherein consists the clarity, the intelligibility? The clarity of an explanation seems to depend upon the degree of satisfaction that it affords. An explanation 'explains' best when it meets some need of our nature, some deep-seated demand for assurance. 'Explanation' may perhaps be roughly defined as a restatement of something – event, theory, doctrine, etc. – in terms of the current interests and assumptions. It satisfies, as explanation, because it appeals to that particular set of assumptions, as superseding those of a past age or of a former state of mind. Thus it is necessary, if an explanation is to seem satisfactory, that its terms should seem ultimate, incapable of further analysis. Directly we allow ourselves to ask 'What, after all, does this explanation amount to?' we have really demanded an explanation of the explanation, that is to say, we have seen that the terms of the first explanation are not ultimate, but can be analysed into other terms – which perhaps for the moment do seem to us to be ultimate. Thus, for example, we may choose to accept a psychological explanation of a metaphysical proposition, or we may prefer a metaphysical explanation of a psychological proposition. All depends upon our presuppositions, which in turn depend upon our training, whereby we have come to regard (or to feel) one set of terms as ultimate, the other not. An explanation commands our assent with immediate authority, when it presupposes the 'reality,' the 'truth,' of what seems to us most real, most true. One cannot, therefore, define 'explanation' absolutely; one can only say that it is statement which satisfies the demands of a particular time or place.[6]

American Studies scholars and teachers tend to explain, as I say, by making sequences, by chronology, by telling a story. When that will not do, when questions continue to arise about cause and connection, they are in a quandary. It is not that they confront philosophically new questions. Aristotle, after all, discriminated between kinds of causes. It is only that in American Studies the old questions about explanation have not been very extensively or self-consciously dealt with.

Thus, when sequence fails to provide assurances, the appeal is to some common sense notion of multiple cause and effect, which is a very unsystematic and unsatisfactory guide to intelligibility. What seems to common sense most real and true may not, on examination, hold up. I want to avoid dealing with any of the lecturers specifically on this matter. Characteristically, instead of making the difficulty of answering problematic — that is, making the difficulty itself the problem — the lecturers tried to give substantive answers, inadequately I thought (and so, often, did they). Consider instead a characteristic and hypothetical example. How would scholars in American Studies "explain" Watergate? Presumably the analysis would go something like this: first there is Richard Nixon (individual, perhaps a psychological explanation), then there is the set of images and beliefs the right wing of the Republican Party brings out of the Cold War (myth, symbol), then there is the discovery of the burglars in the act, the way some elements of the media pushed the story, the judge who persisted in making inquiries (accident), then there is the nature of American political campaigns (institutional), then there is the struggle between the Presidency and the Congress over power, with the Presidency winning out in the past few decades (internal institutional conflict), then there is the inevitability of such events given the growth of the national security bureaucracy since WW II (institutional history, maybe even functional institutional analysis), then there is the nature of the cultural system as a whole, which inevitably generates such incidents (culture, structuralism perhaps), and so on. This list is reminiscent of textbook multiple explanations of the coming of the Civil War.[7] My objection is not that some one or several of these lines of explanation might not be forceful. Nor do I argue that one cannot sometimes offer something like multiple explanations. On the contrary, I myself would explain in several of these ways, and on the principle of complementarity, often multiple explanations can re-inforce each other and be clarifying. [8] What I do mean to suggest is that (a) explanations should make some kind of coherent, systematic sense, they should not be *obiter dicta* or *ad hoc* appeals to common sense; and (b) scholars and teachers identifying themselves as engaged in American Culture Studies ought to be working at establishing self-consciously and collectively paradigmatic explanations of culture. Anyone wishing to retain a multiple-explanation model ought to feel obliged to articulate the arguments by which it becomes plausible.

The problem of the nature of explanation in socio-humanistic studies has been present and confronted often in the history of thought. Basil Willey's 1934 commentary is not peculiar or even special conceptually. The problem has barely begun to be re-addressed seriously and extensively in the context of American Studies, however. To be sure, at the Institute, Professors Ahlstrom, Cawelti, and Martin seemed particularly sensitive to it in their ways. Bruce Kuklick, in an *American Quarterly* essay analyzing the assumptions of the myth/symbol school of American Studies, takes it as his central problem. Other scholars in the Department of American Civilization at the University of Pennsylvania have made useful contributions, notably Murray Murphey. So also have David Noble and Roland Delattre at the University of Minnesota, and there are others. Gene Wise in his new and exciting *American Historical Explanations: A Strategy for Grounded Inquiry* (Homewood, Illinois: The Dorsey Press, 1973) proposes a new field: Explanation in American Historical Studies. The influence of Thomas Kuhn's *The Structure of Scientific Revolutions* (1962) is apparent in Professor Wise's work, as it is elsewhere in recent reflections on American Studies methodology. My own anthology, *American Studies: Essays on Theory and Method* (1968), has had some success in generating methodological self-awareness in graduate introductory courses in American Studies. The examples can be multiplied, but such interests have still not been adopted by large numbers of scholars, teachers, and students in American Studies, even though theory and method — of which explanation is a part — ought to involve everyone, including high school teachers, not merely those with special interests in abstraction. After all, how is illuminating research or teaching at any level possible without a coherent and adequate view of the subject, at a relatively high level of abstraction and with a clear idea of the relation between methods of inquiry and ends?

Culture: The point about the centrality of theoretical concerns is most forceful, it seems to me, when it is brought to bear on the basic question of what exactly it is we are studying in American Culture Studies. There seems at first to be loose consensus here again, as in the cases of chronology and multiple explanation. We are studying American *culture,* as the repeated use of the term in American Studies scholarship would suggest. We are not doing political history so much as some combination of social-cultural-intellectual history. We read literary documents not only for aesthetic but for "cultural" reasons. Popular literature is important because it articulates the formulas expressing the tensions of large masses of people. We explore architecture because it tells us about lifeways. We dig for ancient artifacts not for purely antiquarian reasons, but because from them we learn about past ways of life. We read the landscape not as a sentimental fable of God's ways but as a document embodying the values and processes of a culture, if only we can make them out. And so on.

As I say, it would seem that we agree. Yet the concept of culture deployed in all the lectures — with the possible exception of Jay Martin's — was loose and, with the exception of John Cotter's formulations, chiefly literary or at best humanistic. The orientation such a minimally rigorous, inveterately humanistic controlling idea gives to American Culture Studies is nearly as unsatisfactory as no orientation at all. We learn some things, but their status is never very clear, and what we learn has chiefly to do with superstructure and epiphenomena. Combined with the tendency to let sequence serve as explanation and with the tendency to engage in non-paradigmatic common sense comments on cause, it leads to a potpourri American Studies where nearly anything goes dealing with belief, value, myth, symbol, image, or idea. I do not want to reverse the error by arguing that only institutions, social relations, quantifiable data, behavior, action, or systemic structures should make up the content of culture and the objects of inquiry. I do want to urge that the concept of culture is best formulated, for American Culture Studies purposes (and for educational purposes at all levels), socio-humanistically, and that it is a comprehensive concept which gets its power not so much from what it excludes as from the way it both arranges all phenomena characteristic of a civilization and focuses inquiry and understanding.

Politics: In his Institute lectures Sydney Ahlstrom informally defined religion as "an orientation toward the totality of being." Everyone with a personality is religious, he said. "Theology" I take to be the articulation of that orientation in metaphysical terms. "Politics" I take as its articulation and acting out in socio-cultural terms, however disguised. In its most general and now unfortunately nearly defunct sense, "politics" deals not only with legitimation and control and with hierarchies and other orders of power, but with the quality and relationships of systems; in short, with the cultural organism as a whole. An ethical politics, as I see it, is one in which the characteristic political subjects are critically analyzed and evaluated from a point of view provided by notions about human "nature" – and then acted upon. Everyone with a personality also has a politics, though not necessarily an ethical politics. The nature of human "nature" is of course a vexed question and a long discussion seems inappropriate here. In my own view, following Maslow and others, it is "natural" that men are loving, courageous, creative, kind, altruistic, playful, humorous, spontaneous, self-regulating, integrated, and so on. The state of psychological health – called variously self-fulfillment, emotional maturity, individuation, productiveness, self-actualization,

authenticity, full-humanness — is natural, though in our
culture unusual. As Maslow remarks, this and other elements
of his psychology make "theoretically possible" a comparative culturology, "transcending and including cultural relativity." The " 'better' culture . . . permits self-actualization.
The 'poorer' cultures do not." [9]

From this point of view, American Studies scholars and
teachers display not only a politics inadequate to the "poor"
condition of American culture in the 1970s but an inadequate sense of the pervasiveness of politics in their
intellectual work. [10] I can hardly imagine serious socio-
humanistic talk or teaching without a political (as well as
theological and psychological) dimension. Even apparently
neutral, academic, objective analyses and discussions have
political implications, and when the stance is objective the
implications are usually conservative. That advocacy should
be forced to make itself explicit and justify itself norma-
tively, I believe, since eventually all such indirect advocacies
in American Culture Studies done by Americans advance
some sort of argument about how Americans ought to live in
the world or about how the world ought to be. My own
communitarian anarchism leads me to see my study of
American culture explicitly as an advocacy study. I advocate
decentralization, simplification, spontaneity, and disclosure;
in short, nature (as I understand it) against culture. I make
inquiries and teach *in order that* (among other things) I might
contribute to the making of a humanly more satisfying
world, as I see it. The historicist emphasis on the given, on
what Daniel Boorstin calls the "seamless web" of American
culture, I oppose in favor of making culture problematic,
because to make culture problematic is inherently revolutionary, at least negatively, and I advocate cultural revolution. Positively, Ivan Illich's definition of a revolutionary act
as the irrevocable establishment of a new cultural possibility,
as the act of beating a new path, seems to me forceful. One
of the questions we should be addressing in American Culture
Studies is the question of how intellect, scholarship, and
teaching might in this sense be revolutionary. Not to address
that question, given the state of American culture in the

1970s, is to violate what I take to be a compelling ethical principle of the profession. In high school, of course, explicit politics of the sort I have in mind is risky. One of the high school workshop participants pointed out that there is "no assumption of academic freedom in high school" and the others largely agreed. We made a short list of important subjects that could seldom be discussed openly: sex, love, revolution, politics, ethics, religion, freedom, and education itself. That is, occasionally one might discuss them "objectively," but one took grave risks dealing with them as live issues. *Not* to discuss them was, as someone else remarked, "a question of survival."

4. What to do Tuesday Morning: Four Special Cases

It may well be, however, that the survival of American culture, if not of some teachers in it, depends on its political transformation and that it is precisely the act of trespassing cultural boundaries and beating a new path that is called for in our time. In education over the past decade a radical reform movement has pointed a way. Can that movement be consolidated in the process of doing American Culture Studies in the high schools, thus establishing the combination of radically reformed educational practices and American Culture Studies irrevocably as a new possibility? On the evidence of the workshop I'm not sure. The difficulties sometimes seem overwhelming. One difficulty is not so much figuring what to say on Monday, as John Holt would have it – on Monday you outline the course – as figuring how to do what needs to be done, and then beginning on Tuesday to do it.

Pursuing John Cotter's proposition that, as in archeology, "education is discovery or it's nothing," I proposed during the second week of the high school workshop a problem-stating/problem-solving process.[11] The workshop would break up into groups of four or five people. Each person in the group would in turn state the "problem" he brought with him to the Institute (personal, intellectual, a course, a curriculum) as precisely as he could and state at the same time all limitations and conditions he felt obliged to put on a workable solution. The other members of the small group

were to ask questions until the problem was very clearly
stated in such a way as to allow for real solutions. Second,
the group was to imagine as many alternative solutions as
possible to the problem as stated, without censorship,
especially without the kind of pre-censorship that rejects
solutions because they are unrealistic. The person whose
problem was being explored would take notes and ask for as
much clarification of detail as he wished. Third, everyone in
the group would criticize the proposed solutions, but the
person stating the problem would decide finally which
solution he goes for and wishes to work out. Fourth, the
chosen solution would be explored in detail by the group.
Finally, the process would be written up in sequence:
problem; solutions rejected, with briefly stated reasons;
solution accepted, described in detail. Those issues and
solutions I have made into case studies. It strikes me that the
case study format may provide a more concretely helpful
way to deal with American Culture Studies in high school
than a generalized description and discussion of course
types. [12] What should be constant in thinking about high
school courses of study are principles, not practices: the logic
of culture study, a coherent and articulated political perspective on contemporary American culture, and some
analysis of the needs of high school age students. Specific
teaching situations and styles are highly variable, though
undoubtedly some situations and styles are more typical than
others. I begin with four distinctive cases which both raise
and clarify fundamental issues. Cases 5-7 seem to me typical
ones, and the final three cases return us to general problems
in mating educational reform and American Culture Studies.
My own general perspective I trust I have established
sufficiently. Throughout, my way of dealing with the cases is
by being insistently and specifically critical. In short, I apply
my view of American Culture Studies, American culture, and
high school to these specific proposals by real teachers in a
real world. I am willing to be specifically critical because in
general the proposals are so good — so obviously sincere,
intelligent, and capable. [13] Often they force me to revise the
bleakness of that image of the high school I began the

Institute with. At the same time, they are not always good enough, given the revolutionary burden I propose must be borne by American Culture Studies in high school.

(1) The problem Jim Seamon posed to the group seems to me characteristic of the moral problems many young, hopeful teachers confront. Jim had taught one year in high school in North Carolina, earned an M.S. in Education, spent three years in the Navy (part of it in Vietnam), and returned straight from Vietnam to USC and the Institute. He had, he said, "become concerned that significant learning can rarely take place within the traditional educational system."[14] Before he could bring himself to return to teaching he felt a "major change in the system" was necessary. Assuming he were in the system, however, he asked how he could "most successfully overcome" its "built-in barriers to learning," particularly (a) the artificial separation of subjects or disciplines, which "ignores ... causal relationships and the patterns and flow of the real world," (b) the notion that the teacher defines what is important to know, not the student, and (c) the teacher's functioning as a judge. He saw American Culture Studies as a solution to (a) because it is comprehensive. Also it emphasizes not "subject matter covered" so much as "thinking, analyzing, integrating," that is, "tools for working with the world." Furthermore, since the student is "both a product and a reflection of his culture as well as a creator and transmitter of it," he will be "intimately related to the subject" of the course, which is not the case in most high school courses. To cope with barrier (b) he would begin the course "by sharing with the students a list of questions" he would himself like answers to. He would then ask them for their own list of questions and meet with each of them individually. Mutually he and each student would decide on individualized problems for the course. Class sessions would be devoted to approaching the culture thematically, "using whatever sources happen to be available plus those suggested by the students." At the end, there would be a paper "documenting" the way each student went at his "quest, indicating thoughts, actions, [and] new problems." There would also be a final examination which would ask students

"to suggest an approach for studying a problem or theme, including what questions should be asked, what are the approaches that might be useful in gathering information," and so on. Neither paper nor exam would be graded. Students would earn an automatic pass for taking the exam, raised to an automatic *C* for the paper, raised higher through negotiation if the student wished.

Toward the conclusion of the Institute Jim was reading *Teaching as a Subversive Activity*. Radical educational reform clearly was what interested him. He sees many of the problems he confronts accurately, but there are both educational and conceptual flaws in his solution. For example, he says he would begin with his own questions: e.g., "Why are we spending billions of dollars flying to the moon when babies in the ghettos are being chewed by rats? . . . Could a Jew or Black be elected President . . . ?" The questions are rhetorical and inauthentic. He already has the answers and he is not really expressing himself. (His real questions involved identity and the educational system and his vocation.) Is he not from the beginning providing a misleading model for students in his hypothetical course? Indeed, beginning with questions is a conventional device in classes and probably should be abandoned in favor of assertions (if only on the therapeutic principle that questions either serve as devices to deflect seriousness or are implied assertions). Surely it is one's deeply held assertions that ought to be tested by inquiry. The grading system, paper, and exam are also relatively conventional, despite Jim's emphasis in the latter on the process of inquiry. Finally, it is clear neither what relation his "thematic approach" in classes has to the student-projects at the center of the course design, nor what the content and procedure of the approach will be — which is, after all, a crucial day-by-day question.

Two other flaws seem to me conceptually important in thinking about high school and American Culture Studies in terms of Jim's problem. First, American Culture Studies adequately conceived is not so much comprehensive — Jim remarks that it "consists of everything ever done, said, worn, watched, eaten, applauded, built, smoked, or otherwise acted upon by Americans" — as it is *convergent*. That is, it tries to make intellectual and human sense out of all available data by means of paradigms (or models or schemes for understanding or the ordering of concepts, as you will) that overlap, revise, or extend traditional disciplinary paradigms. It abstracts from, though it does not ignore, the flow of the real world. The sense it tries to make is cultural (not chiefly psychological or theological) sense. This both circumscribes and clarifies the nature of the activity and puts Jim's comment about multiple data and culture in a specific context. Second, Jim's view of his students seems to me excessively hopeful. That they *are* related intimately to the subject does not necessarily mean they are willing to perceive the importance to their lives of comprehending that relationship. After all, for the most part they emerge from 16 years of living in a one-dimensional culture. Will they be likely to absorb and respond to Jim's hopes easily? To, say, either comprehensiveness or convergence? To radical analysis and criticism? As some members of the workshop put it, what does Jim do if and when the students resist or evade or put him on?

(2) Maggie Bader confronts a similar difficulty. She wished to "come up with an approach to the study of culture" which (a) emphasizes "peace and justice," (b) is applicable to the study of Asian, Third World, and European, as well as American culture, and (c) might satisfy her colleagues. Maggie is a Roman Catholic nun, a Sister of the Holy Child teaching order, and curriculum director at a Washington, D.C., Catholic girls' high school. Her first two conditions — an approach and its extension to cultures other than that of the United States — were relatively easy to satisfy. Explorations of the culturally relative concept of justice, of comparative value systems, of the American dream; ethical decision games, the study of lifeways, the writing of a diary as if one were a sixteen year old in another time or culture; criticism of the concept of "peace" as potentially part of a conservative ideology: all these and other activities were suggested. Her ultimate problem was the third condition, namely satisfying her colleagues. The pro-

blem was simultaneously practical and theoretical. Theoretically, her religious order consents to propositions about
peace and justice that might satisfy the most committed
pacifist, but there is a gaping discrepancy between its theory
and its practice. Maggie thought that, as curriculum director,
she ought to use her position primarily to "focus faculty
thinking and planning" and close the gap. Three related lines
of action were suggested: to serve herself as a witness and
model for the value of concentrating one's study on peace
and justice, to assert (as contrasted merely to defending) the
righteousness of her view and the moral and political error in
denying it, and finally to bring about some community
among the faculty in relation to these questions by means of
a therapeutically oriented workshop (or retreat) with the
help of guest speakers.

Is not the chief difficulty here, however, related to the
critique of Jim's excessive hopefulness, this time at the level
of the faculty instead of the students? The faculty too
emerges from a one-dimensional culture and (in the case of
the nuns) a relatively constricted set of traditions about the
nature of the religious life. Will they be likely to absorb and
respond easily to Maggie's hopes? The discussion of her
problem in the larger workshop sessions brought out a
further difficulty. In her school, as in other such schools,
teachers are obliged to promise they will teach nothing
contrary to the church's position on a whole range of crucial
human issues. Maggie's tendency was to diminish the impact
of such a promise (and the ethos that results) on the quality
of learning, but as it turns out the limitations are severe ones.
If in fact the emphasis on peace and justice covertly means an
emphasis on the church's version of peace and justice, what
we have in Maggie's school and schools like it is not a new,
subversive frame of reference for counter-socialization, but
another socializing, even propagandizing, institution, much
like the public schools where there are also severe restrictions
on subjects and point of view. We are back again to the
schools not as having problems but as being the problem.

(3) Also concerned with justice, Sharlene Vest's program
for those she calls (after Paulo Freire) "culture victims"

constitutes an imaginative and exciting educational strategy. [15] The culture victims she specifically has in mind are young male school dropouts, ages 16-21, who are wards of the State or Court and living in a group home in Boston. In general, culture victims are those who do not fit into the accepted, valued categories of a given culture. Thus if, as in the United States, wealth, success, and formal educational achievement are important, those who are poor, unsuccessful, and unable to be molded by established educational procedures tend to become victims. They share the expectations and values of the culture but are unable to fulfill them and thus unable to reap the rewards which go to those who can. Sharlene's strategy is to "unmask" the culture for its victims, sensitizing them to the dynamics of the system by which they are victimized and making available to them a radical understanding of their condition. With Freire, she supposes that "the form of action men adopt is to a large extent a function of how they perceive themselves in the world." Once culture victims are knowledgeable about cultural formulas, they may choose adaptation and manipulation or resistance and change, one hopes the latter, but whichever, at least with understanding.

Sharlene proposes a number of assumptions: (a) These students will learn most readily in a personal/social/general sequence, in which generalizations about culture come last, after the personal and group experience is articulated. (E.g., the movement should be from *my* detention center experience to others' experience to the treatment in American culture of juveniles; or from *my* family to others' families to the family in American culture.) (b) Many of the young men are unmotivated readers who will read only when reading is seen as having direct value for them. Therefore most of the activities should encourage reading without making it primary. (c) They need to learn to relate to others. Therefore, the learning group should be kept small and a therapeutic group relationship should be built into the daily activity. (d) The content of the program — which will be day-long and controlled to a large extent by the immediate interests of the students — must be concrete and applicable.

It must grow from felt, real questions and lead to clear ideas about the relation between culture victims and culture. The possibilities, as Sharlene remarks, seem nearly unlimited and might include (listed in order of probable applicability to group home residents):

Family backgrounds and current human relationships
Police, courts, law, and justice
Living in Boston, the city
The welfare system, the economy
The biology, psychology, and sociology of sex
Money, time, and leisure
Stimulants and depressants in America
Death
The rights of children
Cars, motorcycles, technology
Environment
Power relationships
Prejudice and ethnic identity
Schools and educational attitudes
Voting, politics, and change
Violence, war

As presently conceived, the course would begin with four concurrent units: living in Boston, jails and justice, families, and welfare and poverty. In the jails and justice unit, the students would: visit the police station (to talk to the police when not being arrested), interview a judge, sit in court sessions, observe and discuss cases, personnel, and the judge's procedures, listen to an American Friends Service Committee worker speak about the court-watching project, then visit court again, visit Roslindale Detention Center, talk to guards, read about juvenile delinquents (who are they? what happens to them?), find out who commits which crimes, evaluate typical sentences, visit Concord Prison, talk to the warden and ex-offenders, interview the men who organized the Prisoners' Peaceful Movement, collect their newsletter and study it, keep a notebook record of crimes reported in the *Boston Globe,* read and discuss stories by or about offenders, and find out about jails and justice in Boston during other periods in history. Sharlene's detailed account of this and other units is valuable, not only for its procedures but also as an illustration of her general case about culture victims and teaching American Culture Studies. I am reminded of the last sentence of Ralph Ellison's *Invisible Man:* "Who knows but that, on the lower frequencies, I speak for you?" As Sharlene remarks, courses similar to this one in aim, though not necessarily in content, are conceivable in a variety of circumstances for a variety of culture victims: women, ethnic minorities, students, children, assembly-line workers, the ugly, the sick. Who is not a victim of culture in contemporary America? Of all the proposals made at the Institute, Sharlene Vest's most articulately and concretely embodies the politics I advocate for American Culture Studies at the high school level.[16]

(4) Her case can be further illustrated by working through Gerard Rossi's proposals for teaching the blind. The subject is not insubstantial in itself, since there are roughly half a million blind people in the United States. For them, nearly everything taken for granted by sighted people in the usual secondary physical environment of Americans becomes problematic, often hostile — cars, freeways, steps, classrooms, TV, restaurants, and so on. The blind are archetypal culture victims. Like other culture victims, they must learn to maneuver in a world not made for them, not supportive of them, certainly not nurturing. Teaching them becomes paradigmatically as well as substantially important.

As Gerry points out, if you are blind even the most basic materials for learning are wanting: visual aids are of no use, most printed material is not available in Braille or on records, many blind students have not had mobility training and therefore do not travel about in their own city environment. Most architecture, most sculpture, and painting are beyond the experience of the blind. (Is the situation much different from the situation of black students in Harlem?) Gerry would rectify the situation by seeking to expand Braille materials, by collecting a number of auditory aids (poets or philosophers reading their own works on records, historical speeches,

recreated history, radio, music), by encouraging guest speakers, by having students conduct interviews, and so on (his list
is long and imaginative). He would teach his students
California culture – its history, governmental system, literary
heritage, art, sociological configurations, religion, economy,
science, geography and climate, environment. (Later we will
explore another proposal for such a curriculum.) But neither
the collection of materials nor the California course seems to
me adequate to the problems the blind confront; both are
adaptive, not assertive. Gerry included in his final written
proposal a pedagogical question I like: "What kind of a world
could the blind construct which would maximize their
opportunities and well being?" My utopian notion – which
Gerry declined fully to share – was that the blind, like all of
us, are fully within their human rights in insisting on a
nurturing, non-hostile world to inhabit. American Culture
Studies in high school for the blind could well become the
foundation and means for a liberation movement, pro-
legomenon to a cultural revolution.

5. What to do Tuesday Morning: Three Typical Cases

Though the situation is changing rapidly, most high
schools still offer no specifically American Culture Studies
courses. Rather, there are standard courses in American
literature, American history, and social studies. A number of
the teachers in the workshop live with such a situation, which
I take as typical. Their general question characteristically
was: what contribution can American Culture Studies make
to my literature (or history or social studies) teaching? My
general answer characteristically is: it can contribute a great
deal, and if you are willing to abandon traditional goals and
to re-orient wholly, it can be transformative.

(5) Elizabeth Paulin, for example, wanted a better
"frame of reference" for a semester course in American
literature and during the workshop devised a "more culture-
oriented approach" to her subject for high school juniors "of
average intelligence." Her stated aim was to "stimulate the
student's cultural awareness" and thus his "self-awareness"
and sense of his "relationship to the American scene." She
planned to "zero in on the idea that each individual" is a

"reflection" of his culture by examining "beliefs" about male and female roles, by studying the youth culture of "cars, booze and sex," and by analyzing American "attitudes" toward the military. (The latter she chose because of her school's proximity to a military base.) The three themes seemed to her to provide a workable balance between continuity and variety. She would engage her subject by the study of literature "in any form."

Elizabeth was inventive in working out units and some of her choices show the influence of the Institute and of American Culture Studies generally: (a) She would begin with a discussion of the statement "I am a reflection of my culture," identifying terms necessary to such a discussion and asking the students to keep a list of them. (b) Moving quickly from generalizations about culture to the students' specific cultural milieu, she would attempt to develop concrete understandings of their time and place by engaging the class in some form of above-ground archeology. (c) After that, she would have the students analyze their reading approximately five years ago (books, comics, magazines) to find out the values "inherent" in their choices and to see what changes they had made. The aim is to see whether the change in reading indicates a change in values and, if so, to explain the change. (d) Next, she would build on the strong sexual interests of the students, asking the boys to "read something that the girls would read today (probably magazines) and vice versa." She would then ask each group to criticize the "subject matter, inherent values and influences, [and] cultural content" found in the readings, focusing particularly on whatever connects with their own ideas, decisions, and visions of the world. (e) Then she would do a unit on the American comic book and comic strip, analyzing them as types. The students, as she remarks, would "work on both literary skills here . . . [and] the cultural aspects of the comics." She would "begin to build a base for the short story." Her description of units goes on at length: analyzing the textbook as a cultural artifact, discussing male and female roles in American culture as they are revealed in short stories, tracing alternative life styles back to the Pilgrims, comparing earlier utopian communities with contemporary communes, comparing past American attitudes toward the military and war with contemporary ones as expressed in such books as *Slaughterhouse Five* and *Catch-22*, analyzing the lyrics of youth culture songs as "a means for teaching the art of poetry, its devices, rhythms, and beauty." In short, Elizabeth saw many of these units as "a good opportunity to explore literary stereotypes and stock characters and how they reflect our cultural values."

Many of these units do provide good opportunities, and if they are to be fully exploited from the point of view of American Culture Studies, often their logic and aims have to be refined and refocused. Individuals are not necessarily a "reflection" of culture, for example. A more descriptive term for the relationship might be "refraction." Or it might be more useful to say that culture provides the terms (the possibilities and limits) within which the individual self is shaped and emerges. Again, when students are asked to explain the causes of the difference between their reading now and five years ago, what model of explanation are they to appeal to? "Why?" and "What is the cause?" are questions too easily asked and much too quickly answered. Fully adequate answers would involve a whole theory of explanation, which obviously is not intended as part of the course. Perhaps it should be. "Choice" and "values" are also concepts too easily and misleadingly deployed, particularly the latter. Again, there is a certain lack of parallelism that will blur the logic of the course as a study of culture: Elizabeth intends her students to study "beliefs" about male and female "attitudes" toward the military, for example, whereas she will study the youth subculture presumably in some more direct fashion. What truth status will the studies have? Again, the relation between analyzing stories and understanding culture is at best problematic and Elizabeth does not address the relation as a problem. On the contrary, it seems as if the comics here are being *used* as a kind of preliminary to the short story, as if the story were a higher art form and as if the real task of the teacher is to tease the students into some interest in it, often by talk about culture.

The extreme instance of this comes when the concept of a cultural frame of reference for studying literature is insensibly transmuted into the concept of using elements out of the lives of students to lure them into the great tradition and to teach them literary (not cultural) analysis. It is that often subtle shift in focus that makes the difference between a literature course with cultural implications and a culture-study course that takes literature as primary evidence.

(6) Kathleen Johnson's proposal for an 11-12th grade history course within an American Culture Studies frame of reference has many similar qualities. The environment within which the course would take place is an independent school in Washington, D.C., where the students spend every Wednesday on Capitol Hill. The course would begin with a study of the 1960s — reading through the year-end issues of magazines, studying White's *Making of the President,* doing some above-ground archeology, learning how to make and administer questionnaires, interviewing, listening to music, artifact-collecting, and using the camera to *see* at least three chief "issues" of the 1960s — the environment, war, and minorities. The idea is to move students toward *doing* history, which echoes the voice of Professor Richard Warch, director of the Yale-New Haven History Education Project, writing in the *Yale Alumni Magazine* (1973): students learn best what they discover for themselves. The idea is also to lead students into the distant past by the carrot of their present interests, however. After the 1960s, then the 1950s and their parents. After the 1950s, then an attempt to deal with "themes" in "historical perspective": e.g., capitalism, "mission," property-rules, environment, minorities, dissent, governmental process. The teacher would also try to provide "some sense of looking at culture."

Here, as I see it, the pedagogy and American Culture Studies are being served up as icing on a cake students are characteristically uninterested in swallowing. As in the literature course, where one function of looking at the comics is to build a base for reading short stories, so here a chief function of working in the 1960s is to lead students into "historical perspective" on issues. I recall a discussion in

the workshop about the college Advanced Placement exams
— how students wanted to pass them so they would not have
to "take" history in college, how teachers were therefore
obliged to teach *for* the exams, and consequently how
American history courses could not move too far or for too
long into culture study. One of the results, of course, is an
attenuated and distorted American Culture Studies in high
school American history courses. Another is inadequate
history. It seems unlikely that the situation will change
without a substantial reconceptualization and re-ordering of
priorities and aims on the part of everyone involved.

(7) Lois Goss's problem was to prepare a teaching unit
on "culture and cultural values" for a 7th grade, racially-
integrated class on "Man and Culture," in which foreign
cultures (e.g., Africa and Asia) are dealt with. Her idea was to
build a base from which the class could do its cross-cultural
study by spending approximately 5 weeks exploring the
students' own culture, focusing particularly on "values." She
would begin by defining values inductively, by means of
playing simulation games such as "Crash Landing on Another
Planet" where students are obliged to make decisions which
(upon analysis) they find reflect their own values. Then she
would have the students examine their own activities (say,
their leisure time activities) to see what and whose values are
being acted out. She would have them analyze their regular
reading in terms of the values it promotes, see the values
taught in the religious schools they attend, look for hypo-
crisies or conflicting values, analyze documents (e.g., the Boy
Scout Handbook) in terms of the values urged in them, read
the values out of poetry and stories, a TV series, popular
music, bumper stickers, male-female stereotypes in textbooks
and advertisements, make their own 8 mm movie films
dramatizing conflicting values they see in the generation gap
or ethnic differences, interview grandparents, prepare a
questionnaire to discover values, and so on. The activities
sound as if they would be fun, nourishing, and contribute to
the students' learning. There is a general concept of culture
controlling the course and the course is not chiefly
historicist.

Two aspects of the course as proposed seem to me problematic, however. First, the attention paid to "values" misleadingly simplifies and ultimately distorts the under- standing of culture, no matter at what age level it is taught. Lois would "teach the concept of values as determining forces in the development of a particular culture" and show that "one's own values determine the direction and develop- ment of a whole culture." But by "values" she means nothing specific and clear: by "value" she can mean anything ranging from a belief, to behavior, to a controlling image, to a view of ends and means and their relationship, to an institution. What does it mean, then, to say that values "determine the direction and development of a whole culture"? If, as I suppose, by "values" we are here to understand belief systems primarily, then is it true that they "determine" the development of a whole culture — more than does, say, its technological level or economic system? I think not. Second, Lois would "prefer to avoid any judgment-making" about values, since (as she remarked) 7th graders are very quick to be judgmental anyway and since the 5-week unit is to serve as an introduction to the study of foreign cultures: ". . . it is particularly important that the students appreciate the fact that a value [behavior?] is not wrong (or negative) just because it is different from one's own. To get into evaluating values requires a whole set of criteria . . . ." Yes, evaluating does require criteria. There is a sense in which the implied aim here is laudable — namely, to teach the "value" of non-judgmental tolerance for foreign ways of life. At the same time, the students are learning that descriptive neu- trality is a virtue and it does not seem to me to be a virtue. "Values" and cultures are better or worse, and to return to the liberal relativism of an earlier anthropological movement seems to me an educational and political mistake, though surely an honorable one. It is exactly judgment and its criteria that are crucial to everyone in the 1970s, particularly 7th graders, whose quickness to make judgments may be a piece of flawed child's wisdom, not merely a developmental stage.

6. What to do Tuesday Morning: Three Larger Cases

In contrast to those teachers engaged in special studies and to those obliged to work within previously established literature, history, or social science contexts, three of the workshop participants worked on broader problems. Each of them succeeded in solving his or her problem and making an admirably ambitious vision into a plan, despite working within overly cramped limits.

(8) Lyssa Axeen's limits were that in a "fairly traditional private school" her 8th grade girls were to be taught American Culture Studies within a chronological structure (though not necessarily a mechanical one) and were to work simultaneously on writing, spelling, and vocabulary skills. She developed a model which she hoped would bring "variety and organization" to the course. The model was a simple one, designed from the point of view of "what affects me":

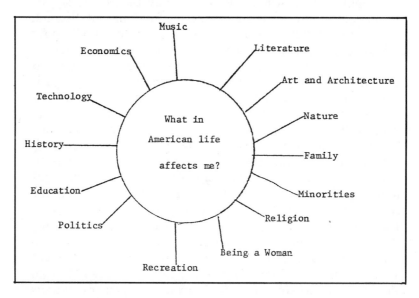

She uses the word "life" rather than "culture" because the term means more to younger students, she supposes. Her aim is to have her students "understand and appreciate American life and their relationship to it." Like the model, her plan is elegantly simple. She will concentrate on "only a few parts of

American life in this model for each unit of study." For example, while studying the early settlement of the country, "we might concentrate on Religion, Nature, Family, Economics, and Minorities. The students will investigate the areas carefully and then, hopefully, discover how they are related to each one and how the areas are interrelated." Moreover, while studying aspects of the past, the students "will also work with the same aspects of American life in the present and observe the similarities, modifications, and differences." They "may not see connections and relationships immediately, but as the course progresses, I hope they will make them automatically . . . ."

The conceptual clarity and simplicity of the model are admirable (though it might be objected at a more theoretical and at a human and political level that there is also the question of "how do I affect American life?"). The sense it gives of a relationship between self and system is heuristically helpful (though, again, the relationship seems too passive), and it represents a distinct advance in the ordering principle and conceptualization of the course, which was initially a combination of history and literature. In some senses it reminds me of the "survival chart" developed initially for an alternative American Culture Studies curriculum at Davis High School (Davis, California).[17] The chart lists in six increasingly larger concentric circles: A THEME — the survival of man; INSTITUTIONS — e.g., education, government, the family; PHENOMENA — e.g., student drop-out rates, elections, divorces; MODES OF ANALYSIS — e.g., sociological, historical, ecological; TECHNIQUES OF INQUIRY — e.g., participant observation, interviewing, literary analysis; and FORMS OF PRESENTATION — e.g., statistical charts, an analytical essay, film. The idea is to spin the circles on the chart in order to match up the phenomenon the student wants to study with the institution to which the phenomenon is primarily related and with the mode of analysis, the technique, and the form of presentation he has in mind. The chart shows options in both subject and act, allowing the student to see his possibilities and make his choices, and the theme of the course (survival) can be understood at a number of levels.

(9) The theme of Peggy Peterson's proposal for a curriculum in American Culture Studies at Esparto High School (Esparto, California) is that not only Spaceship Earth but the cultural system is being abused and needs to be "understood, nurtured, and explored." "Just as people need to be committed to the understanding and awareness of ecosystems, in a biological sense, people also need to commit themselves to obtaining and maintaining a continual awareness of cultural systems . . . ." "Intentionally" the course aims at "consciousness raising" and it focuses on California both because of its "microcosmic relationship to the rest of the country" and because it is home for Esparto students. The plan is for three teachers over the year each to teach four mini-courses of approximately 10 weeks during the same time of day. The arrangement would look like this:

Instructor	1st quarter	2nd quarter	3rd quarter	4th quarter
A	Geography	Literature	Geography	Literature or Educational Systems
B	Media	Popular Culture	Media	Popular Culture or Educational Systems
C	Above-ground Archeology	History and Racial Conflict	Above-ground Archeology	Politics and Economics

There is some flexibility in the design, and the intention is to make inquiries of students to determine their interests before the schedule is finally established. Those students taking the year "course" will choose one mini-course each ten weeks. The course is not limited to any specific age group. Furthermore, each instructor will work with a particular sub-group for the entire year as their advisor, field trip sponsor, facilitator, and friend, even as students are separately enrolled in the mini-courses. He will meet with his group at least every two weeks, if only to pass on information about what is happening in all the mini-courses that quarter, hopefully also to find out where students are in relation to the mini-courses they are taking. In addition to the sub-group meetings, there will be a number of whole-group meetings throughout the year in order to nurture a sense of unity in the class and "to dispel fragmentation" and "hear group ideas." Finally, the aim is to make considerable use of community experts and informants. ("In our community alone there are families whose ancestors came to Esparto in covered wagons, there are professional people, artists, businessmen, and people who have an intimate knowledge of California history and heritage through their own and through family experiences.") One of the exciting elements of the proposal is its sense that there remains unfinished business. As Peggy says, "there are many areas that need to be dealt with that cannot possibly be included this year as separate entities." She names the feminist movement, problems of the future, and the environment as three of them. Her solution for now is to see them as "so pervasive and all-encompassing that they need to be an integral part" of all the classes.

There are some potential flaws. The focus on California, for example, poses the danger of not seeing the American system as a whole and allowing the course to become an extension of the local historical society. "Home" may be a matter of class and caste status as well as a geographical place, or perhaps a psychic location as well as a spatial one, especially in a migrant-labor community like Esparto. Why the "media," which characteristically in the United States are national more than local? How *do* we cope with the present and future? What happens when 50 students want to study above-ground archeology and only a few want to study geography and media? These are quibbles, however; my only serious objection is that, by splintering subjects into a number of mini-courses, a steady and full view of the whole of the cultural system may not develop in the students. The counter to that is to make culture and system — like women, the future, and the environment — pervade the course.

(10) Sherry Marron took a long step toward developing

and expanding American Culture Studies in the high school.
A doctoral candidate in American Studies at the University
of New Mexico, she plans to write her dissertation in the
form of a high school textbook for American Culture Studies
courses for juniors. What she offered for the criticism of the
group was an outline of the aims and plan for the text. There
is considerable irony in the straw poll taken during the
discussion of her work: asked who would adopt her text,
there was unanimous agreement in the workshop that it
would *not* be a text for any of the courses worked out by
any of the participants, though some said they would surely
buy it for their own use as a resource book. In retrospect, it
seems clear to me that the irony was inevitable. Sherry was
making a text for a course that does not as yet exist, and it
will not exist widely until there is a text for it. The text
attempted to integrate the vision and practice of the radical
educational reform movement, on the one hand, and a
coherent concept of American Culture Studies as a theory
and learning process, on the other hand. Such integration is a
crucial aim, and to explore critically the nature of Sherry's
failures and the possibilities for her success is to come close
to the central theme of this essay.

Sherry's educational goals are to promote: a love of
learning, critical thinking and problem solving, compassion
and concern for others, and an understanding of the past and
present "in order to better anticipate the future," thus
making "the world and the self more comprehensible and,
hence, more controllable and . . . changeable." She conceives
the text as a means to "stimulate and excite," an "experience
or 'happening' for each reader." It would provide a "series of
projects or topics to explore which radiate from the
immediate interests of the students themselves." In design,
the book would omit title pages and the table of contents,
and either be ordered alphabetically by topics or be provided
with an extensive index. Students can begin "free exploration" anywhere among 32 topics or sections, among which
are: a metal mirror cover with the subscript "You're a
reflection of your culture"; "Looking around: Culture,
Values, and You," a section containing some blank pages to

encourage the students to collect pictures of American people and scenes, some suggestions for projects (e.g., study a Sears Catalogue, decide what you will buy with $1,000, and see how your choices reflect values), and a listing of "Culture is ... [food, dress, house, laws, transportation, etc.]" statements; Music in America; Advertising, U.S.A.; Urbanization (e.g., an in-depth study of some urban center, or the related study of alternative life styles, or the study of Paolo Soleri's archology); "Complexity in the 20th Century" (e.g., make a comparative shopping list for 1930 and 1970, read Hemingway's *In Our Time*); "Literature and What It Reveals"; "Women as Human Beings"; Films; American Utopias; Youth as a Minority; Biography; and so on.

The chief problem with this outline for a text, as I see it, is that it assumes some intimate correlation between liberation and a neutral ordering of possibilities (alphabetical or by index). That is, it would seem to accept the contentions of the radical reform movement in education dealing with student-centered learning and learning processes, but it translates them unaccountably into a neutrally ordered format whose interest is meant to be derived chiefly from visual design (lots of colors, graffiti, doodling, the book as an open system) and the non-imposition of any conceptual scheme for understanding the world and American culture. Real liberation, to the contrary, implies understanding the world in newly conceptualized terms. The book needs a unifying theme built around a concept of culture – let us say culture as a nexus of interconnecting subsystems, to be studied in order to understand how those subsystems collectively control, limit, and make possible *my* experience. The aim here explicitly becomes unmasking an opaque cultural system. Unmasking is potentially politicizing in contemporary America, and at the very least a real aid to individuals as they learn to cope with or even change the world they inhabit. But how might this concept of culture and these aims be integrated with the idea of an "open book"? My suggestion would be to make the theme of the text "survival" and to organize according to the six categories of the survival chart I have referred to earlier. The book would be "open" within each category and it would have a meaningful structure by virtue of the categories. The student's activities are not coerced and may be freely chosen; at the same time, the concept of culture remains controlling. Further,"survival" simultaneously is a very student-centered concern and encourages consistency and focus in the book. After all, it is coping and survival at all levels — survival as individuals, as a civilization, as part of a planet — that in the 1970s animates all of us. It *is* a small world. Survival now requires an understanding of the cultural process as never before.

7. *A Postscript on Being Practical*

My Disneyland experience with my kids — especially my tears on the Small World ride — was clarified somewhat when Roderick Nash, during one of his Institute lectures, showed a slide of Disney's Matterhorn and it seemed to me for a long moment as if I were seeing the real mountain. Triple illusion: of the slide projector and screen, of the camera, and of Disney's imitative craft, as if seeing what is real and what is not is a perspectivist problem, which of course in one sense it is. That is, as I discovered in discussing my experience with colleagues later in the summer, by not bringing my tears to my children's attention I was depriving them of my perspective on our common experience. I was contributing to their learning *not* to acknowledge what was up and to a cultural agreement *not* to unmask. I re-inforced their simply accepting Disney's version of the world. What I might well have done is to have gone through the experience again alone and without crying, paid attention to the differences in the experiences and to what was happening, and reported my findings to my kids. I assume that they would have agreed to my report. ("O sure, Dad, we know that Disney's a shuck.") That is, when I declined to talk about my tears, I was contributing to my children's learning to not pay attention to what they in fact know. To paraphrase the conclusions of the late summer discussion: human beings in culture all commonly understand what's up and often repress and refuse to acknowledge what they understand. Some people articulate their understandings; most people decline to pay attention.

Survival depends on paying attention. [18]

  I take this interpretation of my Disneyland experience as educationally paradigmatic for American Culture Studies in high school. That is, in the high school classroom, the teacher's task is himself to experience and understand what's up culturally, articulate it, and bring others to see it too by meeting them in their own psychic-cultural space. He provides his students with room and the means by which to do their own acknowledging. In some ways such a scheme is not student-centered so much as it is reality-centered, except that the realities I have in mind are neither the consequence of being practical nor of using common sense, and they include the self at the center. Being practical and using common sense are often resistances, ways to avoid acknowledging what's up and acting on the acknowledgement. There is a higher practicality and an *un*common sense, and it is to those that I want American Culture Studies teachers to appeal. Such an appeal may entail what Ivan Illich calls a "revolutionary" act – a trespass of cultural boundaries which beats a new path – and a subversive vision. It may lead to resisting the dreariness of high school and a celebration of its real fascinations – insisting on the beauty of subjects, for example, and eschewing games-playing and moralisms, insisting on freedom to pursue the forming figure, attacking oppressive order, making the "problem" of teaching a liberating difficulty, rejecting the repetitive endless lament. It may entail reconsidering nature and American civilization as we plan our syllabi, seeing ourselves reflexively, making our world problematic, understanding our dehumanized time as pivotal in the history of civilizations, thinking of our work as contributing to the coming of a cultural revolution, focusing on counter-socialization and humanistic frames of reference, thinking about de-schooling as we rethink curriculums and re-do courses, paying attention to historicist assumptions, explanatory modes, the politics of teaching and thinking, and culture as our ultimate subject and source of being. It may entail, in short, a vast critical apparatus and an intensely felt political perspective brought to bear on what seems after all to be a routine problem in designing an American Culture

Studies course at the high school level. The USC high school workshop did not resolve that routine problem completely, but the problem does seem to me resolvable in a number of ways, the most appealing of which is the focus on survival, self, and culture suggested by the survival chart. Many of the courses proposed verged on the survival theme. To repeat, it is, after all, survival that is ultimately at stake in all this routine activity. If we were to move further, to say that what is required is not merely surviving but flourishing, would we be moving too far too fast? Perhaps. The statement would probably not be a practical one. Undoubtedly whoever makes it will be called a utopian dreamer.

NOTES

1. Ivan Illich, "Dissidence, Deviance and Delinquency in Style," Appendix to *The Dawn of Epimethean Man and Other Essays* (Cuernavaca, Mexico: CIDOC Cuaderno No. 54, 1970).

2. My colleagues Jay Mechling and David Wilson and I have proposed a change in the name of our activity: from "American Studies" to "American Culture Studies." Jay Mechling explains the proposal at length in note No. 35 to his essay in this volume. I will merely note here that when I use the earlier term "American Studies" I mean to refer to older practices and concepts.

3. See Peter L. Berger and Thomas Luckmann, *The Social Construction of Reality: A Treatise in the Sociology of Knowledge* (Garden City, N.Y.: Doubleday and Company, 1966).

4. Becca Livingston, "A Matter of Course," a senior essay in American Studies at the University of California, Davis, 1972-73. There is very little else written on American Culture Studies and high school. "A Matter of Course" was distributed to participants in the USC high school workshop and became part of the everyday talk of the group.

5. Robert Merideth, "Reflexive Learning: Notes Preliminary to Making Interdisciplinary Models for General Education Courses in Community Colleges," in William A. Gager, Jr., and Martha W. Brownlee, eds., *Perspectives in Interdisciplinary General Education* (Tallahassee, Fla.: State of Florida Department of Education, 1972), pp. 4-9, also pp. 10-14. See also my " 'Color It Gray:' A Report on the National American Studies Faculty in Florida," *Connections* (Winter 1972), pp. 31-48.

6. Basil Willey, *The Seventeenth Century Background: Studies in the Thought of the Age in Relation to Poetry and Religion* (Garden City, N.Y.: Doubleday Anchor Books, 1953 [1934]), pp. 12-13.

7. See, e.g., Howard K. Beale, "What Historians Have Said about the Causes of the Civil War," in *Theory and Practice in Historical Study: A Report of the Committee on Historiography* (New York: Social Science Research Council Bulletin #54, n.d.), pp. 55-102.

8. See Henry Wasser, "Principled Opportunism and American Studies," in Marshall W. Fishwick, ed., *American Studies in Transition* (Philadelphia: University of Pennsylvania Press, 1964), pp. 166-80.

9. These comments are all too brief. See Abraham H. Maslow, *Toward a Psychology of Being,* 2nd ed. (New York: Van Nostrand Reinhold Company, 1968) and *The Farther Reaches of Human Nature* (New York: The Viking Press, 1971). For a translation of Maslow into more systematic socio-cultural terms than he himself provides, see Mary Ellen Goodman, *The Individual and Culture* (Homewood, Ill.: The Dorsey Press, 1967). My phrases in the passage above are derived from *Toward a Psychology of Being,* pp. 194-98, 207. For a way to connect such a notion of human nature to politics, see Walt Anderson, *Politics and the New Humanism* (Pacific Palisades, Calif.: Goodyear Publishing Company, 1973). One of the students at the Institute, Kathryn Forte, wrote a final paper entitled "American Studies and the Educational Process: An Intimate Encounter," in which she argued cogently for the introduction of psychology into American Studies as an orienting perspective. I agree with her.

10. The inadequacy becomes explicit and unmistakeable in reading through the ten responses to the "forum question" – "Has American Studies had an implicit political ideology?" – in *The American Examiner: A Forum of Ideas, 2,* No. 1 (Fall 1973).

11. My previous experience with this process, which itself seems appropriate for high school classes, came from the American Studies Summer Institute on Programs and Teaching at Kirkland College in Clinton, New York, August 23-27, 1972. See the special issue of *Connections* (Fall 1972), ed. by Nancy Banister and Robert Scarola.

12. Richard Huber, "A Theory of American Studies," *Social Education,* 18 (Oct. 1954), 267-71, reprinted in Robert Merideth, ed., *American Studies: Essays on Theory and Method* (Columbus, Ohio: Charles E. Merrill, 1968), pp. 3-13, proposes a standard series of "alternative forms of organization" for courses and curriculums, mostly derived from a theory of what I call Classic American Studies. Briefly, the alternatives are: a period course, a regional course, an institution course, a subject or topic course, a theme course, an observer course, a discipline or department course, and a "major approaches to American Civilization" course.

13. I am grateful to all of the participants for their candor during the Institute and specifically to a number of them for their critical comments on an earlier draft of this essay: Maggie Bader, Sherry Marron, Peggy Peterson, David E. Russell, Sharlene Vest, and a couple of others who remained anonymous. I am also grateful for the comments on this essay by the following colleagues, high school teachers, and students: Larry Chisolm, Joe Collier, Michael Devine, John Hague, Richard Livingston, Luther Luedtke, Virginia McNeill, Jay Mechling, Pam Paris, and David Wilson.

14.   Here and throughout the case studies, I draw on and quote the teachers' own proposals. As I see it, often the language in which the proposal is formulated makes an important difference. A number of the objections I raise here I raised in the workshop itself, sometimes persuasively and sometimes not.

15.   See Paulo Freire, *Pedagogy of the Oppressed* (New York: Herder and Herder, 1970).

16.   Her proposal was funded in the middle of the 1973-74 academic year and she will be able to test a number of her assumptions and hypotheses. It would be useful to follow up a number of these proposals.

17.   The history of the chart's development suggests the value of mutual aid among people in American Culture Studies and high school teachers. The idea for it came out of the discussion of Lyssa's chart. I passed it on in the Fall 1973 to Richard Livingston, who with three other Davis High School teachers involved in an alternative American Culture Studies course (Hadassah Steen, Linelle Glass, and Janet Hughes) made a much more complicated version. I sent that version to Sharlene Vest, who returned to me a more simplified and workable version, which I have again revised, increasing the circles (and categories).

18.   I am grateful to my friends in the National *Connections II* American Studies Collective for helping me clarify these matters. Our talk (August 1973) was taped and translated into "Concentric Circles: A *Connections II* Dialogue," an abbreviated version of which appears at the beginning of *Connections II,* 1, No. 1 (Winter 1974). The subtitle of the special issue – "Toward a Theory of Education as Transformative Action" – was derived from Freire and the issue as a whole is related to some of the questions brought up in this essay.

CHAPTER 12

Not so Common Ground: Controversies in Contemporary American Studies

By Luther S. Luedtke

LUTHER S. LUEDTKE received his doctoral degree in American Civilization at Brown University in 1971 and is now Assistant Professor of English and Co-Director of American Studies at the University of Southern California. He has been a Fulbright lecturer in American Studies at the University of Kiel, Germany and a member of the Executive Council of the American Studies Association. The author of articles on Dickens, Emerson, Hawthorne, Frederic, Cummings, Sherwood Anderson, and Salinger, he currently is studying Near Eastern influences in American literature and culture.

The following essay, a *vade mecum* through several issues and controversies in American Studies, argues for the continued importance of humanistic attitudes amid competing theories of knowledge from literary, historical, and social studies.

> Every fact is related on one side to sensation, and on the other to morals. The game of thought is on the appearance of one of these two sides, to find the other .... This head and this tail are called, in the language of philosophy, Infinite and Finite; Relative and Absolute; Apparent and Real; and many fine names beside.
>
>   R. W. Emerson, "Montaigne; or, The Skeptic"

> Memory without passion would be better lost.
> But memory and passion, and with these
> The understanding of heaven, would be bliss
> If anything would be bliss.
>
>   Wallace Stevens, "Lytton Strachey, Also,
>   Enters Into Heaven"

American Studies has espoused an exceptional variety of philosophies, cultural attitudes, and research interests. Its thought is in flux, and controversy continually rages over fundamental principles of scholarship and the interpretation of American experience. In this final chapter I will examine the present state of American Studies with attention primarily to the role of literature in historical studies, the importance of myth and symbol, and the interplay of scientific and humanistic approaches to culture. These issues, which have inspired volumes of learned scholarship, remain the subjects of fervid discussion in American Studies, as in other fields. My purpose is — by reviewing representative cases from recent scholarship — to describe the overall configuration of modern American Studies, and to offer a convenient guide to its critical literature. At the same time, this exposition will embody ideas and understandings about the study of our culture that differ substantially from those stated by the last two essayists. Where both have argued that the history of ideas and literary criticism are of declining consequence, that a new discipline of American Studies is in the making, and that its method is a predominantly *scientific* approach to the structure of culture, I would emphasize an alternative ideology. The type of knowledge and self-understanding we are seeking through American Studies, in my view, attributes lasting importance to ideas and individual achievements, and to the critical and intuitive modes which, as in the past, will continue to shape our perspectives on man in the United States.

In the formative period of American Studies its scholars cherished the humanistic notion that reason and imagination work together harmoniously in life, as in art; consequently they long favored literature and intellectual history as being the most luminous and profound records of the nation's life and thought. But as time passed, American Studies has suffered with special intensity the rapid evolution of thought in both the humanities and the social sciences. The humanist today must justify his critical and speculative judgments about culture and human behavior in the light of what is known empirically through work in sociology, anthropology, psychology, and allied disciplines. Simultaneously, however, the social scientist has discovered that objective procedures for studying man and culture also have their limits, and so is turning again to the insights of philosophy, history, and literature.

In its Janus-like position among the disciplines, American Studies may remain isolated for a time from the developing thought of any one area. Yet as an arena where diverse humanists and social scientists meet, it eventually is affected by all the theories of knowledge and explanation in its associated fields. For many scholars this meeting of the minds is the most exacting and engaging part of their work, re-enforcing their commitment to a unified understanding of American culture, and provoking a constant evaluation of basic assumptions about the nature of history, ideas, and expression. The American Studies scholar, by the nature of his work, is obligated to know the theory and scholarship of a half dozen disciplines. Indeed, in the last years he perhaps has been distinguished as much by his readiness to assimilate the epistemological concerns of the related fields of study as by his substantive reinterpretations of American history and culture.

Much of the recent writing in American Studies has been concerned with methodology, as a new generation of critics reappraises the scholarship of the past by the light of proliferating theories of culture in other disciplines. Although discussion of theory and experiments in methodology are particularly appropriate to American Studies, which thrives on new ideas and modes of analysis, there also are hazards in the highly conceptual nature of much recent writing that should be made clear from the outset. In their efforts to give structure and depth to the evolving field of American Studies, scholars have been tempted to borrow the most complex and profound procedures from other fields. We find, too often, that sophisticated methods which in the traditional disciplines have evolved from long consideration of a stable body of materials are ill-suited to an interdisciplinary approach and to the fresh documents of American culture. Imagination, common sense generalizations, and established methods of research are still our most important guides to understanding American history and culture. New theory and methodology, like the old, finally will be judged by the substantive scholarship it produces, and by its ability to speak meaningfully of the American experience.

From Area Studies to the Culture Concept

Assumptions about the nature of American Studies have gravitated between two poles of thought. The earliest notion of American Studies was basically geographical and political; it designated a body of subject matter including all the ideas and events, beliefs and behavior, human institutions and natural phenomena that exist or have existed in the United States. Defined in this way, American Studies has been able to draw upon all disciplines that have interpreted American materials and thus has employed a variety of methodologies: formalist criticism and literary history, political theory and social history, and so on. Such an eclectic interpretation tends to be highly individualized. The outer limits of this type of *area study* have been shaped at least minimally by the intention to describe the national "civilization" or "character"; or, as Tremaine McDowell proposed, by the need to render "the complex design of American life." McDowell, writing the first book-length history of the American Studies movement in 1948, described a *synthetic* approach based on the bridging and interpenetration of the existing disciplines and encouraged his colleagues to teach "the fundamental diversity of human experience within which the student should eventually find an equally fundamental unity."[1] In practice, the borders of American Studies have remained exceedingly difficult to draw because all meaningful statements about the life of the nation have their place within its precincts. Even the natural sciences play a role in American Studies inasmuch as no area of thought or behavior in our society has been immune from the forces of science and technology.

Increasingly throughout the 1950s scholars emphasized a *holistic* alternative to the synthetic approach to American Studies. Robert Walker, taking account of the expanded participation of the social science disciplines, conjectured in 1958 that its proper goal is to study "a civilization as a whole greater than the sum of its parts." He predicted the possibility of "a discipline of American Studies — a single comprehensive method for examining and organizing the multi-fold data and phenomena which describe a group of people living in a given place at a given time."[2] Although Walker recommended the model of cultural anthropology, scholars were uncertain even then about the nature of the comprehensive method for which he called. In his provocative essay "Can 'American Studies' Develop a Method?" Henry Nash Smith warned in 1957 that the transformation of American Studies into an autonomous discipline was by no means accomplished. In its present state, neither cultural anthropology nor any other ready-made methodology could offer the relational analysis of fact and value called for in American Studies. "A new method will have to come piece-meal," Smith cautioned, "through a kind of principled opportunism, in the course of daily struggles with our various tasks."[3] The anthologies of essays that traced the progress of American Studies through the 1960s commonly bore out his prediction that scholars would continue to work out of several old-line disciplines, striving thereby to broaden their own particular competence.[4]

The development of a holistic approach led in one direction to what has become known as the *culture concept,*

according to which American Studies is seen as an interpretation of the uniformity and functional wholeness of the
national culture through its customs, behavior, institutions,
and values. This perspective attributes significance to particular acts and beliefs only insofar as they reveal the
underlying structures of our culture and help to distinguish it
from other cultures. Specific behavior and ideas, of course,
stand in a reciprocal relationship to the culture within which
they appear, and so to an extent distinctive phenomena must
be dealt with no less in a *culture* study than an *area* study.
But here the individual act has its first meaning not *per se,*
but rather as it typifies or challenges the coherence of the
culture. Richard E. Sykes gave a landmark formulation to
this idea in 1963 in his article "American Studies and the
Concept of Culture: A Theory and Method." Sykes argued,
as Robert Walker earlier had surmised, that the methodological home of the holistic approach is in the social sciences.
"What then is American Studies?" asked Sykes. "Briefly
defined, it is the study of American culture. Culture is the
key concept, the unifying concept, the root word which
suggests both theory and method. It is a branch of culture
studies, and as such is closer to the social sciences theoretically than to the humanities. It is a specialized branch of
cultural anthropology." He adopted A. L. Kroeber and Clyde
Kluckhohn's definition of culture as "an abstract description
of *trends toward* uniformity in the words, acts, and artifacts
of human groups." Sykes did not disavow the use of
intellectual history, imaginative literature, and humanistic
criticism, but he warned assertively that the American
Studies approach to literature "will be that of the student of
culture, not the critic." [5]

The area concept is inclined to be centrifugal, favoring
the overt products and expressions of culture. The culture
concept is centripetal and emphasizes masked or avowed
patterns. [6] If fully articulated, the culture concept would
transform the interdisciplinary study of several fields into a
new discipline with its own prescriptive criteria and techniques. There are signs that it has begun to eclipse the more
individualized and methodologically mixed forms of scholar-

ship that historically have been included in American Studies; yet the eclectic, synthetic approach to American Studies also is strongly supported. Separately, in collaboration, or in rivalry, the interdisciplinary area approach and the disciplinary cultural approach to American Studies together have strengthened and clarified the movement. [7]

High Culture and the Problem of Imaginative Literature

Although discriminating between the humanities and the social sciences often throws more smoke than light on discussion, American Studies is involved in a perpetual controversy of Two Cultures. To be sure, the labels *humanities* and *social sciences* are more often used today to identify idealized tendencies — "truth" versus "fact," etc. — than to distinguish the questions, methods, or types of thought actually at work within the academic departments that commonly appear under these headings. Linguists, Cliometricians, and English scholars who use computer technology in their prosody studies all employ the statistical method and content analysis once considered the resources of the social sciences. Since the turn of the century, the influence of the behavioral and social sciences on literary studies has been profound, as sharply demonstrated by the psychological criticism of the twenties and the sociological criticism of the thirties. Conversely, modern philosophical anthropologists, sociologists of knowledge, and historians of science — affirming that no system of thought is value-free — all have emphasized the social importance of language, philosophy, and the history of ideas. Still, despite the cross-fertilization of the great divisions of knowledge in this century, there is more than a heuristic value in continuing to contrast the humanities and the social sciences when discussing American Studies. One unresolved issue that frequently represents this dialectic is the relation of high culture — particularly *imaginative* literature* — to historical and cultural investigation.

---

*I realize that objection might be made to the seemingly casual manner in which I speak, synonymously, of *imaginative, serious, great,* and *high* literature in this essay. Although the terminology may be rather forward, an evaluative discrimination between orders of literature is intended, for which the distinction

For at least the last half century imaginative literature has enjoyed a special status in the interpretation of American character and culture — alongside the study of religious thought, political theory, and other forms of intellectual history. Concentration on these high cultural forms has wedded Matthew Arnold's idea that culture is "The best that has been thought and said in the world" to the notion that, in an historical as well as an ontological sense, elite achievements of thought and literature constitute *civilization* in America. At heart is the conviction that great literature, before all other forms of expression, reveals a realm of consciousness that cannot be exhausted through simple analysis of content — and furthermore, the belief that literature bears the accumulated culture of the past, exercises normative force in the present, and affects the ethical progress of man and society. As Henry Nash Smith stated, "The range of possible human experience beyond the limits of paraphrasable meaning is the province of imaginative or poetic language. The complex modes of statement which characterize the truly imaginative use of language (and I would be understood here as referring to the different vocabularies of the several arts) are the only instruments we have for embodying and communicating the full content of consciousness."[8] When he contrasted the functions of the literary critic and the sociologist, Smith in effect was repeating Aristotle's distinction between poetry and history:

---

of *imagination* and *understanding* is still serviceable. At heart I am less concerned with the 'transcendental' origins of literature (what Coleridge denominated the Primary Imagination) than with the power of individual authors to look backwards and forwards from their historical standpoint and, *perceiving* the spiritual ethos and direction of their cultures, to create *images* which become our consciousness of past, present, and future (the Secondary Imagination). These powers are by no means restricted to visionary and prophetic writers (one thinks immediately of Blake and Whitman), nor even to the broad class of Romanticism (Hawthorne, Thoreau, Fitzgerald, Faulkner), but may be found in he enduring works of Washington Irving and Henry James, Mark Twain and Sinclair Lewis — all those, in other words, who have crystallized our cultural consciousness in dramatic terms. (Coleridge described the Secondary Imagination thus: "It dissolves, diffuses, dissipates, in order to re-create; or where this process is rendered impossible, yet still at all events it struggles to idealize and to unify. It is essentially *vital* even as all objects (as objects) are essentially fixed and dead." — *Biographia Literaria,* chap. 13.)

"One relates what has happened, the other what may happen. Poetry, therefore, is a more philosophical and a higher thing than history, for poetry tends to express the universal, history the particular." [9]

Correlating aesthetics with culture and society has troubled many American Studies scholars, who argue the degree to which the imaginative work of art may be considered either a product of, or an influence upon, its culture. The nature and purpose of high art, the humanist believes, is to organize experience, to hypothesize form, to bring order from chaos. The religiously minded critic, moreover, looks to art iconically, as a means of communication between the spiritual and the temporal worlds; with the classicist, he regards art as an agency through which prophetic individuals shape their cultures. Is our great literature a symbolic expression of what precedes and brings culture into being? Or does it work in less mysterious and more functional ways? It should be apparent that imaginative literature, by virtue of its intensity and self-consciousness, is unamenable in form as well as substance to mainly quantitative approaches. Yet at the same time, from their diverse epistemological positions Leo Marx, Roy Harvey Pearce, Cecil Tate, and other critics of American culture have denied that literature is epiphenomenal and have defended its central importance in the study of culture.

Serious literature is more than simply a reflection of its culture or one among many social documents. But there has been a tendency among modern social and cultural historians to minimize the role of high art in the development of culture, to deny its existential and spiritual status (except insofar as communities of cognoscente may develop around it), and to look for more straightforward statements about life in the United States. [10] Although the majority of teachers and scholars in American Studies have not abandoned their former humanistic attitudes for a 'scientific' disposition, there is a clearly evident trend away from both literary studies and intellectual history towards social and cultural history. The privileged position of literature and intellectual history has been assailed on both political and theoretical grounds. During the social and political ferment of the 1960s, critics attacked the ideas of a strong national character and democratic faith that had been articulated in American literary and historical studies, finding there the germs of chauvinist ideologies which, if they were not directly culpable for the nation's invasions of Asia and Latin America and the repression of ethnic minorities at home, at least had helped to rationalize acts of cultural imperialism. In the eyes of these critics, delusive myths of American individualism, mission, and the frontier spirit too long had diverted the attention of the American people from sobering social realities. In his cogent essay "American Studies & the Realities of America" in 1970, Robert Sklar indicted the kinds of high literary and intellectual history that flourished from the 1930s into the 1960s for limiting our perceptions of American culture and society: notably the emphasis on *mind* in the writings of Perry Miller, F. O. Matthiessen, and their contemporaries. Linking the decline of high cultural history to the current crises of American culture, he predicted that the most fruitful approach to our culture in the near future would be "an intensified study of society and social structure."[11]

Although political dissent has deepened the distrust of traditional literary and intellectual approaches to American character and culture, scholars also have been troubled by the thought that the sophisticated expressions of art and ideas may really have little to do with socio-historical realities. John Kouwenhoven enunciated this issue in 1964 in "American Studies: Words or Things?" "Verbal symbols," remarked Kouwenhoven, "are inherently 'defective' " tools for approaching American experience — "at best a sort of generalized, averaged-out substitute for a complex reality comprising an infinite number of individual particularities." He contrasted the child's immediate perception of objects to the patterns and filters of language through which adults receive their world and then charged that our understanding and our appreciation of cultural realities are distorted by a high dependence on language. Literary scholars, historians, and social scientists alike have based their ideas of America "primarily upon ingenious verbal generalizations that are sometimes laughably and sometimes tragically unrelated to actualities." Thus Kouwenhoven questioned the importance of words, which only convey artificial meaning, and encouraged a return to the universe of concrete particulars where meaning originates, namely the "vernacular arts": those "objects shaped empirically by ordinary people in unselfconscious and uninhibited response to the challenges of an unprecedented cultural environment" — like tools, toys, buildings, and machines. Although Kouwenhoven confessed his respect for the powers of language, and for subjects like philosophy, theology, history, and art criticism which the generalizing properties of language have made possible, he deprecated the tendency to overlook "sensory thinking." Intellectual and verbal constructions of reality have blurred our vision of cultural facts, he concluded, in a manner that only a return to concrete and sensual perceptions can correct. [12]

Material history and the use of non-verbal records of the past have attracted strong attention lately, particularly in the American Civilization Department of the University of Pennsylvania, where literary and non-literary documents have been assimilated in an approach to American culture that is heavily weighed towards quantitative analysis and the social sciences. Murray Murphey reported in 1970 that at Pennsylvania

> American civilization [had] moved from an interdisciplinary to a disciplinary approach, which defined its subject matter as American society and culture, past and present, and its methods as that of the social sciences, applied to both contemporary and historical data. [13]

Three years later, in *Our Knowledge of the Historical Past,* Murphey acknowledged that at present "the methods and standards of the contemporary social sciences can be applied only imperfectly to study of the past," due to the character of historical data and the problems they generate for confirmation of hypotheses and theories. He was confident, however, that in time the problems would be resolved through the perfection of statistical analysis and the "covering law model" of explanation. By these means, he expected, future historical problems might be stated in a manner admitting "mathematical attack." [14]

The "hard data" approach to culture study is surrounded by a difficult conceptual language which for many humanists has implied a mechanistic world view and intolerance towards subjective and speculative modes of thought. In two recent essays ("The Social Sciences in American Studies" and "Quantitative American Studies"), Stanley Bailis and Richard Jensen have sought to dispel some of the persistent stereotypes of reductionism and methodological absolutism which surround social science procedures. They have professed that with the new methods analysis can become unexpectedly subtle, and more complex causal relationships can be elucidated than heretofore. [15] Within a quantifying system of analysis, however, individual acts and expressions often do, in fact, take on negative values; and a complex scientific methodology is ever in danger of becoming an end in itself rather than a means of historical understanding. The challenge is obvious as literary critics and intellectual historians see their great documents and historical personages reduced to averages, means, and charts. Lines of controversy have been drawn between scholars who insist on the centrality of individuals and ideas and those who regard culture principally in mathematical and structural terms.

One of the more vigorous assaults on the use of imaginative literature and literary criticism in American Studies is R. Gordon Kelly's "Literature and the Historian," printed in the *American Quarterly* in 1974. For purposes of contrast his statement may be considered alongside Leo Marx's essay "American Studies – A Defense of an Unscientific Method," which appeared in *New Literary History* in 1969. Their respective stands represent an antithesis in the continuing dialogue over the place of imaginative literature in American Studies. First, a look at the position defined by Leo Marx.

In 1967 Marx was invited by a symposium on public

opinion and the historian to describe and defend "the methodology" of American Studies. Because he insisted that no method should be prescriptive for American Studies, Marx set for himself the larger task of contrasting "two ways of studying group consciousness: that of the empirical historian (or sociologist) who is a practitioner of content analysis, and that of the humanistic scholar working in American Studies." He separated these two modes of thought along the lines of "statements of fact and judgments of value." The empirical historian is obligated to produce quantifiable results and assumes that "the paraphrasable 'message,' either manifest or latent, is the truly significant feature of every verbal construct." The humanist, on the other hand, recognizes no sanctions or limits that could be called objective. He makes value judgments in the choice of his data and refuses to recognize the authority of any criteria that would exclude major works of thought and expression. The designation of these works of high culture relies on the "impersonal process of critical scholarship" and the eventual achievement of a scholarly consensus. The social historian's concern with works of literature is essentially one of defining public opinion; the humanist's is culture. Although both approaches to the study of literature are legitimate, Marx believed that serious works of art have a more sustaining importance in the life of a culture than the works of transient popularity often preferred by social historians.

Marx illustrated his argument by citing the example of *Moby-Dick.* He admitted that Melville's novel had no immediate public appeal and probably did not *reflect* the spirit of the times more accurately than many now forgotten works of fiction. Yet it has had a special kind of significance for historical understanding: "It is useful for its satisfying power, its capacity to provide a coherent organization of thought and feeling, or in a word, for its compelling truth value." Both the literary and the historical value of *Moby-Dick,* finally, rest "upon its continuing — one might say, growing — capacity . . . to provide us with satisfaction, and to shape our experience of past and present." When the purpose of the scholar is to "represent the common life," then, Marx

allowed, perhaps literature should be put aside altogether.
However, in the longer perspective (as compared, for instance, with an editorial from 1851), *"Moby-Dick* clearly
must be credited with having had the greater influence upon
American action as well as thought." With the passage of
time the enduring work of art comprises an ever larger part of
our consciousness of the past; it *"becomes* the culture which
produced it" as that culture is alive in the present. 16

Marx acknowledged that the true relation of the aesthetic
work to the history of culture often has been obscured by
extravagant and uncritical uses that have been made of
imaginative literature in historical studies. He attempted to
prepare a basis for reconciliation. Instead, his essay has
brewed a small storm of protest which reveals how earnestly
many scholars regard the ties between historical writing and
empirical data, and how sternly they insist on an "objective"
interpretation of culture.

Gordon Kelly chose two tasks for his essay on "Literature and the Historian." First, he wished to explore "the
problem of using imaginative literature as historical evidence," and to propose a solution consistent with convergent tendencies in other disciplines, although at variance
with the myth-symbol school of interpretation. Second, he
intended to illustrate this position with reference to a body
of late-nineteenth-century American children's fiction. By
selecting popular periodical literature for his demonstration,
Kelly implied from the outset that, as concerns the cultural
historian, there is no essential difference between the order
of consciousness and achievement one finds in works of great
literature like *Moby-Dick* and the level of expression in
writing for children. He objected that the doctrine of
"inherent power" by which Marx accounted for the
emergence of Melville's novel as a cultural force is based on a
"rudimentary theory" that simply focuses attention on "the
elements of aesthetic form of a few cherished texts, and
implies an appropriate method – close textual analysis." The
true historical interest of these great works has nothing to do
with aesthetic form but rather concerns the index they
provide to group behavior, and the institutional machinery

which selects, transmits, and preserves literary documents within society. In historical studies, argued Kelly, the concept of society and culture must be established first; the commitment of a functional elite to great literature is a secondary matter. Since children's fiction and other types of popular literature represent a wider social base and are more susceptible to quantification than high literature — and the institutions of their distribution are more transparent — the historian who uses imaginative literature at all will want to look here for insight into the formation of values.

> The assumptions frequently carried over into American Studies from the study of literature — namely that great literature constitutes a qualitatively superior kind of cultural evidence, that it is autonomous, and that inferences from such works can be readily generalized to society as a whole and to a wide range of behavior — must be severely qualified, if not abandoned completely; for these assumptions appear now to hold only for the simplest model of culture and have little predictive or explanatory power for American society, past or present.[17]

Leo Marx's argument, as Kelly observes, was incomplete inasmuch as he failed to particularize just how the great work of literature should contribute to a clearer historical understanding of its period. Nevertheless, Kelly misconstrues the intent of Marx's essay in a manner that represents the social historian's general difficulty in grappling with truly imaginative literature. In his desire to render literary achievement and recognition (or in his words: production and consumption) as a matter of socialization, Kelly readily associates Marx with the school of New Criticism which rose to prominence in the late 1930s and still remains influential. But Marx's statement cannot be labeled, and thereby dismissed, as one more manifesto from an exclusive literary school. In its pure form, the New Criticism regarded the literary object as a phenomenon equally independent of its cultural context and the personality of its author. Marx, on the other hand, accentuated the intimate relationship of literature and culture, arguing that the great work of art expresses a type of consciousness which may lie too deep to be reflected in the social forms of its time but which progressively acts itself out in the history of the culture. Although he ascribed the literary power of *Moby-Dick* to "the intrinsic (or esthetic) value of the novel" and its "inherent capacity . . . to generate the emotional and intellectual response of its readers," he did not limit that power, as Kelly too quickly assumes, to formal devices and the precepts of New Critical theory. There are other compelling explanations — metaphysical, psychological, and mythical — for the inherent power of those works of literature that endure. Melville's writings, in any case, were made widely known by the pioneering work of Raymond Weaver and Lewis Mumford in the 1920s quite independently of the New Criticism, and the intensive study of Melville and Hawthorne in the forties and fifties certainly is more attributable to neo-orthodox currents in modern thought than, as Kelly implies, to the tenets of a particular movement in literary criticism. [18]

The historian's frequent impatience with poetry and imaginative literature — as with idealist philosophies and the notion of human will — is self-explanatory, since by its nature great literature deals with characteristics that transcend a particular social milieu and the research problems it generates. Yet to repudiate the study of great literature and other forms of humanistic criticism, and to draw inferences about human consciousness exclusively from hard data, predisposes the historian to leveling explanations of culture and obscures the roles of accident and creativity, of human genius and the irrational in history. Whatever position the modern scholar may take epistemologically on propositions of free will, man's relation to the sacred, and the meaningfulness of history, these questions have troubled the minds of American authors from the time of Anne Bradstreet down to William Faulkner and Saul Bellow. De-emphasizing value-laden and subjective matters such as these when studying the shape and meaning of the authors' works or the times in which they lived blinks away a good deal of perspective on the conditions and consciousness of the past, and therefore of the present.

Literature can be examined as a social phenomenon

without exhausting all of its meaning for the study of historical cultures. Starting with a focus on historical explanation, Gordon Kelly has represented two types of knowledge — the social-historical and the creative-critical — as mutually exclusive ideologies. American Studies must accomodate both approaches to cultural reality and out of their reciprocal criticism thresh a more complete understanding of the total cultural experience than either the humanist or the social scientist alone can provide. Kelly's critique of literature and historical explanation is an adequate comment on the place of literature in American Studies only if, by supplying a missing axiom, we consider American Studies an exclusively objective historical activity. History, empiricism, culture, and American Studies are too nicely equated here. Fortunately, the "increasingly divergent emphases in the two disciplines" of history and literature that he mentions are now at least a decade behind us, and the generation succeeding the New Criticism, which itself became a kind of cold literary science, is exploring new forms of social, historical, and literary analysis in its efforts better to understand the interpenetrations of literature and culture.

Between the poles of thought represented by Marx and Kelly varied efforts have been made to define the relations of language, literature, and culture. Scholars in American Studies usually have not upheld the New Critics' hieratic view of great literature or worked with the theoretical fineness of aesthetic philosophers like Susanne Langer, who argued her thesis in *Philosophy in a New Key* (1942) and *Feeling and Form* (1953) that art is a highly articulate form of expression symbolizing direct or intuitive knowledge of life patterns. They have, however, learned from linguists, aestheticians, and style critics that verbal structures are intricately related to other classes of cultural experience and that disclosing these connections requires the refined sensibility of critic and historian alike.

In his recent essay "The Whorf Hypothesis as a Critique of Western Science and Technology," Peter Rollins has examined the religious motivation at the root of one linguistic anthropologist's influential work. Benjamin Lee

Whorf and his teacher Edward Sapir, founders of the
American school of anthropology, formulated a relativist
theory of linguistics which left the phrase "language and
culture" firmly planted in our critical lexicon. They hypothesized that language radically *is* culture; that culture is
conceived, stated, and communicated in terms of the
language of a people; and that a culture has no knowledge of
behavior or reality save through its system of language. Sapir
wrote:

> Human beings do not live in the objective world alone, nor alone in the
> world of social activity as ordinarily understood, but are very much at
> the mercy of the particular language which has become the medium of
> expression for their society . . . . The worlds in which different societies
> live are distinct worlds, not merely the same world with different labels
> attached. [19]

According to Sapir's model the evolving philosophies,
life-ways, and "real worlds" characteristic of particular
cultures are determined by their distinctive styles of language. Culture study, therefore, properly begins with a
knowledge and description of language.

Whorf extended Sapir's hypothesis that language and
culture are inseparable, but he gave less emphasis to the
tyranny of language over culture and held that language
patterns and cultural norms grow up *together* in response to
immaterial forces. Whorf's interest in linguistics arose from a
deep-seated Christian moralism and from his desire to defend
religious experience against the proud scientism of the 1920s
and 1930s. In his statements of linguistic relativity he was
severely critical of the limited world view generated by
Western science and technology and of its disdain for the
many forms of religious consciousness. Linguistic study, in
his view, offers religion a sophisticated defense of its own
primary status, for what the world's cultures have had in
common is a core of religious wonder, reverence, and ritual.
Linguistics, the new anti-positivistic science of the human
spirit, promised a way of getting behind sensory data to the
underlying modes of thought and feeling that give form to

culture and meaning to its expressions. Whorf balanced intellect with emotion, science with piety, not only to elaborate the concept that language is one with culture, but also to shape a dialogue between objectified knowledge and spiritual vision that the culture scholar still finds powerful today. [20]

As a means of organizing imagination and experience through language, literature has a special importance for studying culture. The nature of this importance was discussed by Seymour Katz in " 'Culture' and Literature in American Studies." Challenging Richard Sykes's notion that "criticism and culture studies, however legitimate both may be, approach literature with different needs and purposes," Katz installed literature at the center of the concept of culture and argued that the literary critic and the culture scholar perform the same kind of study. He endorsed the view expressed by Leslie White that culture, as it concerns the scholar, is a heuristic device which designates a class of phenomena for study—"the class of things and events consisting of or dependent upon symboling"—and then poses questions about the relation of the symbols to each other. Literary and culture scholars alike, he observed, work with ideal constructs and explicate and compare classes of symbols. Accordingly, one important form of culture studies is the analysis of "particular works of imagistic literature . . . in their formal and temporal relationships to each other." When the relationships between image and idea, experience and concept have been established in a particular body of literature, comparison then becomes possible with other classes of symbols. The final product to be gained by connecting imaginative literature with other forms of symbols is a "cognitive model of experience, a hypothetical construction by means of which we may come to know more about experience than experience alone can show."

The theoretical model described by Katz attributes both intellectual and creative significance to imaginative literature. By abstracting characters, places, and values from a total cultural experience, literature brings forward the essential,

defining qualities of the culture. Simultaneously, it participates in the developments of the abstractions made in
language. "And to say that literature plays a central role in
the development of language is to say that it plays a central
role in the development of culture." Katz demonstrated his
thesis by considering the process of characterization in *The
Scarlet Letter*, which he saw as an illustration of interrelated
literary and cultural symbols. [21]

The concept of connected literary and cultural symbols is
one part of the study of literary and cultural *style* which has
been pursued saliently by Roy Harvey Pearce. In *The
Continuity of American Poetry* (1961) and "Historicism
Once More" (1958), Pearce has examined *style* as "a bridge
between literature and its cultural environment" and defined
the principles of a new "kind of criticism which is, by
definition, a form of historical understanding." This new
form of analysis he calls "critical historicism." While
assuming the close interrelatedness of language and thought
that T. S. Eliot articulated in "Tradition and the Individual
Talent," critical historicism restores language forms to their
historical-cultural setting. Pearce differentiates three levels of
style. Each culture has a *general style* which embodies
"shared, 'communal' assumptions, conscious and unconscious." Within the general style of a culture are *basic styles*
which belong to its many aspects and areas of thought. The
basic literary style of the culture, in turn, invests the poet's
individual style with both the character of the discipline and
of its culture. Consequently, the author's style—that is, his
use of language and his characteristic way of arranging
experience for asethetic ends—necessarily reflects both his
social conditioning and the general style of the culture. The
language of literature in its historical-cultural aspect is a
vehicle for the values of a culture, and literature approached
in such a manner is "a way, perhaps the most profound, of
comprehending that dialectical opposition which characterizes our knowledge of ourselves in our history."

> Studying language, we study history. . . . Studying history, we study
> culture. Studying a culture, we study its poetry. Studying its poetry, we

study its language. The system is one and whole. If it is closed, that is because it encloses us.

Pearce found the style of American culture to be rooted in an Adamic impulse that has narrated itself through a mythology of dynamic individualism and personal freedom. 22

The idea of symbolic forms remains abstract and largely conceptual in current scholarship; yet it opens a way to linking the formal properties of literature (image, symbol, style) to patterns of social behavior, neither discrediting the individual achievement of literature nor denying its application to interpreting culture. The study of language, culture, and style also leads, inevitably, to the broader question of culture and myth.

Myth-Symbol-Image and American Studies

When he proposed his "Unscientific Method" of American Studies, Leo Marx spoke as the representative of a group of literary and cultural historians commonly called the Myth-Symbol School. Their writings, which have dominated American Studies for more than two decades, were inspired by Henry Nash Smith's *Virgin Land: The American West as Symbol and Myth* (1950), and have included, among other works, R. W. B. Lewis's *The American Adam: Innocence, Tragedy, and Tradition in the Nineteenth Century* (1955), John William Ward's *Andrew Jackson: Symbol for an Age* (1955), Charles Sanford's *The Quest for Paradise: Europe and the American Moral Imagination* (1961), Marx's own *The Machine in the Garden: Technology and the Pastoral Ideal in America* (1964), and Alan Trachtenberg's *The Brooklyn Bridge* (1965). Together these scholars have chronicled an authoritative myth of American origins and character built upon images of pastoral innocence, new beginnings, and Adamic freedom. By using imaginative literature and other symbolic forms of expression to interpret the central experience of America they have also exposed themselves to incisive attacks by objective historians.

The scholars of myth and symbol, it is important to notice, have been less concerned with developing theories of explanation than with articulating dramatically patterns they have discerned in American history and consciousness. Consequently, they customarily have avoided extended definitions of terms and methodology in their works. Henry Nash Smith used *myth* and *symbols* simply "to designate larger or smaller units of the same kind of thing, namely an intellectual construction that fuses concept and emotion into an image." They have the further characteristic, he explained, "of being collective representatives rather than the work of a single mind."[23] Myths and symbols thus would appear to precede and affect the formation of images, which are products of interaction between experience, language, and imagination. Leo Marx offered the reciprocal idea that images, symbols, and myths are progressively more complex stages of the same phenomenon, moving from direct perception to idealization: "If a symbol may be defined as an image invested with significance beyond that required for referential purposes, then a myth is a combination of symbols, held together by a narrative, which embodies the virtually all-encompassing conception of reality — the world-view—of a group."[24] Notwithstanding its minimal theoretical basis, the impact of the myth-symbol mode of explanation has been immense, and in the last years has provoked strong opposing critiques.

In his assault on "Myth and Symbol in American Studies," published in the *American Quarterly* in 1972, Bruce Kuklick demonstrated what a *bete noire* myth-symbol analysis has become to one school of historians and cultural theorists. "The imputation of collective beliefs is an extraordinarily complex empirical procedure that ought not to be undertaken lightly," warned Kuklick; for many scholars, great works of art and cultural archetypes have become "a shortcut around masses of historical data." In a series of arguments (which are more logically consistent than true to the practical intentions of the myth-symbol critics), he criticized this mode of explanation for espousing a "crude Cartesian view of mind" which makes a strict dichotomy between consciousness and the world, or eventually leads to a form of platonic idealism. For the myth-symbol scholars, images, symbols, and myths at best *reflect* empirical facts;

they are products of the imagination and complex mental constructs. The most serious flaw in the reasoning of "the American Studies humanists," argued Kuklick, is this belief that ideas, consciousness, and the external world exist in different planes, which therefore makes it impossible to bring them together into any meaningful relationship that would provide "a straight-forward theory to explain past American behavior."

In response to this dilemma, he recommended the alternative view of consciousness discussed by Gilbert Ryle in *The Concept of Mind.* "Mental concepts," Ryle claimed, "cannot be understood as things which exist in our head . . . . Having a mind is for an organism to be disposed to behave in a certain way, to possess certain propensities to action. The realm of the mental is not the realm of inner things, but a realm of observable activities and processes." With this view of idea and image, mind and consciousness, the historian can reach understanding of particular thoughts and actions in past time through an empirical study of the context in which they took place — and avoid accusations both of presentism and of solipsism. The myth-symbol approach might do for literary criticism, Kuklick allowed, but not for history. [25]

In an earlier essay entitled "The Mind of the Historian," Kuklick had described the characteristics of the ideal historian in similar terms. Because "contemporary 'non-cognitivist' theories in meta-ethics are all loosely associated in some way with 'subjectivism' or 'relativism,'" he proposed that the "ideal observer" should be empirical and objective even in his statement of ethical terms. This mode of analysis would recognize no distinction between evaluative and scientific terms. Both factual and moral truths are learned directly from the world, which is fundamentally intelligible to objective analysis; and there is only "one correct evaluation in every situation calling for evaluation." [26]

In "Myth and Symbol in American Studies" Kuklick adopted Gilbert Ryle's "concept of mind" out of his desire to circumscribe reality objectively. The philosophical grounds of the proposition, however, were left unexplained. The connections of history, human consciousness, and "what in fact exists" — deftly equated here — beg for further criticism. The crude Cartesianism Kuklick decried has not ended for humanists in an uncritical mind-body fallacy, the humanists retreating into the world of imagination; it has been earnestly transformed in the social and speculative thought of Kant, Bergson, Husserl, Heidegger, and their successors. Nor does a reaction against Descartes' isolation of thought from total being lead inevitably to Ryle's "dispositional" concept of reality. T. S. Eliot and Allen Tate, who traced the origins of modern secularism to the "dissociation of sensibility" that followed Descartes, saw the possibility of reintegrating culture through a religious view of man that is quite the obverse of Ryle's concept of mind.

Kuklick closed his article on myth-symbol studies with the impatient judgment that "philosophical criticism is much easier to do than constructive empirical research." All the more, his argumentation is good reason for American Studies humanists not to abandon their critical practices, but rather to continue the equally rigorous tasks of interpreting and sustaining the underlying principles of their statements about history, culture, and human consciousness. (Not all American Studies humanists, of course, are myth-symbol critics; and no myth-symbol critic would pretend to have an exclusive claim on historical truths.) The problems of relating history and consciousness are too complicated to be resolved by strictly empirical approaches. The construction of ideas and images in history is a complex process that will leave man always in center-stage, surrounded by a good deal of mystery.

Shortly after Kuklick's essay had appeared, Cecil Tate published his book *The Search for a Method in American Studies,* which has elucidated the achievements of the myth-symbol scholarship and may reconstruct it on new grounds. Tate's primary intention was to demonstrate that American Studies has developed the theoretical foundations, the shared practices, and the growing body of knowledge that merit the honor of a discipline. By examining the implicit assumptions behind Smith's *Virgin Land,* Ward's *Andrew Jackson,* Lewis's *The American Adam,* and Pearce's *The*

Continuity of American Poetry, he demonstrated that the American Studies scholars have developed highly sophisticated techniques in the areas of myth analysis, symbol formation, and language and culture. Taken together, these four works yield a half-articulated methodology that transcends the limitations of the older methods of the humanities and the social sciences alike and opens a vision of the whole that American Studies has so long sought. Recent advances in knowledge theory, principally in the areas of linguistics and anthropology, now make it possible to understand the accomplishments of earlier writings in American Studies and to direct myth-symbol analysis into systematic procedures. The use of myth and symbol contains more than the rudiments of an American Studies method, Tate believed. Language and myth are the heart of any cultural analysis.

Tate arranged the exemplary works by Smith, Ward, Lewis, and Pearce under the headings of *myth* and *holism.* Holism is a "broad methodological assumption" of each work; myth, "a more specific analytic concept each uses." In varying degree all four works adopt an attitude of "organic holism" towards American culture. This inference about the nature of our history and society Tate found misleading and restrictive inasmuch as it assumes that each culture has its autonomous physiology and teleology and that each part of a culture is unique to that one organism. As an alternative to organic holism, Tate proposed a system of structural analysis that would transcend the parochialism of regarding American culture as a wholly unique event in history. In so doing, he also sought to salvage the important contributions which the holist critics have made to understanding the nation, namely their deep insight into the relationship of language and culture.

Where Kuklick had stressed the idea that myths and symbols are "products of the imagination," Tate represented myths and symbols as "unconscious outgrowths reflecting deeper-lying, nonrational patterns of the culture." He investigated the premise, which has been stated variously by Ernst Cassirer, Mircea Eliade, and Claude Levi-Strauss, that myth is deeply rooted in human nature and in the nature of reality itself. Philosophical anthropologists may disagree about the origins of myth-making — Eliade relating myths to innate human religious interests, Levi-Strauss analyzing the content of myth in terms of the local and particular aspects of a given society — but they share the belief that mythological thinking is the fundamental level of consciousness, that it is "the way man organizes all of his experience initially" and "the primary cognitive form under which all reality is viewed." Myths, Tate concurred, are indissolubly related to culture, bringing it to wholeness and sustaining it. They cannot be judged by standards of truth or falsity. The scholar can only watch their life and development and narrate their transformation through time.

According to this theory, myth is both an active force in creating culture and the primary standpoint from which it is seen — fusing fact, need, and value into one whole. Therefore the study as well as the making of historical cultures operates in a mythical framework, and our interpretation of reality depends upon the cultural lens through which we perceive it. The attempt to explain culture by restoring empirical facts thus is ill-fated because facts are neutral neither at the time of occurrence nor in the act of memory; both are stages in working out a cultural myth and its inherent form. Understanding the relation of consciousness to culture, of thought to event, requires a perspective that neither empirically derived data nor intuition alone can provide; but poetry and other literary forms, which provide a narrative or story for the culture, can reveal its deepest values and preoccupations. As Robert Penn Warren expressed this circuit of creation and study in the "Foreword" to Brother to Dragons: "Historical sense and poetic sense should not, in the end, be contradictory, for if poetry is the little myth we make, history is the big myth we live in, and in our living, constantly remake."

Tate argued that aside from its tendency toward cultural nationalism, the concept of organic holism is limited by its interior view and its blindness to the "continuity of mythic themes across cultures throughout history." He advised American mythographers to adopt a new comparative and structural approach to myth studies and to understand that, if our national myths are partly idiosyncratic, they also express fundamental human concerns which have been embodied in the mythologies of other peoples. Scholars can better determine which symbolic experiences lie deeply in the structure of human existence and which are unique to our culture by observing the appearance or nonappearance of particular myths across cultures and by comparing the way they are articulated. Tate found the linguistic theories of Noam Chomsky and the anthropology of Claude Levi-Strauss of particular moment because they challenge the notion that language is acquired solely as a cultural function and hypothesize that consciousness is determined by an innate "language environment" on which cultures perform incidental changes. Myths may differ in their surface structure, but in their deep structure they remain constant from culture to culture. The task of the culture scholar, therefore, is to chart the constants and the variables.

Tate conceded that there is a tendency in structuralism to ignore the historical dimension of events by focusing on synchronic structures (relations across one moment of time) and neglecting diachronic structures (through time), but he emphasized that structural analysis does not necessarily preclude the study either of historical causes or of particular acts of genius. Questions of *why, how,* and *what* can all be asked simultaneously in American Studies. 27

Structuralism is stirring heated controversy among humanists, who are as skeptical of the deterministic implications of this approach to culture as they have been of earlier sociological and anthropological methods. Nevertheless, structuralism can be employed as a means of analysis and comparison without its becoming a reductive philosophy. Despite its criticism of the Herderist notion that cultures have their autonomous destinies, it does not necessarily proscribe a progressive view of human history in which each culture has its place.

Studying the stages of mythic development within our nation and comparing the chapters and versions of the national myth with myths worked out in other cultures is a task that demands a high degree of detente between humanists and social scientists. European backgrounds commonly have been included in American Studies curricula to provide the comparison and perspective that Tate recommends. European studies, however, have been more successful for demonstrating the roots of American culture and the genetic continuities from Europe to America than for providing a genuinely outside vision. Women, ethnic subcultures, and other communities within the nation also have been singled out for contrast to the dominant culture. They, too, fail to lend satisfactory perspectives when the culture we intend to study is one that incorporates all of them.

Two further statements on the subject of image and myth studies, although written outside the community of American Studies, may be mentioned here to recapitulate the controversy between humanists and social scientists. Both authors have rejected the notion of a value-free, objective approach to reality and have argued persuasively that all systems of thought are necessarily metaphorical and expressive. In his penetrating *The Image: Knowledge in Life and Society,* Kenneth Boulding recommended "a new science, or at least a cross-disciplinary specialization" of the image, which he proposed to call *eiconics.* There are no "facts" in human culture, science, or humanities, he wrote. "There are only messages filtered through a changeable value system," messages which are received and interpreted according to images which exist in the mind. Facts cannot be regarded as objective data and the proper goal of scientific study, values simply as subjective topics for the humanities. The process by which we create images of the factual world is no different from the process by which we build up images for our evaluative world. The scientific method is only "one among many of the methods whereby images change and develop." Moreover, the final correspondence of image with reality is validated neither in the field of fact nor in the field of value. Boulding's system recalls Sapir and Whorf's relativist doctrine of language and culture, wherein the consciousness of a culture is contained by its own language. It is also consistent with Thomas Kuhn's demonstration in *The Struc-ture of Scientific Revolutions* that analytic systems even in the natural sciences are built upon man-made paradigms and interpret "messages" according to their structures. The extreme implication of this theorem is to strip away the scientist's character of objective rationality and to leave him, as Boulding wrote, "degraded to the status of the servant of a subculture, trapped in the fortress of its own defended public image, and straining the grains of truth through its own value system."

Against the shattering skepticism of such relativist thought, images have the power to organize the lives of individuals and societies. Cultures crystallize around faiths, religions, and myths which supply the "manifest image of their destiny toward which they feel themselves to be drawn." Every culture in its expansive phase is humbly sensitive of the deep and unconscious forces of history at work within it. All efforts to produce a wholly rational and manifest image of history, however, are fated to disappoint-ment, for the most sophisticated explanations invariably prove in the longer view to have been pseudo-sophisticated. Only genuine religious ideologies, it seems, are capable of providing "the kind of manifest image of life, history, and purpose" that is satisfying to mankind and sustaining to culture. Boulding's organic philosophy of knowledge and images suggests a corresponding method of culture study.

[It] leads in the direction of a broad, eclectic, organic, yet humble epistemology looking for processes of organization rather than specific tests of validity and finding these processes in many areas of life and experience: in art, religion, and in the common experiences of daily life, as well as in science . . . . Most of all, perhaps, it brings the actor into the act; it looks beyond mechanism without falling into vitalism.[28]

In his recent monograph *The Critical Path* Northrop Frye has placed cultures in an apposite tension between forms of mythological thinking. A *Myth of Concern* — a unifying religious or political belief like Judaism, Mohammedanism, or Marxism — brings the culture into being, expresses its faith, establishes its ethos, creates its values, and concentrates its energies. Then a *Myth of Freedom* — characteristic of the liberal, rational, and progressive mind — rises to evaluate and criticize the Myth of Concern. In reality the myths do not exist independently, nor could culture live save in their dynamic equipoise. By clarifying and criticizing the *concerns* of culture, the scholar may help restrain and channel their vitality — as Frye wrote in *Anatomy of Criticism*, "reforging the broken links between creation and knowledge, art and science, myth and concept"[29] — but total rationality in either the making or the study of culture is an abstract and static ideal, true neither to the life, movement, and semi-rationality of history, nor to the ineradicable subjectivity of the historian and critic. Literature is an especially sensitive record of the creative forces of a culture because it "displays the imaginative possibilities of concern, the total range of verbal fictions and models and images and metaphors out of which all myths of concern are constructed." The narrative form of a culture is a group of stories which, in time, takes on a central and canonical importance. "When a mythology crystallizes in the center of a culture," Frye remarked, "a *temenos* or magic circle is drawn around that culture, and a literature develops historically within a limited orbit of language, reference, allusion, belief, transmitted and shared tradition."[30]

Neither Boulding nor Frye is concerned with discussing the metaphysical reality of the mythologies from which societies and cultures take their life forms. They do, however, agree on the radical importance of shared faiths, mythic narratives, and symbolic languages within culture. According to the line of thought which they and others have developed, the myth-symbol criticism may be the most profoundly *true*, if indeed not the most factual, way to an understanding of our cultural nationhood.

Culture, Consciousness, and Politics

On the basis of the dialogues I have been tracing several conclusions can be stated. *Culture*, which once designated the great works and ideas at the center of a developed civilization, is increasingly defined in terms of the consciousness and behavior shared by a group of people. Both old and new concepts of culture are too broad to be explained by a strictly empirical mode of thought. Not an exclusively rational process, nor accidental, culture develops in relation to a shaping theme, or myth, which progressively defines itself in the course of history. It can be approached structurally, comparatively, and historically in various ways. However, as the most abstract and symbolic of human constructions, language and literature offer unique advantages for getting at the ethos of culture and essentializing the consciousness of its members.

Where does this leave us, then, in American Studies? Most scholars, of course, as in the past, will continue to subordinate such matters of theory and concept to specific research and teaching problems. However, those Americanists who are becoming concerned with issues of methodology must confront the same prior questions of knowledge and explanation that are struggled over in the array of fields connecting history, sociology, philosophy, ethics, and literature. These modes of thought go by many names: philosophical anthropology, historicism, the sociology of knowledge, phenomenology, existentialism. Their borders are indistinct. Yet all deal with the phenomena of consciousness — idea, intuition, knowledge, perception, image — and the question of how we know the reality of ourselves and our cultural environment. Collectively these modern disciplines have criticized the undefined status of scientific knowledge and have demonstrated that objective systems of historical explanation are incompatible with our experience as free and responsible beings. The nonempirical "science" of phenomenology, with its emphasis on intentionality, the intuitional method, and (in Husserl's middle period) a transcendental ego, might be particularly attractive to scholars in American Studies. Opposed to reductive or mechanistic descriptions, it is similar in many respects to the pragmatism of William James, who likewise refuted the empiricism of Hume and the naturalism of Spencer. The entire historicist impulse in modern thought, romantic in its origin and often aesthetic in sentiment, stands in revolt against systematic methodologies.

Process and individuality, change, the transiency of time and the concreteness of historical facts have remained the cornerstone of historicism; "Instead of trying to contain reality within a system, we have dismissed the empty figment of one linear history and learnt appreciation of the subtle shades of individuality, respect for irreducible particularity, acceptance of the untold multitude of facts, and awareness of endless formation and transformation, of achievement without end."[31]

Although the problems of returning from latitudinous theories to specific cases are considerable, American scholars have taken exciting steps towards reconciling the social scientist's search for data with the humanist's respect for individual achievement, and towards correlating historical explanation with the world of lived experience. Let us look for a moment at two recent books which, although in other respects quite dissimilar, represent the new interest of American historians in the intersections of cultural traditions, academic disciplines, and individual talent.

In *A Behavioral Approach to Historical Analysis* (1969), Robert Berkhofer has stressed the concept of culture and insisted on the historian's need to know the discussion of philosophy, theory, and method that is currently taking place in the social sciences. Berkhofer believes that the historian's traditional reliance on a little popular psychology and his innocence of the theories of culture developed in the social sciences bar the way to adequate historical explanation. Uncritical narrative and chronology cannot satisfy our desire to know the state of consciousness of a historical culture; concepts and theories of historical explanation must be treated explicitly. The historian's task, he writes, is twofold: 1) to relate the historical situation to the mind of the historical subject, and to distinguish his professed from his actual intentions; 2) to establish the contemporary commentator's position in relation to the occasion which he seeks to understand. In order to achieve these connections the modern historian must adopt much stricter criteria than he has been accustomed to practice – criteria such as social scientists have developed for explaining group behavior. Furthermore, argues Berkhofer, historical writing shall have a new form. Without forsaking narrative altogether, the historian must abandon the "omniscient viewpoint" of older literature, which assumed that the truth of an event is known directly, at least at the time of occurrence, and build instead on the "multiple viewpoint" of such innovative novelists as Joyce and Faulkner.[32]

The type of history for which Berkhofer called has been elaborated by Gene Wise in *American Historical Explanations: A Strategy for Grounded Inquiry* (1973). Beginning with modes of "seeing" in William Faulkner's *The Sound and the Fury* (and later commending Lionel Trilling's criticism and Kenneth Burke's studies of language and symbolic action), Wise argues that history exists not "out there," but rather in the interaction of the individual with his cultural environment. Historical forms and patterns occur "in an ongoing dialogue between human projections and environmental givens." Historical events not only are viewed retrospectively through frames of reference, or "perspectives"; they occurred that way in the first place. The writing of history recreates this process, for the historian brings to his work experience with his culture, a disciplinary paradigm that is at best partially conscious, and a personal perspective. This interaction of the individual historian, his scholarly milieu, and the historical occasion which he observes is mediated by the innately symbolizing character of man's perceptions. An historical explanation, therefore, is equally remarkable for its content and for its form, and the proper concern of the historian is no less "thought" than "the act of think-ing." Wise has grounded his own inquiry in the writings of selected Progressive historians. Through the evolution of Progressive history he traces the emergence of a dominant theory, its internal elaboration but gradual divergence from the style of the culture in which it is expressed, and a subsequent revolution in paradigms of explanation.[33]

Wise emphasizes again that imaginative literature and written history both are ways of ordering and constructing man's world in an act of consciousness. The historian, he insists, must utilize the same criteria of evaluation that the New Critics have applied to literature: attention to coherence and ambiguity, to imagistic language and individual talent.

Post-New Critical analysis also is brought to mind. The reciprocities of historical subjects and objects, of cultural events and the modern commentator that Wise describes have inspired, for example, the schools of thought represented in Georges Poulet's "Phenomenology of Reading" and Stanley Fish's "Literature in the Reader: Affective Stylistics." [34] Each wants history and literature to be read dramatically, as the dialogue of man and event, intuition and experience. The importance of this dramaturgical view of history has been stated concisely by Roy Harvey Pearce:

> It may well be that one of the main achievements of the American Studies movement will be its contribution toward a new kind of historiography, in which intellectual history becomes not a matter of ideas analyzed but of ideas dramatized, ideas so placed in their cultural matrix that they are shown to be possible beliefs. [35]

Reading history as "a story" assumes complicity between the audience and the narrator both in the making and in the telling of that story.

The phenomenologist's stress on interpreting experience directly, the new historian's perspectives on man in the act of writing history, the affective stylist's insistence that the literary work becomes a new event each time it is read — these distress scholars by the relativity and imprecision they encourage unless scrupulously criticized. Objective historians reduce the problems of relativity by a narrowed definition of reality; but even scholars who do not share an empirical view are tempted to question the cloudy imperatives that are professed by more extreme forms of thought like humanist psychology. It may be instructive, at this point, to reconsider the views Robert Merideth expressed in the preceding chapter on the inutility of the past and to look briefly at the values in which he has girded his culture study. His plan to carry the reflexive study of culture out of the stage of theory and into the classroom — blending older, sharper definitions of scientific objectivity and humanistic ideals into a new "scientific humanism" — demonstrates the malleability of American culture studies in its current state to personal politics.

Santayana's admonition that those who forget the past shall be doomed to relive it is not dissuasive to Merideth. He has muted the voice of the past precisely in order *not* to relive it, not to allow it to determine or taint the lives of his students. Because he believes that students do not inevitably benefit from knowing about their past, he has proposed a type of systems analysis that would locate them in a grid of contemporary institutions and social forces. Yet we should not forget, as a committed young teacher recently observed, that the situation of high school and college students today typically is one of profound *fragmentation;* furthermore, that in order to understand their life experiences students require a coherent world-view that extends not only laterally through social institutions but also backwards through time.[36] Learning their culture in "chronological depth" — tracing the dramatic story from beginning to end through political history, art, literature, religion, or another discipline — is less important, finally, for providing a series of hooks on which to hang particular facts than for demonstrating the inter-relatedness of human experience with time and enabling the student to perceive himself as a purposeful being historically, socially, and spiritually. Human freedom is inseparably wedded on one side to acceptance of cultural heritage. Studying the history of our culture, however severely we may criticize it, situates us and instills faith and commitment to the developing culture.

Historical subject matter is not necessarily inert for students, as Merideth has claimed, nor is radical social transformation so obviously the goal of education. Even at a functional level, questions of character formation and cultural maintenance will have to be answered before we can conclude that all social institutions and codes are to be made problematic for students. Sociologists Peter Berger and Thomas Luckmann, while they argued for the radical "social construction of reality," also have accentuated the role of human and cultural biography in sustaining man's sense of place and purpose and warding off anomic terror.[37]

Like his politics of time, Merideth's ethical values are presented as if experientially self-evident. Love, courage, creativity, kindness, altruism, spontaneity, and humor certainly are traits to be cultivated, but it is not at all clear in what sense self-actualization, "grace, excitement, growth, peak experience, health, friendship, community, a good sexual life, useful work, and the like" are *natural* characteristics, as Abraham Maslow and the humanist psychologists have told us. The complexity and inscrutability of man, proved tragically in the politics of the last half century and explicated by neo-orthodox critics, is not so easily forgotten. To such religiously minded writers as Flannery O'Connor and Iris Murdoch, a dream-like faculty pervades all attempts to escape the reality of habits, tradition, and culture, or to avoid the hard reflective effort to understand morality. In the view of such humanists, human character is *by nature* opaque. Some of the newest discussion of theories, methods, and strategies for American Studies has assumed all too easily that the philosphical and moral issues basic to cultural understanding have been answered. At the point where American Studies moves from research problems to resocializing students, our politics and metaphysics — as Merideth has advised — must be mutually criticized.

Perhaps humanists can contribute best to culture study by keeping alive a sense of human limits and human freedom founded on historical experience, and by reminding us that, whatever the exigencies of daily scholarship, man is more than a sociable creature or an object of research. In support of such an ideology Peter Berger admonished readers of his sharp-witted *Invitation to Sociology* against the belief that sociological and other principally scientific perspectives can account for experience and consciousness. "It must be clear at once," he declared, "that we cannot accept or resurrect our old Comtean hope ... to the effect that sociological science will be able to come up with an objective morality." "The humanistic scope of sociology ... implies an ongoing communication with other disciplines that are vitally concerned with exploring the human condition. The most important of these are history and philosphy."[38] In *The Sacred Canopy: Elements of a Sociological Theory of Religion* Berger later discarded the notion of "dialogue" between the empirical discipline of sociology and the nonempirical and normative discipline of theology. But thereupon he stated a fundamental principle of human knowledge that shall continue to guide humanists and social scientists in their collaborative study of culture. "To say that religion is a human projection," wrote Berger, "does not logically preclude the possibility that the projected meanings may have an ultimate status independent of man." Man may project "ultimate meanings into reality because that reality is, indeed, ultimately meaningful, and because his own being (the empirical ground of these projections) contains and intends these same ultimate meanings."[39]

The rigorous standards set by science are not antagonistic to the humanistic spirit. Precision, consistency, and verification of thought are ideals respected throughout the disciplines. The foe of humanism, rather, is a proscriptive dogmatism, reductionism, or behaviorism of whatever sort. In this sense R. S. Crane, leader of the Chicago neo-Aristotelian school of criticism, warned against:

> the spirit that . . . seek[s] always to direct our attention away from the multiplicity and diversity of human achievements, in their rich concrete actuality, to some lower or lowest common denominator; the spirit that is ever intent on resolving the complex into the simple, the conscious into the unconscious, the human into the natural; the spirit for which great philosophic systems are nothing but the expression of personal opinions or class prejudices, the forms of art nothing but their material or their sources in the unconscious mind.[40]

The tasks of American Studies perforce are humanistic. They require the erudition of the historian, the objectivity of the scientist, the perception of the literary critic, and the faith, tolerance, and imagination of all three. In view of the materials and interests of American Studies, its prudent course will continue to be a genuinely pluralistic methodology, the readiness to engage in new controversies, and alertness to unexpected reconciliations. Towards these ends philosophical consensus is less important than a liberal appreciation for the ways in which humanists and social scientists are finding themselves and their common ground.

American Studies and the National Image

Tremaine McDowell closed his history of the young American Studies movement in 1948 with an appeal for its scholars to define the *cultural nationality* of the United States. Only a true understanding of our culture and firm national self-trust, he predicted, would enable the country to exercise its authority in the world with wisdom and restraint and avert another atomic war. In the 1930s regionalism had contributed to the internal unity of the American nation; in the 1940s and 1950s an enlightened sense of cultural nationality could likewise foster the creation of "one world" among the nations. The duty of American Studies, as McDowell saw it, was simultaneously the purification of national loyalties and the exposure of diseased political and economic nationalisms. [41]

No less than in McDowell's time, contemporary scholars have a twofold obligation to disinterested scholarship and ethical citizenry, and an opportunity to contribute constructively to the development of our culture. Particularly since the 1960s, political and social experiences have complicated the wedding of these goals insofar as they have caused scholars gravely to question their cultural loyalties and the destiny of the nation. Asked to recognize a positive national image in their work, they often, like Melville's Bartleby, would "prefer not to." We have good reason, of course, to be suspicious of civil religions and uncritical myths of nationhood. Yet we cannot ignore the great consequence of images, symbols, and faiths to our life as a nation, or overlook the creative force that they have exerted in the past. If we fail to forge our own image within the family of nations, we must accept the image made of us. Two centuries of foreign commentary — from Crevecoeur, Trollope, and De Tocqueville to Jean-Jacques Servan-Schreiber (*The American Challenge,* 1968) and Jean-Francois Revel *(Without Marx or Jesus: The New American Revolution Has Begun,* 1970) — remind us of the fact. The image of nationhood has the same importance for the world community that ethnicity has for our pluralistic society. A positive self-image, infused with motive and will, is equally the basis of national ethos and human personality. Although the culture will decide whether, in Kenneth Boulding's terms, its images are "self-realizing" or "self-negating," American Studies scholars can strive to kindle the feelings that are the impulse to duty: the belief in individual achievement and the purposefulness of history.

NOTES

1. Tremaine McDowell, *American Studies* (Minneapolis: University of Minnesota Press, 1948), p. 51.

2. Robert Walker, *American Studies in the United States: A Survey of College Programs* (Baton Rouge: Louisiana State University Press, 1958), p. 158.

3. Henry Nash Smith, "Can 'American Studies' Develop a Method?," *American Quarterly*, 9 (Summer 1957), 207.

4. These collections provide a library of documents for charting the developing idea of American Studies. Edwin T. Bowden's *American Studies: Problems, Promises and Possibilities* (Austin: University of Texas, 1958) is a panel discussion dealing with general matters. Still one of the most valuable collections is Joseph J. Kwiat and Mary C. Turpie, eds., *Studies in American Culture: Dominant Ideas and Images* (Minneapolis: University of Minnesota Press, 1960), which reprints Bowron, Marx, and Rose's "Literature and Covert Culture" among other essays. *American Perspectives: The National Self-Image in the Twentieth Century*, ed. Robert E. Spiller and Eric Larrabee (Cambridge, Mass.: Harvard University Press, 1961) was an experiment at achieving synthesis by asking ten specialists from diverse fields to contribute essays on a common topic. Two anthologies appeared in 1964: John A. Hague, ed., *American Character and Culture: Some Twentieth Century Perspectives* (DeLand, Fla.: Everett Edwards Press) and Marshall Fishwick, ed., *American Studies in Transition* (Philadelphia: University of Pennsylvania). The collection by Ray B. Browne, Donald M. Winkelman, and Allen Hayman, eds., *New Voices in American Studies* (Lafayette, Ind.: Purdue University Studies, 1966) contains essays from the Mid-America Conference on Literature, History, Popular Culture and Folklore. *Frontiers of American Culture*, ed. Ray B. Browne, Richard H. Crowder, Virgil L. Lokke, and William T. Stafford (Lafayette, Ind.: Purdue University Studies, 1968) comprises papers mainly on unexamined aspects of popular culture. Three other anthologies appeared in 1968: Robert Merideth edited *American Studies: Essays on Theory and Method* (Columbus, Ohio: Charles E. Merrill); *The American Experience* and *The American Culture* (Boston: Houghton Mifflin), both edited by Hennig Cohen and subtitled *Approaches to the Study of the United States*, are collections of scholarship from the first twenty years of the *American Quarterly*. Followers of American Studies in Europe will be interested in A. N. J. Hollander and Sigmund Skard, eds., *American Civilization: An Introduction* (London: Longmans, 1968), and Skard's two-volume history *American Studies in Europe: Their History and Present Organization* (Philadelphia: University of Pennsylvania, 1958). The Summer 1970 issue of the *American Quarterly*, ed. Robert Lucid, contains lengthy descriptions of ten representative "Programs in American Studies."

5. Richard E. Sykes, "American Studies and the Concept of Culture: A Theory and Method," *American Quarterly,* 15 (Summer 1963) 254, 256.

6. Like culture, national character can be defined both organically and structurally, that is, either as an ontologically real entity or as a useful hypothesis for research. In regard to this issue, see David M. Potter, "The Historians and National Character," *People of Plenty: Economic Abundance and the American Character* (Chicago: The University of Chicago Press, 1954), pp. 3-31; Daniel Bell, "National Character Revisited: A Proposal for Renegotiating the Concept," *The Study of Personality: An Interdisciplinary Appraisal,* ed. Edward Norbeck, Douglass Price-Williams, and William M. McCord (New York: Holt, Rinehart and Winston, 1968), pp. 103-20; and Walter P. Metzger, "Generalizations About National Character: An Analytic Essay," *Generalizations in the Writing of History,* ed. Louis Gottschalk (Chicago: The University of Chicago Press, 1963), pp. 77-102.

7. For a recent statement of this view, see Robert E. Spiller, "Unity and Diversity in the Study of American Culture: The American Studies Association in Perspective," *American Quarterly,* 25 (Dec. 1973), 611-18.

8. Smith, "Can 'American Studies' Develop a Method?," pp. 205-206.

9. *On the Art of Poetry,* trans. S. H. Butcher (Indianapolis: Library of Liberal Arts, 1956), p. 13.

10. In "Art, Values, Institutions and Culture: An Essay in American Studies Methodology and Relevance," *American Quarterly,* 24 (May 1972), 131-65, Stuart Levine performs an analysis that readers will find useful, especially those who, like Levine, are approaching social behavior from an essentially humanistic orientation. Beginning with the arts as "a group of institutions among many," Levine suggests criteria by which their cultural meaning can be abstracted and categorized. Although he makes two classes of "universal" and "sacred" values, he does not, however, account for the status of the high works of art in which he admits his own interest.

11. Robert Sklar, "American Studies & the Realities of America," *American Quarterly,* 22 (Summer 1970), 598, 600-601.

12. John A. Kouwenhoven, "American Studies: Words or Things?," in *American Studies in Transition,* ed. Marshall Fishwick (Philadelphia: University of Pennsylvania, 1964), 16, 20, 29, 32-33.

13. Murray G. Murphey, "American Studies at Pennsylvania," *American Quarterly,* 22 (Summer 1970), 497.

14. Murray G. Murphey, *Our Knowledge of the Historical Past* (Indianapolis: Bobbs-Merrill Company, 1973), pp. 203-205.

15. Stanley Bailis, "The Social Sciences in American Studies: An Integrative Conception," and Richard Jensen, "Quantitative American Studies: The State of the Art," *American Quarterly,* 26 (Aug. 1974), 202-24, 225-40. In his address

to the California American Studies Association, November 10, 1974, entitled "The Agony of a Social Historian," Allen F. Davis sounded a stirring alarm against attempts to turn American Studies into a social science discipline: "The social sciences with a few exceptions are rapidly cutting themselves off from a general readership, and often, in their attempt to become more scientific, they are actually becoming less precise, less able to offer a perspective on the human condition in America. This is not to say that the American Studies scholar should not utilize demography, content analyses, or whatever technique seems appropriate to his research problem, but at the same time we should remember what Charles Beard said years ago, that objective history is history without object."

16. Leo Marx, "American Studies – A Defense of an Unscientific Method," *New Literary History,* 1 (Oct. 1969), 89.

17. R. Gordon Kelly, "Literature and the Historian," *American Quarterly,* 26 (May 1974), 145. Other references to Kelly's position are taken *passim,* pp. 141-59. For a like-spirited indictment of tendencies to impose new categories on the past, and of the historical misjudgments which can result from the expressionist style, see D. W. Robertson, Jr., "Some Observations on Method in Literary Studies," *New Literary History,* 1 (Oct. 1969), 21-33. Kelly's own methods of research through literature are demonstrated at length in his book *Mother Was a Lady: Self and Society in Selected American Children's Periodicals, 1865-1890* (Westport, Conn.: Greenwood Press, 1974).

18. We need not embrace the New Critics' strict formal requirements in order to appreciate their doctrine that literature is a unique mode of apprehending reality and a form of truth different from that which can be achieved by scientific discourse. John Crowe Ransom stated this proposition in relation to poetic forms, but it can also apply to imaginative literature in other genres:

> [Poetry] treats an order of existence, a grade of objectivity, which cannot be treated in scientific discourse.
> ... Poetry intends to recover the denser and more refractory original world which we know loosely through our perceptions and memories. By this supposition it is a kind of knowledge which is radically or ontologically distinct. – *The New Criticism* (Norfolk, Conn.: New Directions, 1941), p. 281.

Although they disagreed in the finer points of critical theory, Ransom, Allen Tate, Robert Penn Warren, and other colleagues were guided in their writing by a devout sense of the moral purpose of man and the spiritual orderliness of his universe. Regarded under this aspect, works of serious literature become expressions of man's enduring search to explain the spiritual structures of the world in which he lives and, as such, are fundamental to understanding the generation of culture.

Aerol Arnold demonstrated the classical New Critical argument that "without attention to the form of any art work there is no arriving at its meaning" in "Why Structure in Fiction: A Note to Social Scientists," *American Quarterly,* 10 (Fall 1958), 325-37.

19. Edward Sapir, "The Status of Linguistics as a Science" (1929), in *Selected Writings in Language, Culture, and Personality*, ed. David G. Mandelbaum (Berkeley: University of California Press, 1949), p. 162.

20. The comments on Whorf derive mainly from Peter C. Rollins, "The Whorf Hypothesis as a Critique of Western Science and Technology," *American Quarterly*, 24 (Dec. 1972), 563-83.

21. Seymour Katz, " 'Culture' and Literature in American Studies," *American Quarterly*, 20 (Summer 1968), 320, 323, 327-28.

22. Roy Harvey Pearce, *The Continuity of American Poetry* (Princeton, N. J.: Princeton University Press, 1961), pp. 12-13; "Historicism Once More" (1958), reprinted in *Historicism Once More* (Princeton, N.J.: Princeton University Press, 1969), pp. 4, 14.

Richard Poirier has extended this line of investigation in *A World Elsewhere: The Place of Style in American Literature* (New York: Oxford University Press, 1966). The characteristic conflict in American literature since the time of Emerson, he proposes, has been the struggle between the Hegelian idea that " 'freedom is a creation not of political institutions but of consciousness, that freedom is that reality which the consciousness creates for itself," and the idea that time-space and social, natural, and historical necessities encompass man's world (p. 4).

Walter Sutton discusses Pearce's theory of style and culture in *Modern American Criticism* (Englewood Cliffs, N.J.: Prentice-Hall, 1963), pp. 273-75. In Sutton's own judgment, "The broadening of the base of formalism in such a way that structural elements of the work are identified with environmental and historical factors promises the best resolution of the social-aesthetic critical dichotomy" (p. 275). In *Beyond Formalism: Literary Essays 1958-1970* (New Haven: Yale University Press, 1970), Geoffrey H. Hartman expresses the perhaps dominant critical view of the moment that the precepts of New Criticism will be widened through genre and myth studies in such a way as to reveal the intrinsic role of the arts, high and popular, in all cultures and the archetypal bases of social mythologies.

23. Henry Nash Smith, *Virgin Land: The American West as Symbol and Myth* (New York: Vintage Books, 1959 [1950]), p.v.

24. Marx, "American Studies – A Defense of an Unscientific Method," p. 86. For a fuller consideration of these terms, see Rene Wellek and Austin Warren, *Theory of Literature* (New York: Harcourt, Brace and Company, 1949), chap. 15: "Image, Metaphor, Symbol, Myth." "An 'image' may be invoked once as a metaphor, but if it persistently recurs, both as presentation and representation, it becomes a symbol, may even become part of a symbolic (mythic) system" (p. 194).

25. Bruce Kuklick, "Myth and Symbol in American Studies," *American Quarterly*, 24 (Oct. 1972), 436-40, 445, 447, 449-50.

26. Bruce Kuklick, "The Mind of the Historian," *History and Theory*, 8 (1969), 316.

27. Cecil F. Tate, *The Search for a Method in American Studies* (Minneapolis: University of Minnesota Press, 1973). Reference has been made especially to passages on pp. 7-8, 15, 103, 118, 127-28, 147-48.

28. Kenneth E. Boulding, *The Image: Knowledge in Life and Society* (Ann Arbor: University of Michigan Press, 1956), p. 175; see also pp. 14-16, 126-29, 171-75.

29. Northrop Frye, *Anatomy of Criticism: Four Essays* (Princeton, N.J.: Princeton University Press, 1957), p. 354. While myth participates in the creation of culture, it is also compulsively traditional in preserving cultural values in the face of change. Vague and unarticulated in its origins, with time the cultural myth develops into patterns and literary narratives that can be clearly charted. Frye has divided the cultural cycle into five stages, each with its literary mode (mythic, romantic, high mimetic, low mimetic, ironic), its distinctive attitude towards symbolism, and its hero-protagonist. For side-taking on his scheme of culture, history, literature and myth, see *Northrop Frye in Modern Criticism,* ed. Murray Krieger (Selected Papers from the English Institute; New York: Columbia University Press, 1966).

30. Northrop Frye, *The Critical Path: An Essay on the Social Context of Literary Criticism* (Bloomington: Indiana University Press, 1971), pp. 34-35.
    The following writings are a few of the many points at which to enter the field of myth studies. Relevant essays have appeared in *History and Theory,* including Ben Halpern, "'Myth' and 'Ideology' in Modern Usage," 1 (1961), 129-49; M. I. Finley, "Myth, Memory, and History," 4 (1965), 281-302; and Hans H. Penner, "Myth and Ritual: A Wasteland or a Forest of Symbols?" in *On Method in the History of Religions,* ed. James S. Helfer (Beiheft 8 of *History and Theory,* 1968), pp. 46-57. Penner juxtaposes the "reductionist" use of myths by sociologists and psychologists, who are concerned with functional social solidarity, and more illuminist uses by religionists, who see myths as encounters with Ultimate Reality. Two issues of *Daedalus* are germane: *Myth, Symbol, Culture* (Winter 1972) and *Myth and Myth-Making* (Spring 1959). The nearer backgrounds of modern myth studies are traced in Burton Feldman and Robert D. Richardson, *The Rise of Modern Mythology, 1680-1860* (Bloomington: Indiana University Press, 1972). See also the Winter 1972 issue of *New Literary History,* entitled *On Interpretation* (hermeneutics, phenomenology, myth and allegory), and the collection of thirty-four essays *Myth and Literature,* ed. John B. Vickery (Lincoln: University of Nebraska Press, 1966).

31. Hans Meyerhoff, *The Philosophy of History in Our Time* (Garden City, N.Y.: Anchor Books, 1959), pp. 11-12. The passage quoted by Meyerhoff is from Geoffrey Barraclough, *History in a Changing World* (1956).

32. Robert F. Berkhofer, Jr., *A Behavioral Approach to Historical Analysis* (New York: The Free Press, 1969). In his review, W. H. Walsh tempers Berkhofer's emphasis on social theory with a reminder of the historian's need to use common sense and to explain in laymen's terms — *History and Theory,* 10 (1971), 241-46. For considered attacks on the notion that the unique texture and inner feel of a culture can be reached objectively, by sophisticated forms of quantitative analysis, see, for example, David Brion Davis, "Some Recent Directions in American Cultural History," *American Historical Review,* 73 (Feb.

1968), 696-707, and "Slavery and the Post-World War II Historians," *Daedalus,* 103 (Spring 1974), 1-14. Jacques Barzun, "History: The Muse and Her Doctors," *American Historical Review,* 77 (Feb. 1972), 33-64, distinguishes "history properly so called" from recent methods of social, quantitative, and psychological history. His essay is a fine example of the traditionalist view that history is a story whose criteria are Narrative, Chronology, Concreteness, and Memorability. In "History and Literature: Branches of the Same Tree," *Essays on History and Literature,* ed. Robert H. Bremner (Columbus: Ohio State University Press, 1966), pp. 123-59, Russell B. Nye agrees that "the creative act common to both history and literature . . . is fundamentally one of imagination" and emphasizes the dependence of the historian, like the novelist and poet, upon the metaphoric resources of language.

33. Gene Wise, *American Historical Explanations: A Strategy for Grounded Inquiry* (Homewood, Ill.: The Dorsey Press, 1973), pp. vii, 37, 40.

34. Stanley Fish, "Literature in the Reader: Affective Stylistics," *New Literary History,* 2 (Autumn 1970), 123-61; Georges Poulet, "Phenomenology of Reading," *New Literary History,* 1 (Oct. 1969), 53-68. After reviewing the philosophy of a number of European critics, Poulet praises Raymond and Rousset for moving beyond the position of the structualists, who let a work be explained by the interdependence of the objective elements that compose it. Raymond and Rousset look to what is "beyond form," searching in the objective and formal aspects of the work for the "something which is previous to the work and on which the work depends for its very existence" (pp. 66-67).

35. Roy Harvey Pearce, "'The American Adam' and the State of American Studies," *Journal of Higher Education,* 27 (Feb. 1956), 106.

36. Thomas Valasek, "American Studies in the Community Colleges," a paper presented at the American Studies Institute, University of Southern California, 1973. For useful insights on teaching American Studies, literature, and interdisciplinary topics in general, especially at pre-college levels, see Fred E. H. Schroeder, *Joining the Human Race: How to Teach the Humanities* (DeLand, Fla.: Everett Edwards Press, 1973).

37. Peter L. Berger and Thomas Luckmann, *The Social Construction of Reality: A Treatise in the Sociology of Knowledge* (Garden City, N.Y.: Anchor Books, 1967 [1966]), p. 103. Denying the force of tradition and divorcing students from history invites the type of dystopia Northrop Frye once descried:

> Just as historical criticism uncorrected relates culture to the past, ethical criticism uncorrected relates culture only to the future, to the ideal society which may eventually come if we take sufficient pains to guard the educating of our youth. For all such lines of thought end in indoctrinating the next generation. – *Anatomy of Criticism,* pp. 346-47.

38. Peter L. Berger, *Invitation to Sociology: A Humanistic Perspective* (Garden City, N.Y.: Anchor Books, 1963), pp. 154-55, 168. See especially the chapters "Excursus: Sociological Machiavellianism and Ethics" and "Sociology as

a Humanistic Discipline."

39. Peter L. Berger, *The Sacred Canopy: Elements of a Sociological Theory of Religion* (Garden City, N.Y.: Anchor Books, 1969 [1967]), pp. 179-80.

40. R. S. Crane, *The Idea of the Humanities and Other Essays Critical and Historical,* Vol. 1 (Chicago: University of Chicago Press, 1967), p. xiv. Two issues of *Daedalus* that are important to establishing boundaries and possibilities for the humanities are *The Future of the Humanities* (Summer 1969) and *Theory in Humanistic Studies* (Spring 1970).

41. McDowell, *American Studies,* chap. 7: "Region, Nation, World."

INDEX

The following index is comprehensive for the twelve essays in this volume. Not included are the general "Introduction," title-pages to the essays, illustrations, and notes and bibliographies.

Multiple explanation, 289, 291-294
Mumford, Lewis, 10, 33, 34, 35, 338
  The Culture of Cities, 20, 33, 34
Munich crisis, 8
Murdoch, Iris, 358
Murphey, Murray G., 83, 84, 293, 333
  Our Knowledge of the Historical Past, 83, 333
Murray, Judith, *The Gleaner,* 228
Murrow, Edward, 8
Museum of Modern Art, 29, 147
Mussolini, Benito, 8, 11
Myth, symbol, and image study, 121-176, 179, 180, 181, 182, 186,
  196-208, 221, 222, 229, 253, 263, 324, 332, 341, 342, 343-352,
  355, 360
Myth-Symbol School of American Studies, 198, 242, 243, 252, 261,
  293, 336, 343

Nabuco, Joaquin, 232
Nader, Ralph, 116
Nancy Drew mysteries, 154
Napoleon, 78
Nash, Roderick, 280, 318
National Academy of Design, 41
National Commission on the Reform of Secondary Education, 282
The National Environmental Policy Act of 1969, 82
National Forest Service, 81, 83
National Guard, 6
National mission, 100, 113, 238, 332
National Park Service, 81, 82, 83
National Register of Historic Sites and Buildings, 81, 82
National Resources Committee, 21
National Velvet, 164
Navajos, 252, 254, 258, 259, 260
Nazis, 5, 8, 111
Neal, John, 230
  Brother Jonathan, 230
Neal, Larry, 221, 222
Neo-orthodoxy, 338, 358
Neotechnic phase (civilization), 34, 37

University of New Mexico, 316
University of Pennsylvania, 83, 293
    (American Civilization Department), 333
University of Southern California (USC), 283, 299, 320
Up the Down Staircase, 282
Updike, John, 163, 222
U. S. Geological Survey, 92
Usonian houses (see Frank Lloyd Wright)

Valkyrie, 167, 169
Valla, Laurentius, 64
Van Doren, Mamie, 160
Van Eycks, Hubert and Jan, 28
Vanderbilt University, 12, 23, 24
Vasconcelos, Jose, 234
Vassar College, 54, 140
Vest, Sharlene, 302, 303, 304, 305
Vietnam, 10, 151, 197, 200, 299
Virginia Slims, 124, 169
Voltaire, 228

Walker, Robert, 327, 328
Wallace, Anthony F. C., *Culture and Personality,* 222, 245, 248, 249,
    251, 262, 264
The Waltons, 16
Warch, Richard (Yale-New Haven History Education Project), 309
Ward, John William, 106, 243, 347
    Andrew Jackson: Symbol for an Age, 343, 346
Warner Brothers, 139
Warren, Robert Penn, 12, 24, 348
    Brother to Dragons, 348
Warwick, Ruth, 134
Watergate, 115, 292
Wayne, John, 181
Weaver, Raymond, 338
Webb, Clifton, 2
Webb, W. P., *The Great Plains,* 20
Weber, Max, 66, 225
Webster, Noah, 228, 229